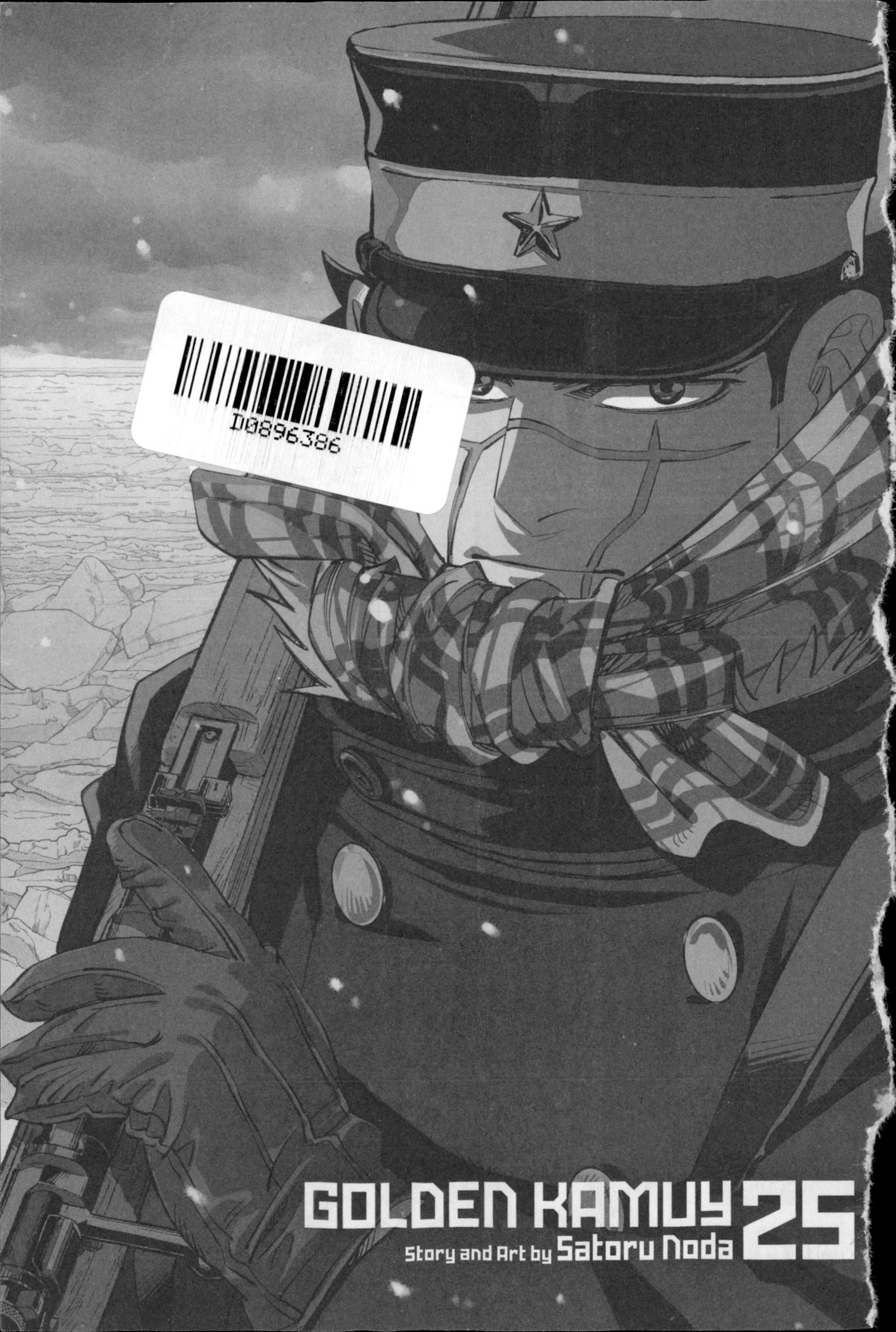
GOLDEN KAMUY 25
Story and Art by Satoru Noda

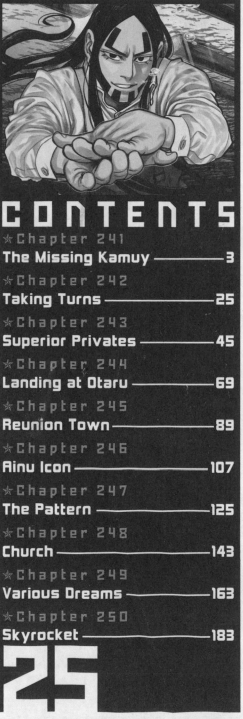

CONTENTS

GOLDEN KAMUY

25

Story and Art by Satoru Noda

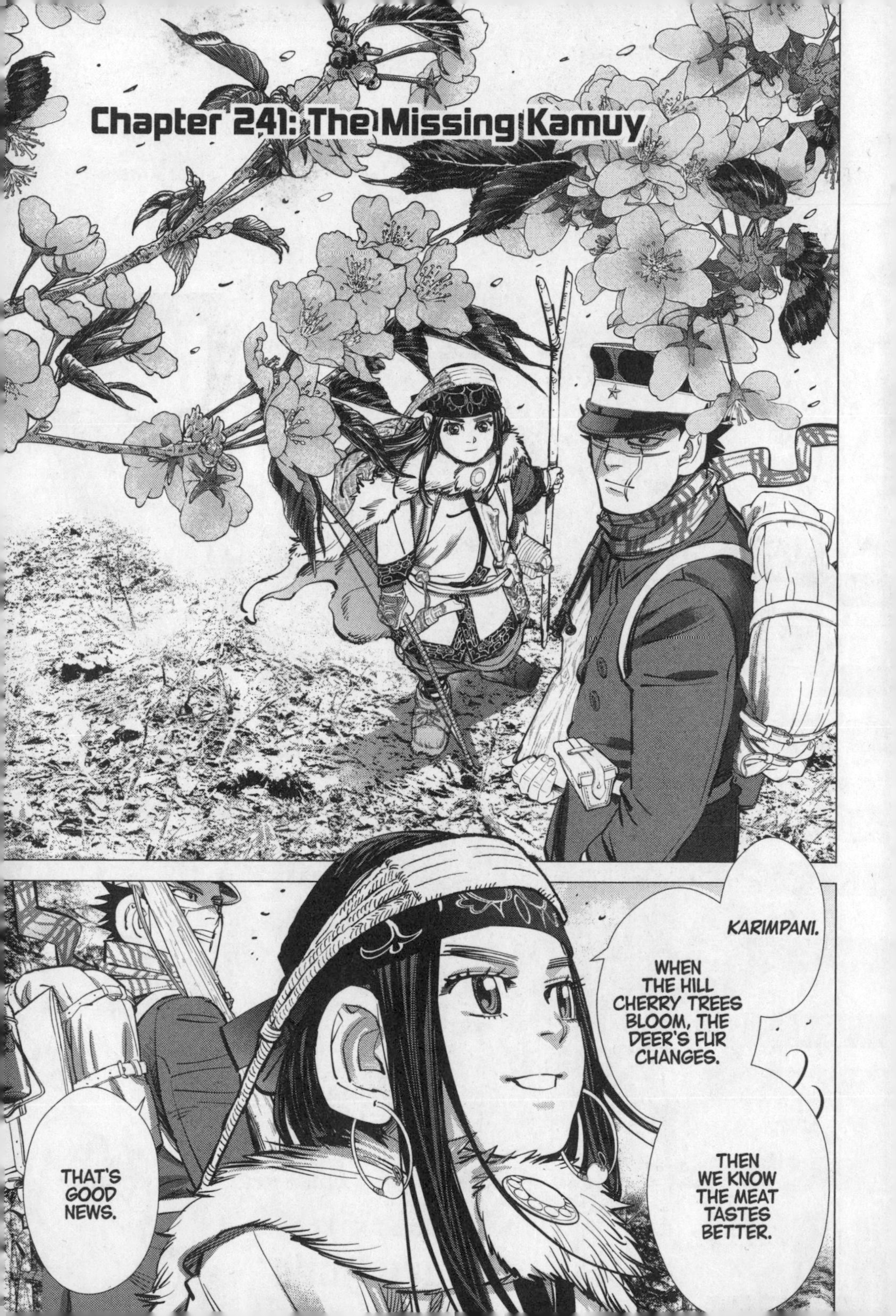
Chapter 241: The Missing Kamuy
KARIMPANI.
WHEN THE HILL CHERRY TREES BLOOM, THE DEER'S FUR CHANGES.
THEN WE KNOW THE MEAT TASTES BETTER.
THAT'S GOOD NEWS.

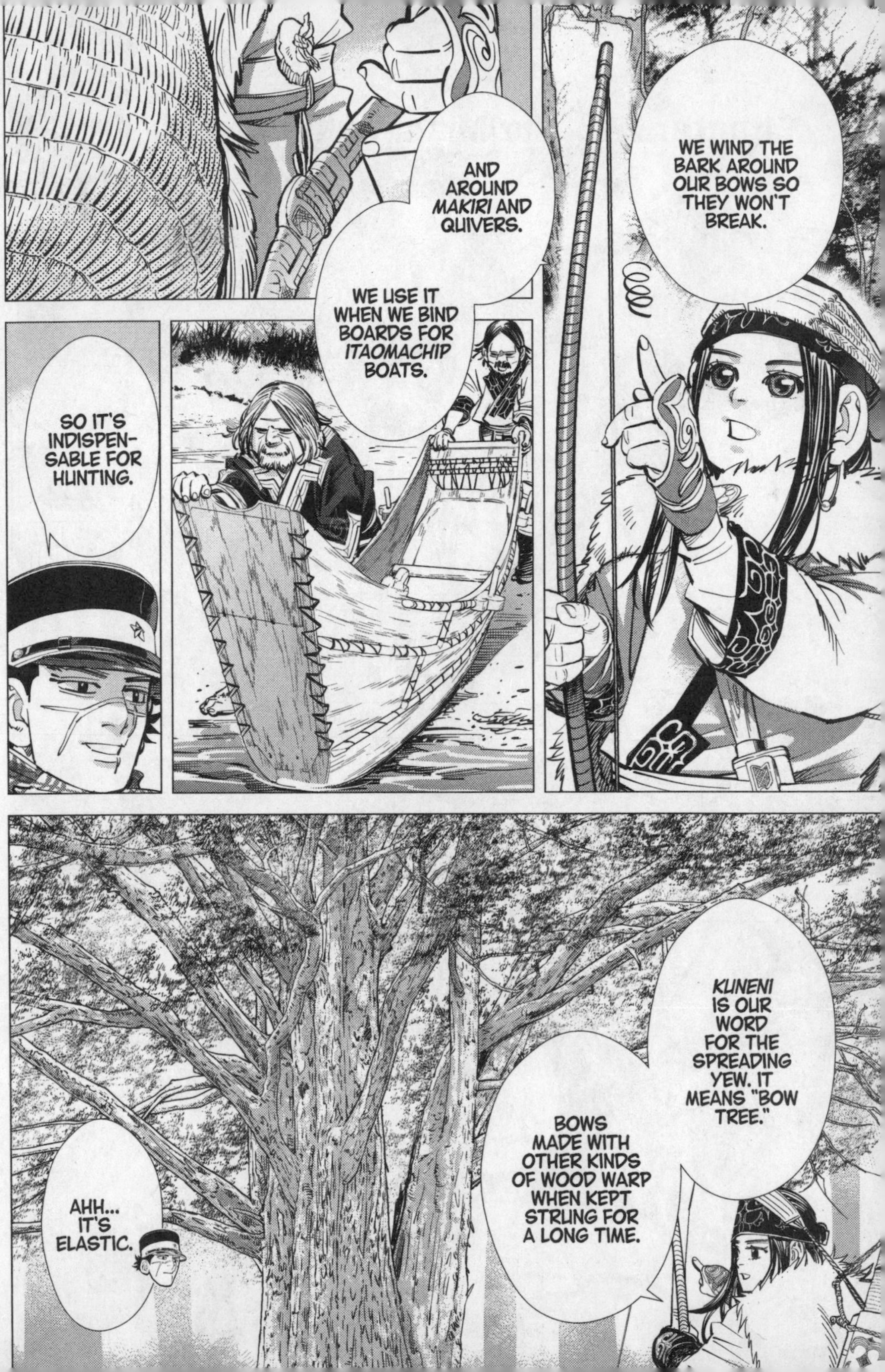
WE WIND THE BARK AROUND OUR BOWS SO THEY WON'T BREAK.
AND AROUND MAKIRI AND QUIVERS.
WE USE IT WHEN WE BIND BOARDS FOR ITAOMACHIP BOATS.
SO IT'S INDISPEN-SABLE FOR HUNTING.
KUNENI IS OUR WORD FOR THE SPREADING YEW. IT MEANS "BOW TREE."
BOWS MADE WITH OTHER KINDS OF WOOD WARP WHEN KEPT STRUNG FOR A LONG TIME.
AHH... IT'S ELASTIC.

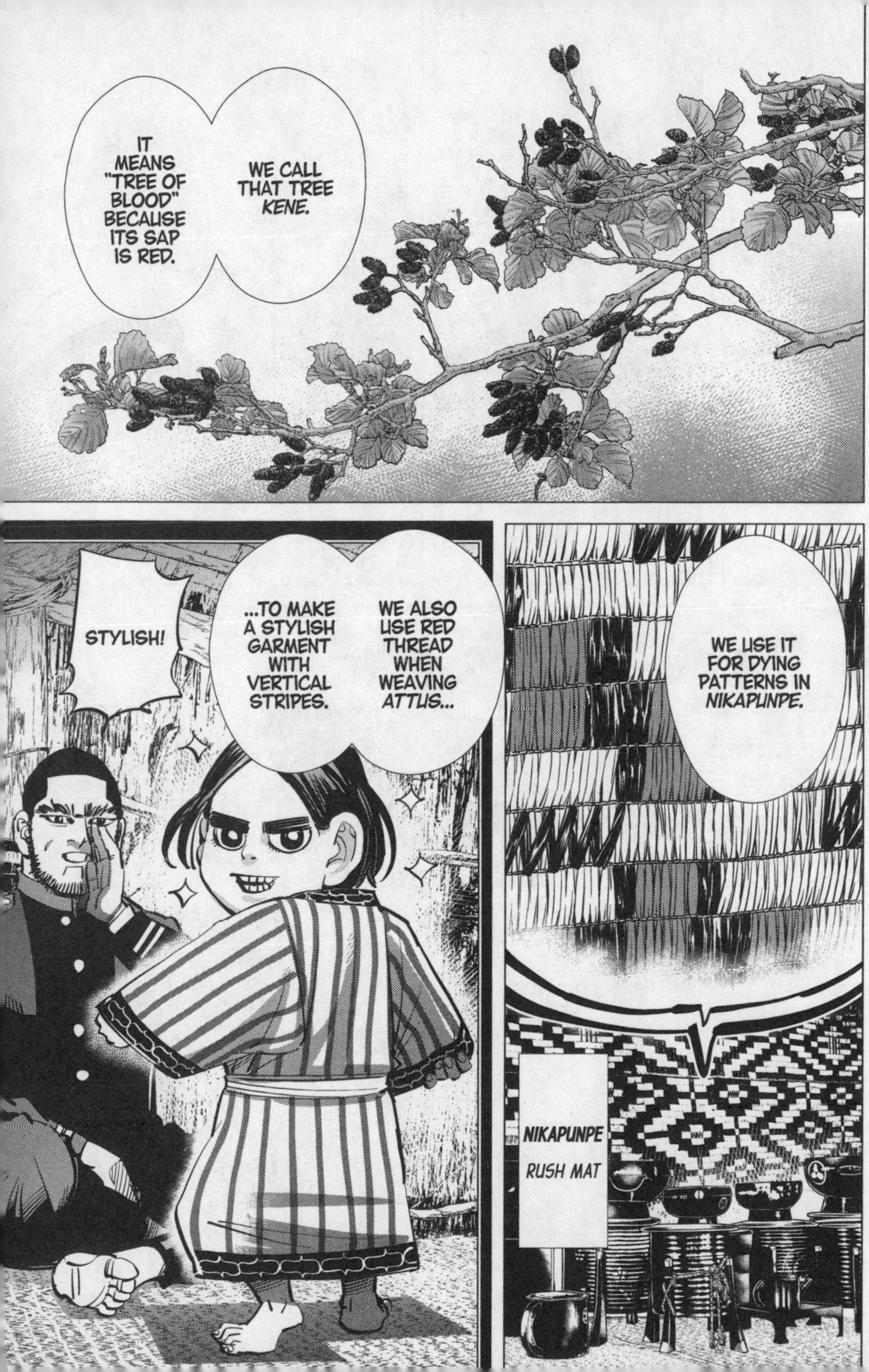
WE CALL THAT TREE KENE.
IT MEANS "TREE OF BLOOD" BECAUSE ITS SAP IS RED.
WE USE IT FOR DYING PATTERNS IN *NIKAPUNPE*.
NIKAPUNPE
RUSH MAT
WE ALSO USE RED THREAD WHEN WEAVING *ATTUS*...
...TO MAKE A STYLISH GARMENT WITH VERTICAL STRIPES.
STYLISH!

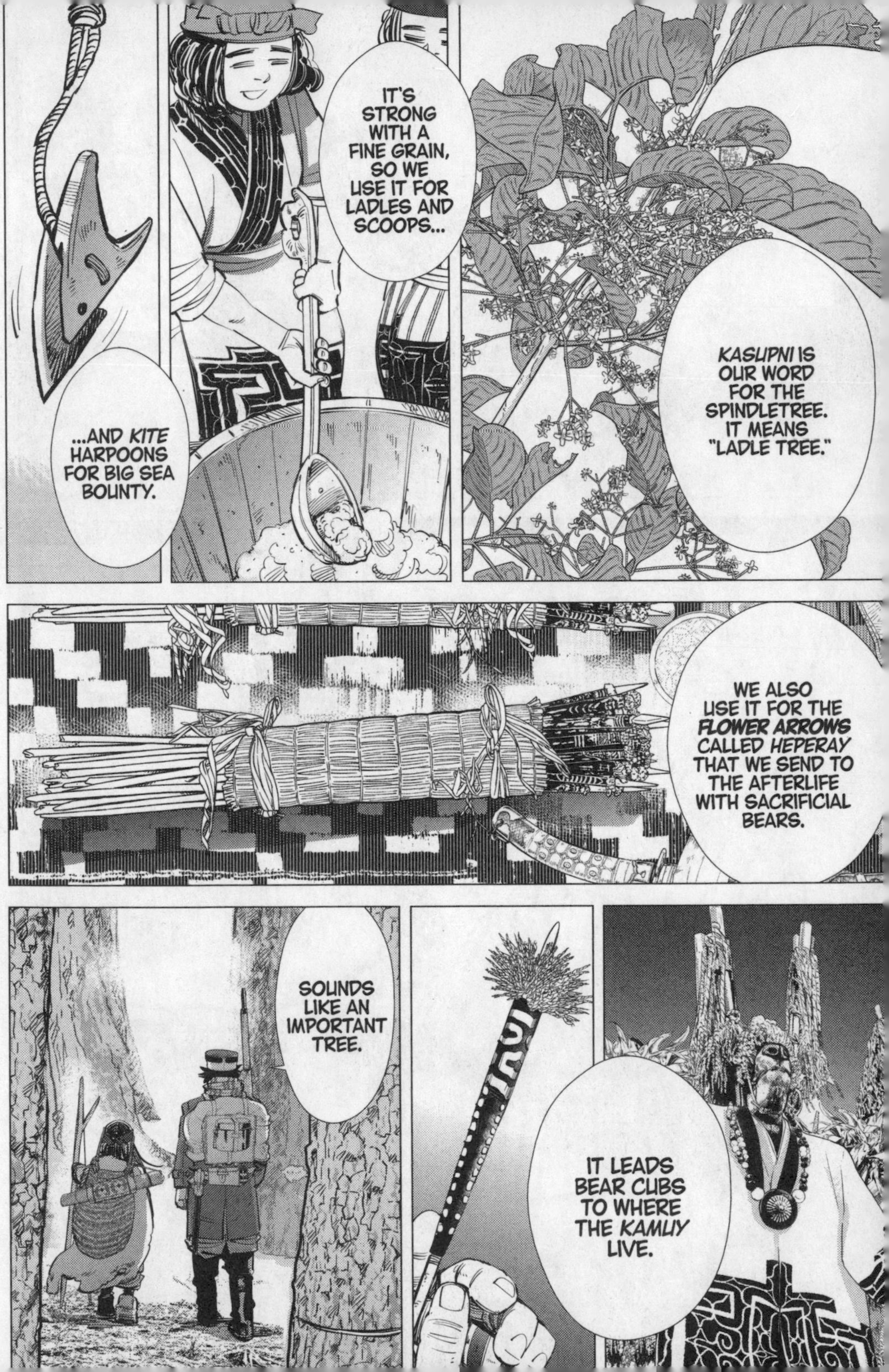
KASUPNI IS OUR WORD FOR THE SPINDLETREE. IT MEANS "LADLE TREE."
IT'S STRONG WITH A FINE GRAIN, SO WE USE IT FOR LADLES AND SCOOPS...
...AND KITE HARPOONS FOR BIG SEA BOUNTY.
WE ALSO USE IT FOR THE FLOWER ARROWS CALLED HEPERAY THAT WE SEND TO THE AFTERLIFE WITH SACRIFICIAL BEARS.
IT LEADS BEAR CUBS TO WHERE THE KAMUY LIVE.
SOUNDS LIKE AN IMPORTANT TREE.

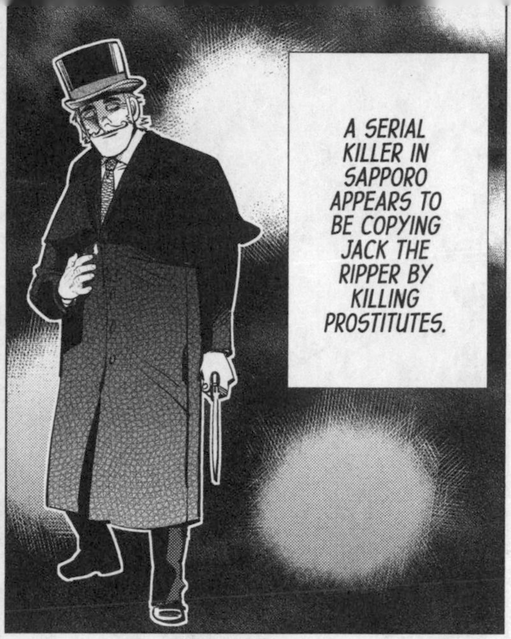
A SERIAL KILLER IN SAPPORO APPEARS TO BE COPYING JACK THE RIPPER BY KILLING PROSTITUTES.

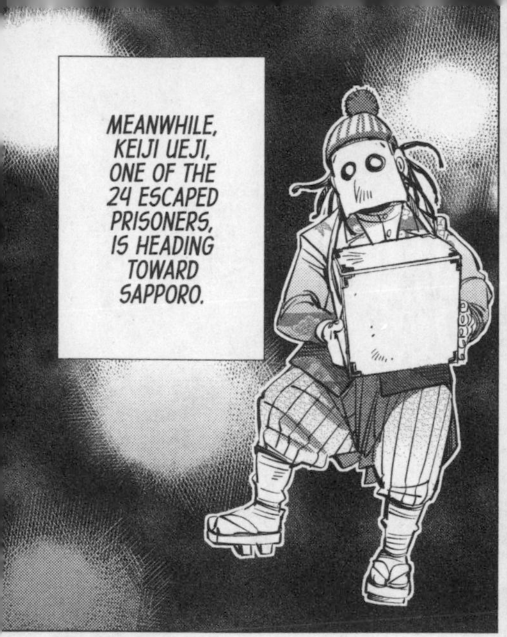
MEANWHILE, KEIJI UEJI, ONE OF THE 24 ESCAPED PRISONERS, IS HEADING TOWARD SAPPORO.

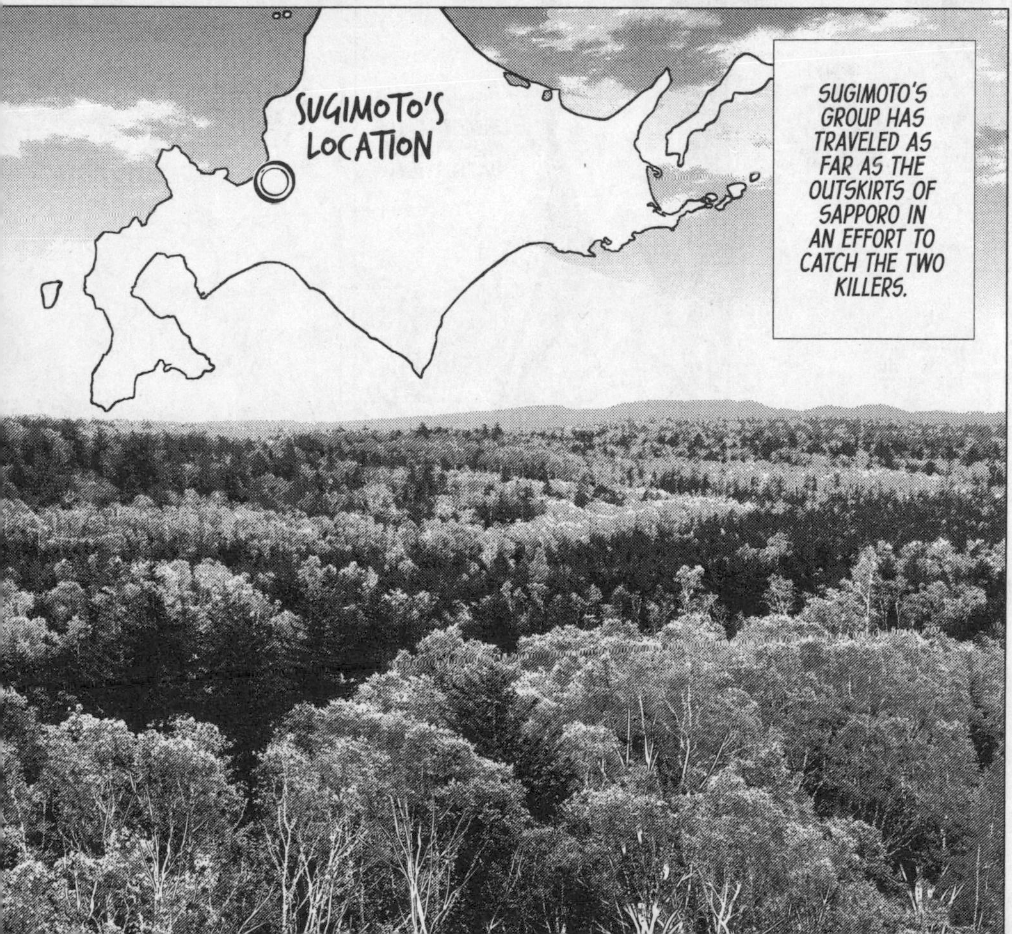
SUGIMOTO'S GROUP HAS TRAVELED AS FAR AS THE OUTSKIRTS OF SAPPORO IN AN EFFORT TO CATCH THE TWO KILLERS.
SUGIMOTO'S LOCATION

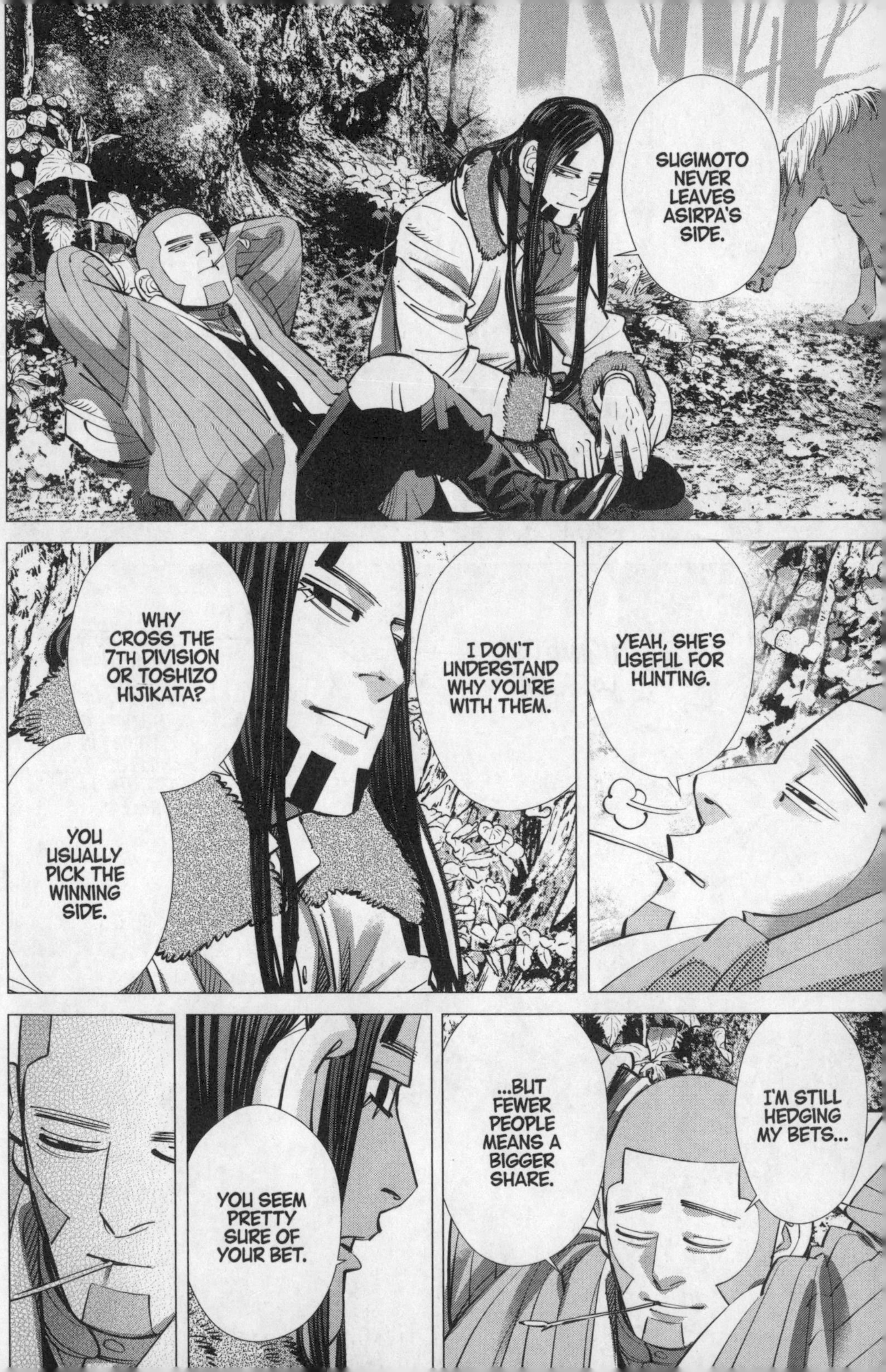
SUGIMOTO NEVER LEAVES ASIRPA'S SIDE.
YEAH, SHE'S USEFUL FOR HUNTING.
I DON'T UNDERSTAND WHY YOU'RE WITH THEM.
WHY CROSS THE 7TH DIVISION OR TOSHIZO HIJIKATA?
YOU USUALLY PICK THE WINNING SIDE.
I'M STILL HEDGING MY BETS...
...BUT FEWER PEOPLE MEANS A BIGGER SHARE.
YOU SEEM PRETTY SURE OF YOUR BET.

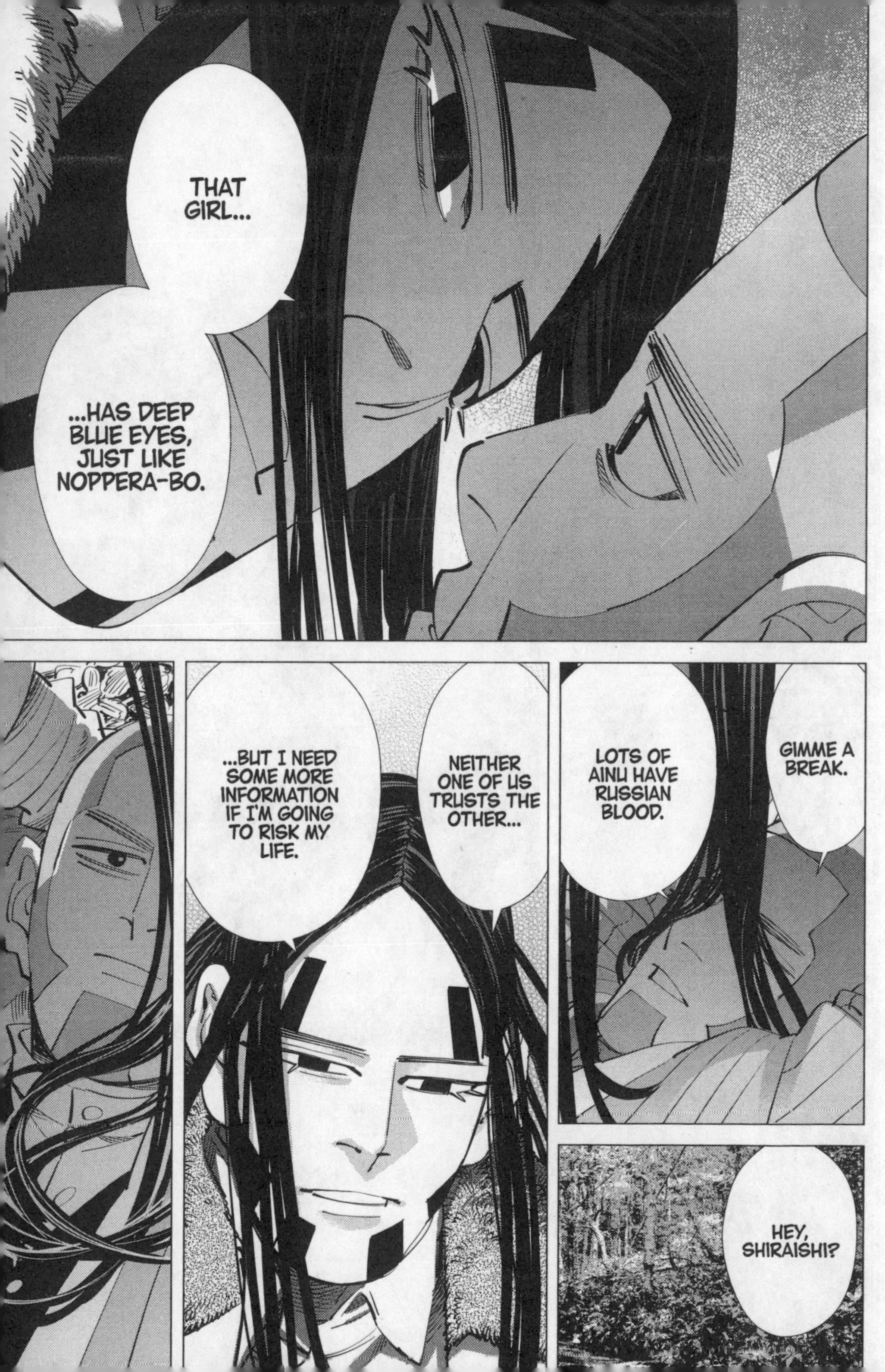
THAT GIRL...
...HAS DEEP BLUE EYES, JUST LIKE NOPPERA-BO.
GIMME A BREAK.
LOTS OF AINU HAVE RUSSIAN BLOOD.
HEY, SHIRAISHI?
NEITHER ONE OF US TRUSTS THE OTHER...
...BUT I NEED SOME MORE INFORMATION IF I'M GOING TO RISK MY LIFE.

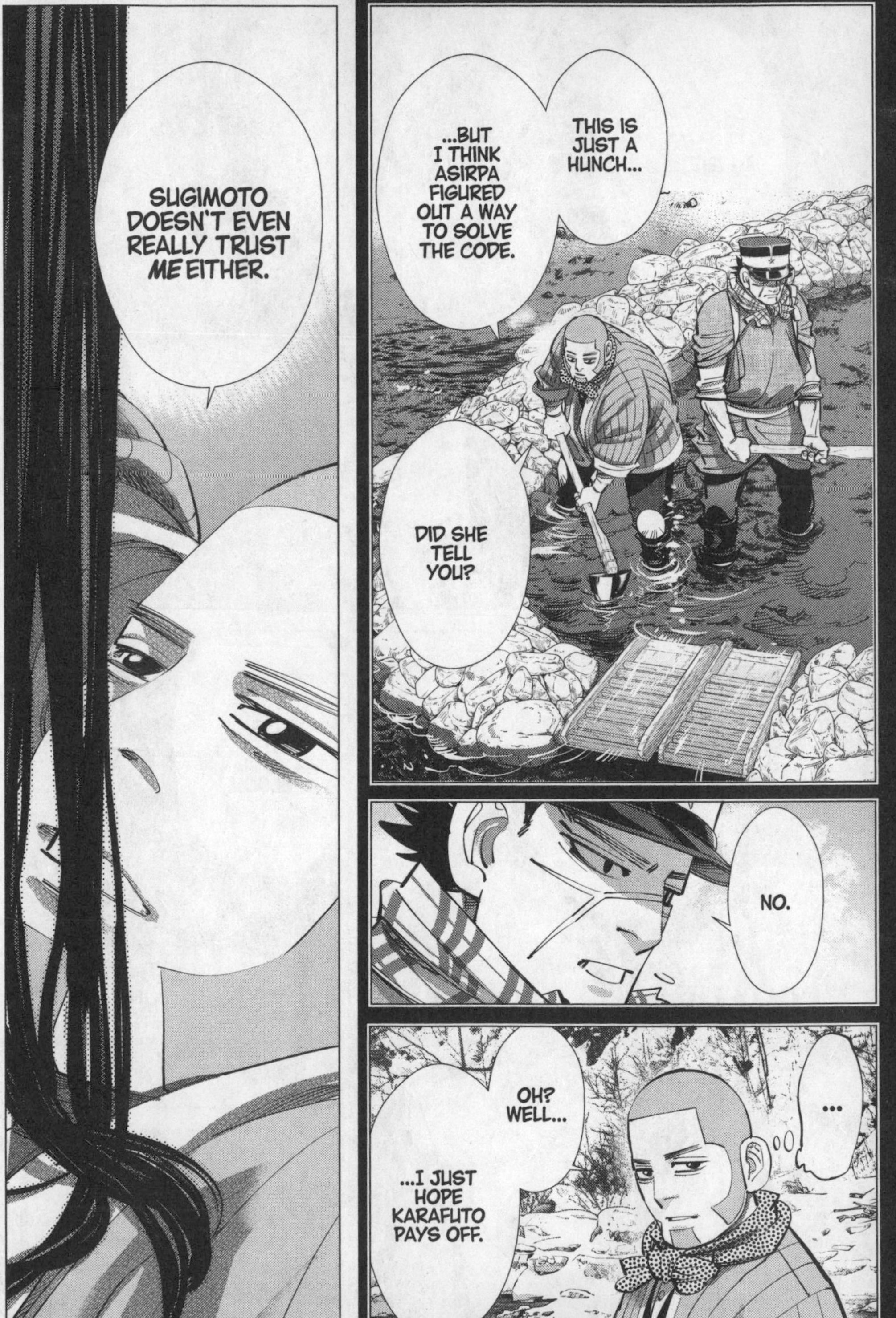
THIS IS JUST A HUNCH...
...BUT I THINK ASIRPA FIGURED OUT A WAY TO SOLVE THE CODE.
DID SHE TELL YOU?
NO.
...
OH? WELL...
...I JUST HOPE KARAFUTO PAYS OFF.
SUGIMOTO DOESN'T EVEN REALLY TRUST *ME* EITHER.

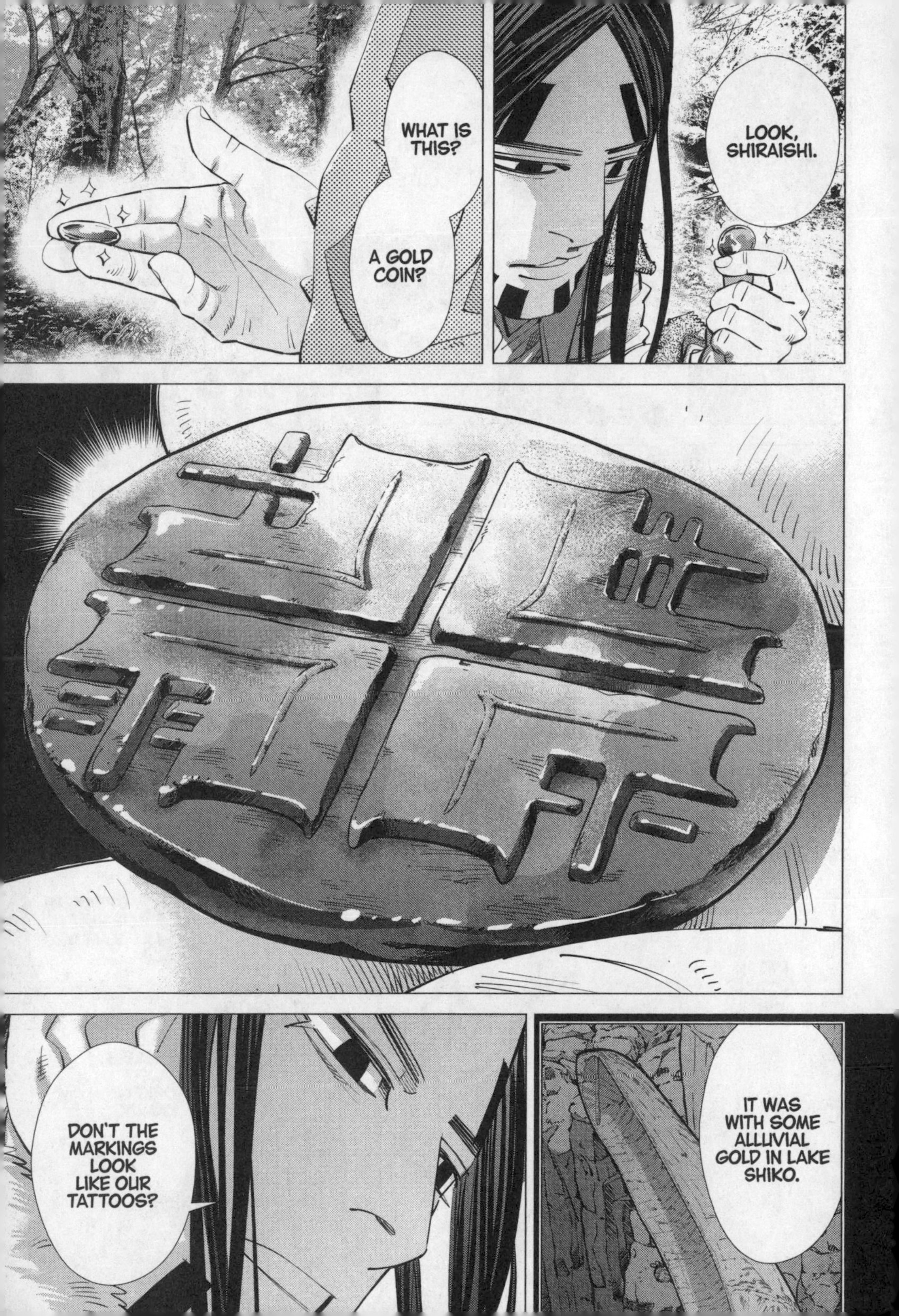
LOOK, SHIRAISHI.
WHAT IS THIS?
A GOLD COIN?
IT WAS WITH SOME ALLUVIAL GOLD IN LAKE SHIKO.
DON'T THE MARKINGS LOOK LIKE OUR TATTOOS?

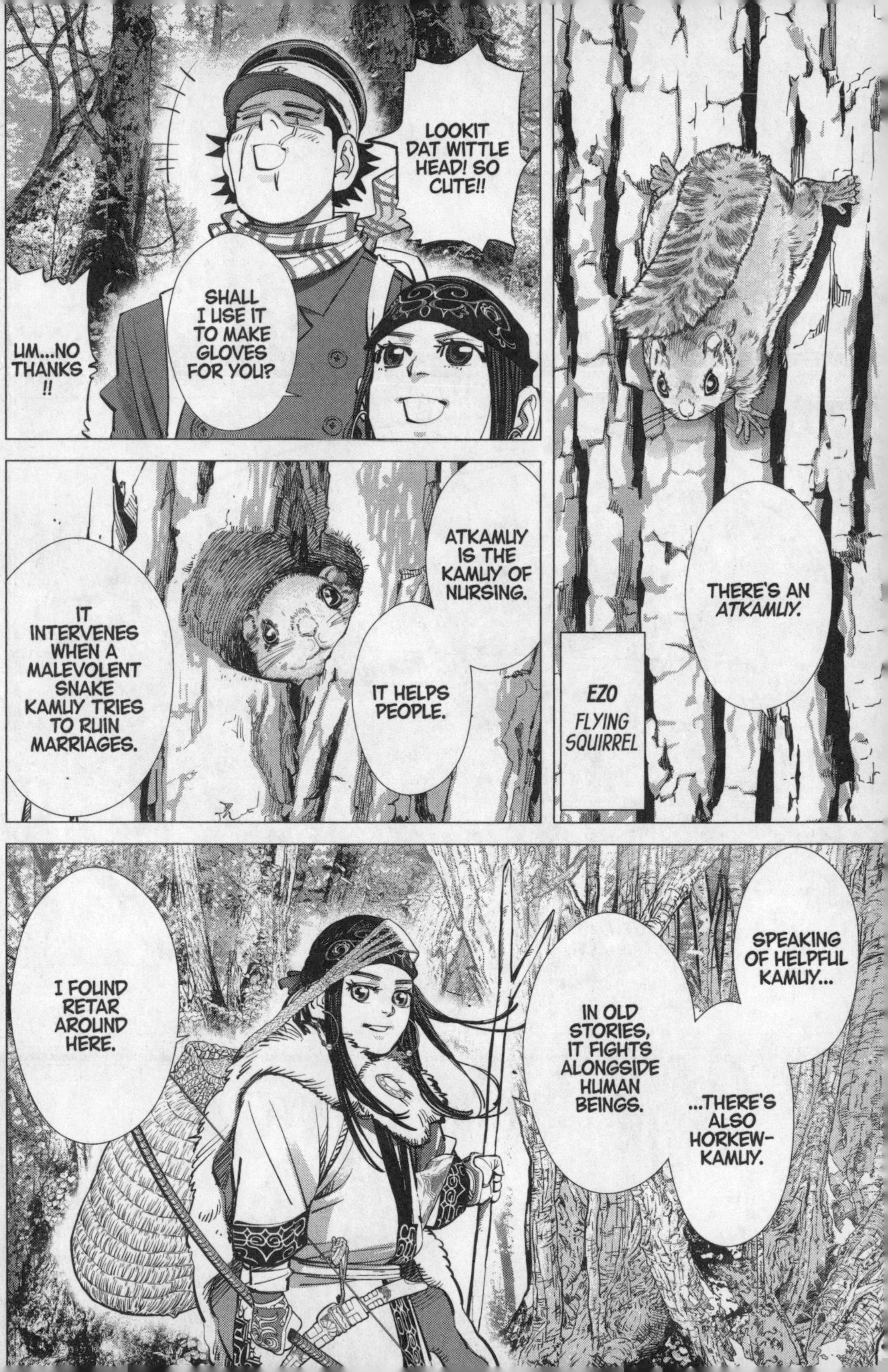
THERE'S AN *ATKAMUY.*
EZO FLYING SQUIRREL
LOOKIT DAT WITTLE HEAD! SO CUTE!!
SHALL I USE IT TO MAKE GLOVES FOR YOU?
UM...NO THANKS!!
ATKAMUY IS THE KAMUY OF NURSING.
IT HELPS PEOPLE.
IT INTERVENES WHEN A MALEVOLENT SNAKE KAMUY TRIES TO RUIN MARRIAGES.
SPEAKING OF HELPFUL KAMUY...
...THERE'S ALSO HORKEW-KAMUY.
IN OLD STORIES, IT FIGHTS ALONGSIDE HUMAN BEINGS.
I FOUND RETAR AROUND HERE.

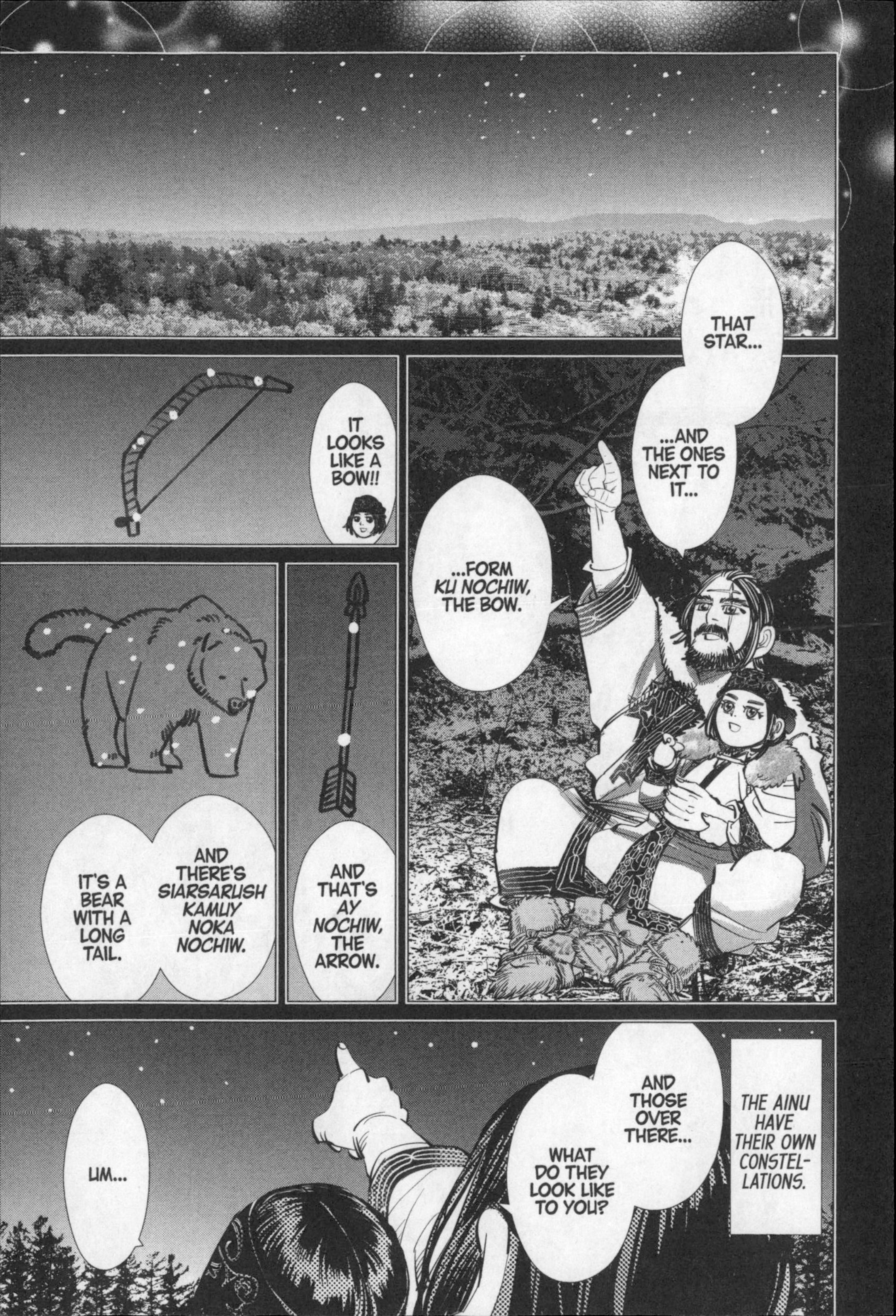
THAT STAR...
...AND THE ONES NEXT TO IT...
...FORM KU NOCHIW, THE BOW.
IT LOOKS LIKE A BOW!!
AND THAT'S AY NOCHIW, THE ARROW.
AND THERE'S SIARSARUSH KAMUY NOKA NOCHIW.
IT'S A BEAR WITH A LONG TAIL.
THE AINU HAVE THEIR OWN CONSTEL-LATIONS.
AND THOSE OVER THERE...
WHAT DO THEY LOOK LIKE TO YOU?
UM...

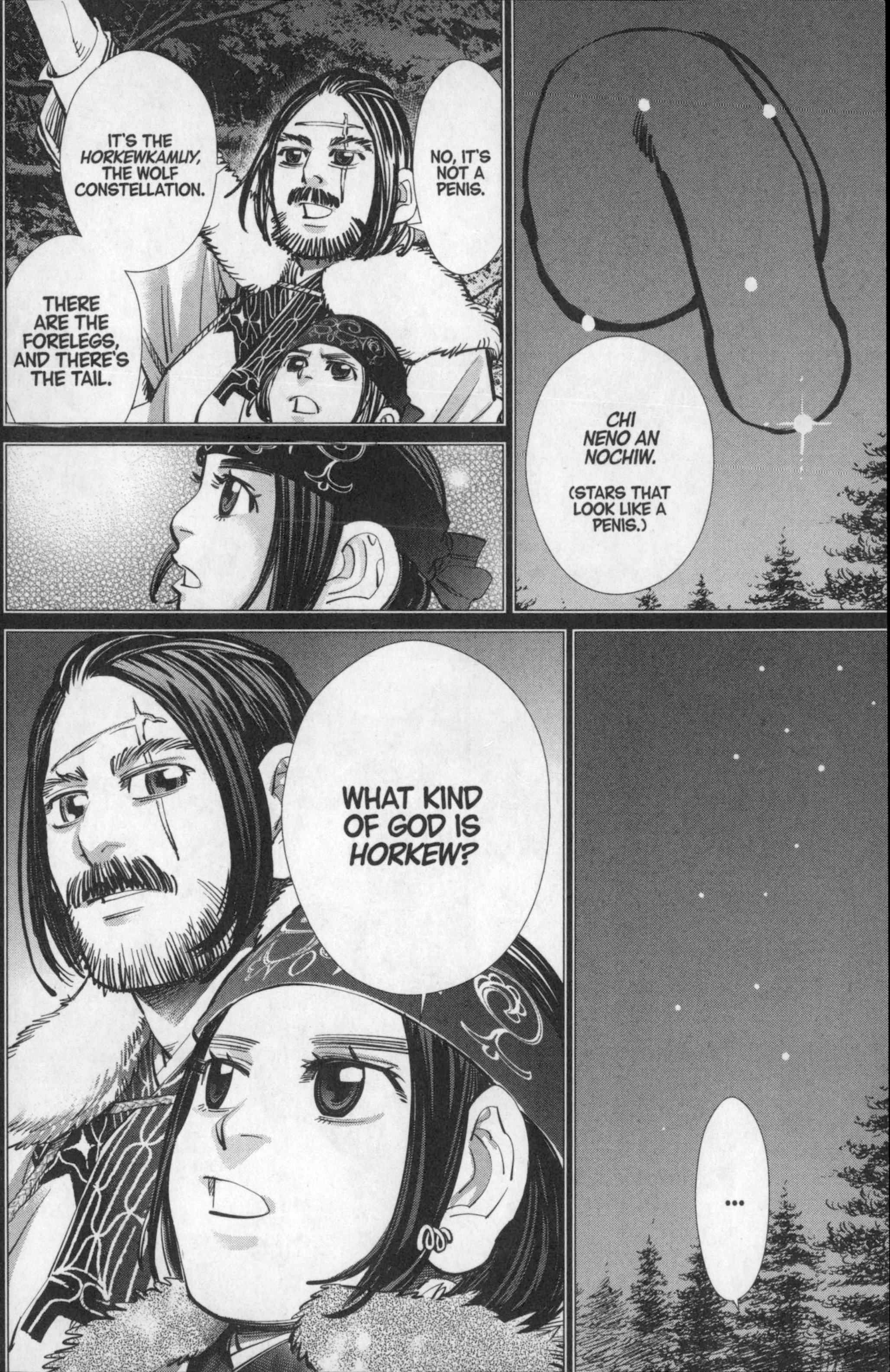
CHI NENO AN NOCHIW.
(STARS THAT LOOK LIKE A PENIS.)
NO, IT'S NOT A PENIS.
IT'S THE *HORKEWKAMUY*, THE WOLF CONSTELLATION.
THERE ARE THE FORELEGS, AND THERE'S THE TAIL.
...
WHAT KIND OF GOD IS HORKEW?

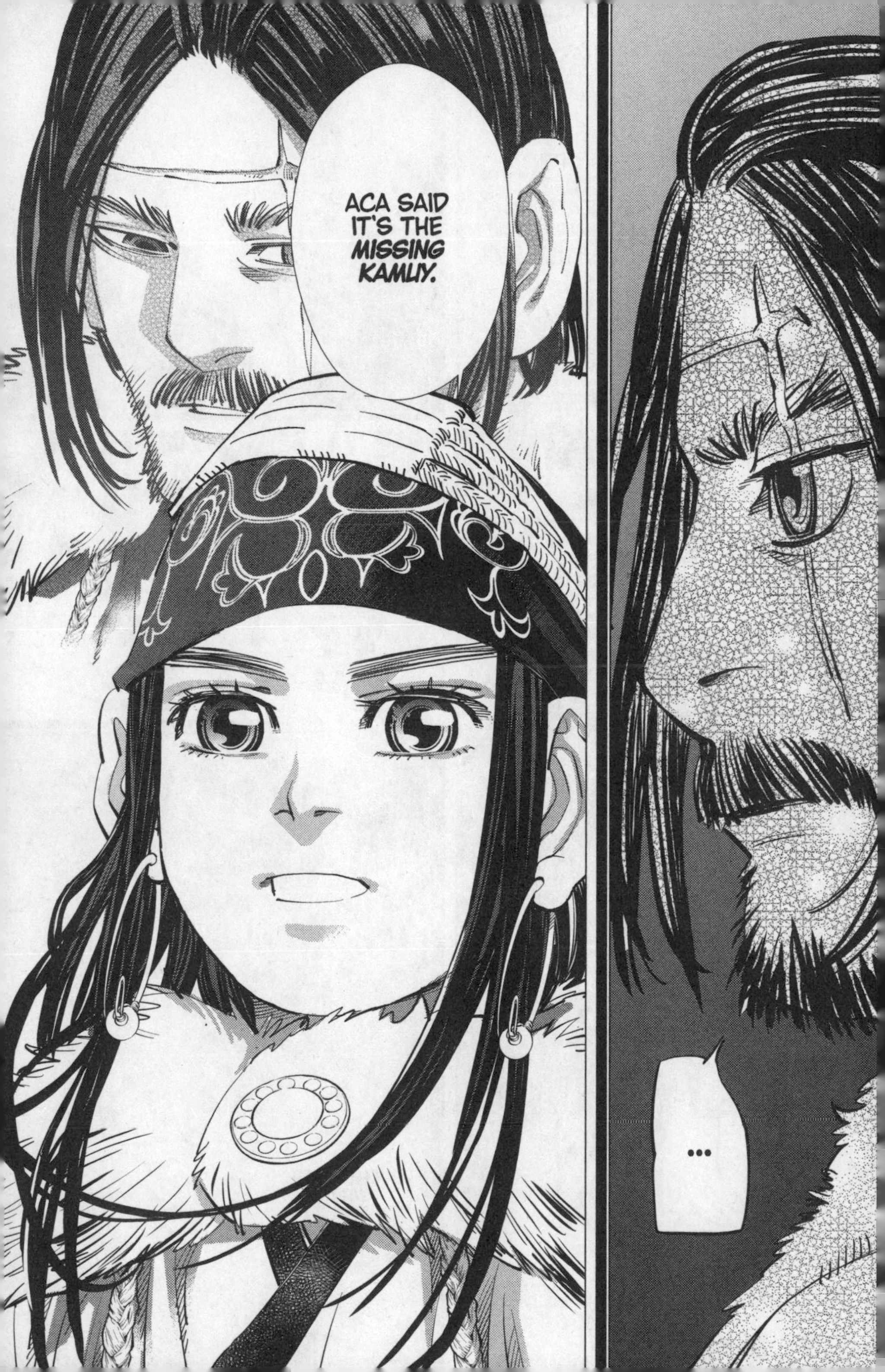
...
ACA SAID IT'S THE MISSING KAMUY.

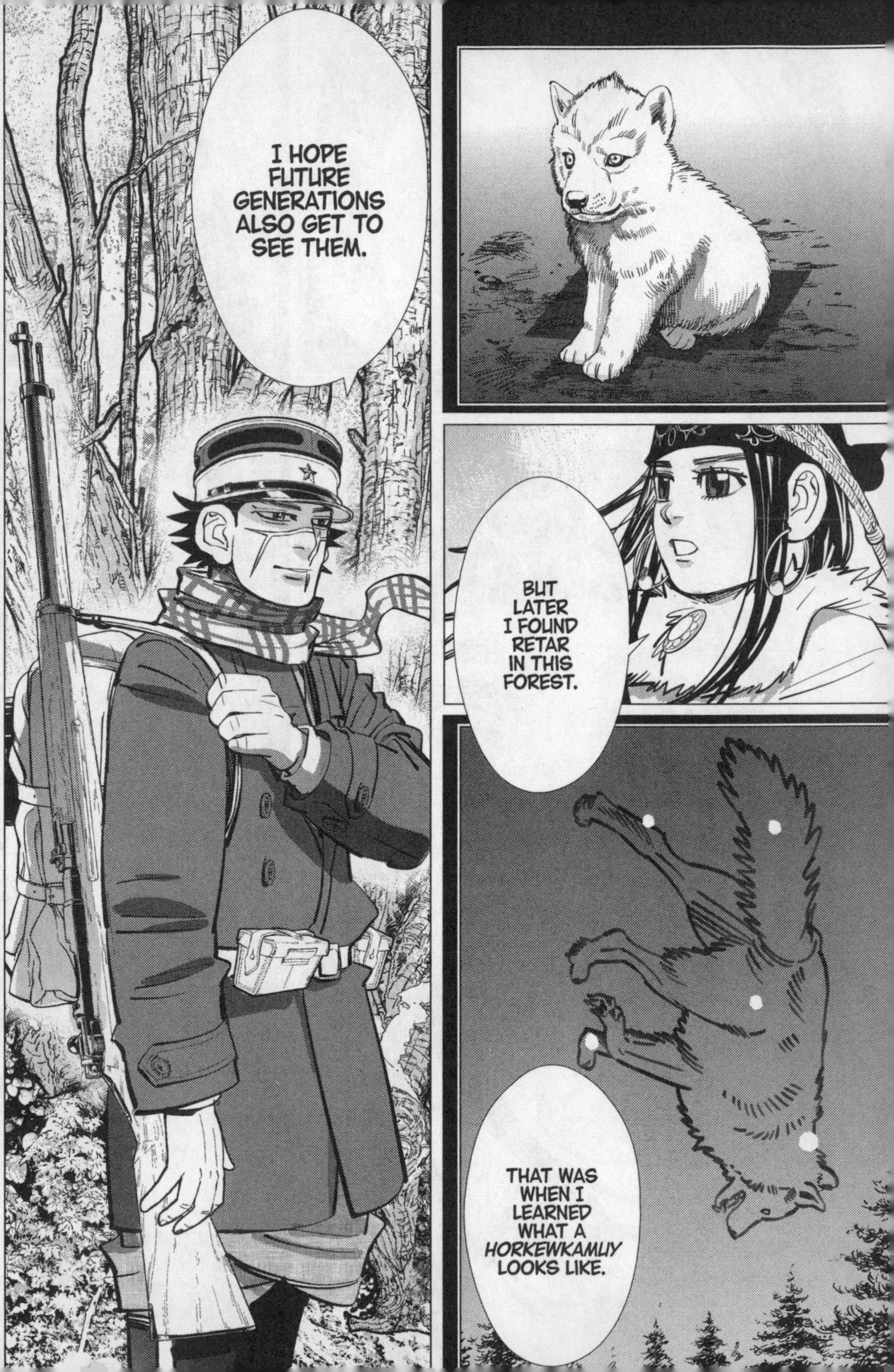
BUT LATER I FOUND RETAR IN THIS FOREST.
THAT WAS WHEN I LEARNED WHAT A *HORKEWKAMUY* LOOKS LIKE.
I HOPE FUTURE GENERATIONS ALSO GET TO SEE THEM.

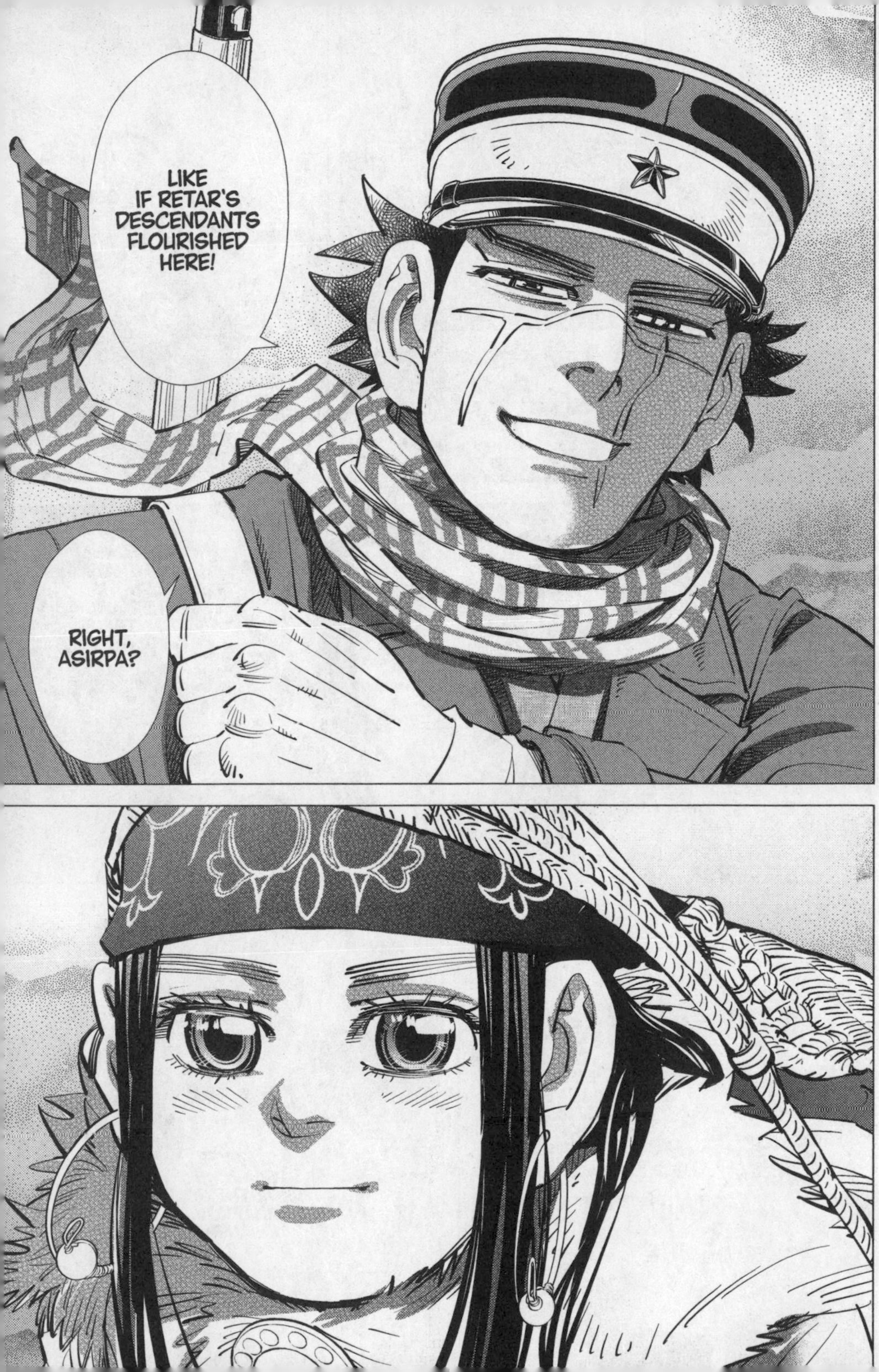
LIKE IF RETAR'S DESCENDANTS FLOURISHED HERE!
RIGHT, ASIRPA?

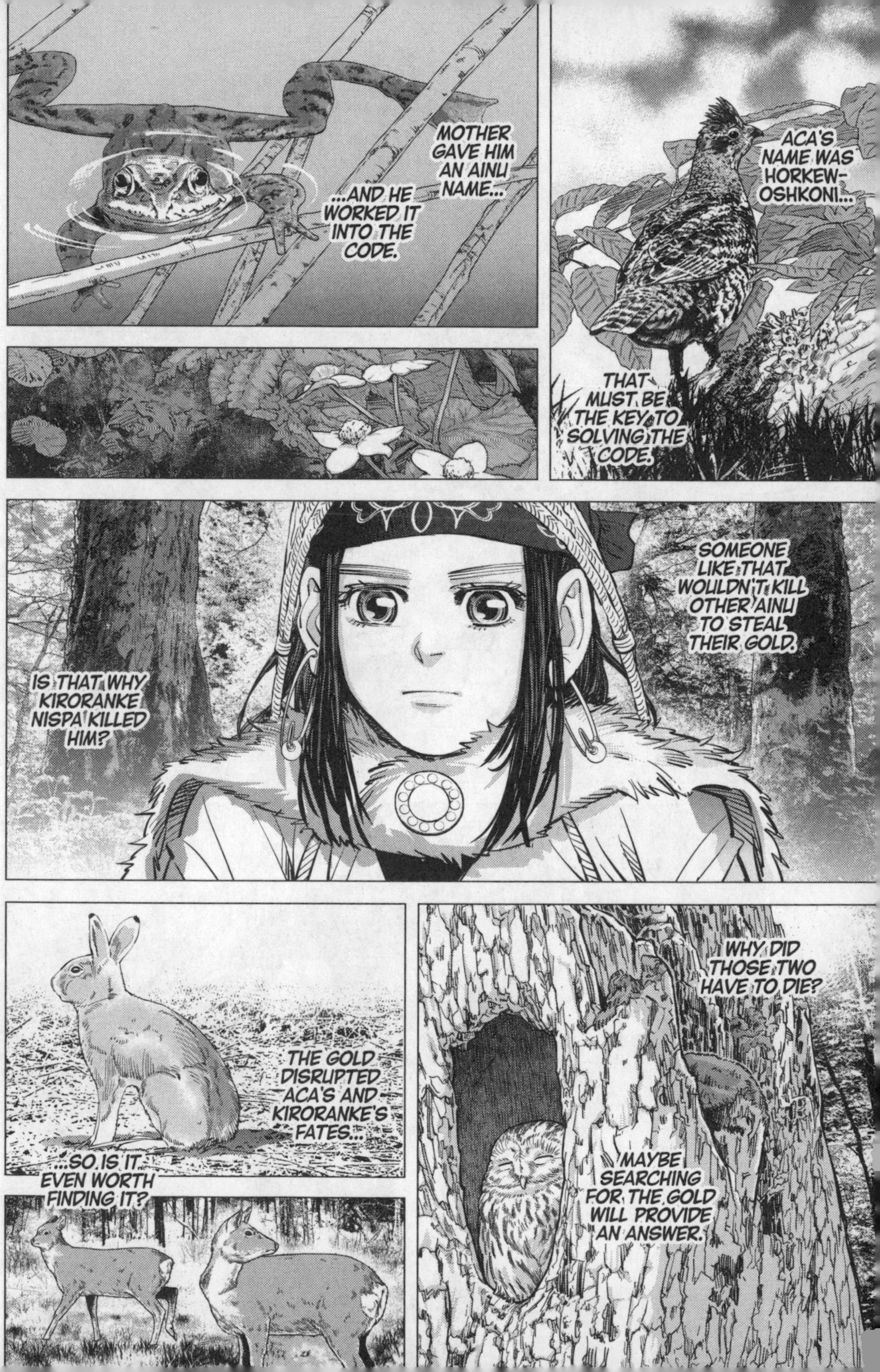
ACA'S NAME WAS HORKEW-OSHKONI...
THAT MUST BE THE KEY TO SOLVING THE CODE.
MOTHER GAVE HIM AN AINU NAME...
...AND HE WORKED IT INTO THE CODE.
SOMEONE LIKE THAT WOULDN'T KILL OTHER AINU TO STEAL THEIR GOLD.
IS THAT WHY KIRORANKE NISPA KILLED HIM?
WHY DID THOSE TWO HAVE TO DIE?
MAYBE SEARCHING FOR THE GOLD WILL PROVIDE AN ANSWER.
THE GOLD DISRUPTED ACA'S AND KIRORANKE'S FATES...
...SO IS IT EVEN WORTH FINDING IT?

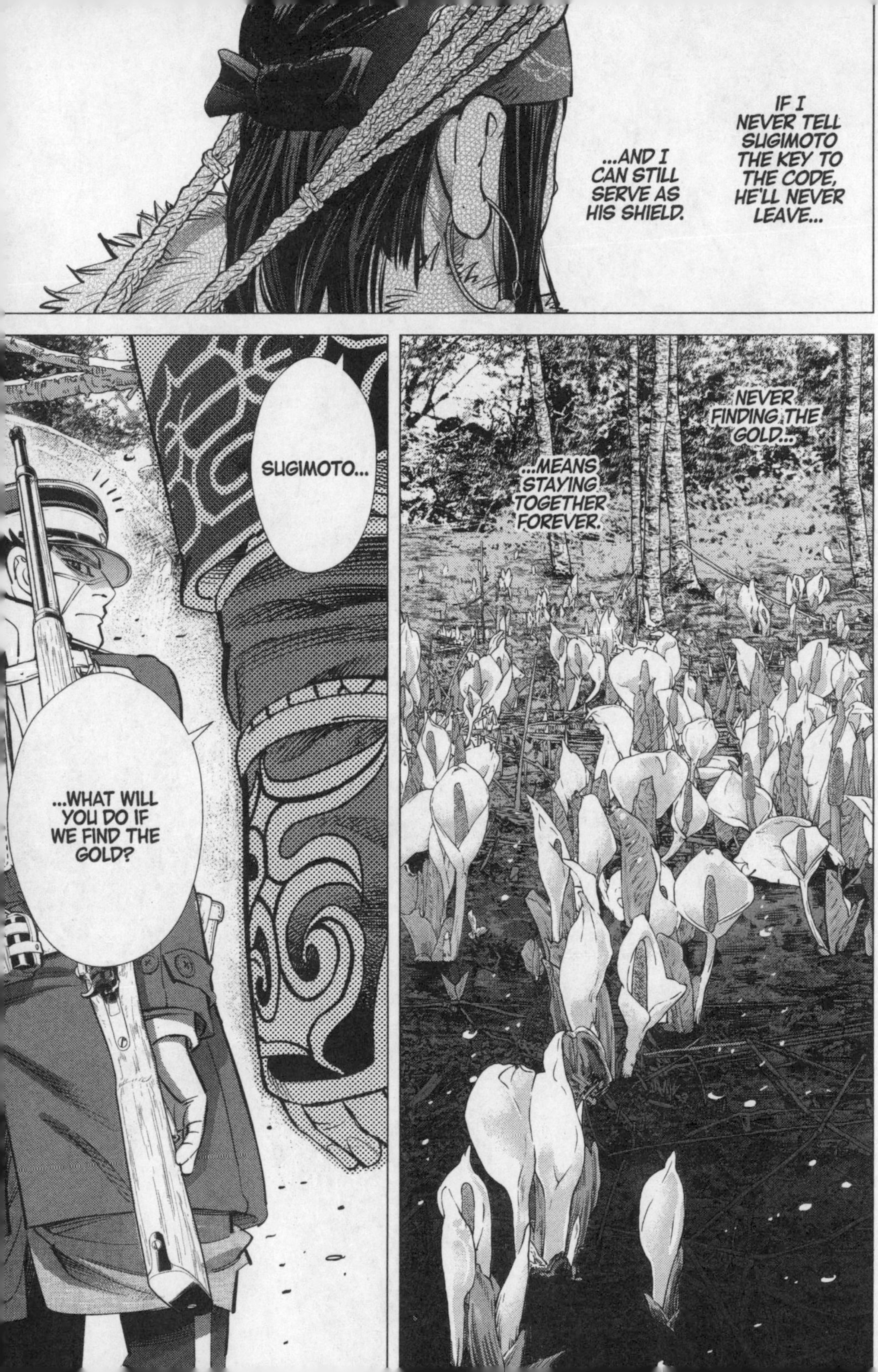
IF I NEVER TELL SUGIMOTO THE KEY TO THE CODE, HE'LL NEVER LEAVE...
...AND I CAN STILL SERVE AS HIS SHIELD.
NEVER FINDING THE GOLD...
...MEANS STAYING TOGETHER FOREVER.
SUGIMOTO...
...WHAT WILL YOU DO IF WE FIND THE GOLD?

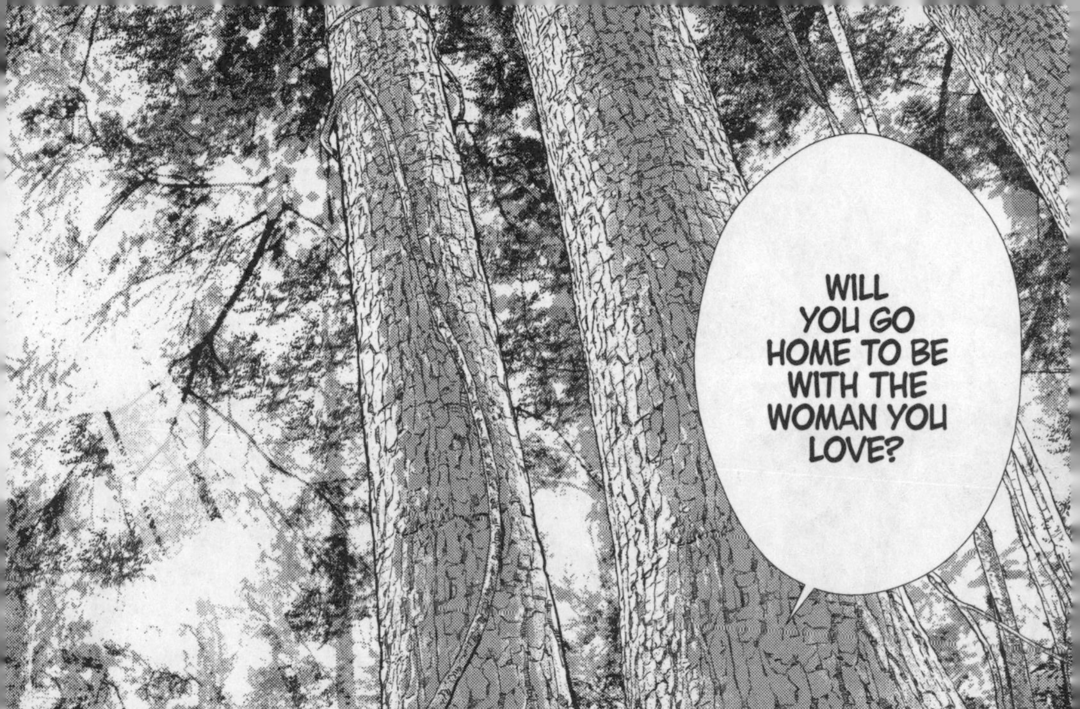
WILL YOU GO HOME TO BE WITH THE WOMAN YOU LOVE?

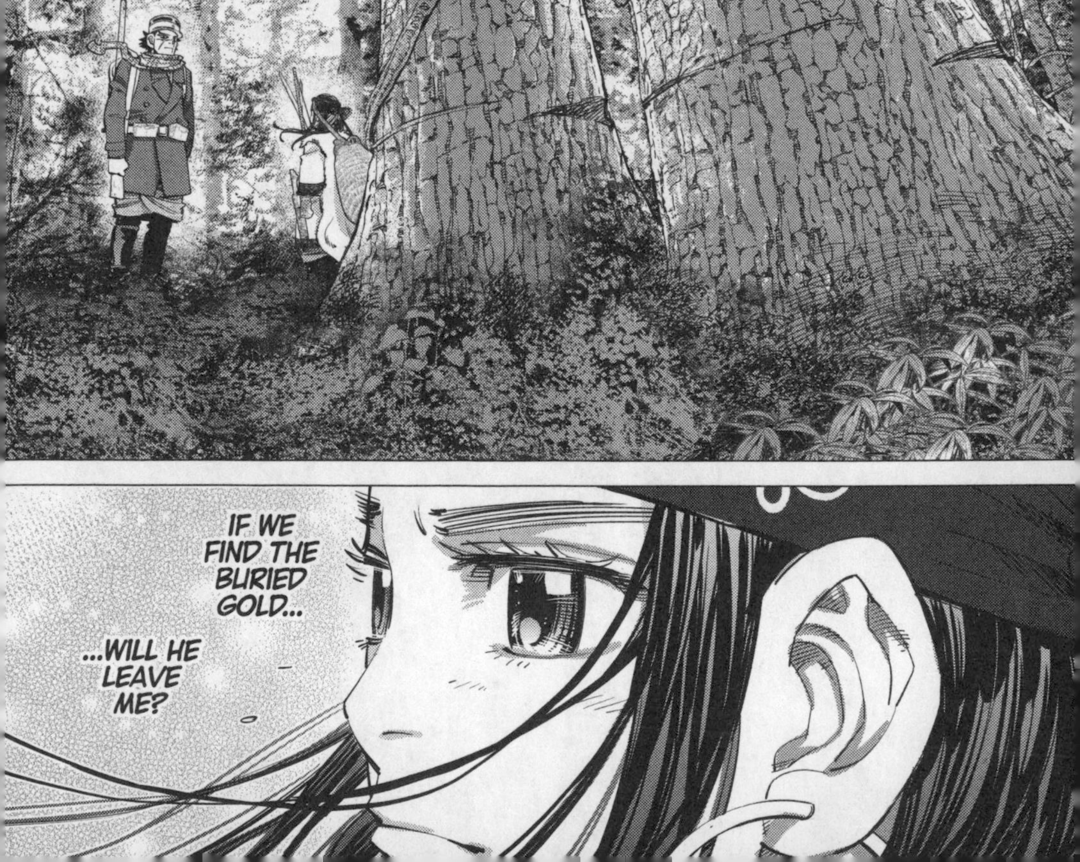
IF WE FIND THE BURIED GOLD...
...WILL HE LEAVE ME?

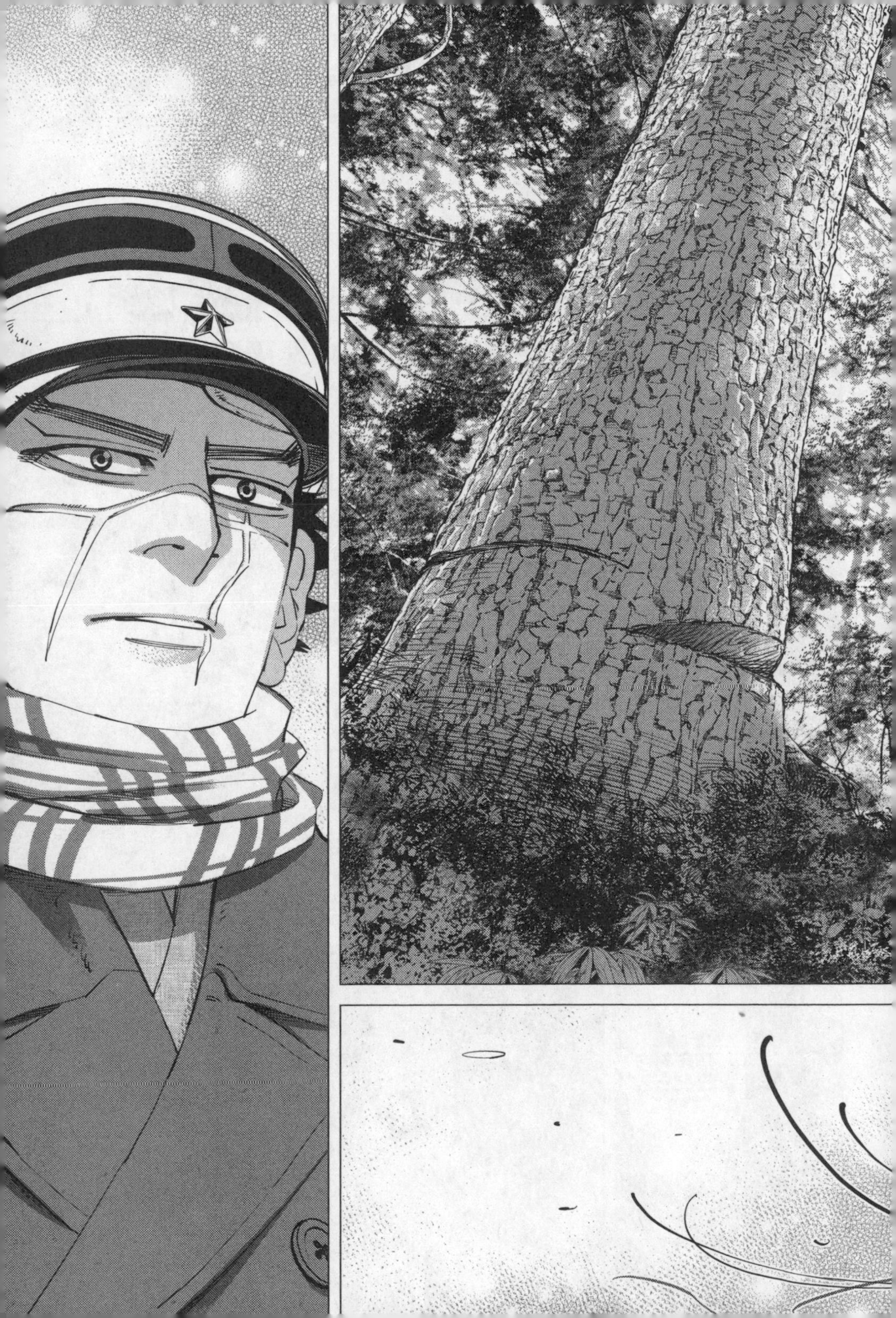

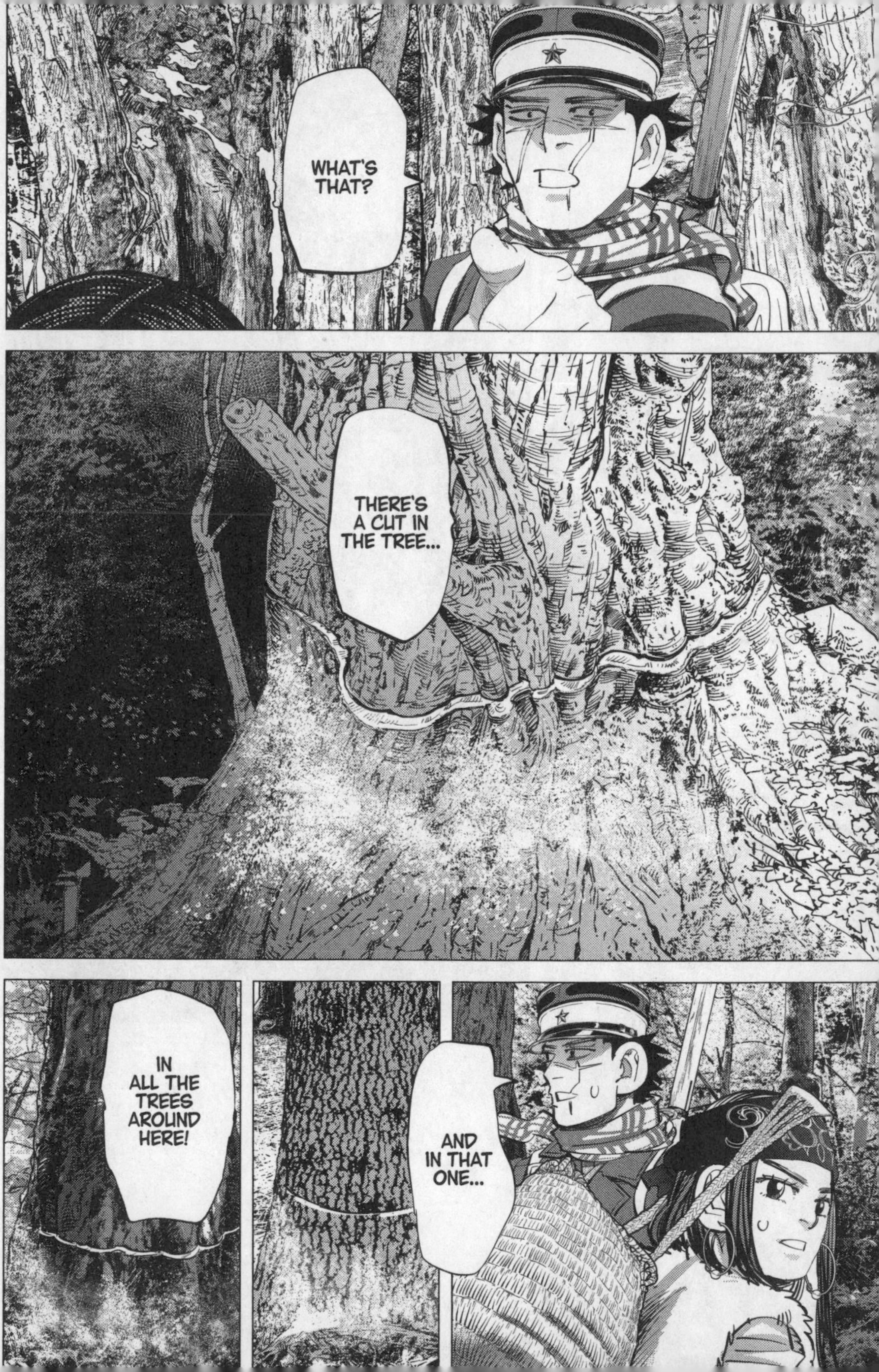
WHAT'S THAT?
THERE'S A CUT IN THE TREE...
AND IN THAT ONE...
IN ALL THE TREES AROUND HERE!

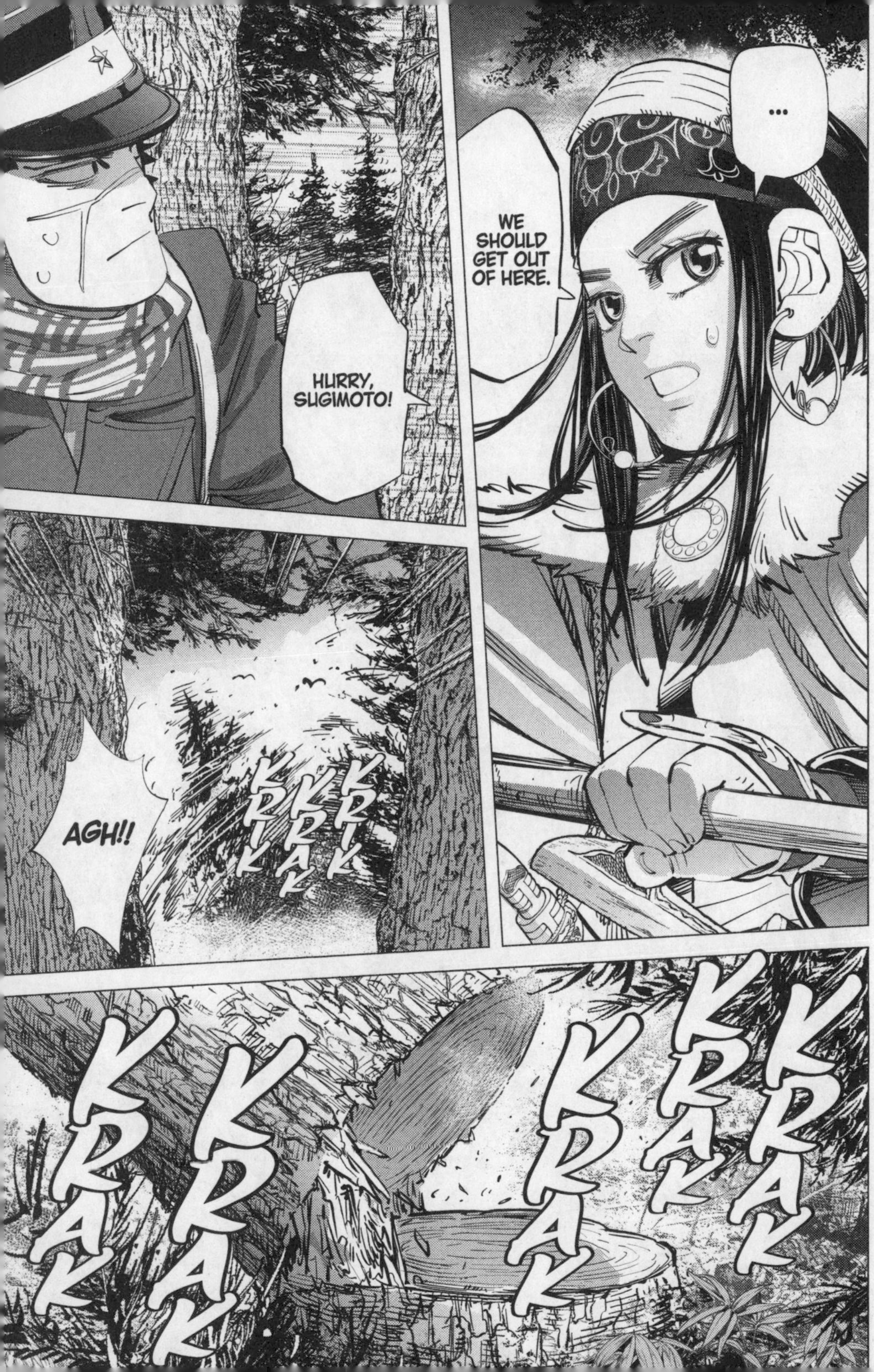
...
WE SHOULD GET OUT OF HERE.
HURRY, SUGIMOTO!
KRIK
KRAK
KRIK
AGH!!
KRAK
KRAK
KRAK
KRAK
KRAK

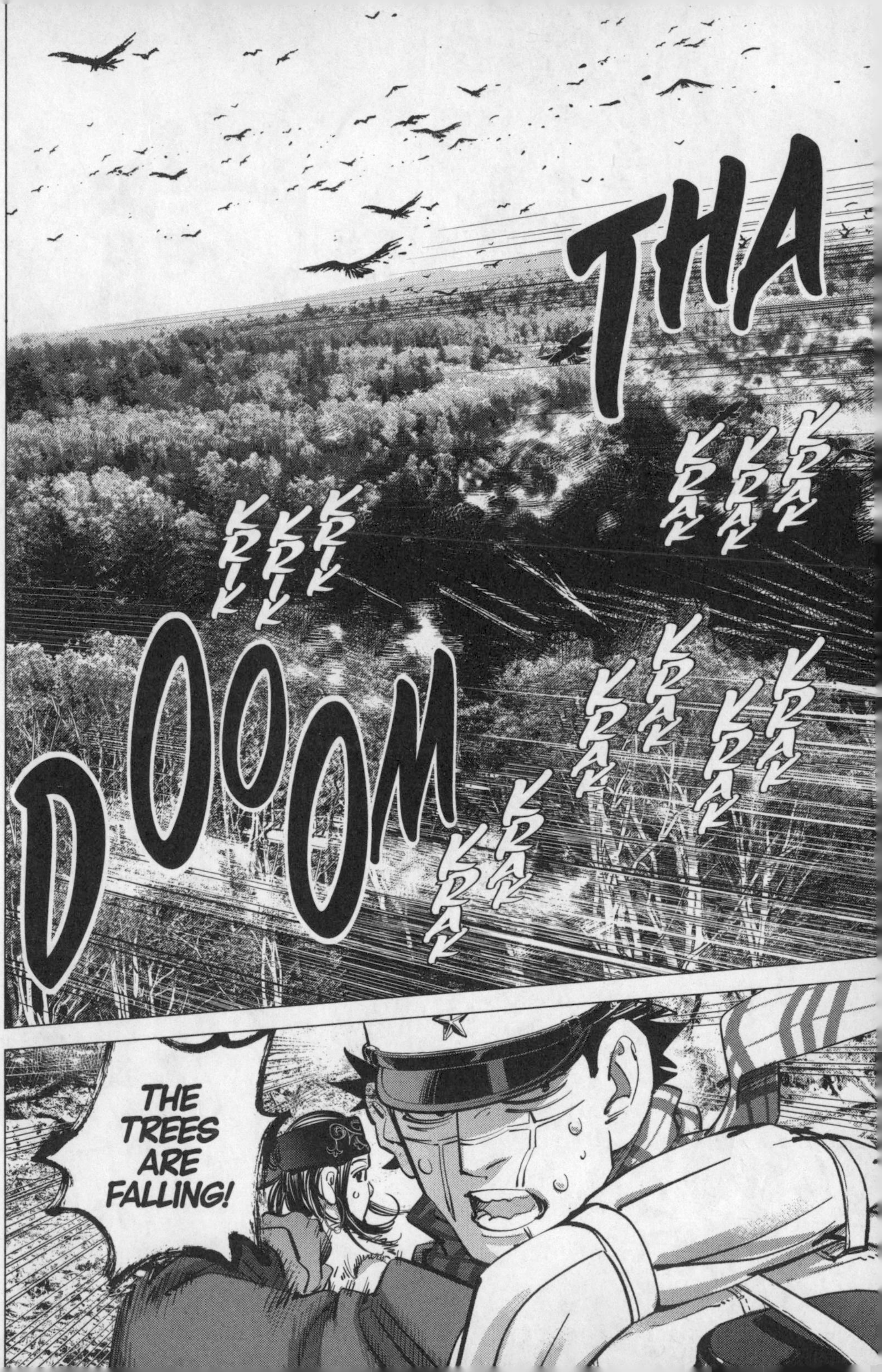
THA
KRAK KRAK KRAK
KRAK KRAK KRAK KRAK KRAK
KRIK KRIK KRIK
DOOOM
KRAK KRAK
THE TREES ARE FALLING!

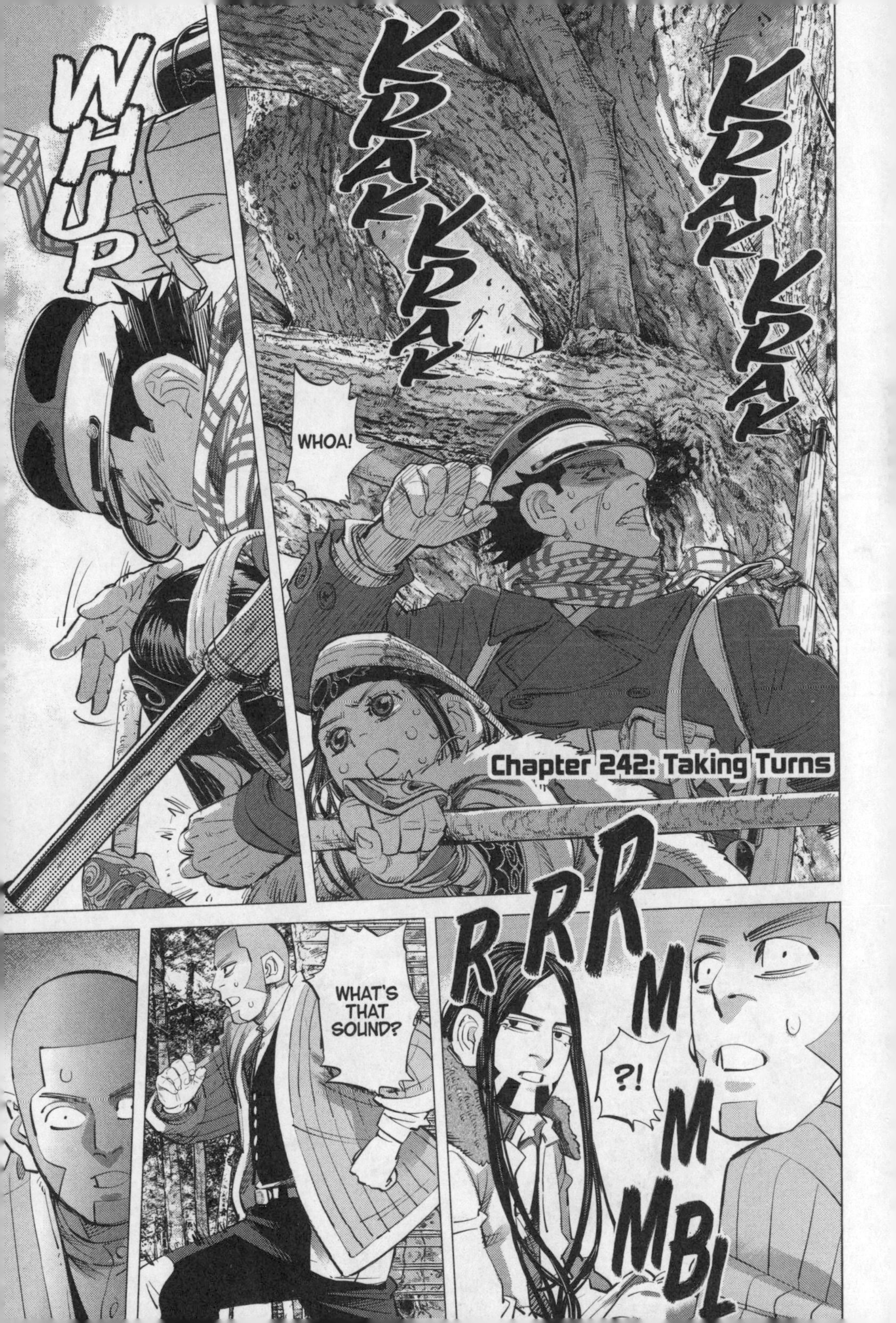
KRAK KRAK
KRAK KRAK
WHOA!
Chapter 242: Taking Turns
WHUP
RRRMMMBL
?!
WHAT'S THAT SOUND?

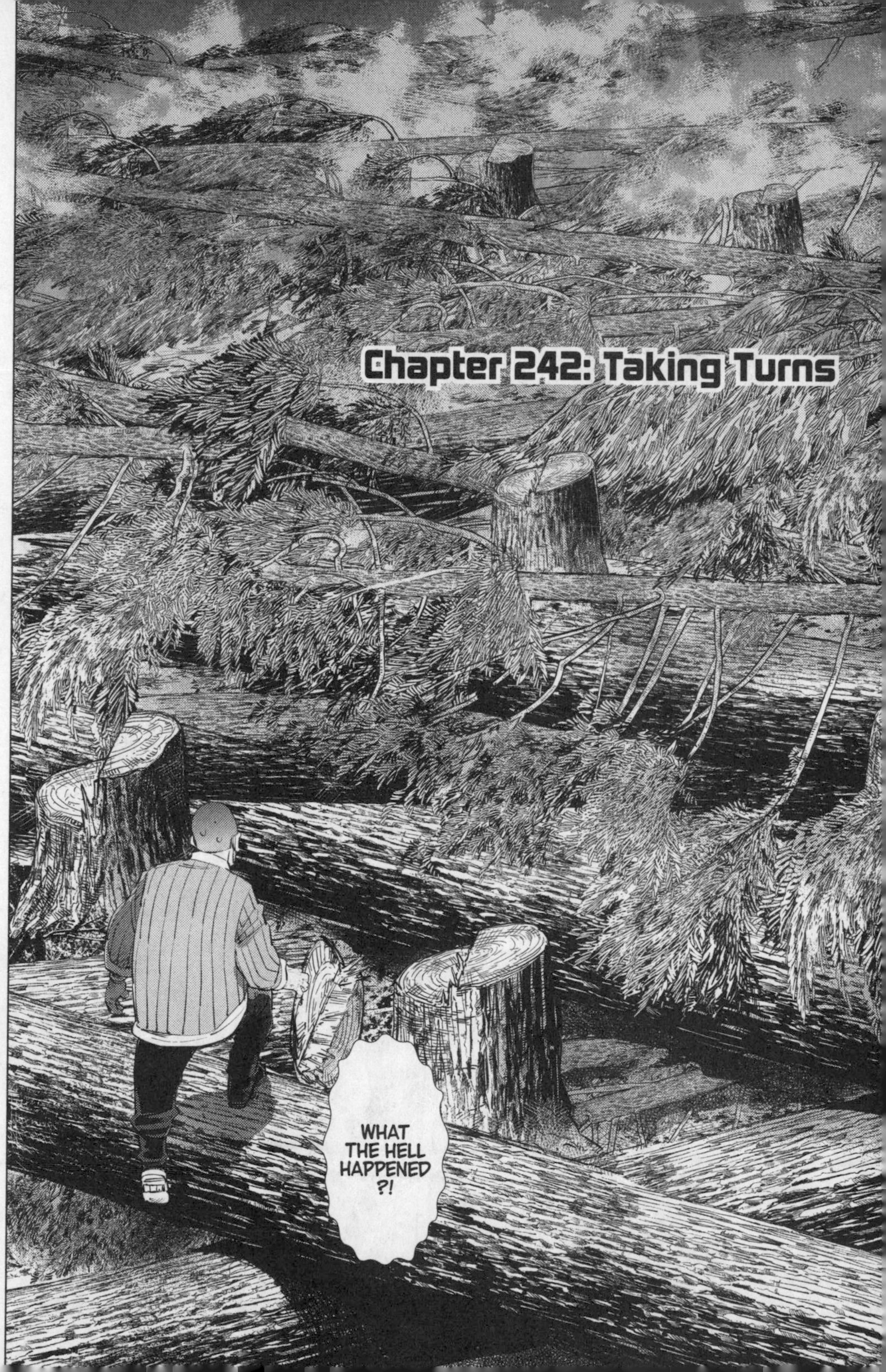
Chapter 242: Taking Turns
WHAT THE HELL HAPPENED ?!

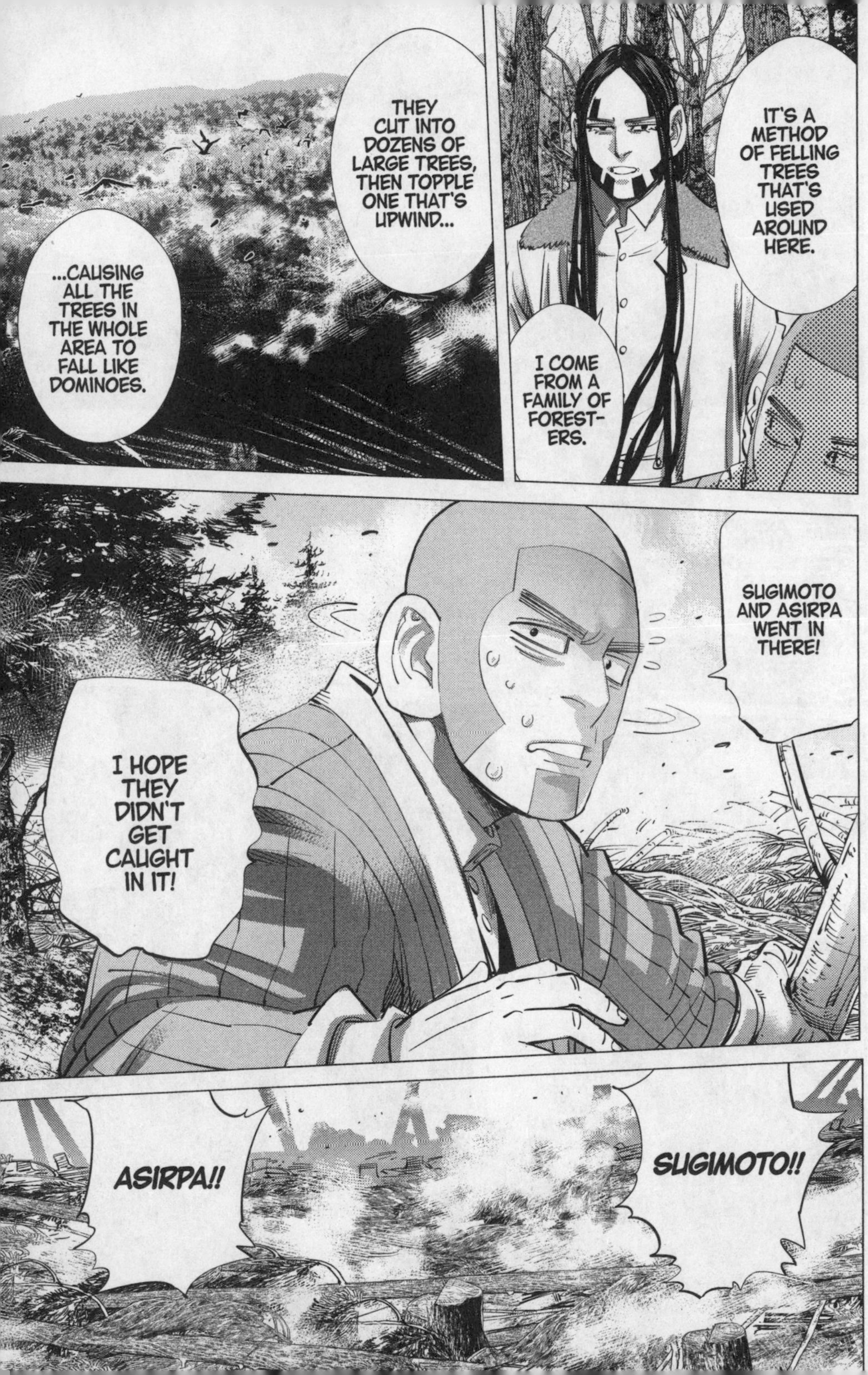
IT'S A METHOD OF FELLING TREES THAT'S USED AROUND HERE.
I COME FROM A FAMILY OF FOREST-ERS.
THEY CUT INTO DOZENS OF LARGE TREES, THEN TOPPLE ONE THAT'S UPWIND...
...CAUSING ALL THE TREES IN THE WHOLE AREA TO FALL LIKE DOMINOES.
SUGIMOTO AND ASIRPA WENT IN THERE!
I HOPE THEY DIDN'T GET CAUGHT IN IT!
SUGIMOTO!!
ASIRPA!!

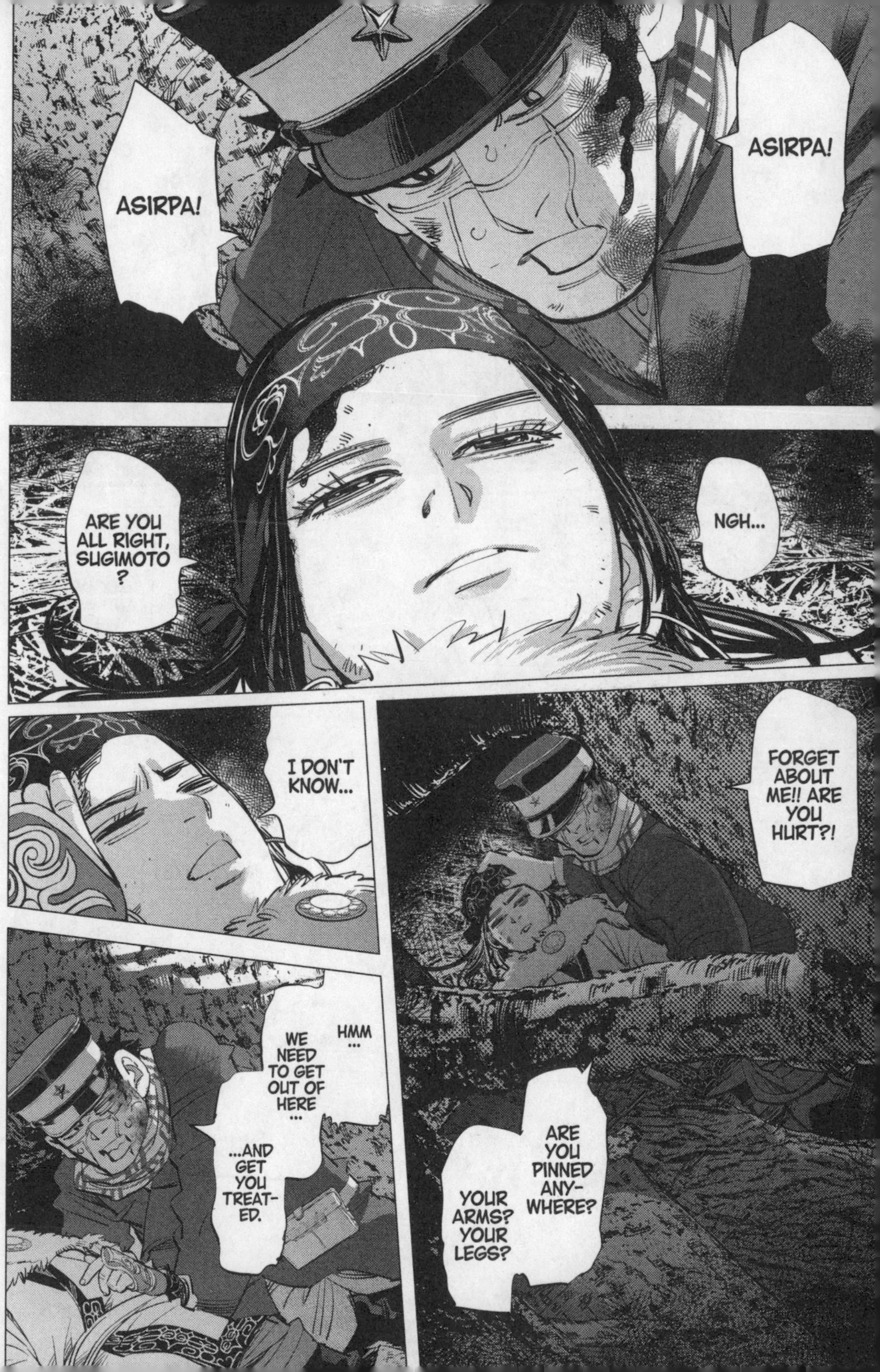
ASIRPA!
ASIRPA!
NGH...
ARE YOU ALL RIGHT, SUGIMOTO?
FORGET ABOUT ME!! ARE YOU HURT?!
ARE YOU PINNED ANYWHERE?
YOUR ARMS? YOUR LEGS?
I DON'T KNOW...
HMM...
WE NEED TO GET OUT OF HERE...
...AND GET YOU TREATED.

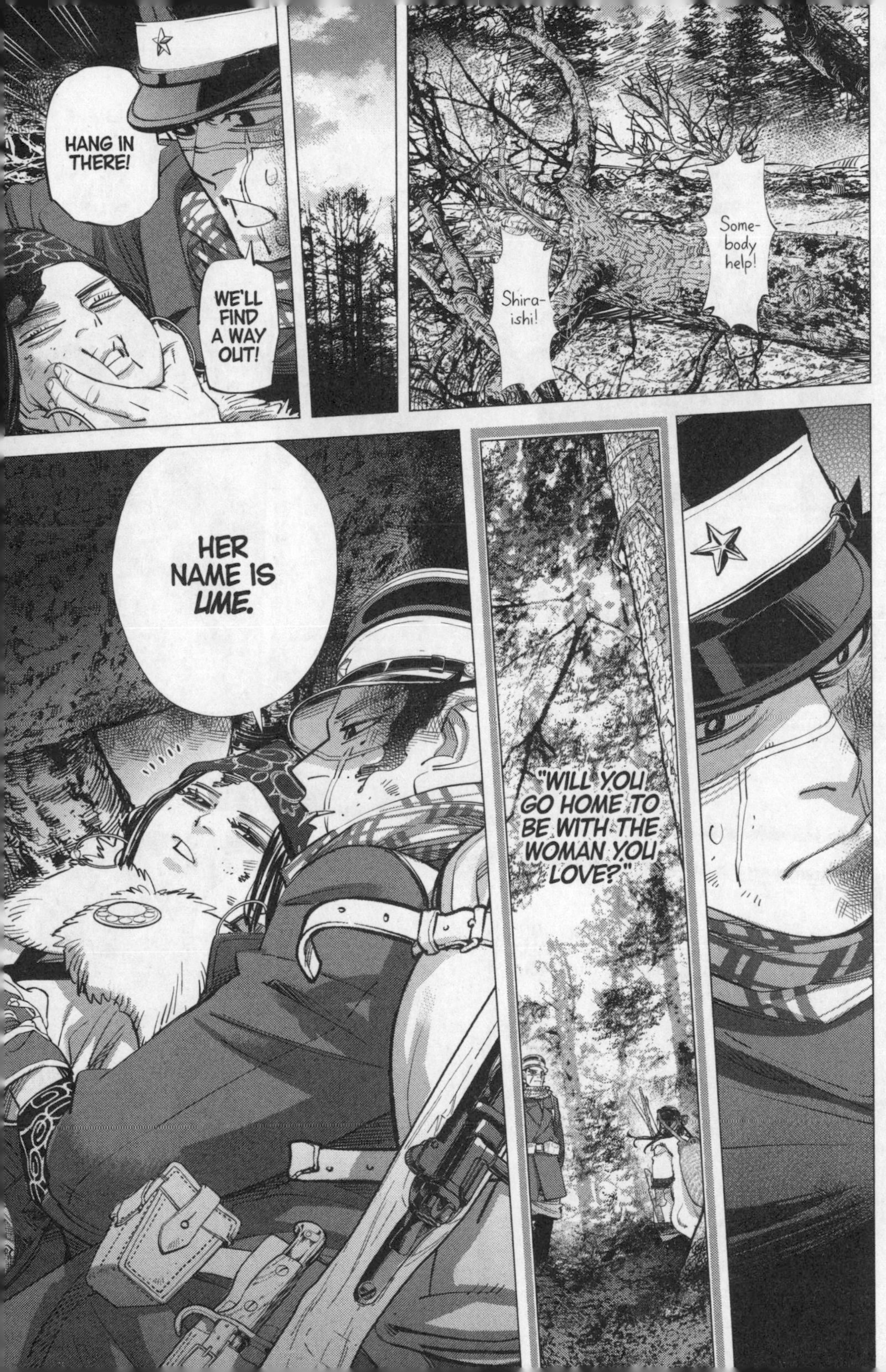
Somebody help!
Shiraishi!
HANG IN THERE!
WE'LL FIND A WAY OUT!
"WILL YOU GO HOME TO BE WITH THE WOMAN YOU LOVE?"
HER NAME IS UME.

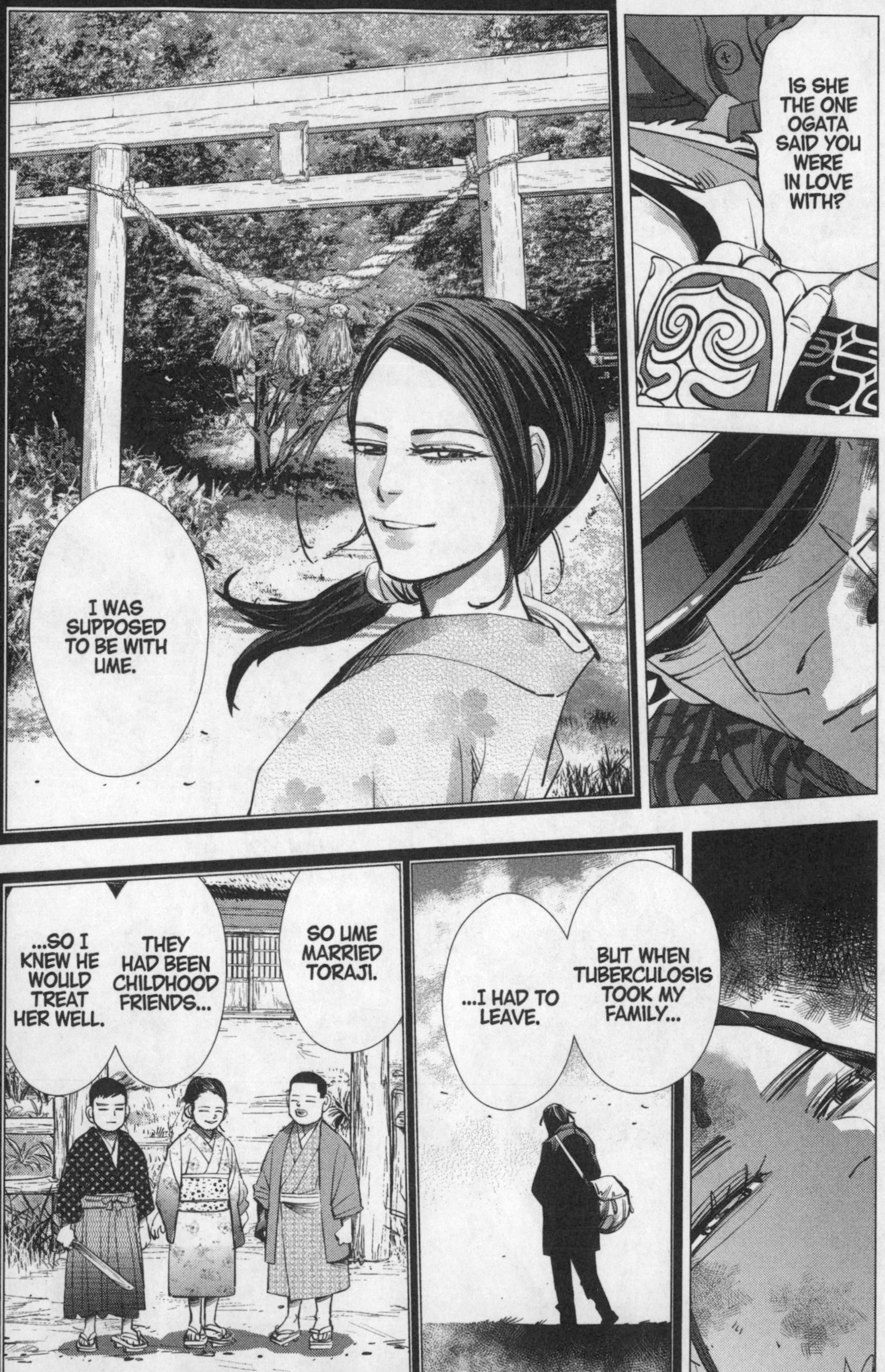
IS SHE THE ONE OGATA SAID YOU WERE IN LOVE WITH?
I WAS SUPPOSED TO BE WITH UME.
BUT WHEN TUBERCULOSIS TOOK MY FAMILY...
...I HAD TO LEAVE.
SO UME MARRIED TORAJI.
THEY HAD BEEN CHILDHOOD FRIENDS...
...SO I KNEW HE WOULD TREAT HER WELL.

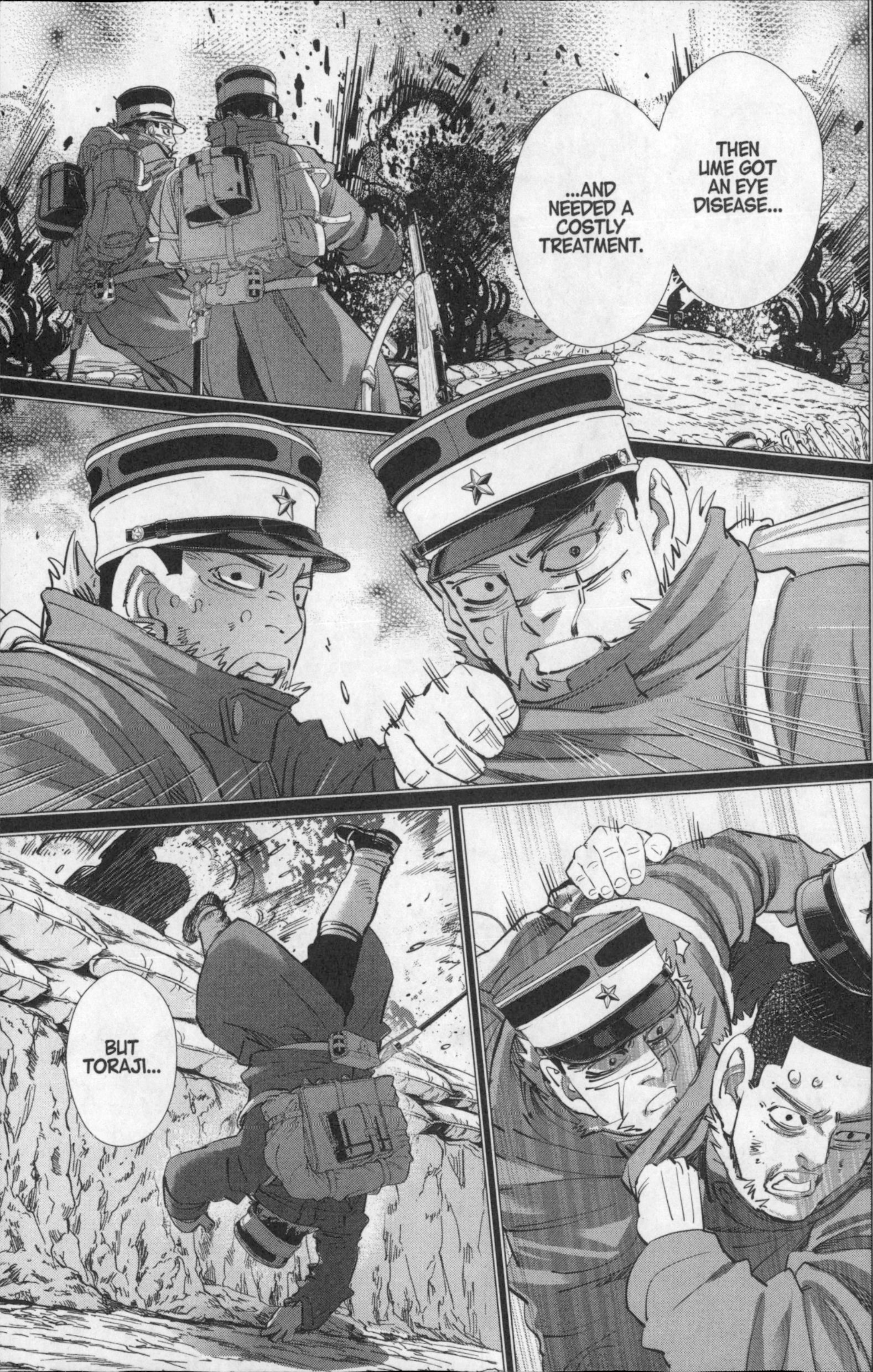
THEN UME GOT AN EYE DISEASE...
...AND NEEDED A COSTLY TREATMENT.
BUT TORAJI...

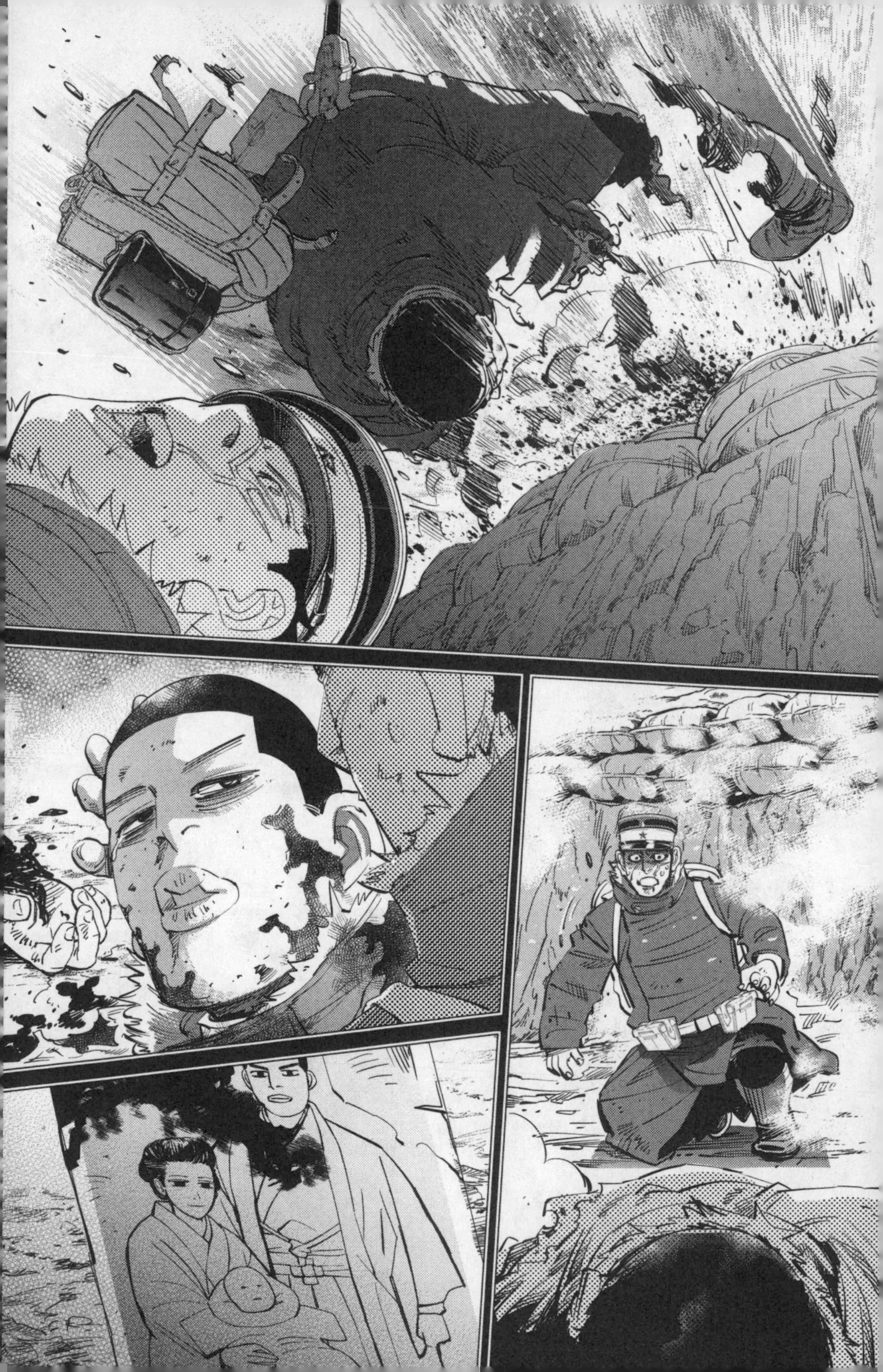

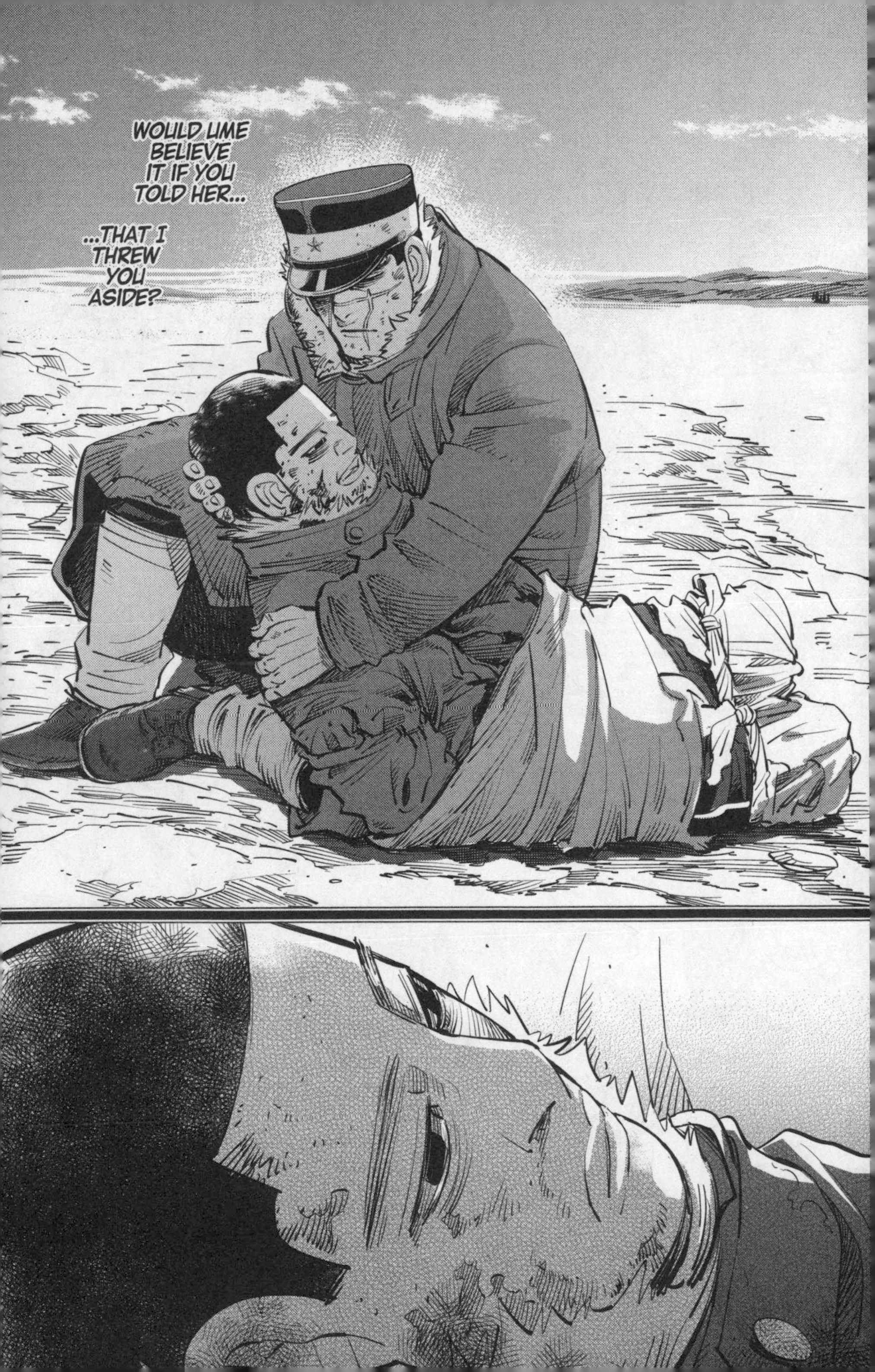
WOULD UME BELIEVE IT IF YOU TOLD HER...
...THAT I THREW YOU ASIDE?

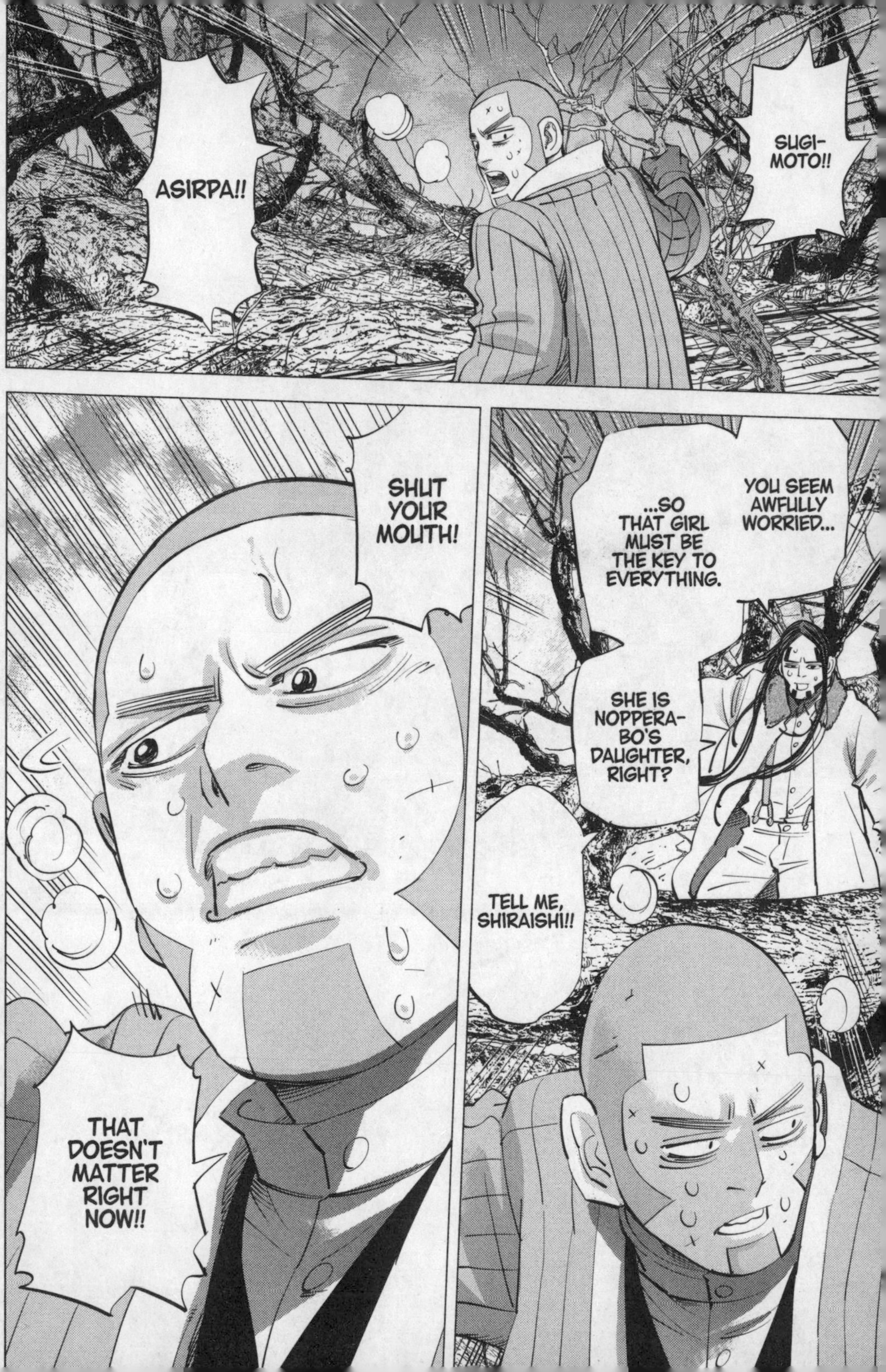
SUGI-MOTO!!
ASIRPA!!
YOU SEEM AWFULLY WORRIED...
...SO THAT GIRL MUST BE THE KEY TO EVERYTHING.
SHE IS NOPPERA-BO'S DAUGHTER, RIGHT?
TELL ME, SHIRAISHI!!
SHUT YOUR MOUTH!
THAT DOESN'T MATTER RIGHT NOW!!

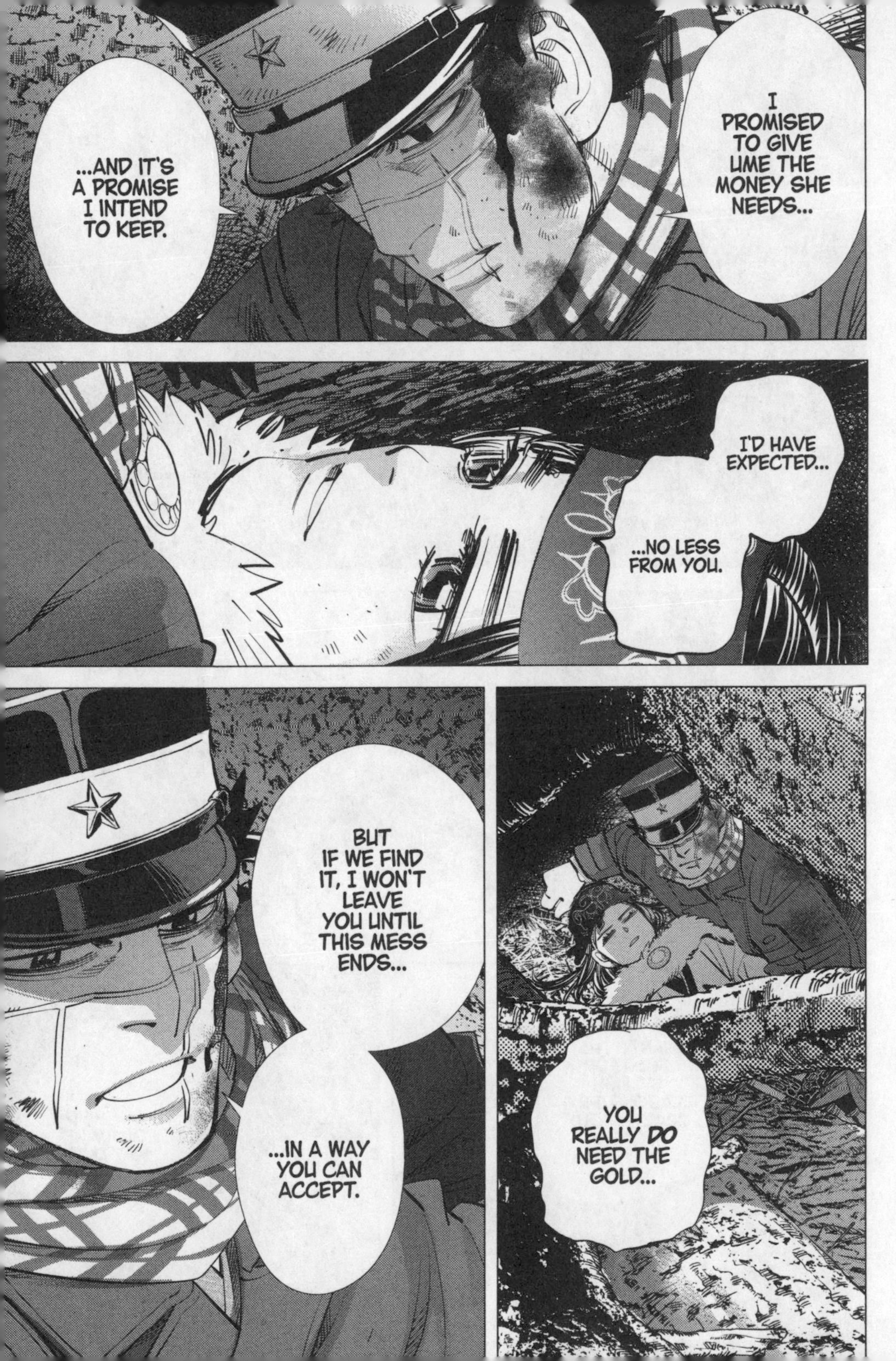
I PROMISED TO GIVE UME THE MONEY SHE NEEDS...
...AND IT'S A PROMISE I INTEND TO KEEP.
I'D HAVE EXPECTED...
...NO LESS FROM YOU.
YOU REALLY DO NEED THE GOLD...
BUT IF WE FIND IT, I WON'T LEAVE YOU UNTIL THIS MESS ENDS...
...IN A WAY YOU CAN ACCEPT.

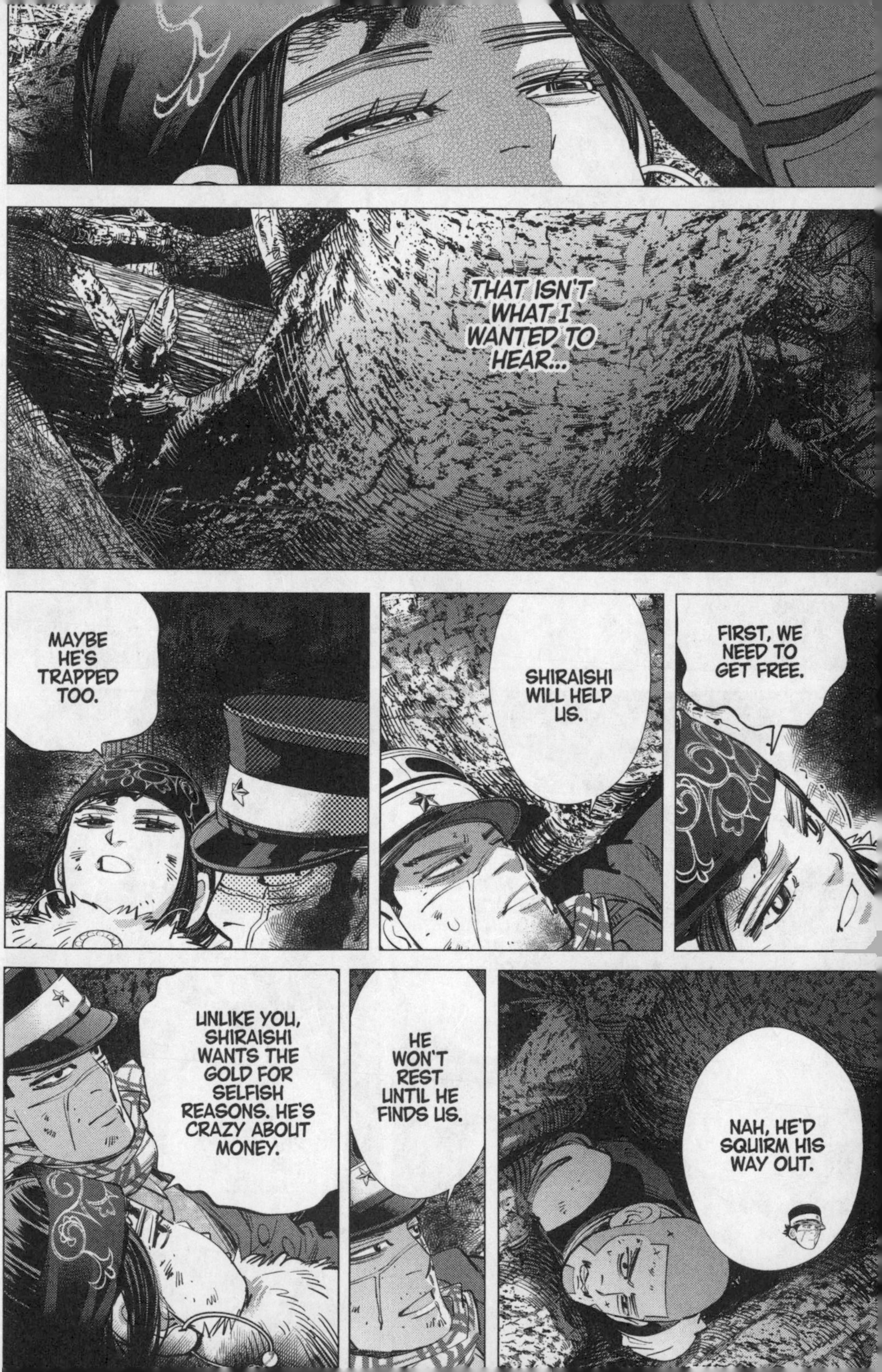
THAT ISN'T WHAT I WANTED TO HEAR...
FIRST, WE NEED TO GET FREE.
SHIRAISHI WILL HELP US.
MAYBE HE'S TRAPPED TOO.
NAH, HE'D SQUIRM HIS WAY OUT.
HE WON'T REST UNTIL HE FINDS US.
UNLIKE YOU, SHIRAISHI WANTS THE GOLD FOR SELFISH REASONS. HE'S CRAZY ABOUT MONEY.

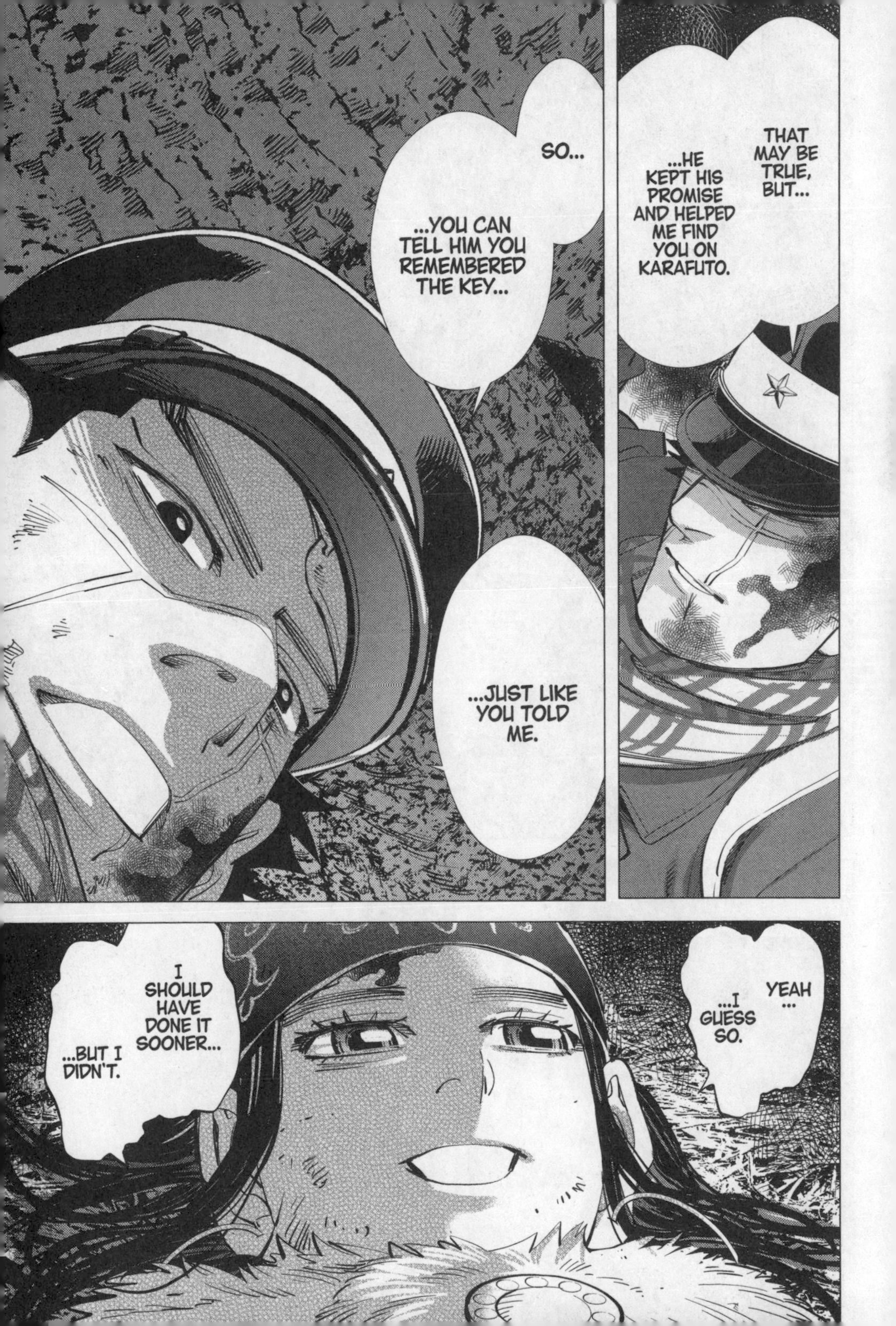
THAT MAY BE TRUE, BUT...
...HE KEPT HIS PROMISE AND HELPED ME FIND YOU ON KARAFUTO.
SO...
...YOU CAN TELL HIM YOU REMEMBERED THE KEY...
...JUST LIKE YOU TOLD ME.
YEAH...
...I GUESS SO.
I SHOULD HAVE DONE IT SOONER...
...BUT I DIDN'T.

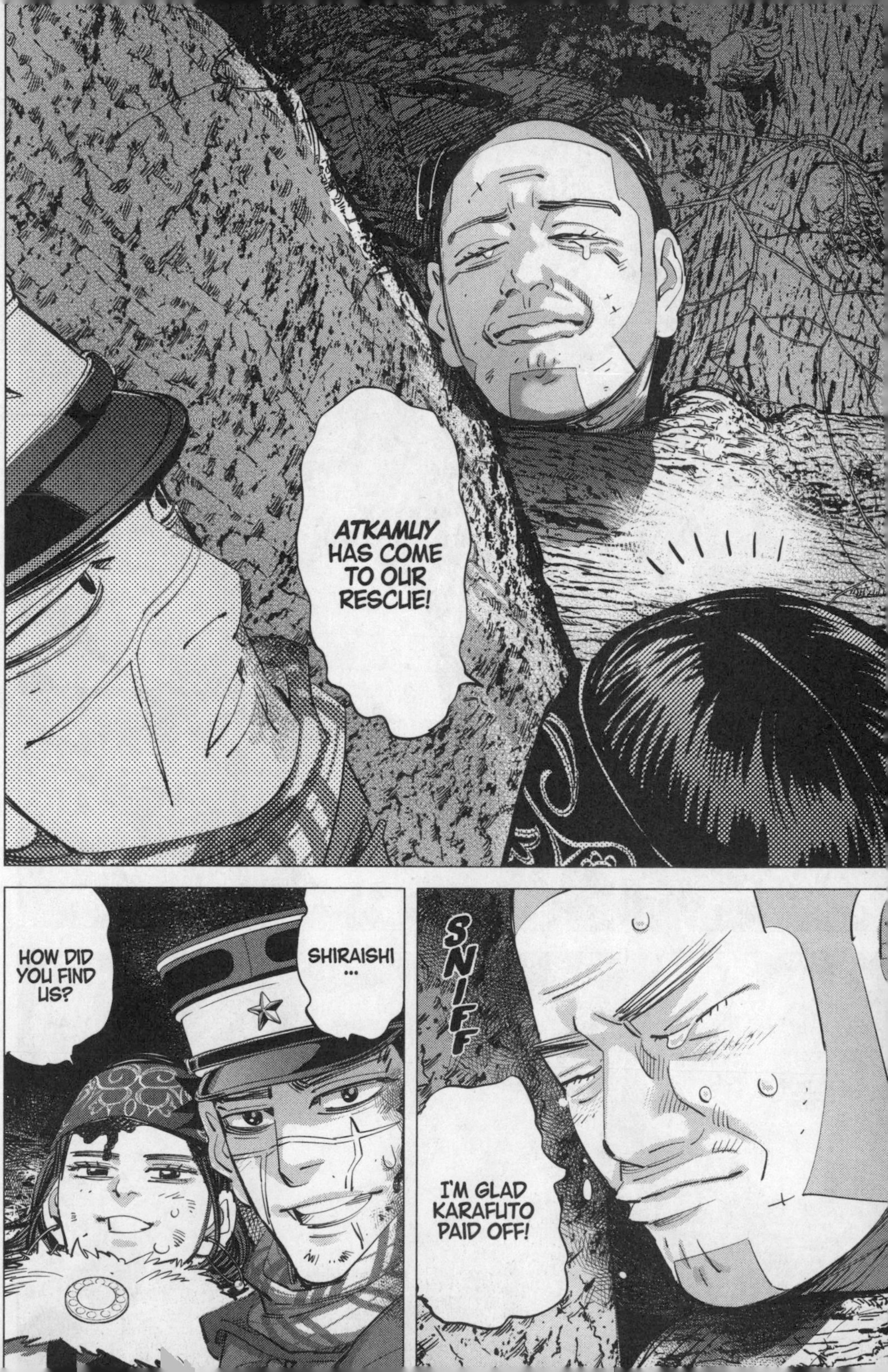
ATKAMUY HAS COME TO OUR RESCUE!
SNIFF
I'M GLAD KARAFUTO PAID OFF!
SHIRAISHI ...
HOW DID YOU FIND US?

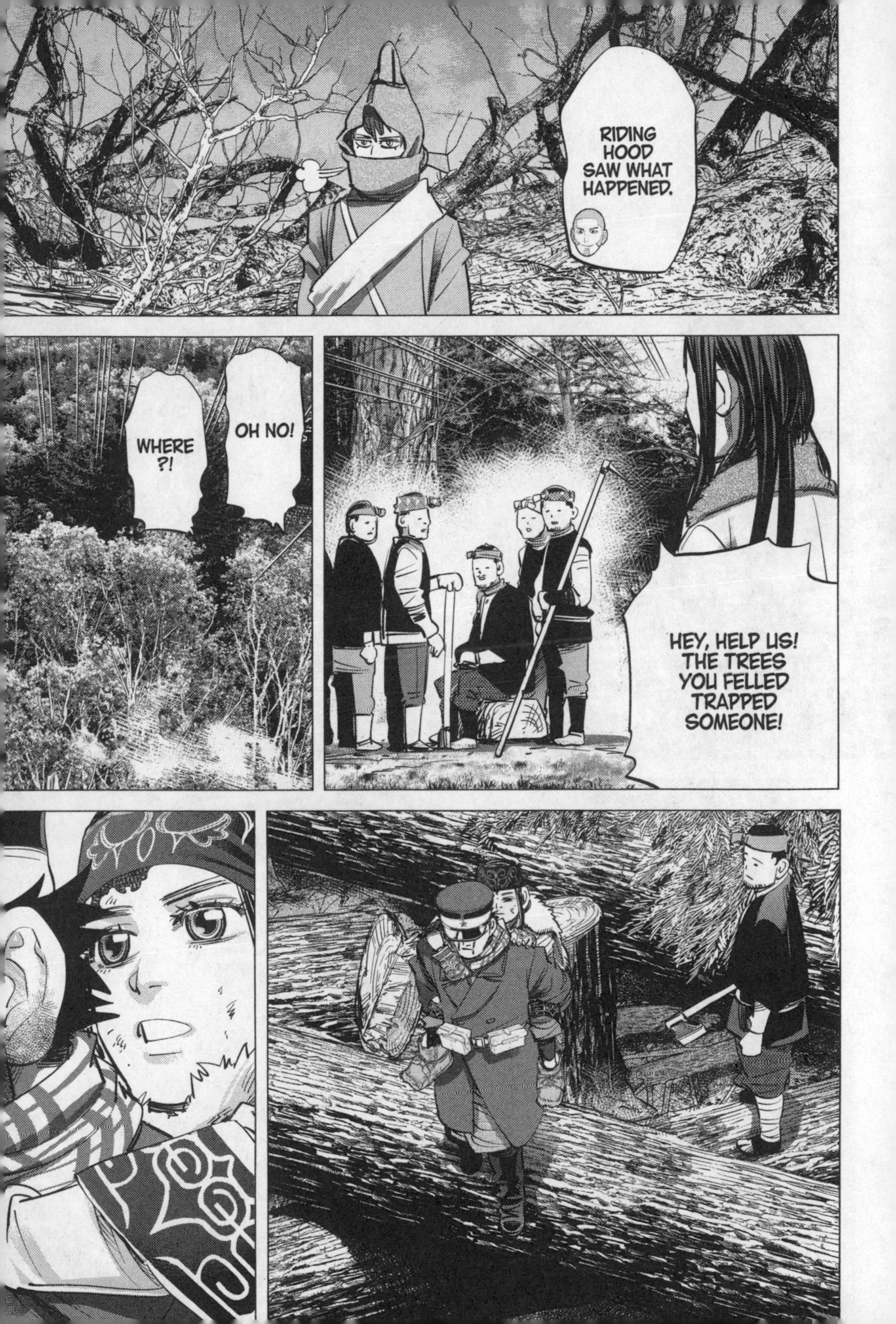
RIDING HOOD SAW WHAT HAPPENED.
HEY, HELP US! THE TREES YOU FELLED TRAPPED SOMEONE!
OH NO!
WHERE ?!

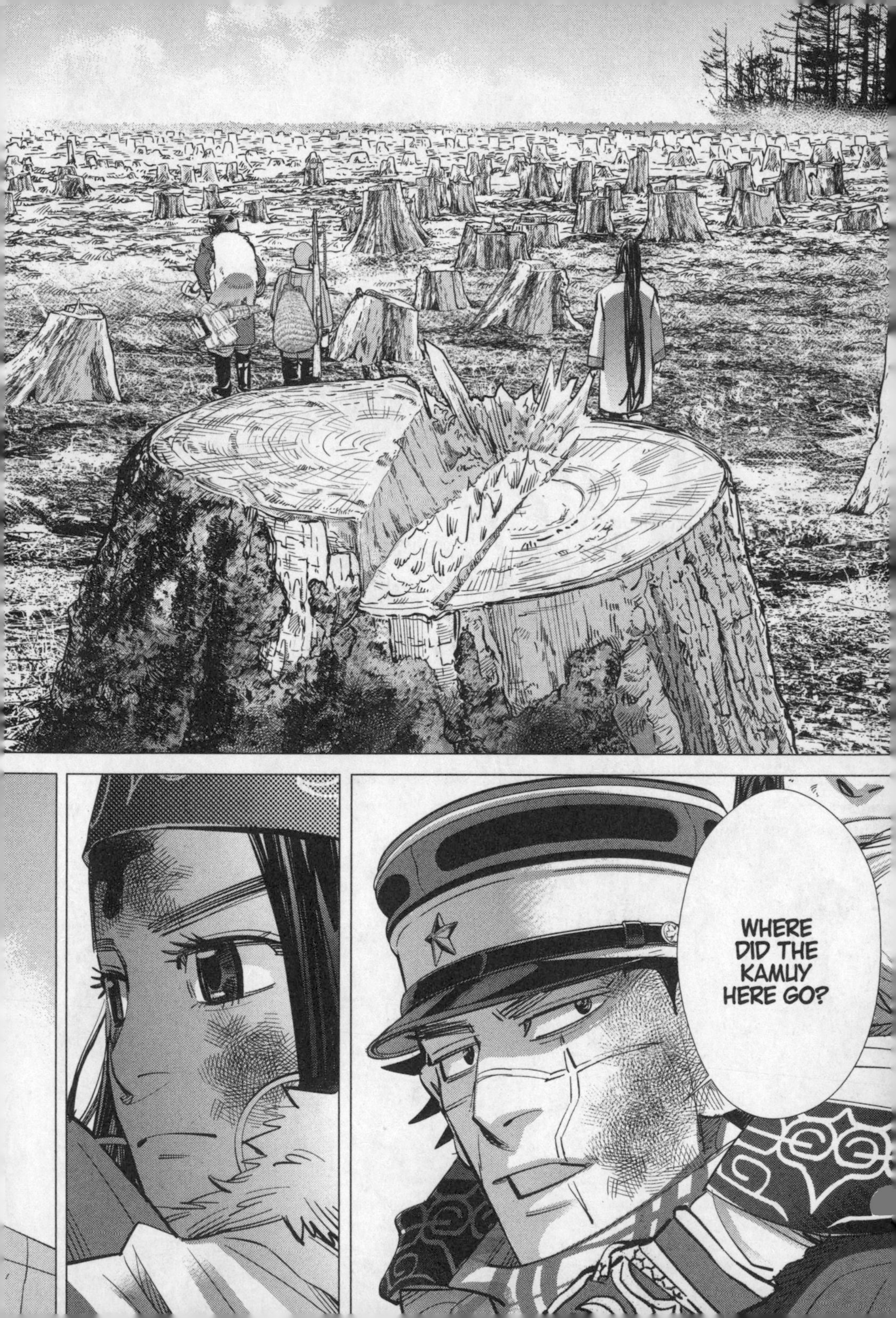
WHERE DID THE KAMUY HERE GO?

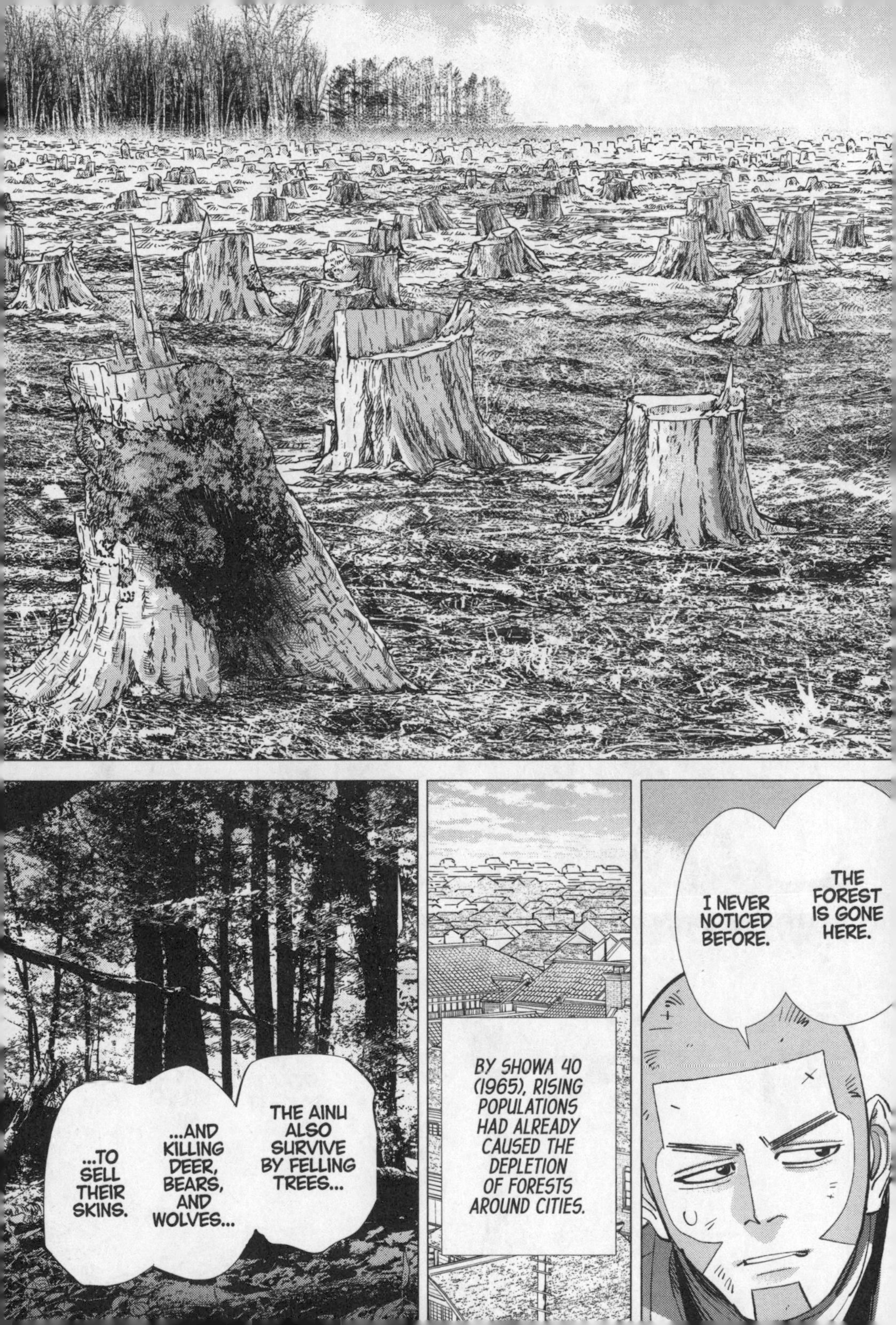
THE FOREST IS GONE HERE.
I NEVER NOTICED BEFORE.
BY SHOWA 40 (1965), RISING POPULATIONS HAD ALREADY CAUSED THE DEPLETION OF FORESTS AROUND CITIES.
THE AINU ALSO SURVIVE BY FELLING TREES...
...AND KILLING DEER, BEARS, AND WOLVES...
...TO SELL THEIR SKINS.

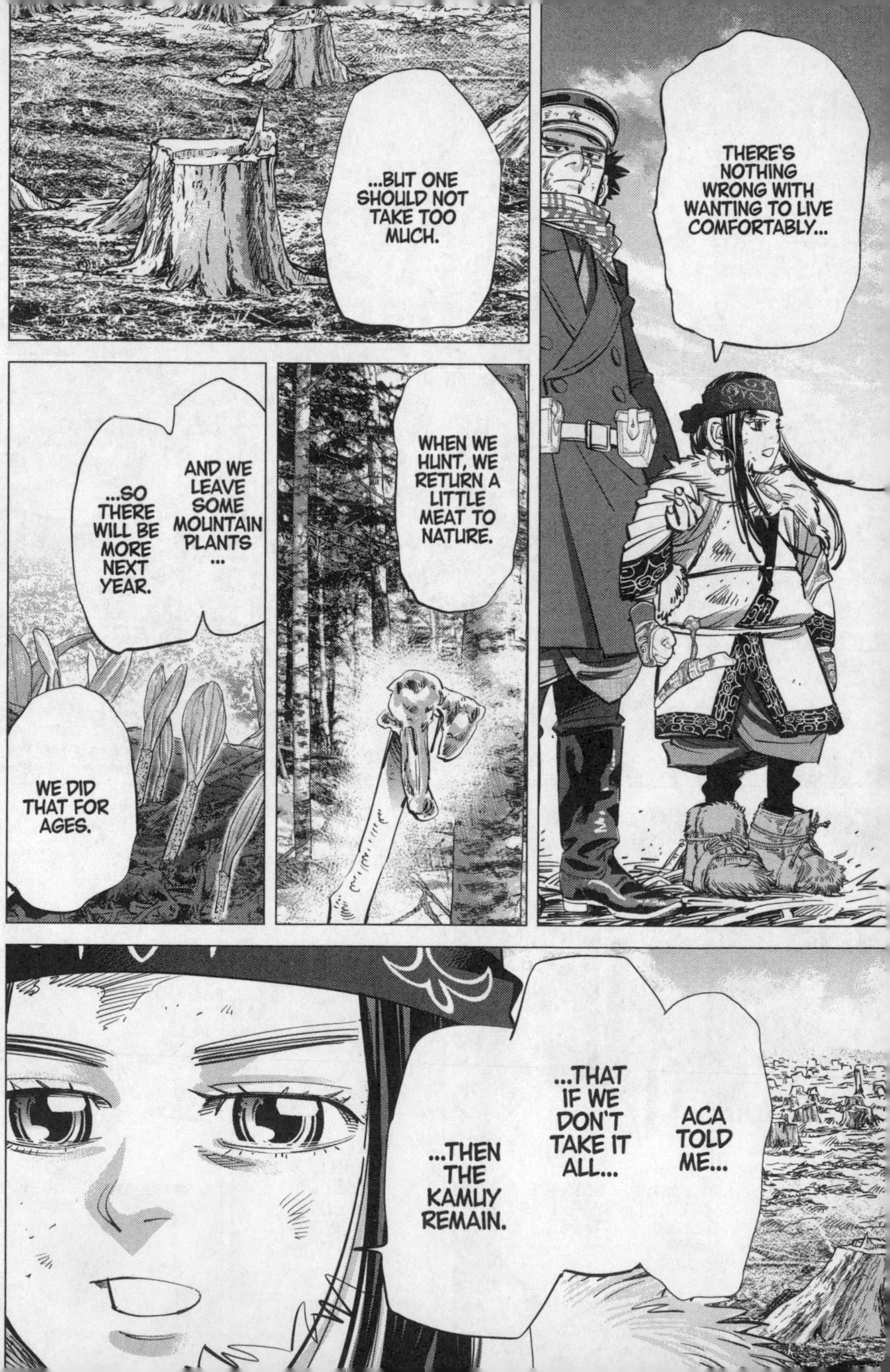
THERE'S NOTHING WRONG WITH WANTING TO LIVE COMFORTABLY...
...BUT ONE SHOULD NOT TAKE TOO MUCH.
WHEN WE HUNT, WE RETURN A LITTLE MEAT TO NATURE.
AND WE LEAVE SOME MOUNTAIN PLANTS...
...SO THERE WILL BE MORE NEXT YEAR.
WE DID THAT FOR AGES.
ACA TOLD ME...
...THAT IF WE DON'T TAKE IT ALL...
...THEN THE KAMUY REMAIN.

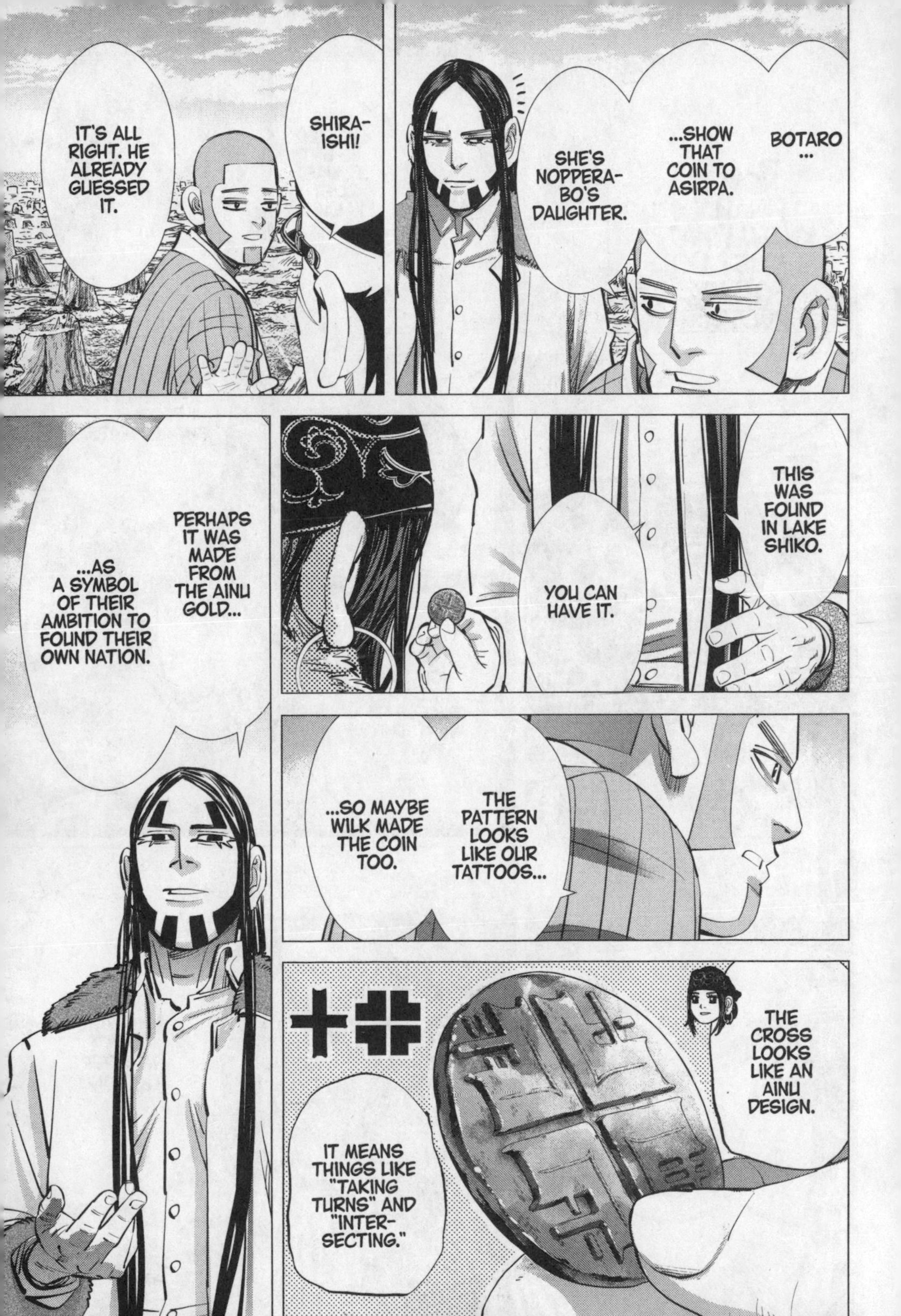
BOTARO ...
...SHOW THAT COIN TO ASIRPA.
SHE'S NOPPERA-BO'S DAUGHTER.
SHIRA-ISHI!
IT'S ALL RIGHT. HE ALREADY GUESSED IT.
THIS WAS FOUND IN LAKE SHIKO.
YOU CAN HAVE IT.
THE PATTERN LOOKS LIKE OUR TATTOOS...
...SO MAYBE WILK MADE THE COIN TOO.
THE CROSS LOOKS LIKE AN AINU DESIGN.
IT MEANS THINGS LIKE "TAKING TURNS" AND "INTER-SECTING."
PERHAPS IT WAS MADE FROM THE AINU GOLD...
...AS A SYMBOL OF THEIR AMBITION TO FOUND THEIR OWN NATION.

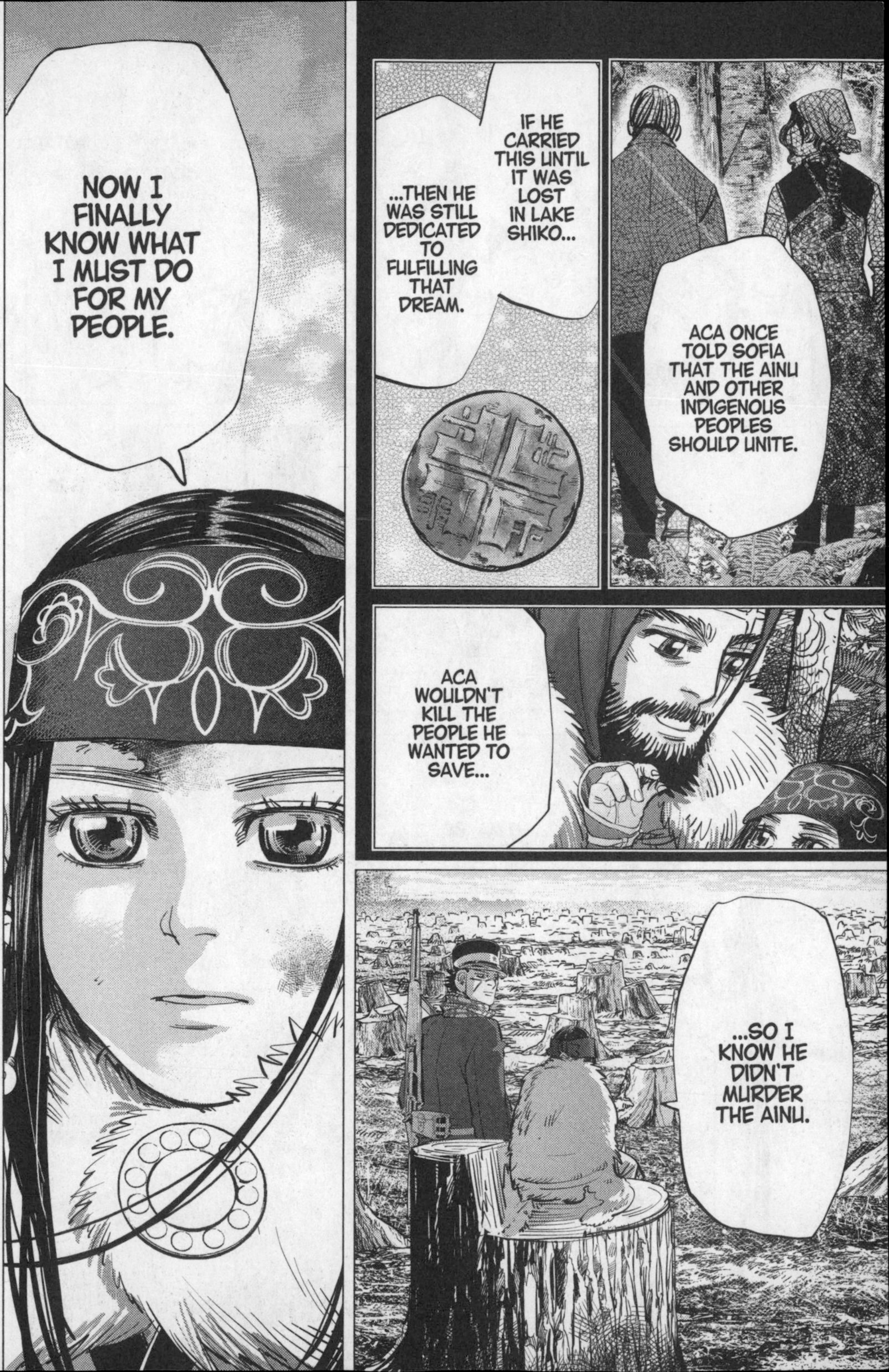
ACA ONCE TOLD SOFIA THAT THE AINU AND OTHER INDIGENOUS PEOPLES SHOULD UNITE.
IF HE CARRIED THIS UNTIL IT WAS LOST IN LAKE SHIKO...
...THEN HE WAS STILL DEDICATED TO FULFILLING THAT DREAM.
ACA WOULDN'T KILL THE PEOPLE HE WANTED TO SAVE...
...SO I KNOW HE DIDN'T MURDER THE AINU.
NOW I FINALLY KNOW WHAT I MUST DO FOR MY PEOPLE.

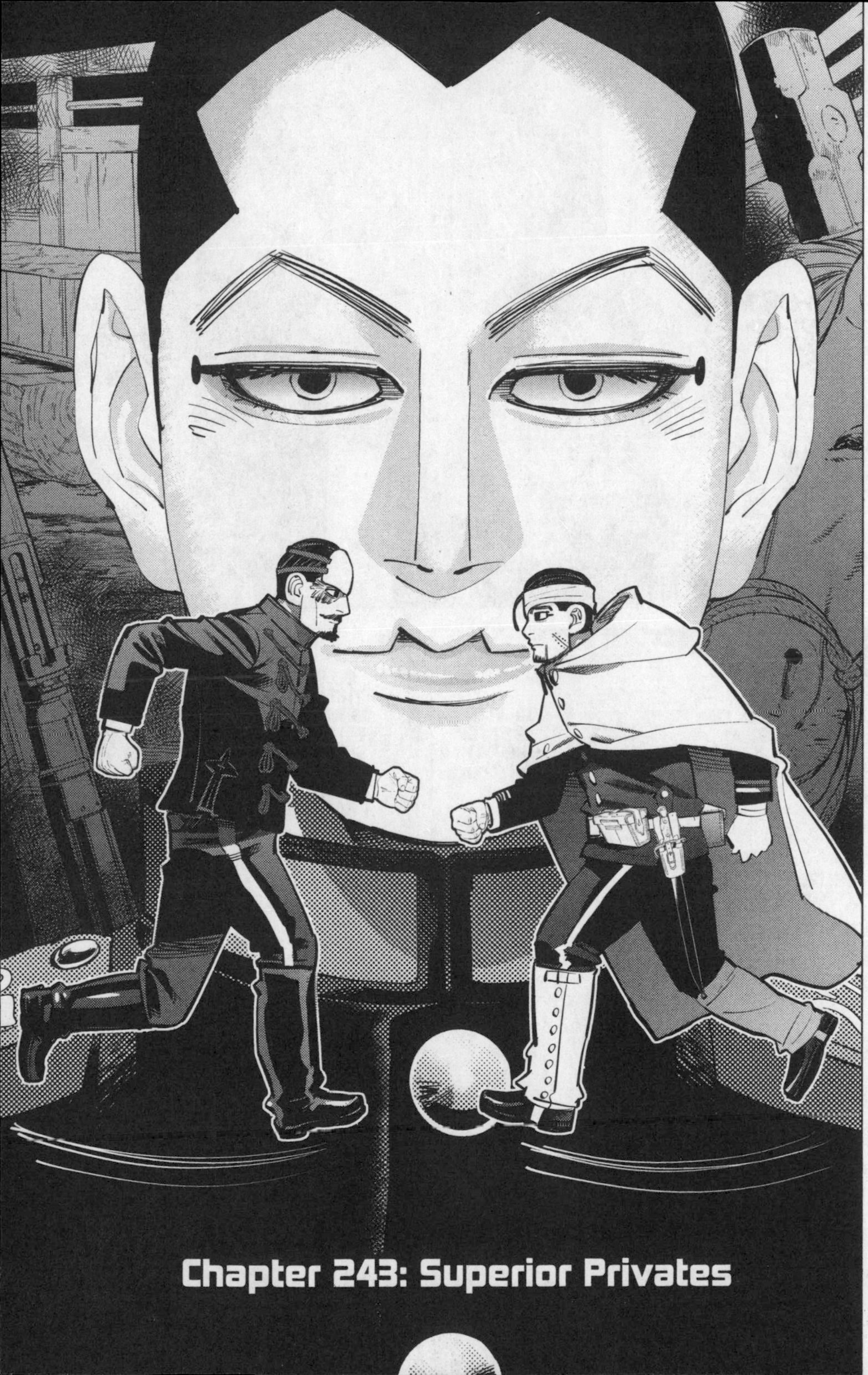

Chapter 243: Superior Privates

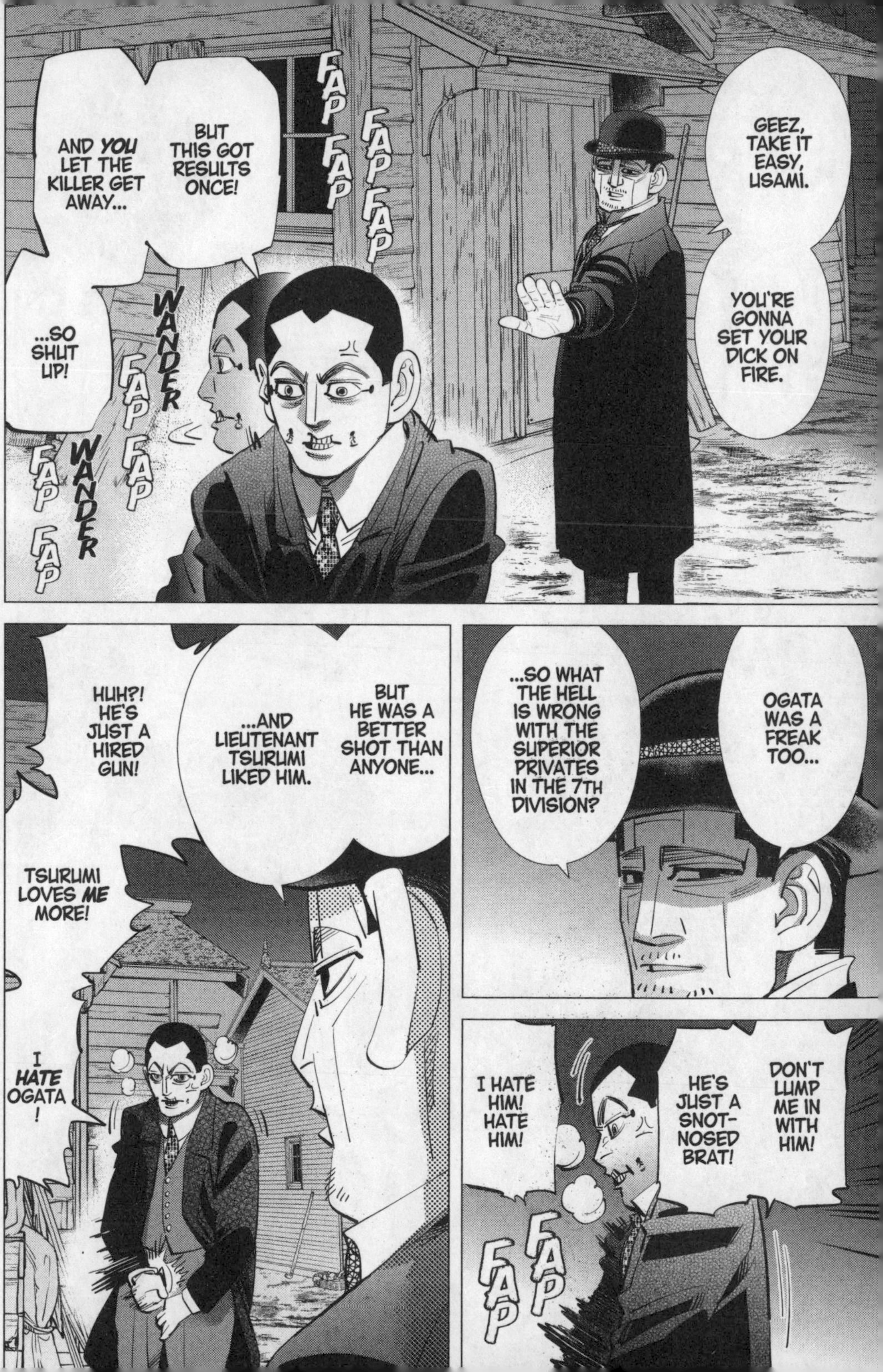
GEEZ, TAKE IT EASY, USAMI.
YOU'RE GONNA SET YOUR DICK ON FIRE.
FAP FAP FAP
FAP FAP FAP
BUT THIS GOT RESULTS ONCE!
AND YOU LET THE KILLER GET AWAY...
...SO SHUT UP!
WANDER
FAP FAP FAP
WANDER
FAP FAP
OGATA WAS A FREAK TOO...
...SO WHAT THE HELL IS WRONG WITH THE SUPERIOR PRIVATES IN THE 7TH DIVISION?
DON'T LUMP ME IN WITH HIM!
HE'S JUST A SNOT-NOSED BRAT!
I HATE HIM! HATE HIM!
FAP FAP
BUT HE WAS A BETTER SHOT THAN ANYONE...
...AND LIEUTENANT TSURUMI LIKED HIM.
HUH?! HE'S JUST A HIRED GUN!
TSURUMI LOVES ME MORE!
I HATE OGATA!

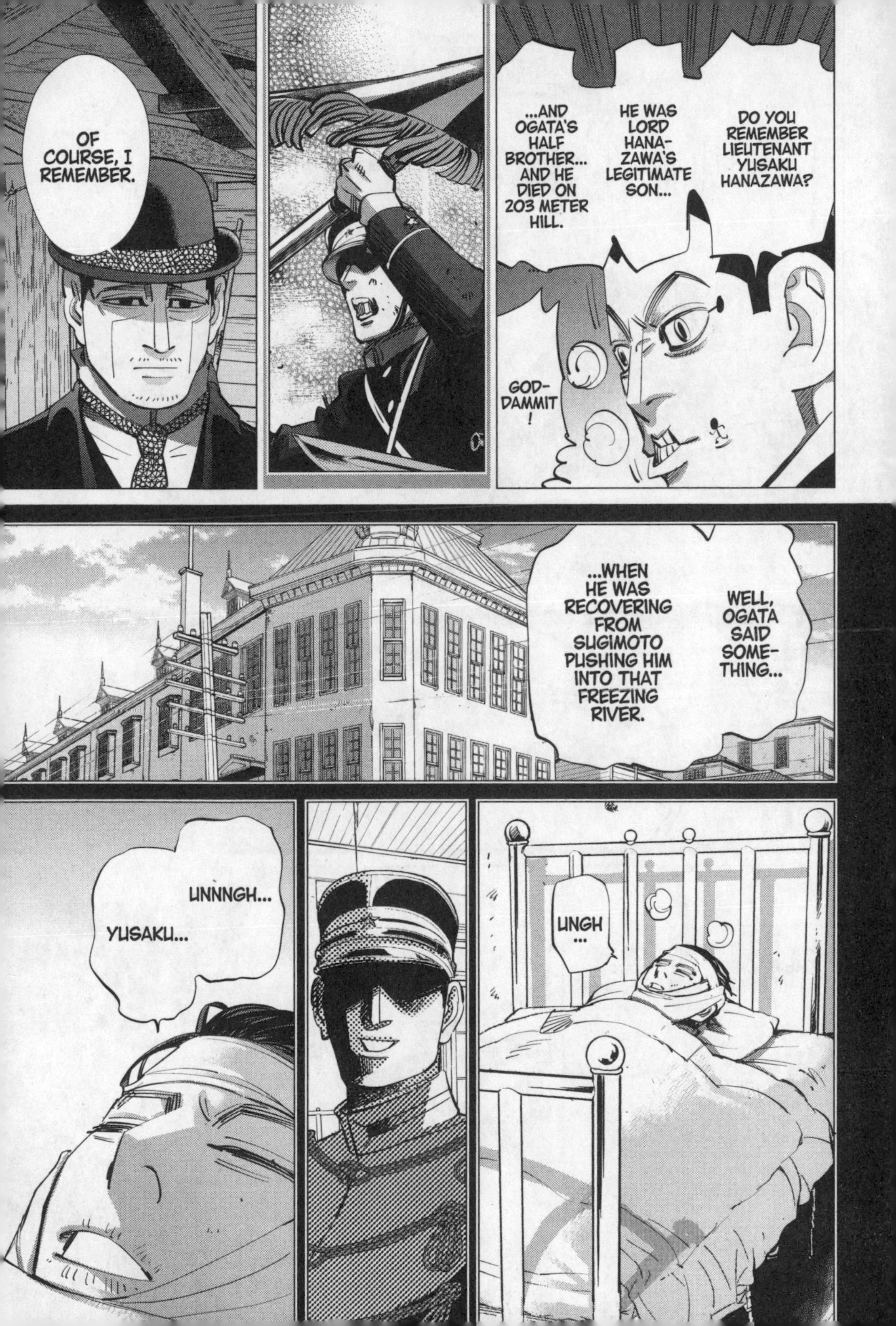
DO YOU REMEMBER LIEUTENANT YUSAKU HANAZAWA?
HE WAS LORD HANAZAWA'S LEGITIMATE SON...
...AND OGATA'S HALF BROTHER... AND HE DIED ON 203 METER HILL.
GOD-DAMMIT!
OF COURSE, I REMEMBER.
WELL, OGATA SAID SOMETHING...
...WHEN HE WAS RECOVERING FROM SUGIMOTO PUSHING HIM INTO THAT FREEZING RIVER.
UNGH...
UNNNGH...
YUSAKU...

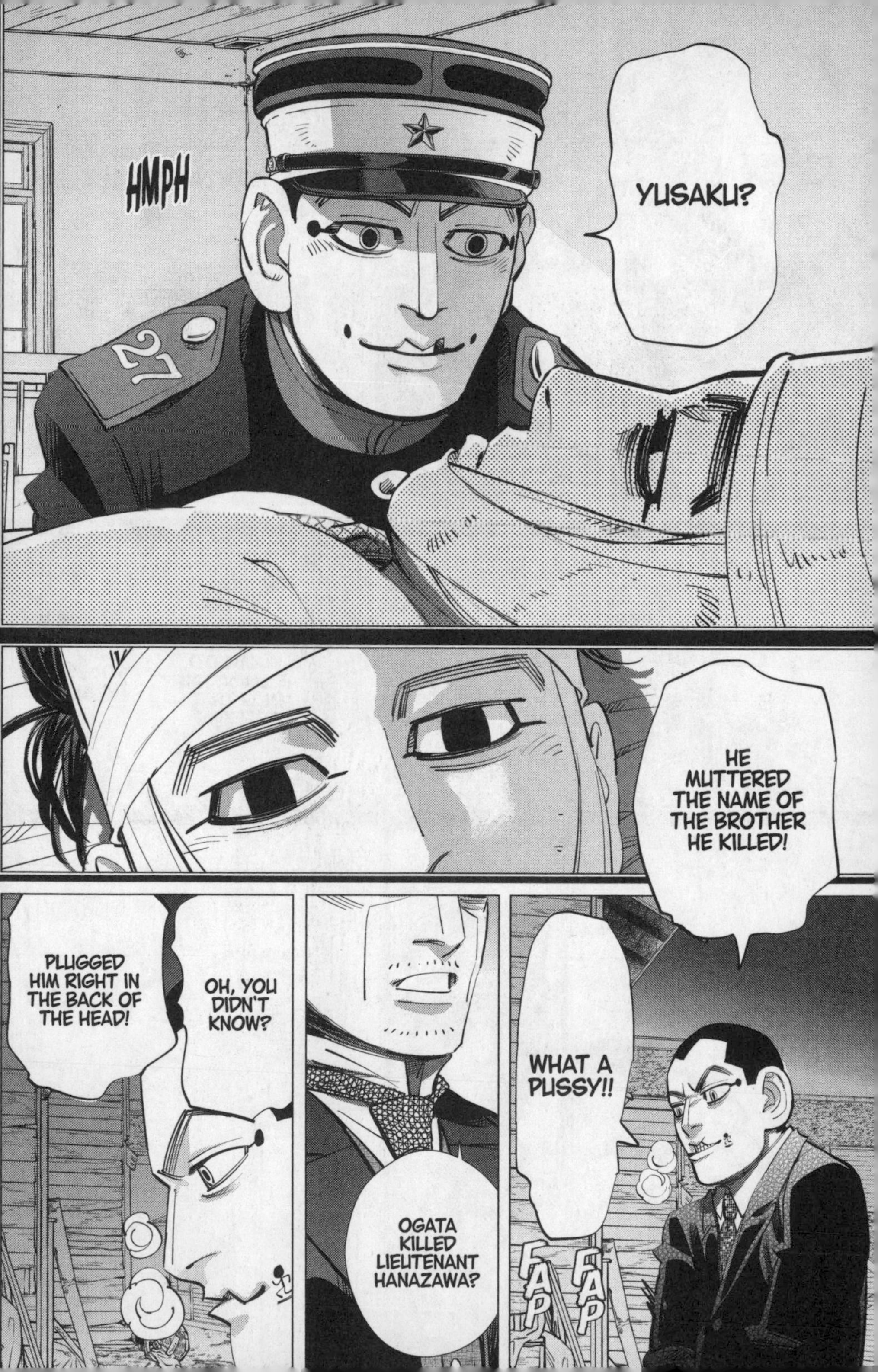
YUSAKU?
HMPH
HE MUTTERED THE NAME OF THE BROTHER HE KILLED!
WHAT A PUSSY!!
FAP FAP
OGATA KILLED LIEUTENANT HANAZAWA?
OH, YOU DIDN'T KNOW?
PLUGGED HIM RIGHT IN THE BACK OF THE HEAD!

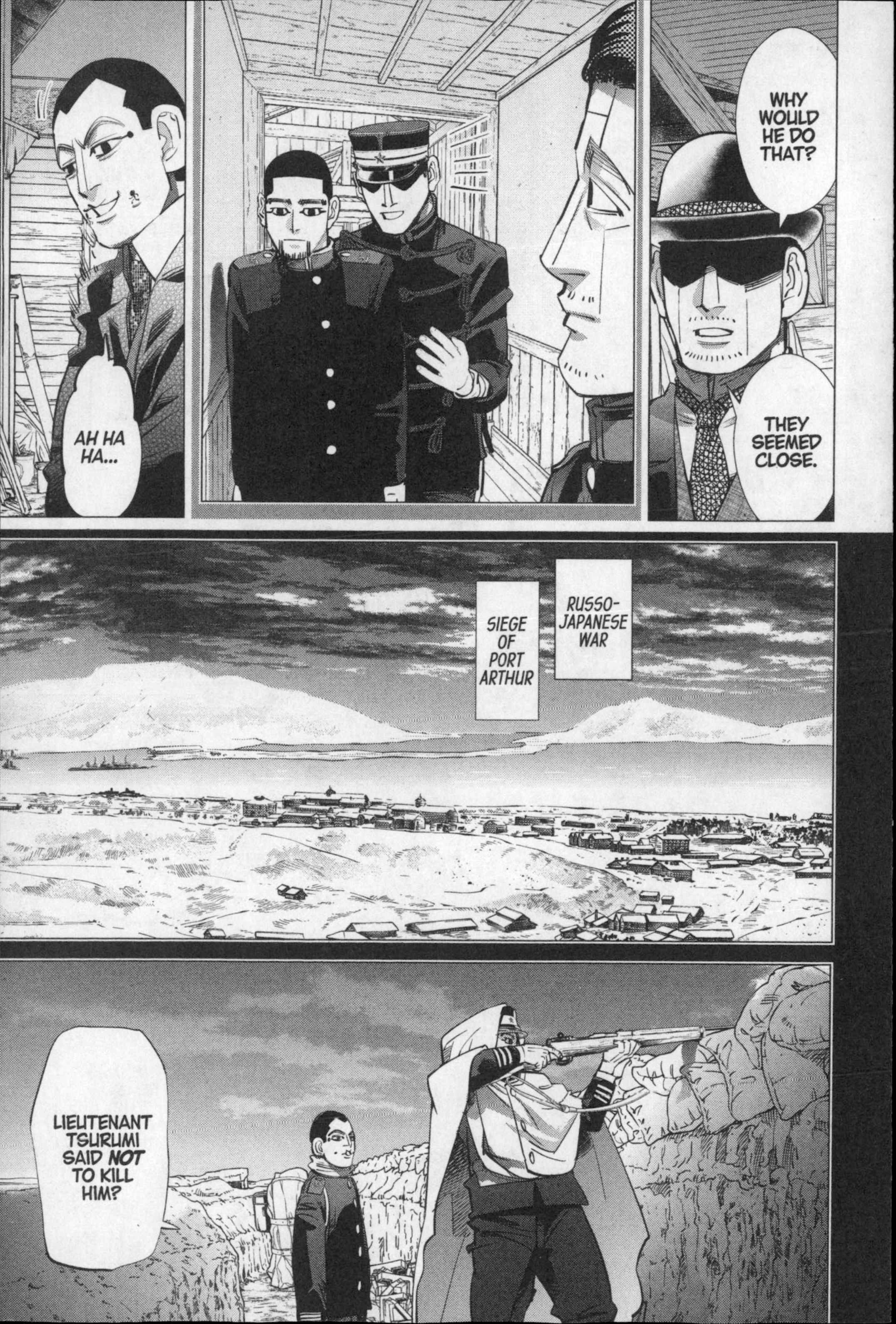
WHY WOULD HE DO THAT?
THEY SEEMED CLOSE.
AH HA HA...
RUSSO-JAPANESE WAR
SIEGE OF PORT ARTHUR
LIEUTENANT TSURUMI SAID *NOT* TO KILL HIM?

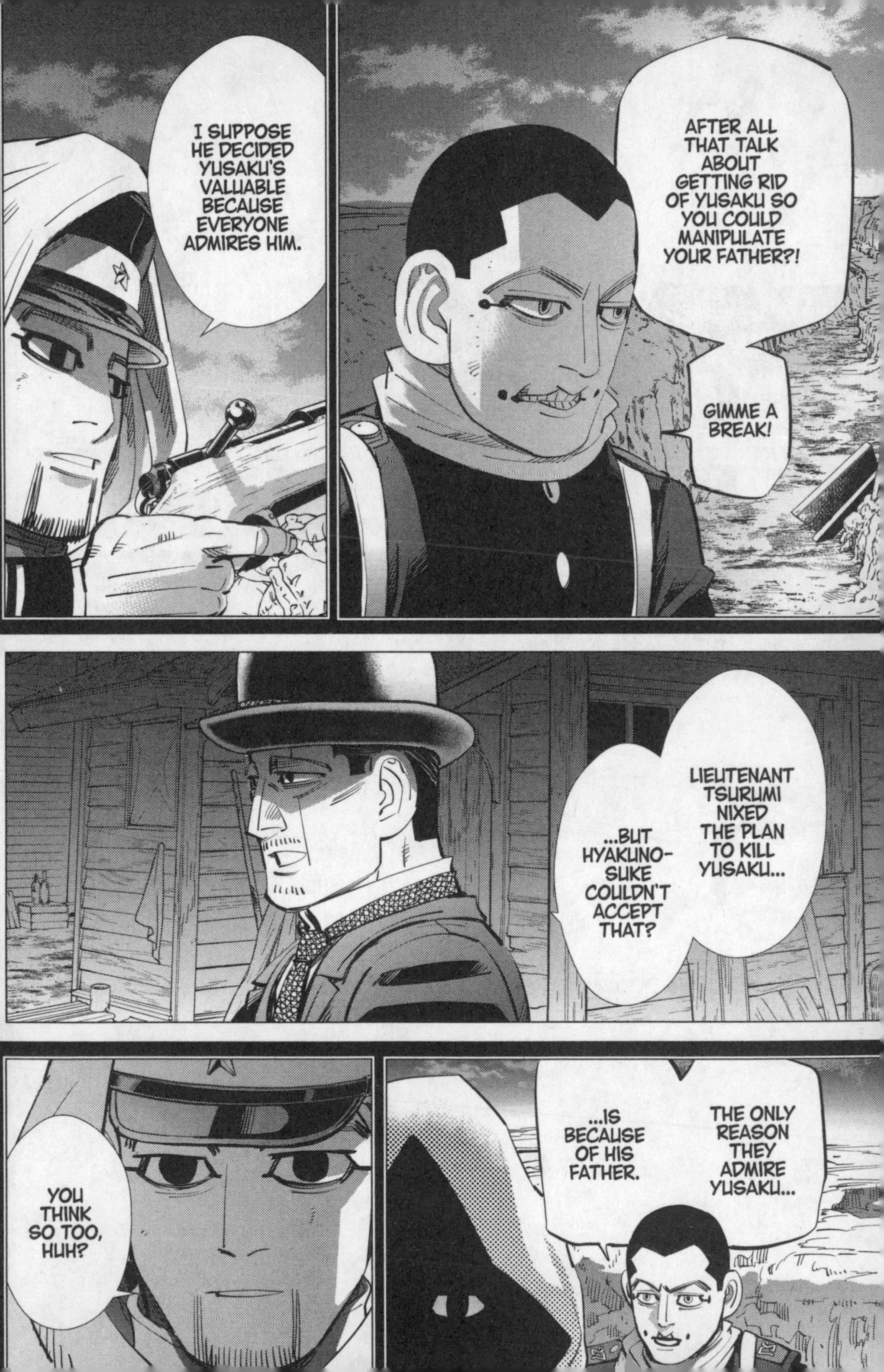
AFTER ALL THAT TALK ABOUT GETTING RID OF YUSAKU SO YOU COULD MANIPULATE YOUR FATHER?!
GIMME A BREAK!
I SUPPOSE HE DECIDED YUSAKU'S VALUABLE BECAUSE EVERYONE ADMIRES HIM.
LIEUTENANT TSURUMI NIXED THE PLAN TO KILL YUSAKU...
...BUT HYAKUNO-SUKE COULDN'T ACCEPT THAT?
THE ONLY REASON THEY ADMIRE YUSAKU...
...IS BECAUSE OF HIS FATHER.
YOU THINK SO TOO, HUH?

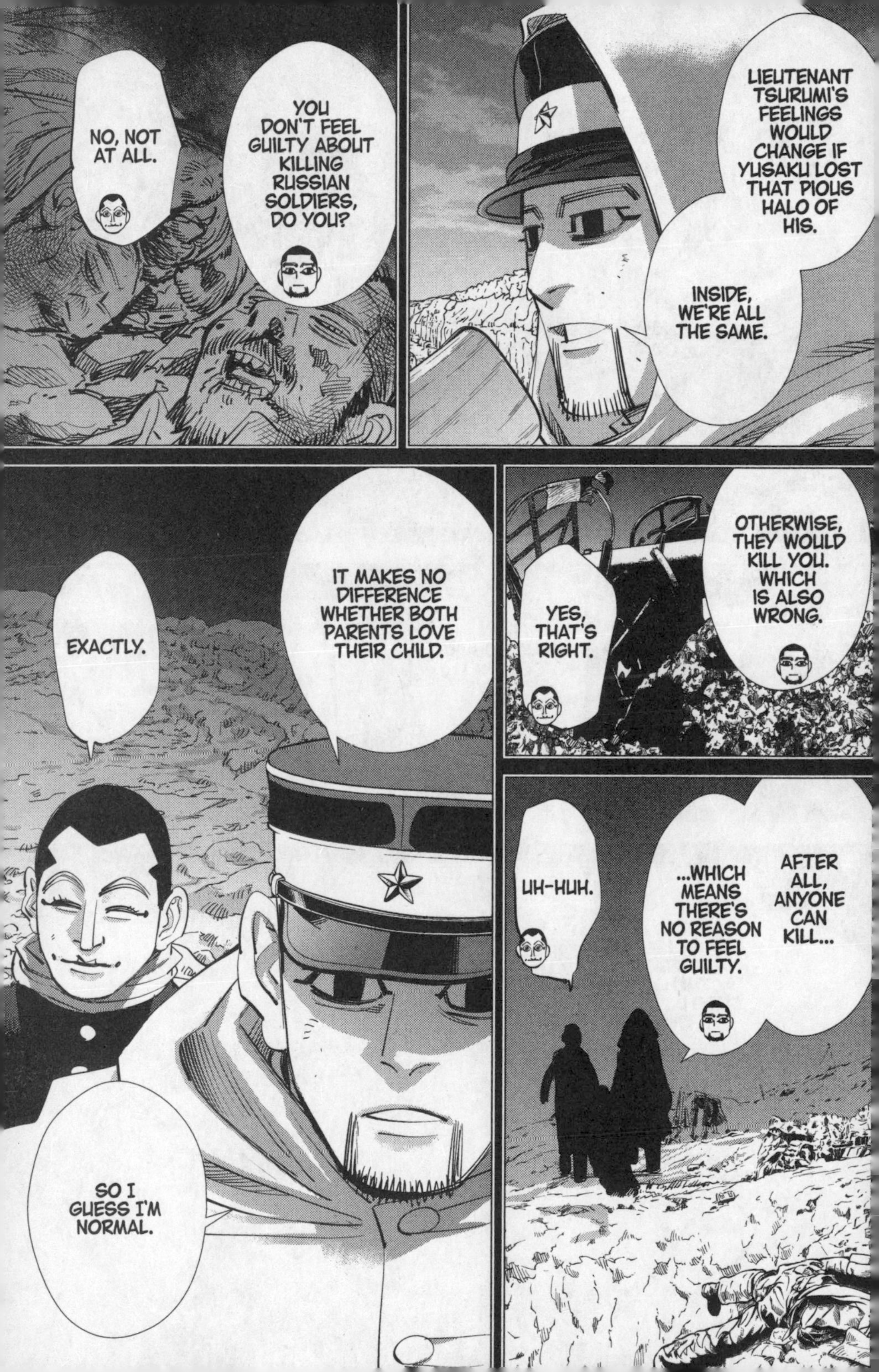
LIEUTENANT TSURUMI'S FEELINGS WOULD CHANGE IF YUSAKU LOST THAT PIOUS HALO OF HIS.
INSIDE, WE'RE ALL THE SAME.
YOU DON'T FEEL GUILTY ABOUT KILLING RUSSIAN SOLDIERS, DO YOU?
NO, NOT AT ALL.
OTHERWISE, THEY WOULD KILL YOU. WHICH IS ALSO WRONG.
YES, THAT'S RIGHT.
AFTER ALL, ANYONE CAN KILL...
...WHICH MEANS THERE'S NO REASON TO FEEL GUILTY.
UH-HUH.
IT MAKES NO DIFFERENCE WHETHER BOTH PARENTS LOVE THEIR CHILD.
EXACTLY.
SO I GUESS I'M NORMAL.

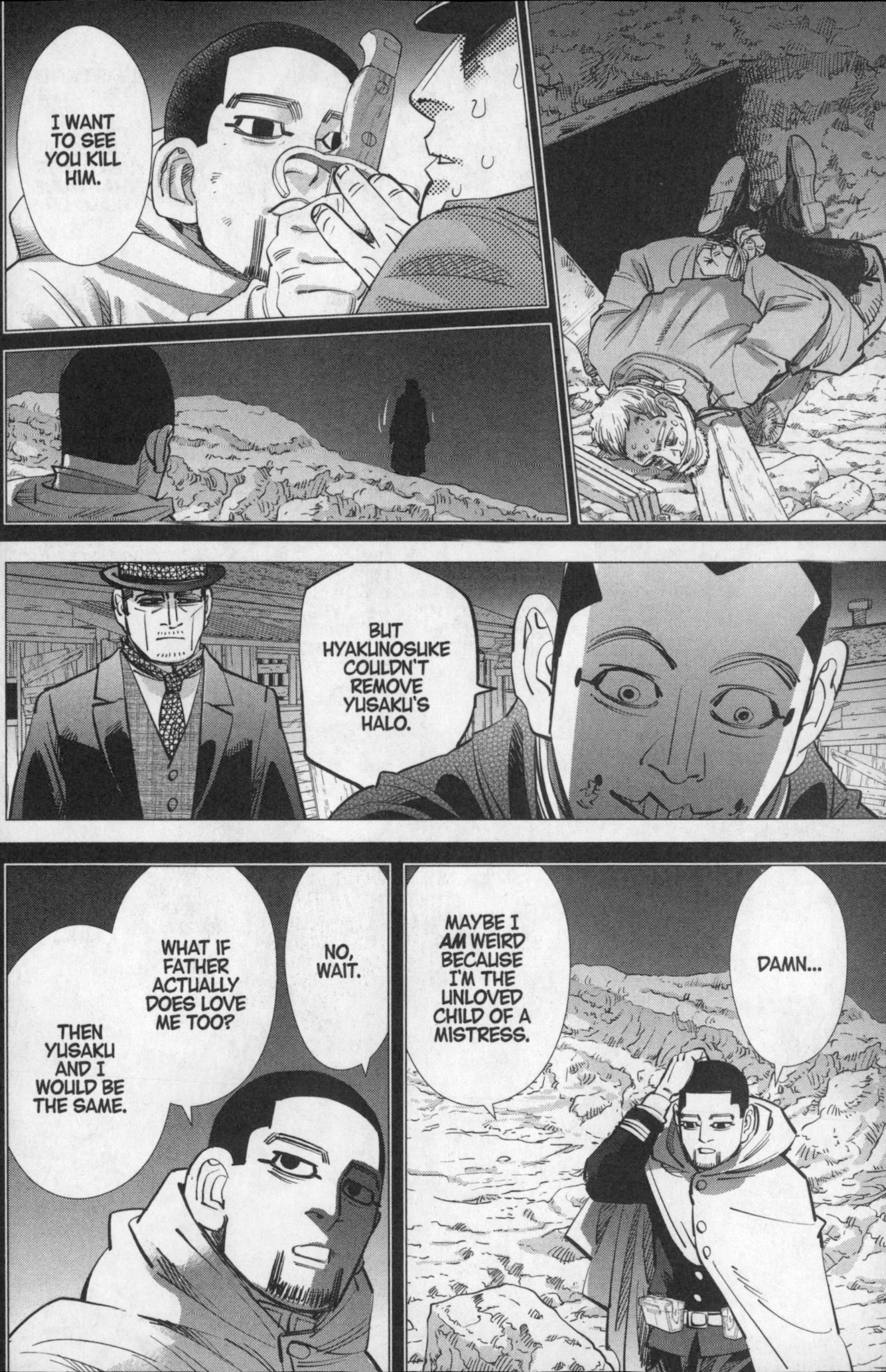
I WANT TO SEE YOU KILL HIM.
BUT HYAKUNOSUKE COULDN'T REMOVE YUSAKU'S HALO.
DAMN...
MAYBE I *AM* WEIRD BECAUSE I'M THE UNLOVED CHILD OF A MISTRESS.
NO, WAIT.
WHAT IF FATHER ACTUALLY DOES LOVE ME TOO?
THEN YUSAKU AND I WOULD BE THE SAME.

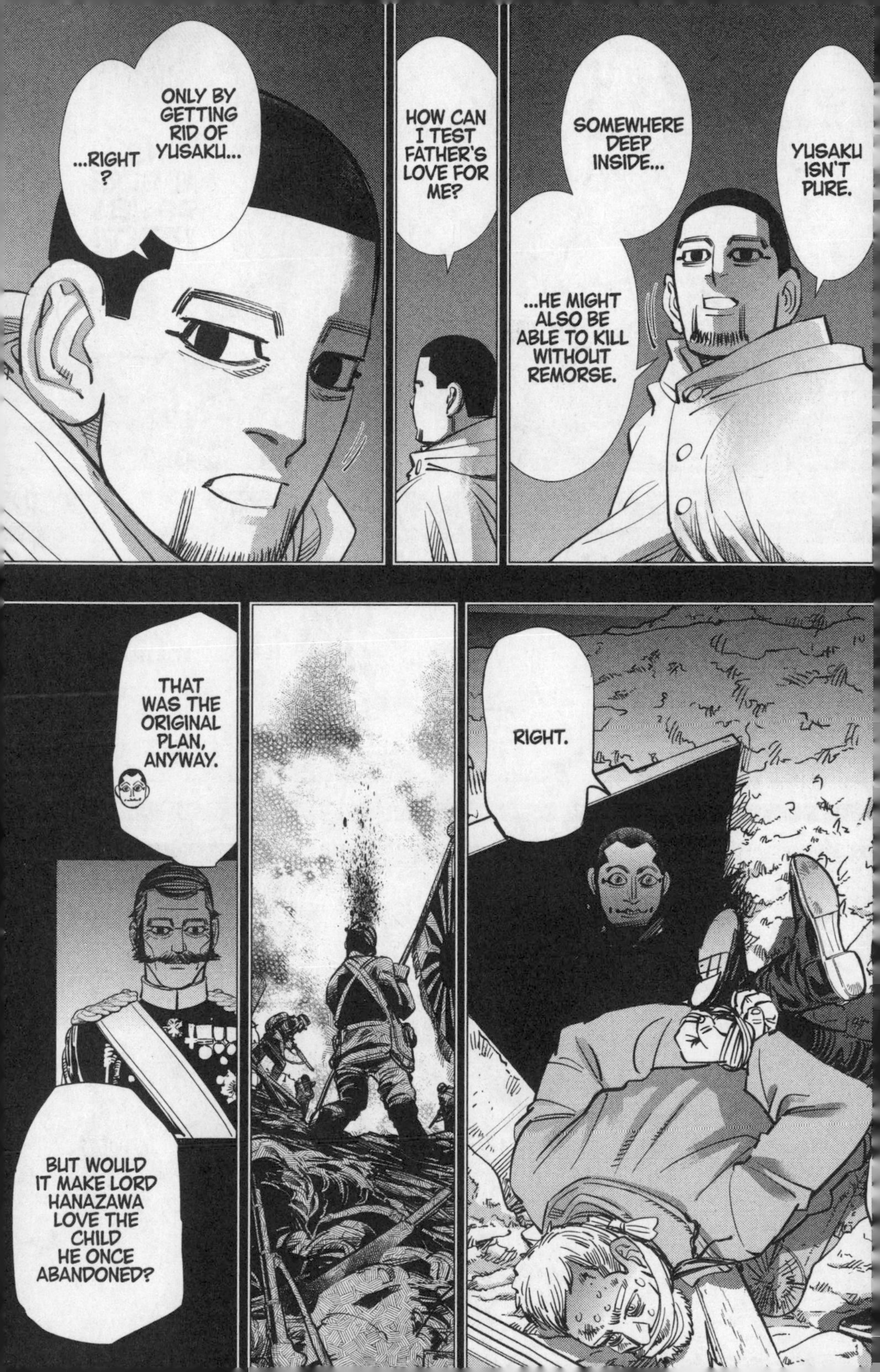
YUSAKU ISN'T PURE.
SOMEWHERE DEEP INSIDE...
...HE MIGHT ALSO BE ABLE TO KILL WITHOUT REMORSE.
HOW CAN I TEST FATHER'S LOVE FOR ME?
ONLY BY GETTING RID OF YUSAKU...
...RIGHT?
RIGHT.
THAT WAS THE ORIGINAL PLAN, ANYWAY.
BUT WOULD IT MAKE LORD HANAZAWA LOVE THE CHILD HE ONCE ABANDONED?

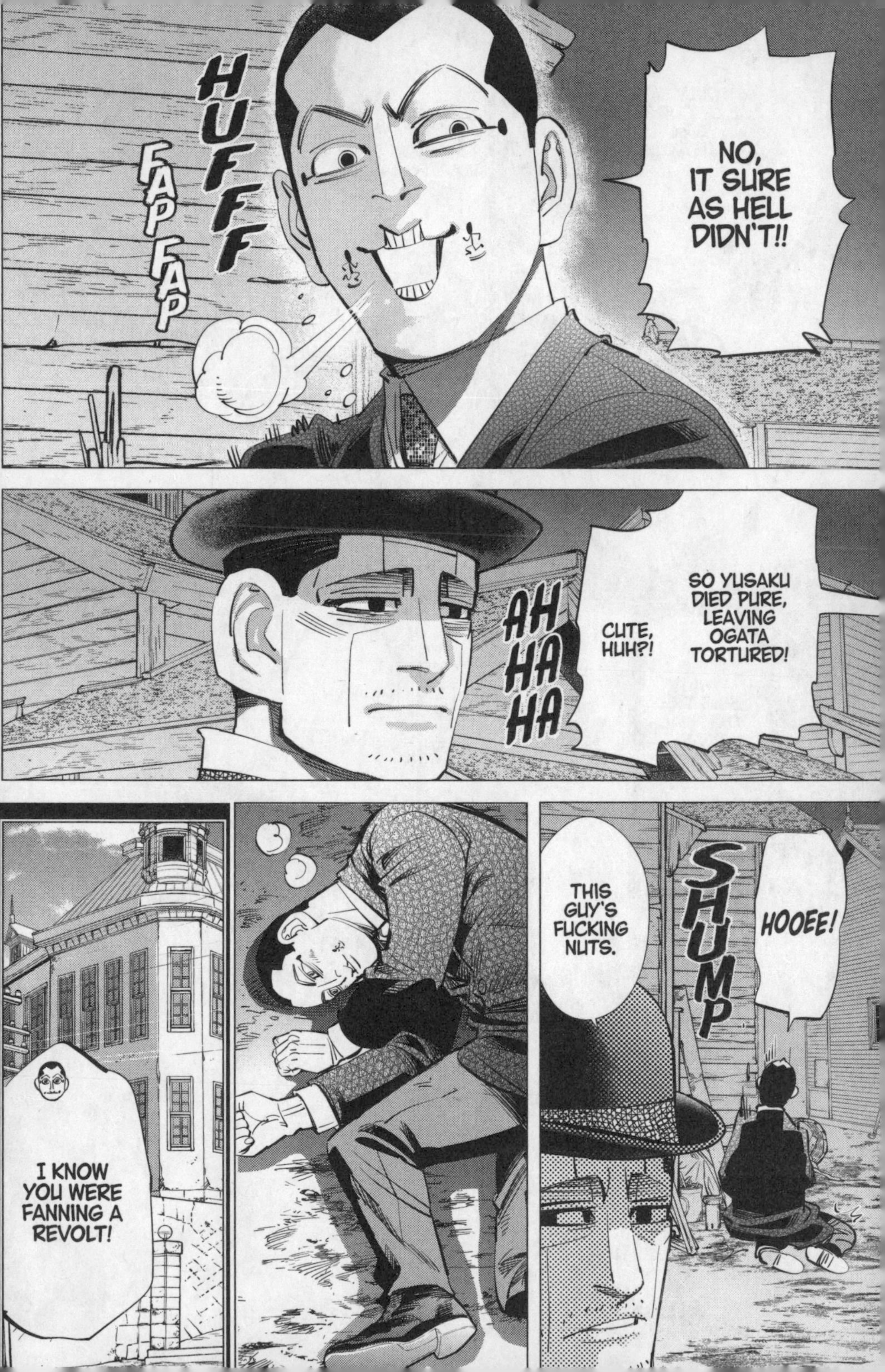
NO, IT SURE AS HELL DIDN'T!!
HUFFF
FAP FAP
SO YUSAKU DIED PURE, LEAVING OGATA TORTURED!
CUTE, HUH?!
AH HA HA HA
HOOEE!
SHUMP
THIS GUY'S FUCKING NUTS.
I KNOW YOU WERE FANNING A REVOLT!

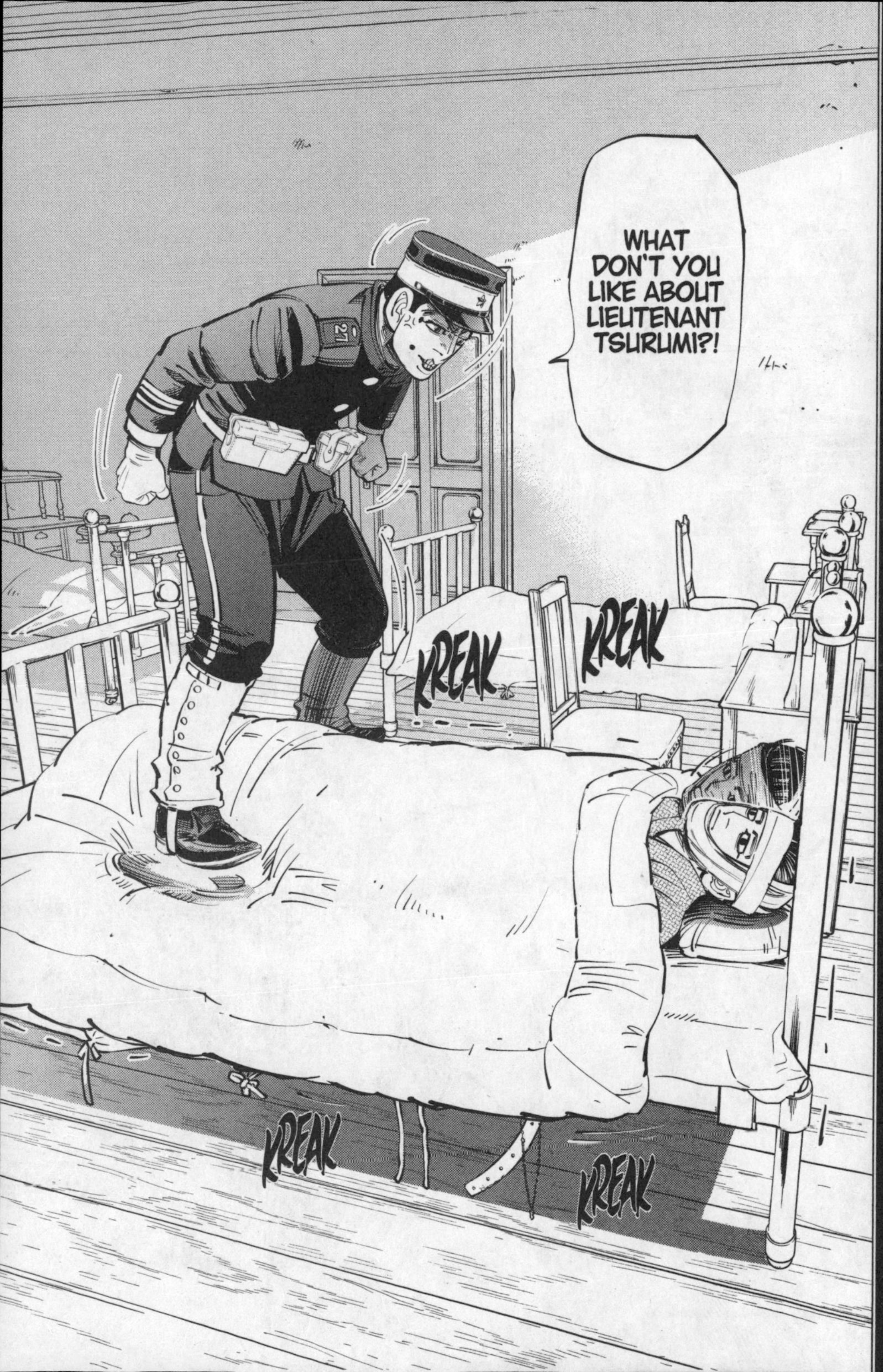
WHAT DON'T YOU LIKE ABOUT LIEUTENANT TSURUMI?!
KREAK
KREAK
KREAK
KREAK

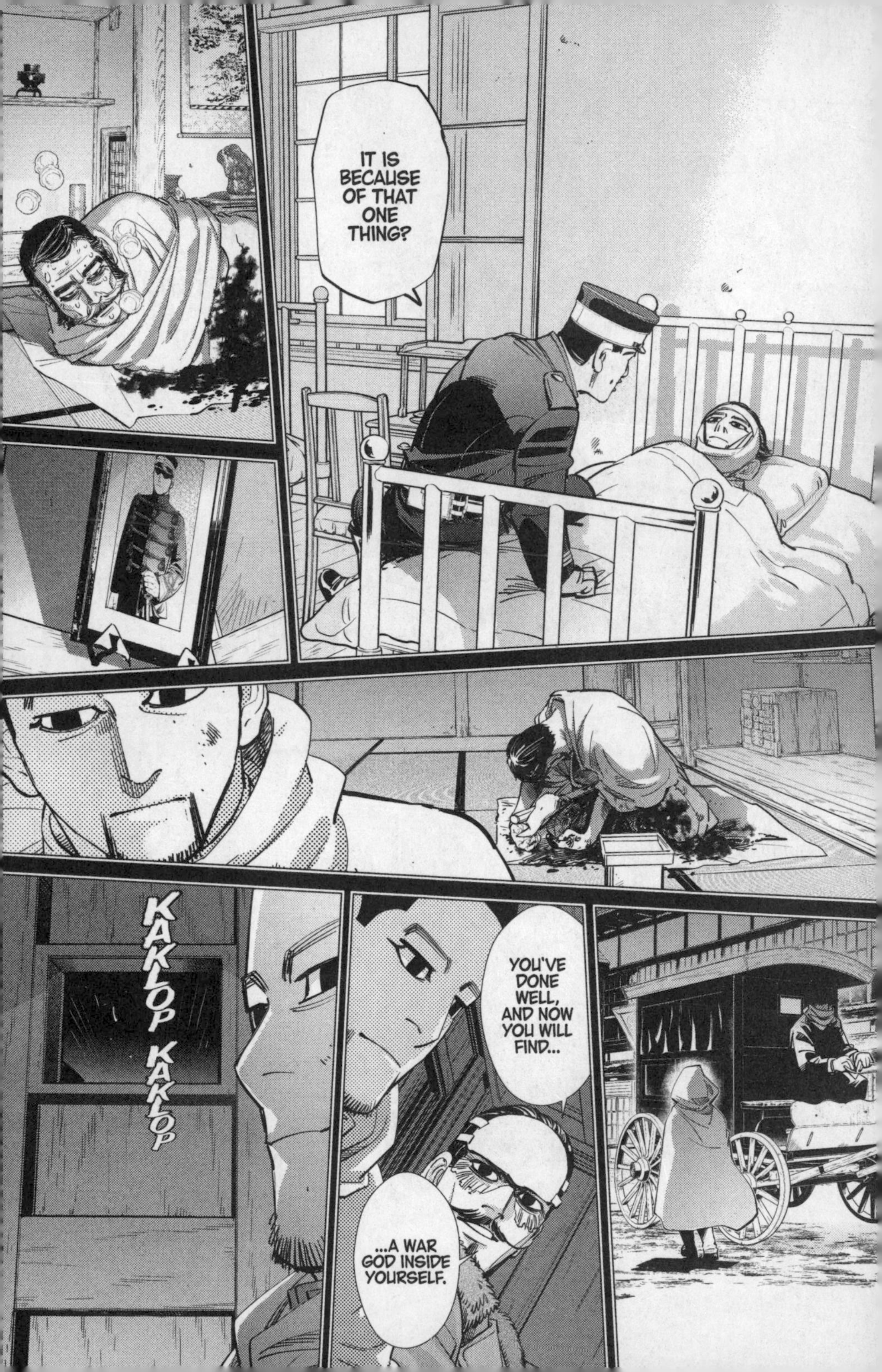
IT IS BECAUSE OF THAT ONE THING?
YOU'VE DONE WELL, AND NOW YOU WILL FIND...
...A WAR GOD INSIDE YOURSELF.
KAKLOP KAKLOP

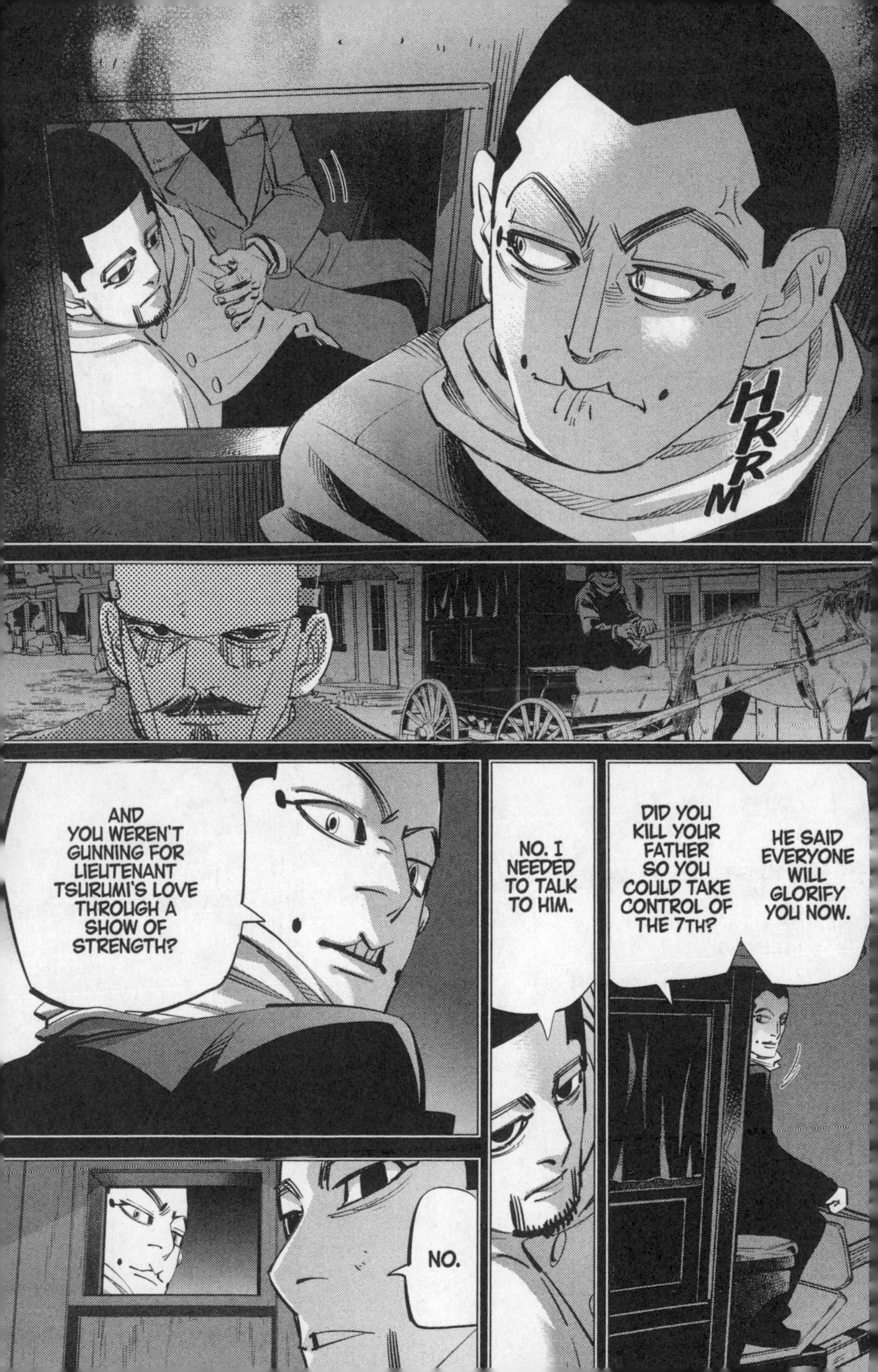
HRRM
HE SAID EVERYONE WILL GLORIFY YOU NOW.
DID YOU KILL YOUR FATHER SO YOU COULD TAKE CONTROL OF THE 7TH?
NO. I NEEDED TO TALK TO HIM.
AND YOU WEREN'T GUNNING FOR LIEUTENANT TSURUMI'S LOVE THROUGH A SHOW OF STRENGTH?
NO.

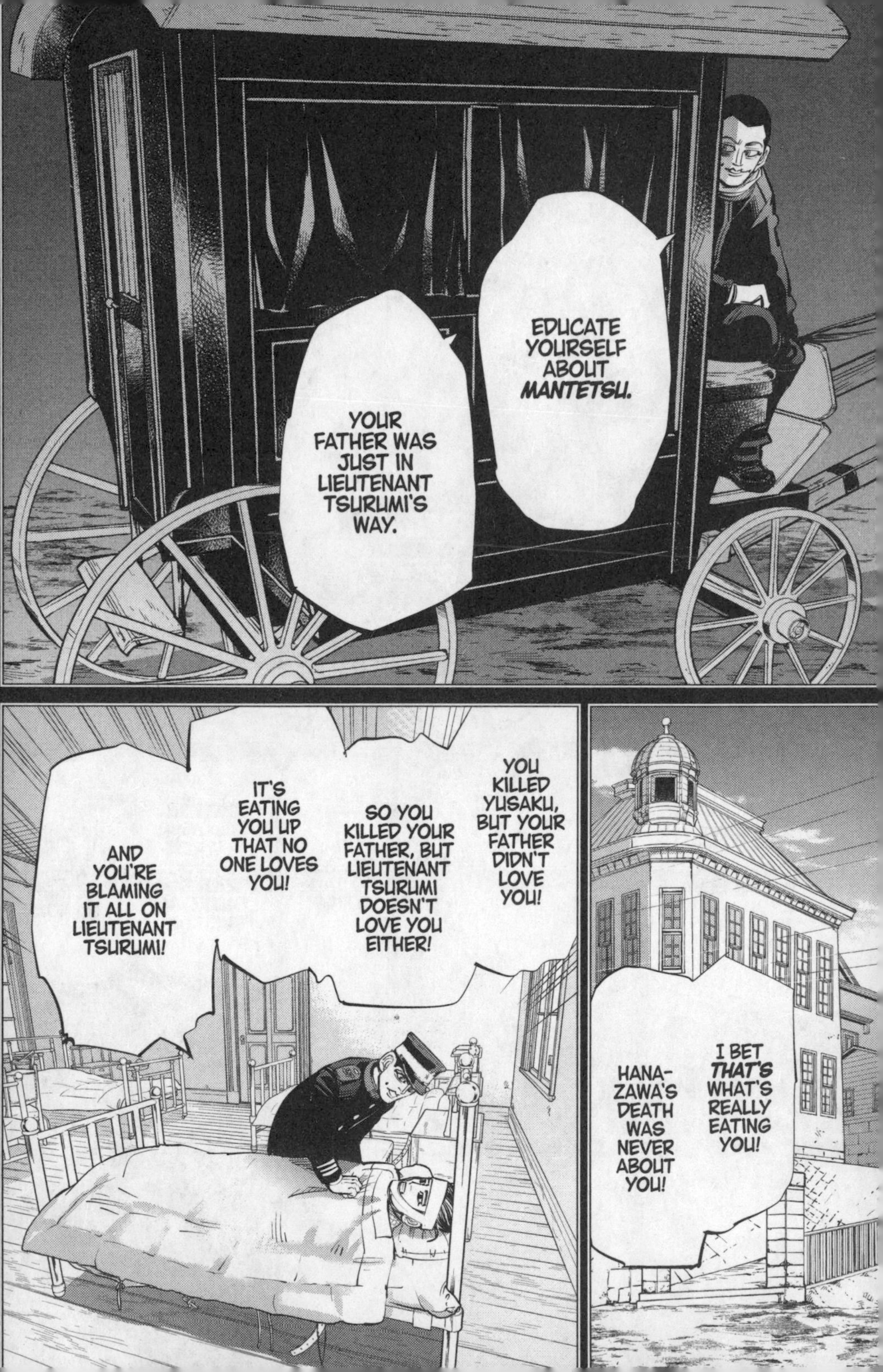
EDUCATE YOURSELF ABOUT *MANTETSU*.
YOUR FATHER WAS JUST IN LIEUTENANT TSURUMI'S WAY.
I BET *THAT'S* WHAT'S REALLY EATING YOU!
HANA-ZAWA'S DEATH WAS NEVER ABOUT YOU!
YOU KILLED YUSAKU, BUT YOUR FATHER DIDN'T LOVE YOU!
SO YOU KILLED YOUR FATHER, BUT LIEUTENANT TSURUMI DOESN'T LOVE YOU EITHER!
IT'S EATING YOU UP THAT NO ONE LOVES YOU!
AND YOU'RE BLAMING IT ALL ON LIEUTENANT TSURUMI!

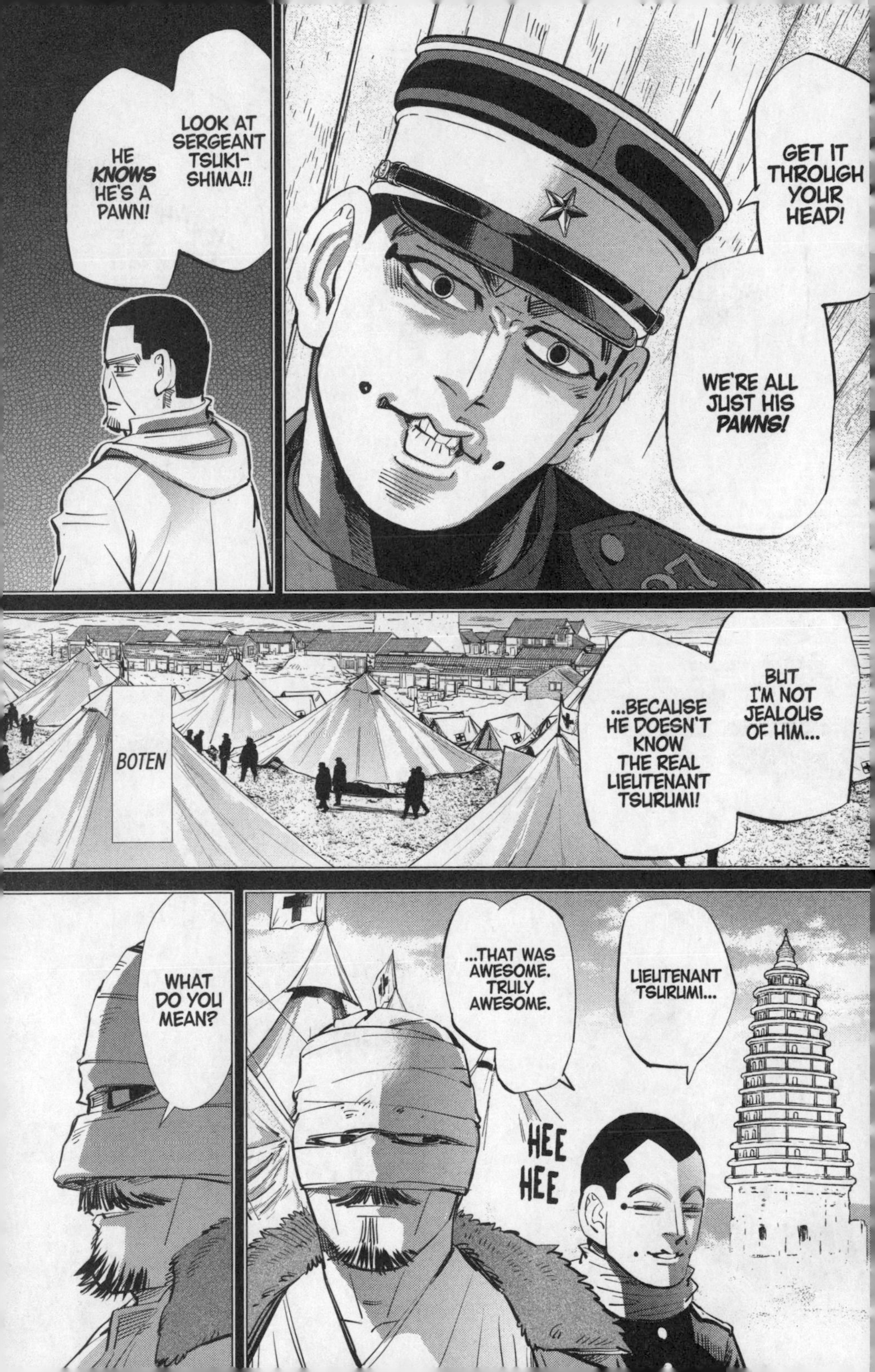
GET IT THROUGH YOUR HEAD!
WE'RE ALL JUST HIS PAWNS!
LOOK AT SERGEANT TSUKI-SHIMA!!
HE KNOWS HE'S A PAWN!
BUT I'M NOT JEALOUS OF HIM...
...BECAUSE HE DOESN'T KNOW THE REAL LIEUTENANT TSURUMI!
BOTEN
LIEUTENANT TSURUMI...
...THAT WAS AWESOME. TRULY AWESOME.
HEE HEE
WHAT DO YOU MEAN?

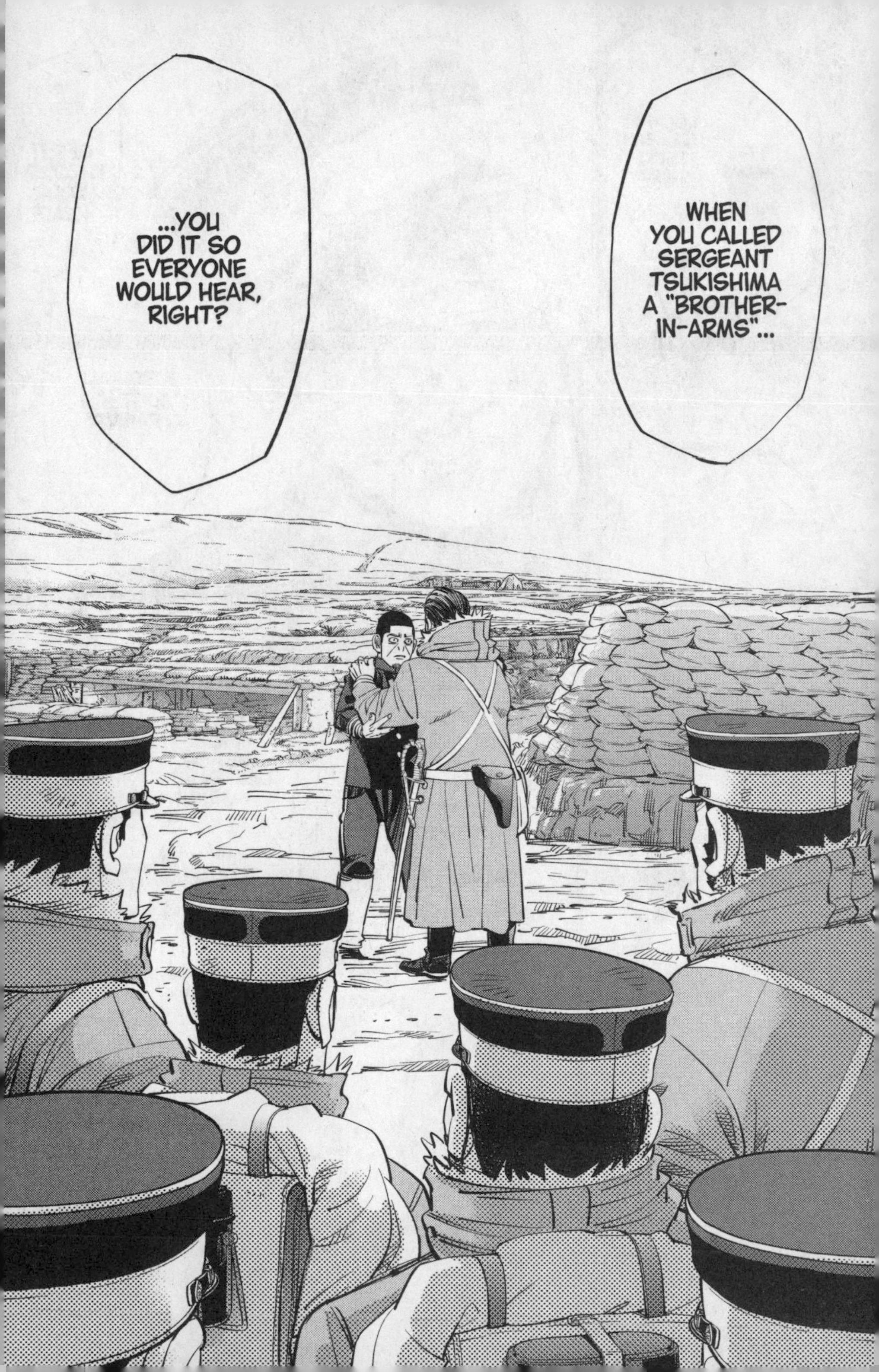
WHEN YOU CALLED SERGEANT TSUKISHIMA A "BROTHER-IN-ARMS"...
...YOU DID IT SO EVERYONE WOULD HEAR, RIGHT?

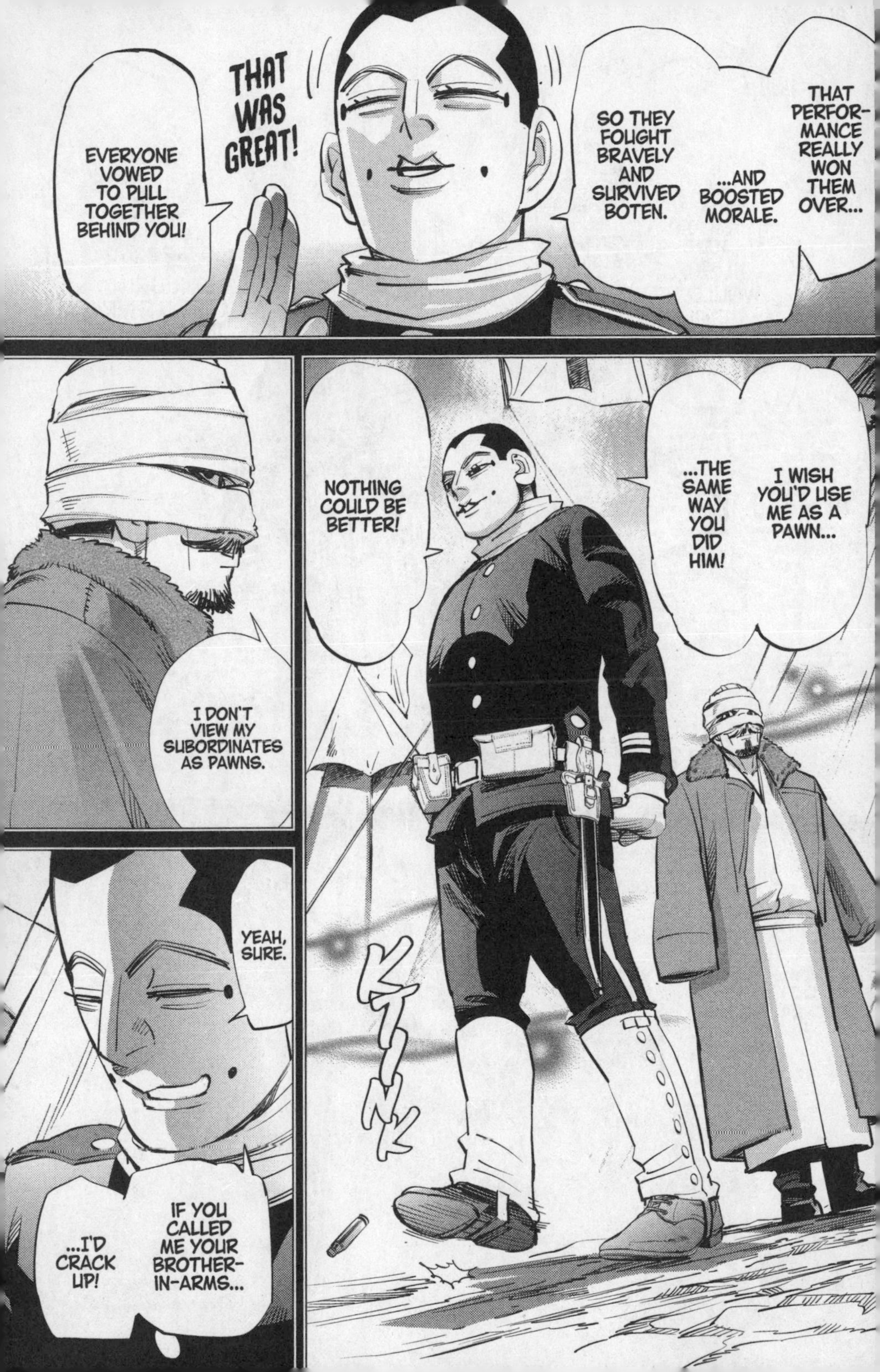
THAT PERFORMANCE REALLY WON THEM OVER...
...AND BOOSTED MORALE.
SO THEY FOUGHT BRAVELY AND SURVIVED BOTEN.
THAT WAS GREAT!
EVERYONE VOWED TO PULL TOGETHER BEHIND YOU!
I WISH YOU'D USE ME AS A PAWN...
...THE SAME WAY YOU DID HIM!
NOTHING COULD BE BETTER!
KTINK
I DON'T VIEW MY SUBORDINATES AS PAWNS.
YEAH, SURE.
IF YOU CALLED ME YOUR BROTHER-IN-ARMS...
...I'D CRACK UP!

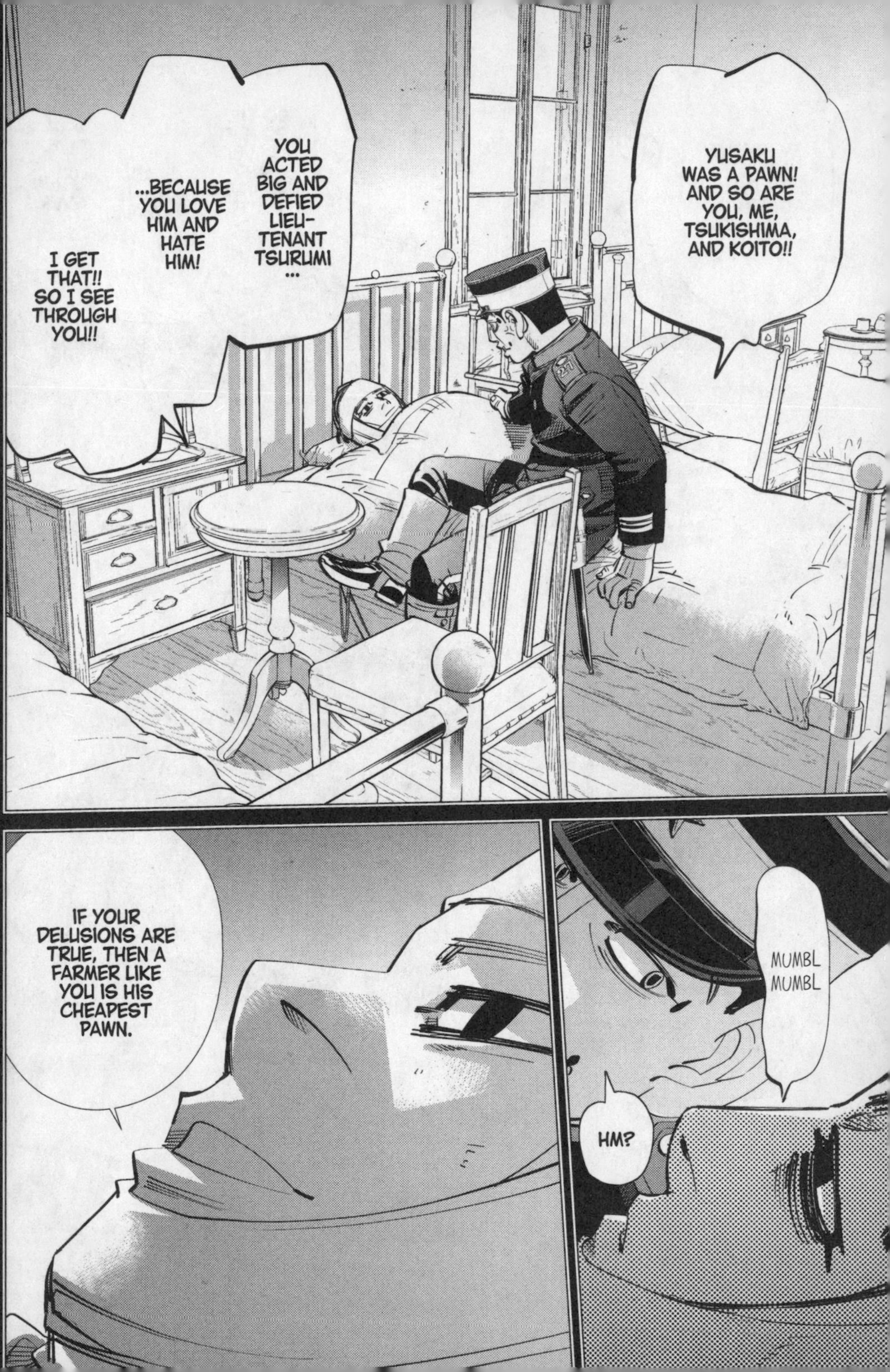
YUSAKU WAS A PAWN! AND SO ARE YOU, ME, TSUKISHIMA, AND KOITO!!
YOU ACTED BIG AND DEFIED LIEU-TENANT TSURUMI...
...BECAUSE YOU LOVE HIM AND HATE HIM!
I GET THAT!! SO I SEE THROUGH YOU!!
MUMBL MUMBL
HM?
IF YOUR DELUSIONS ARE TRUE, THEN A FARMER LIKE YOU IS HIS CHEAPEST PAWN.

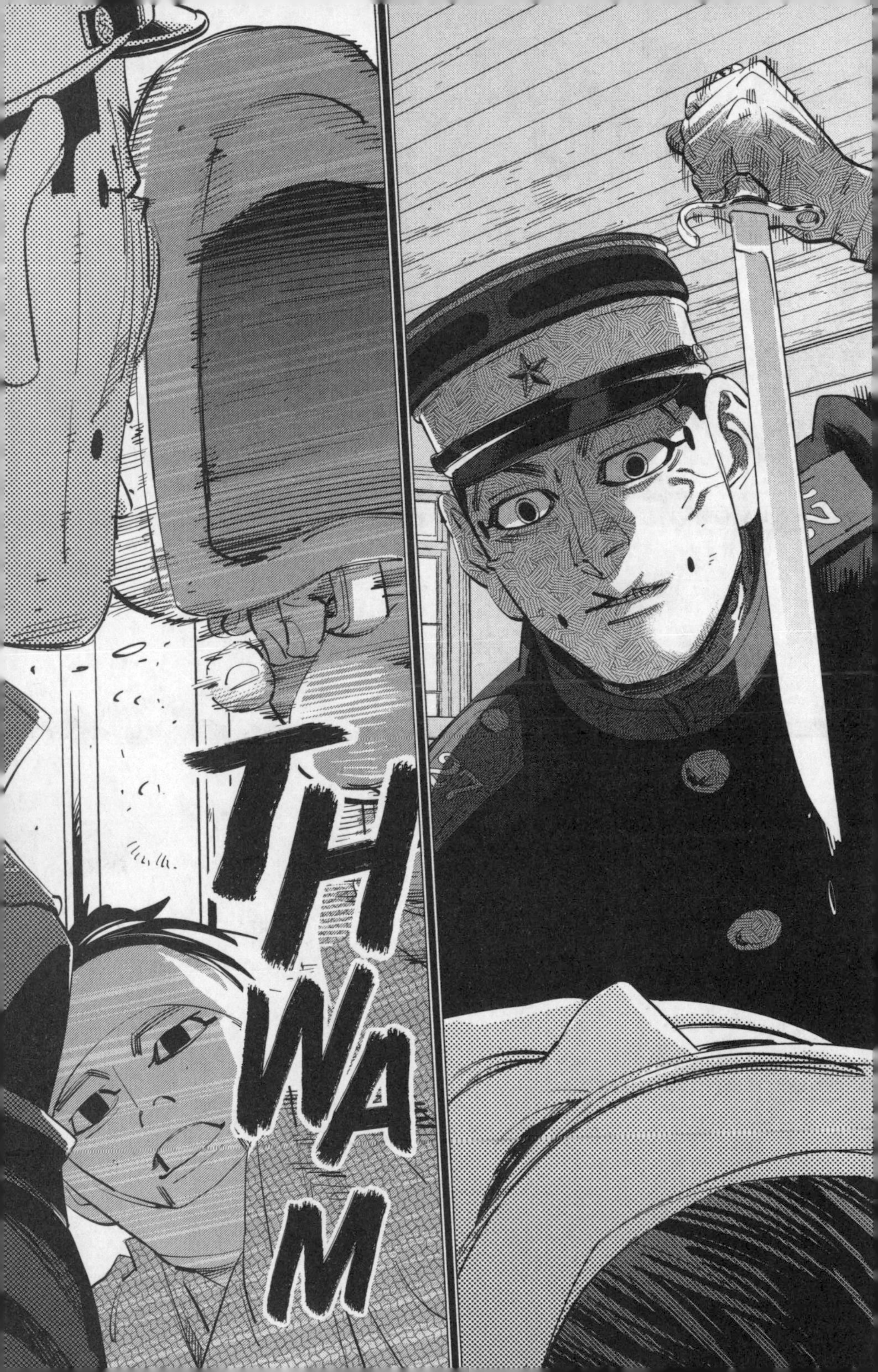
THWAM

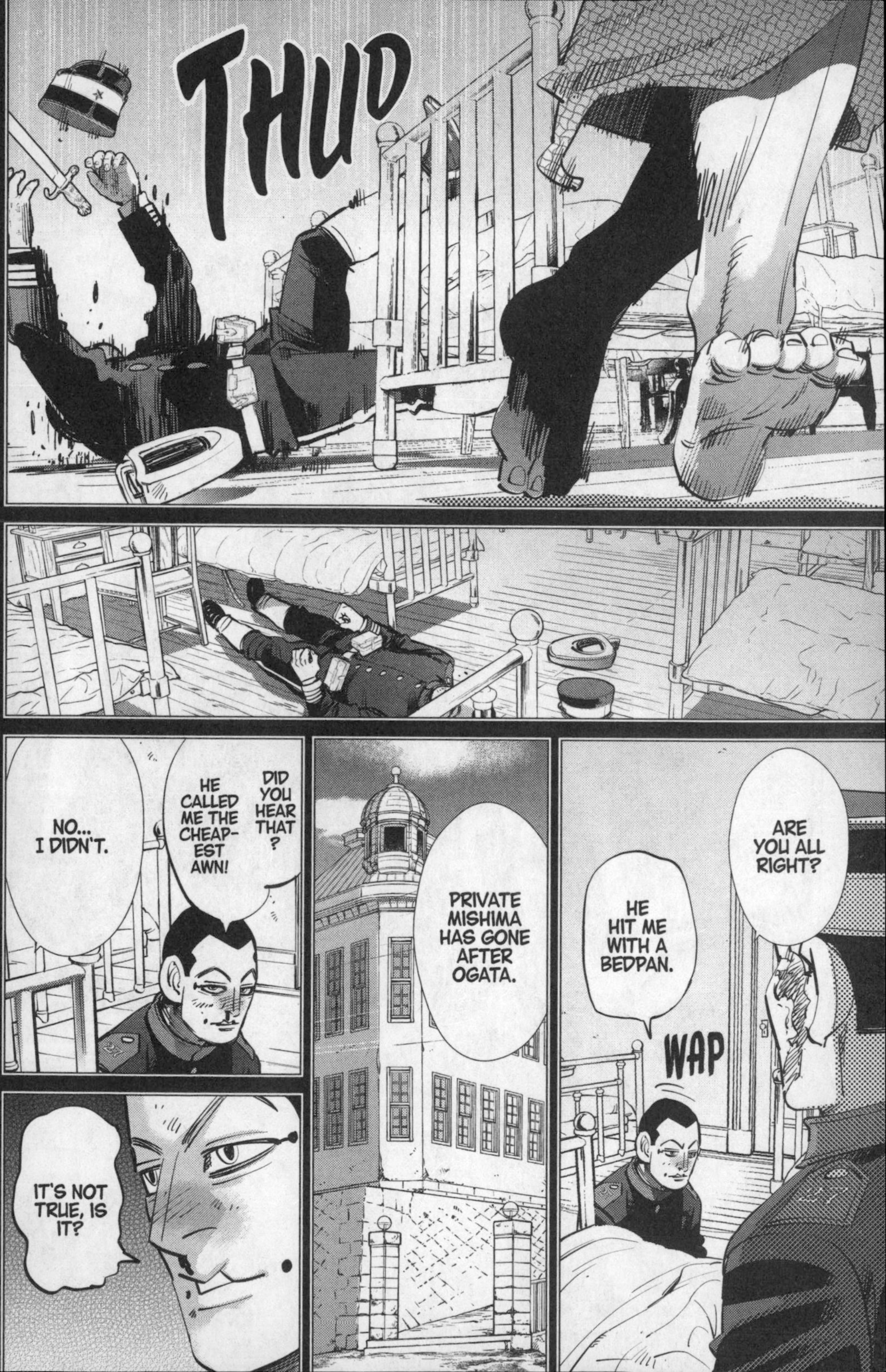
THUD
ARE YOU ALL RIGHT?
HE HIT ME WITH A BEDPAN.
WAP
PRIVATE MISHIMA HAS GONE AFTER OGATA.
DID YOU HEAR THAT?
HE CALLED ME THE CHEAPEST AWN!
NO... I DIDN'T.
IT'S NOT TRUE, IS IT?

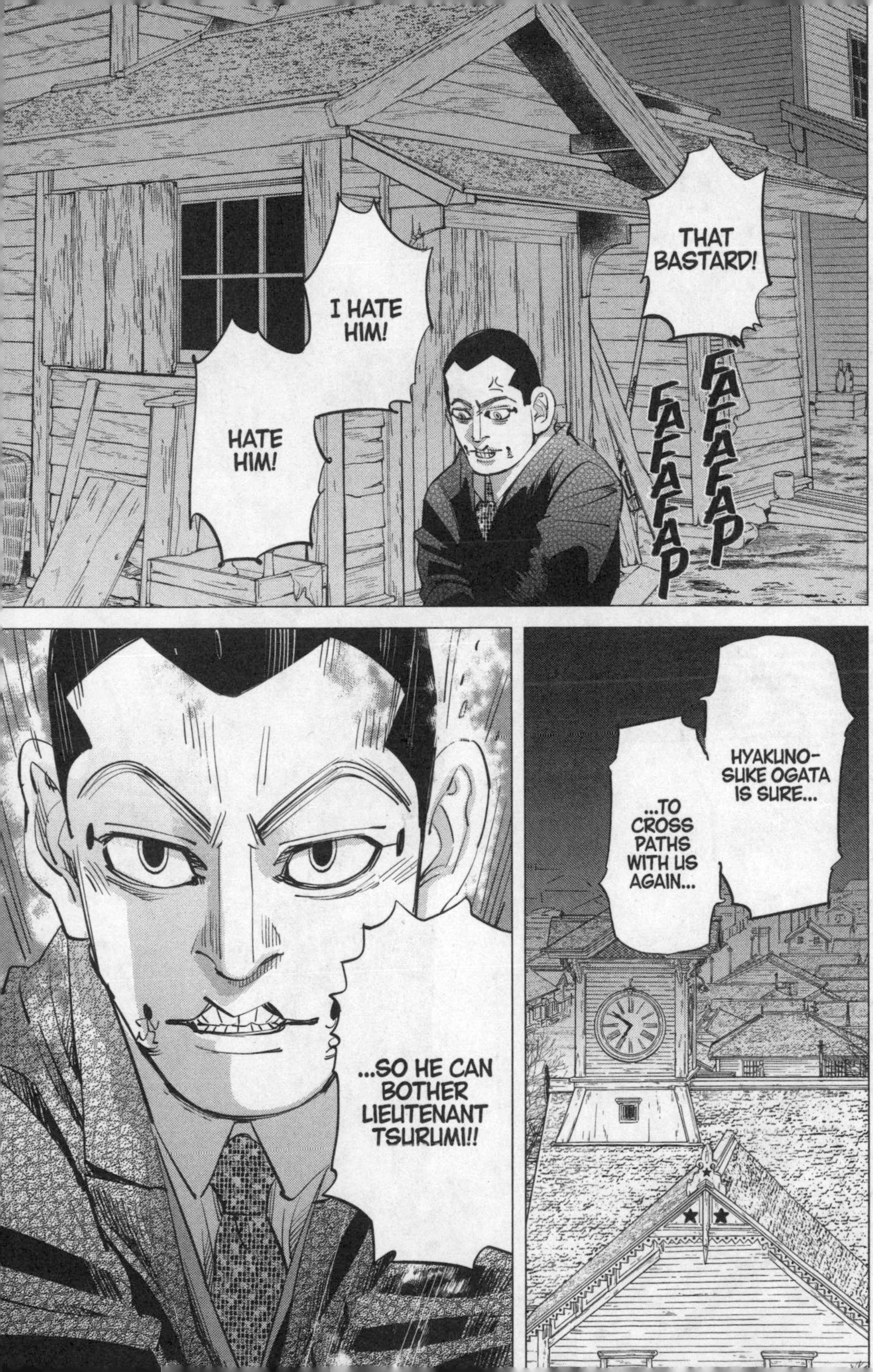
THAT BASTARD!
FAFAFAP
FAFAFAP
I HATE HIM!
HATE HIM!
HYAKUNOSUKE OGATA IS SURE...
...TO CROSS PATHS WITH US AGAIN...
...SO HE CAN BOTHER LIEUTENANT TSURUMI!!

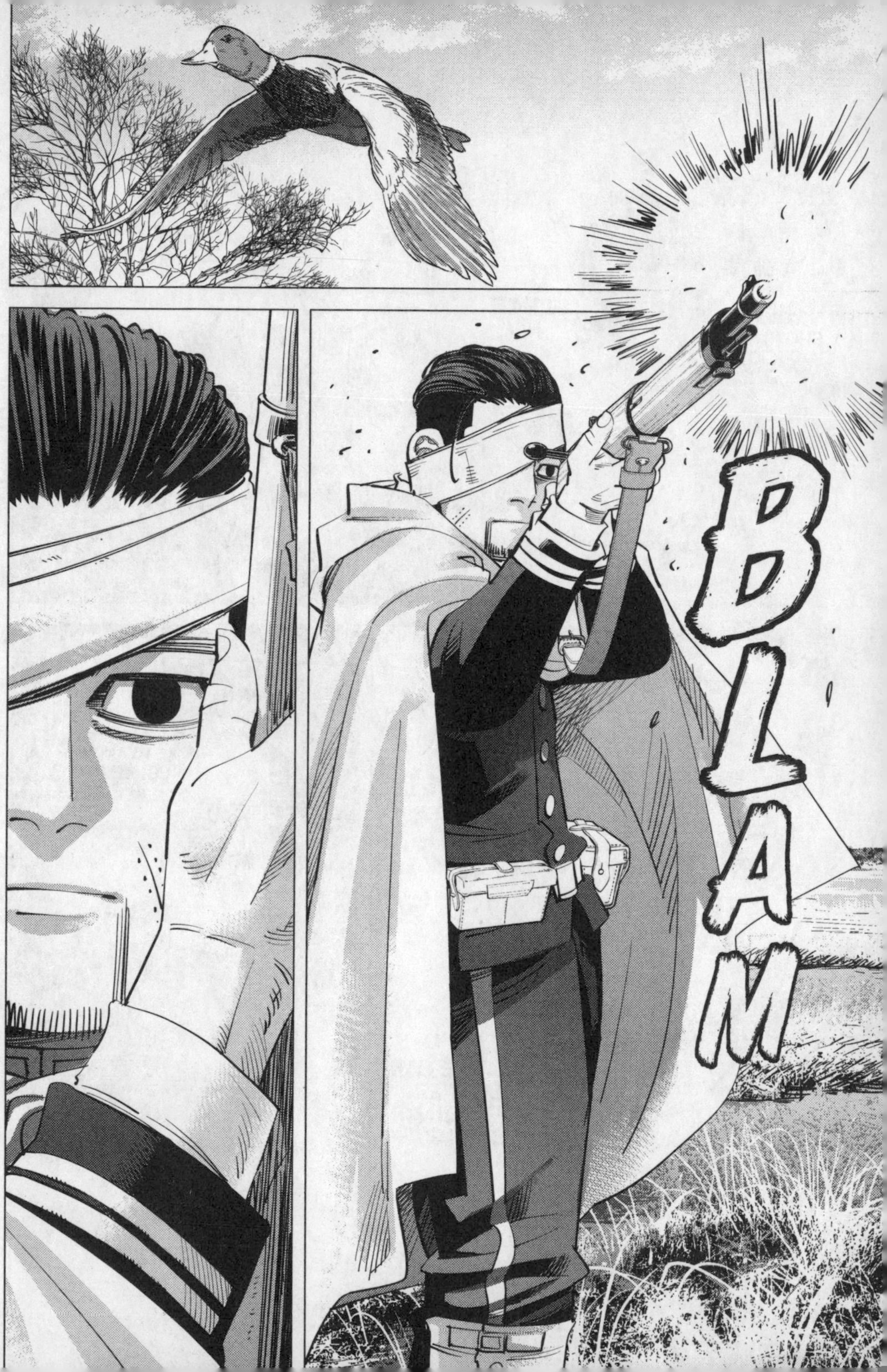
BLAM

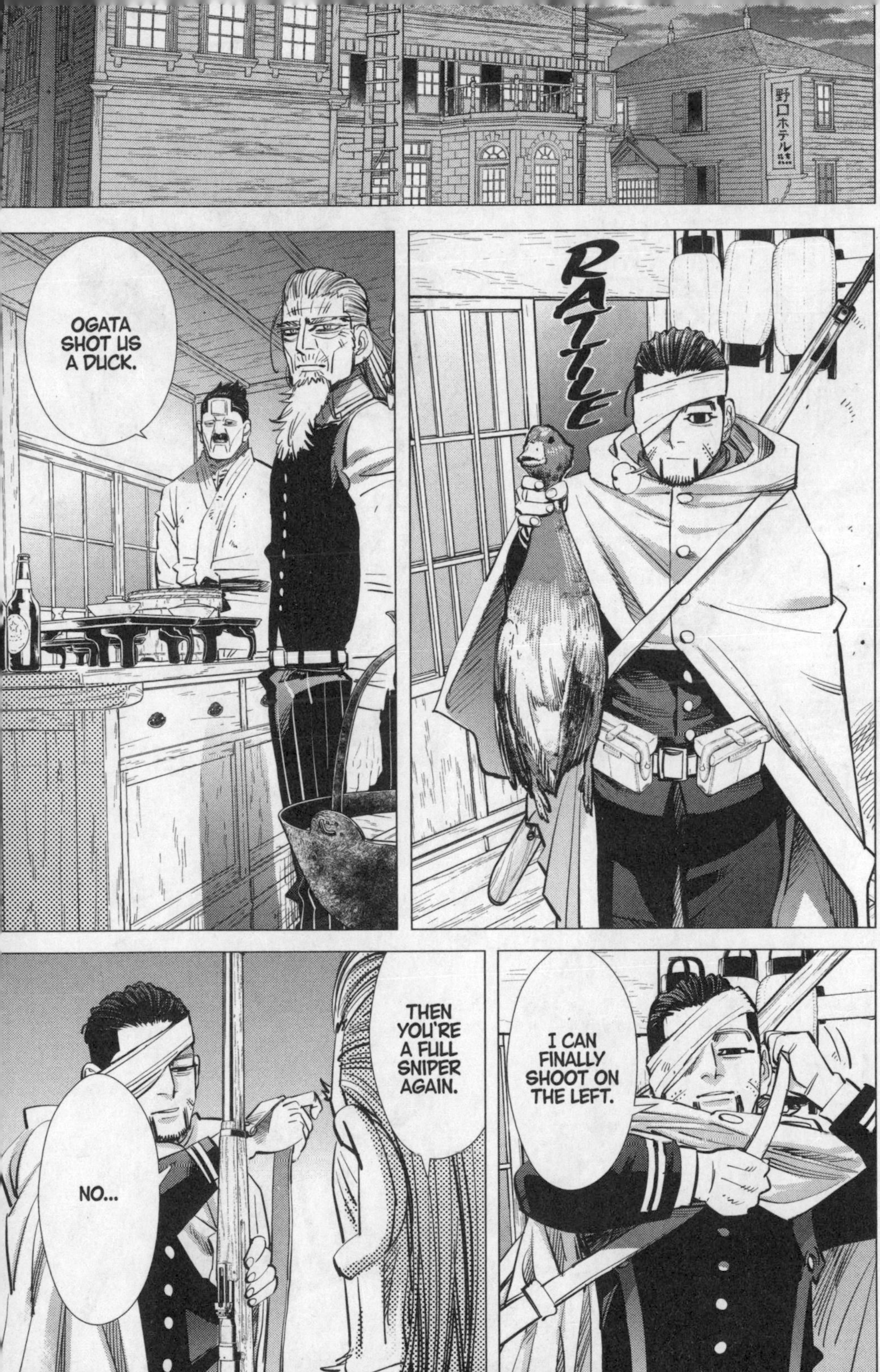
野口ホテル
RATTLE
OGATA SHOT US A DUCK.
I CAN FINALLY SHOOT ON THE LEFT.
THEN YOU'RE A FULL SNIPER AGAIN.
NO...

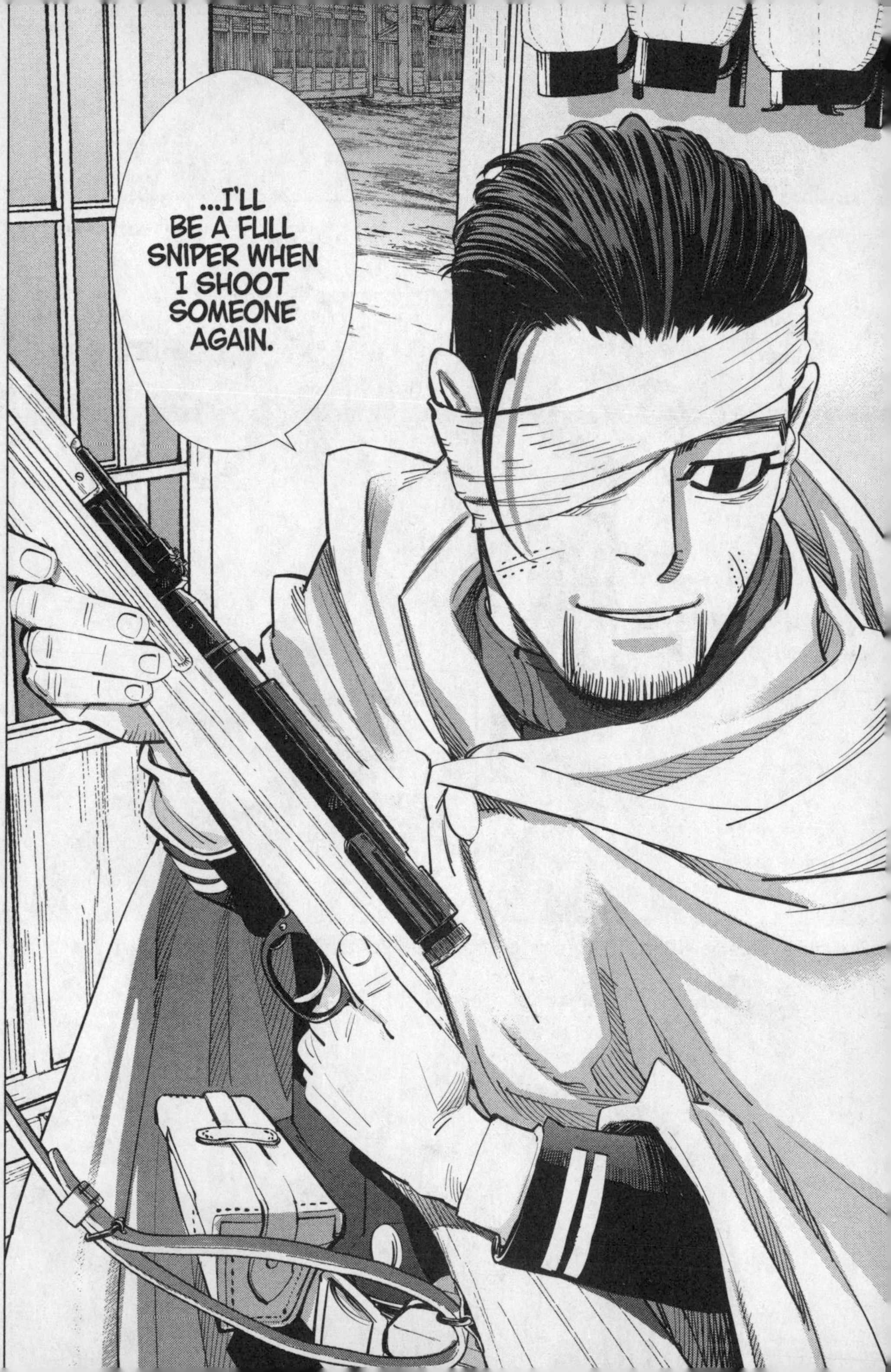
...I'LL BE A FULL SNIPER WHEN I SHOOT SOMEONE AGAIN.

Chapter 244: Landing at Otaru

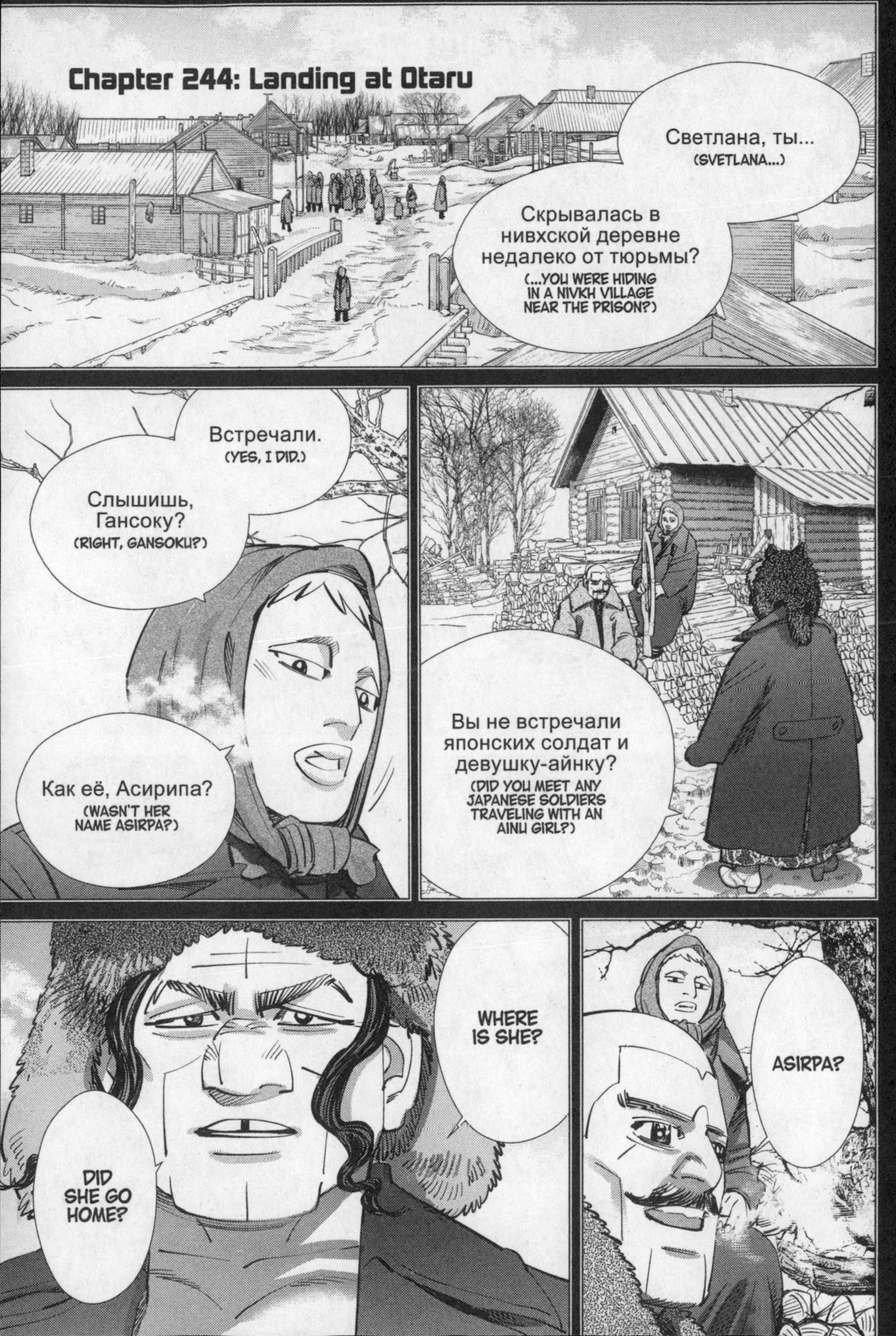
Светлана, ты...
(SVETLANA...)
Скрывалась в нивхской деревне недалеко от тюрьмы?
(...YOU WERE HIDING IN A NIVKH VILLAGE NEAR THE PRISON?)
Вы не встречали японских солдат и девушку-айнку?
(DID YOU MEET ANY JAPANESE SOLDIERS TRAVELING WITH AN AINU GIRL?)
Встречали.
(YES, I DID.)
Слышишь, Гансоку?
(RIGHT, GANSOKU?)
Как её, Асирипа?
(WASN'T HER NAME ASIRPA?)
ASIRPA?
WHERE IS SHE?
DID SHE GO HOME?

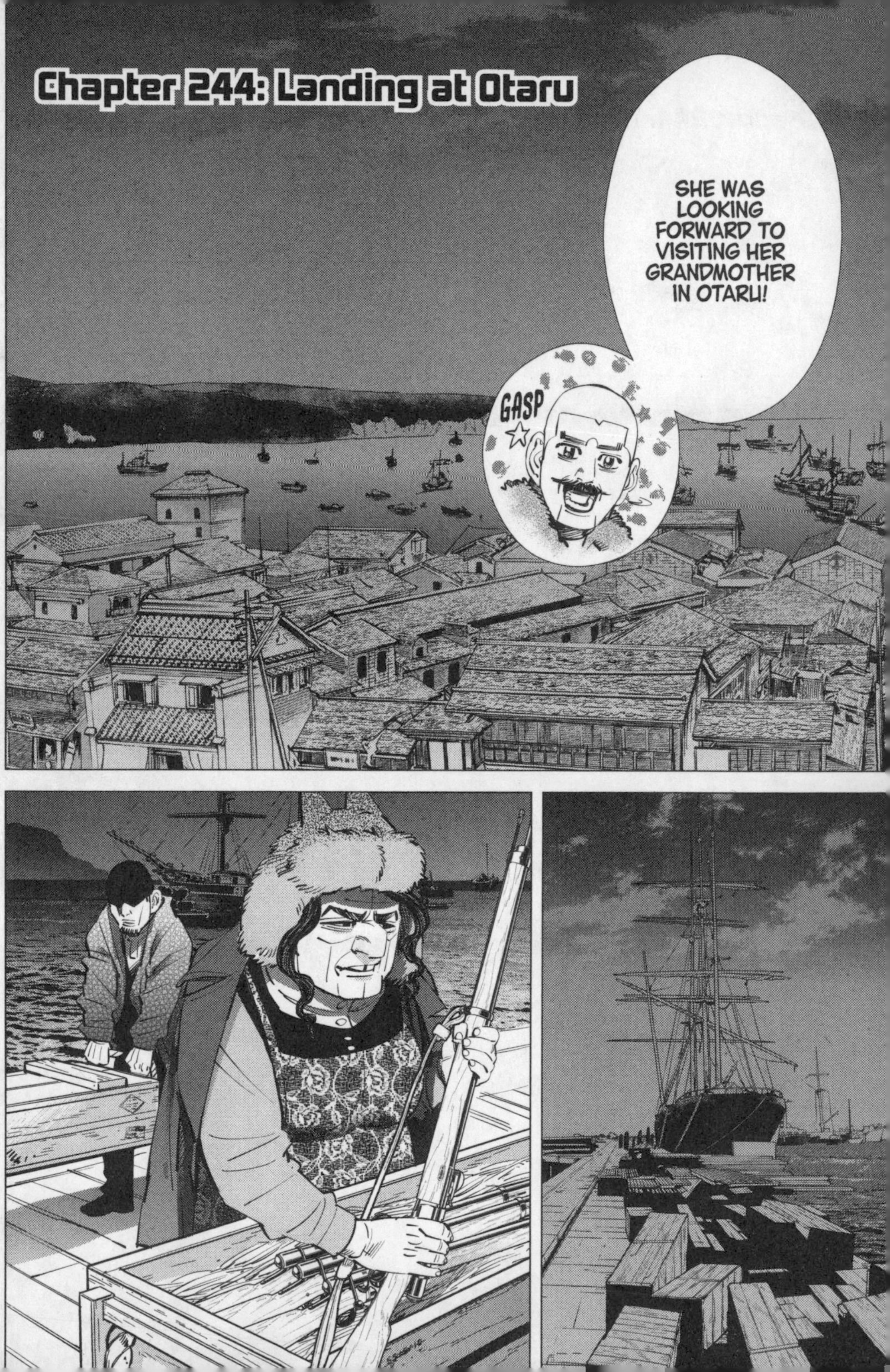
Chapter 244: Landing at Otaru
SHE WAS LOOKING FORWARD TO VISITING HER GRANDMOTHER IN OTARU!
GASP

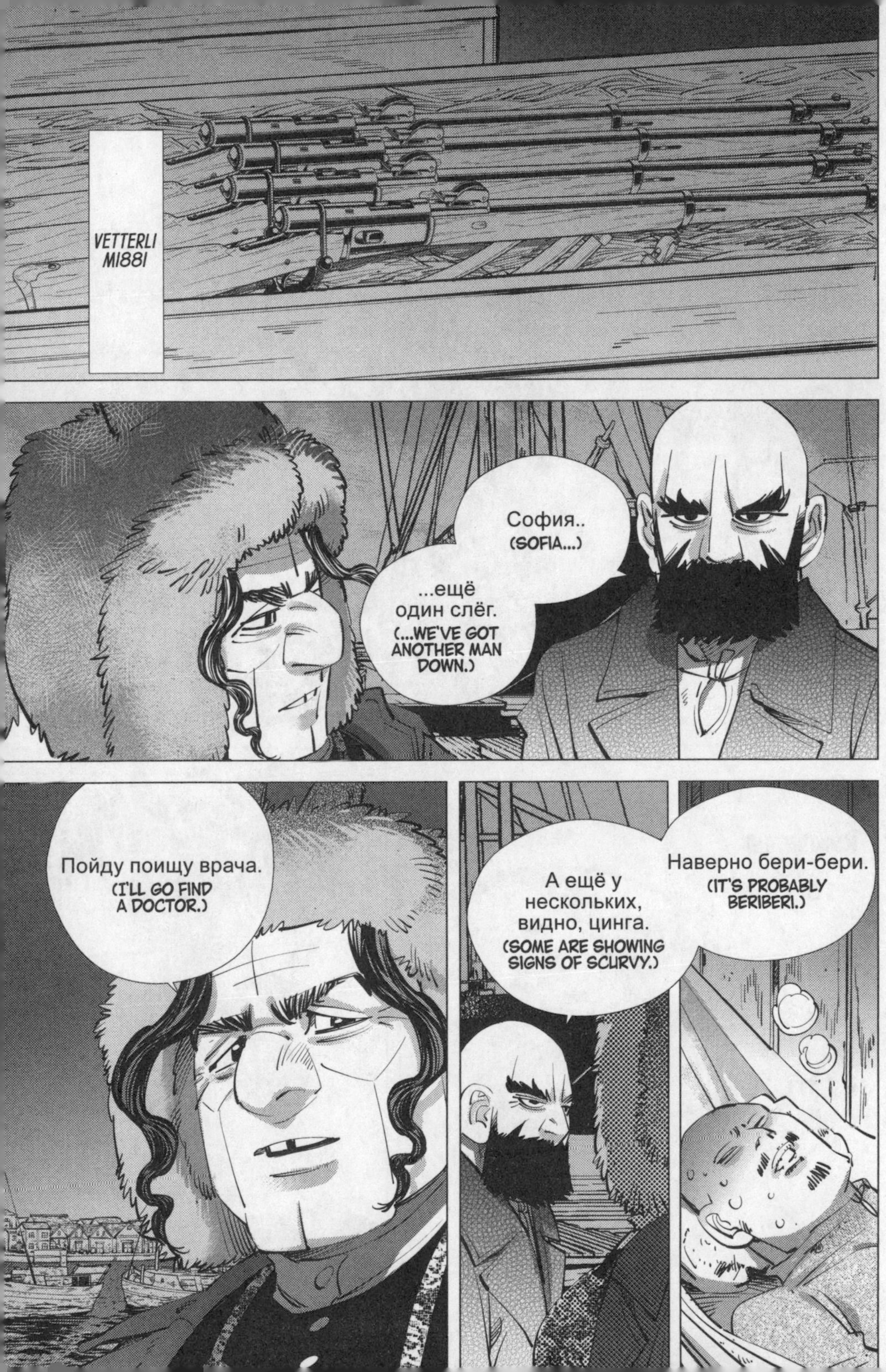
VETTERLI M1881
София..
(SOFIA...)
...ещё один слёг.
(...WE'VE GOT ANOTHER MAN DOWN.)
Наверно бери-бери.
(IT'S PROBABLY BERIBERI.)
А ещё у нескольких, видно, цинга.
(SOME ARE SHOWING SIGNS OF SCURVY.)
Пойду поищу врача.
(I'LL GO FIND A DOCTOR.)

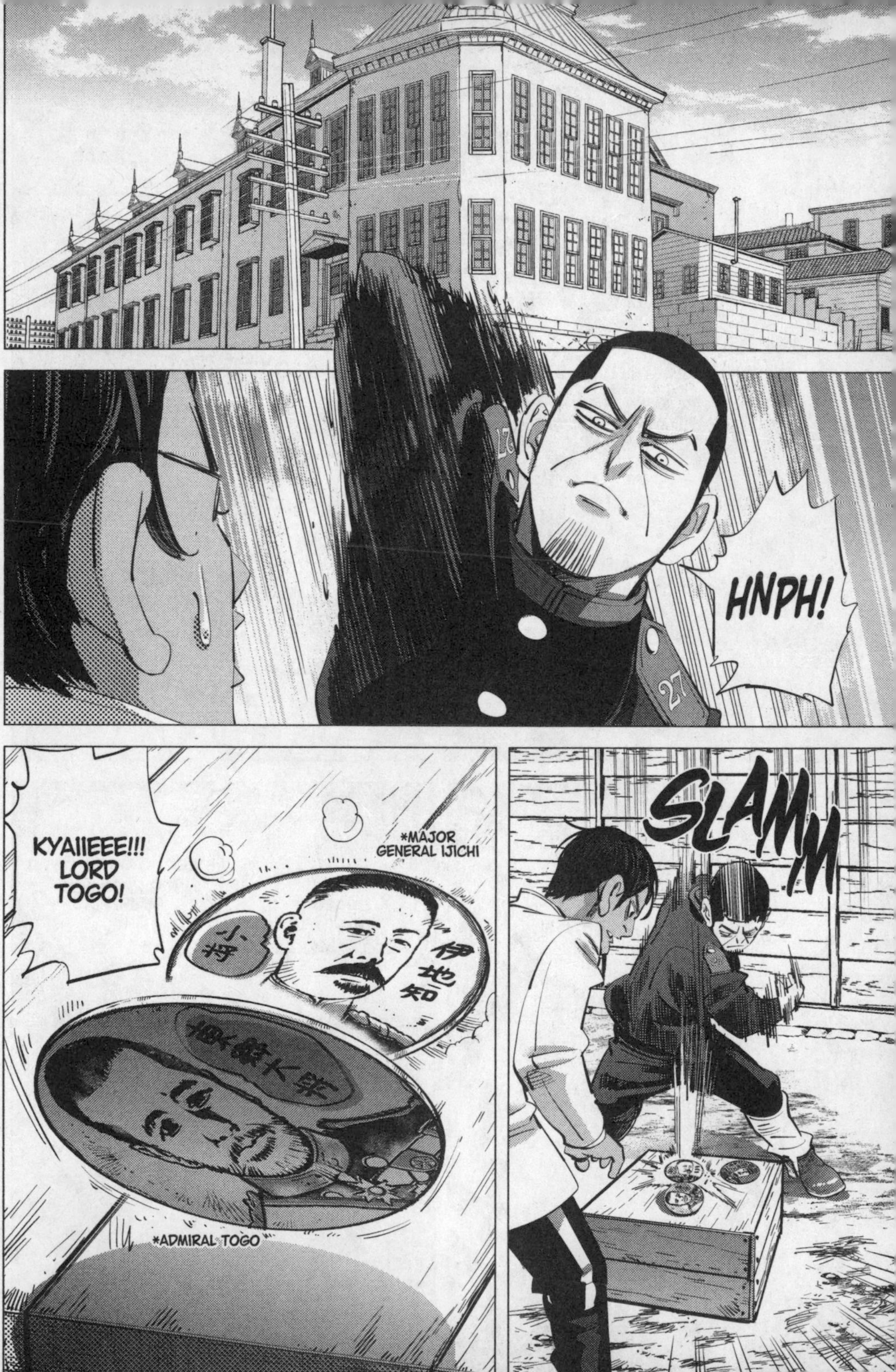
HNPH!
SLAMM
KYAIIEEE!!! LORD TOGO!
*MAJOR GENERAL IJICHI
*ADMIRAL TOGO

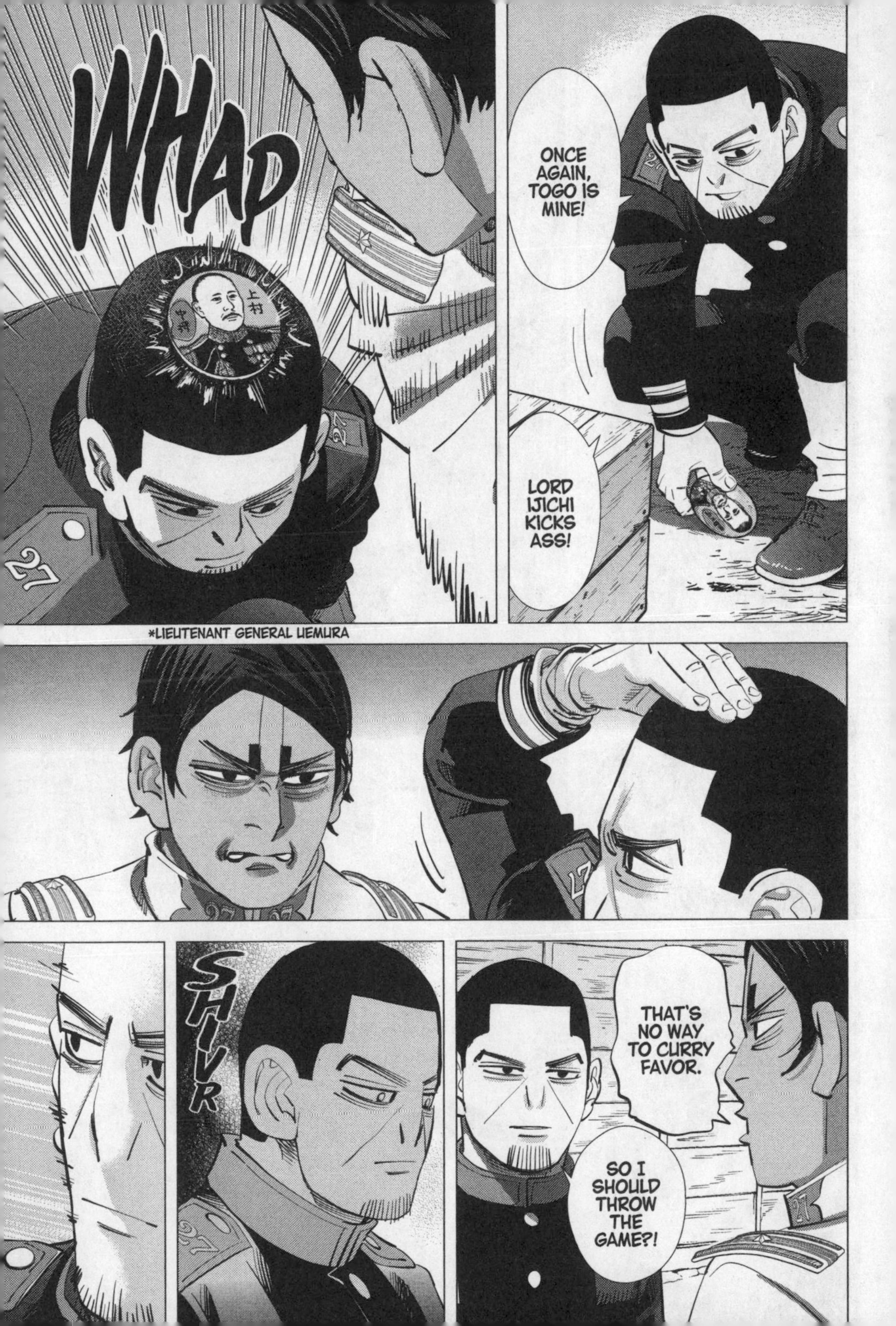
ONCE AGAIN, TOGO IS MINE!
LORD IJICHI KICKS ASS!
WHAP
上村
中将
*LIEUTENANT GENERAL UEMURA
THAT'S NO WAY TO CURRY FAVOR.
SO I SHOULD THROW THE GAME?!
SHIVR

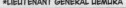

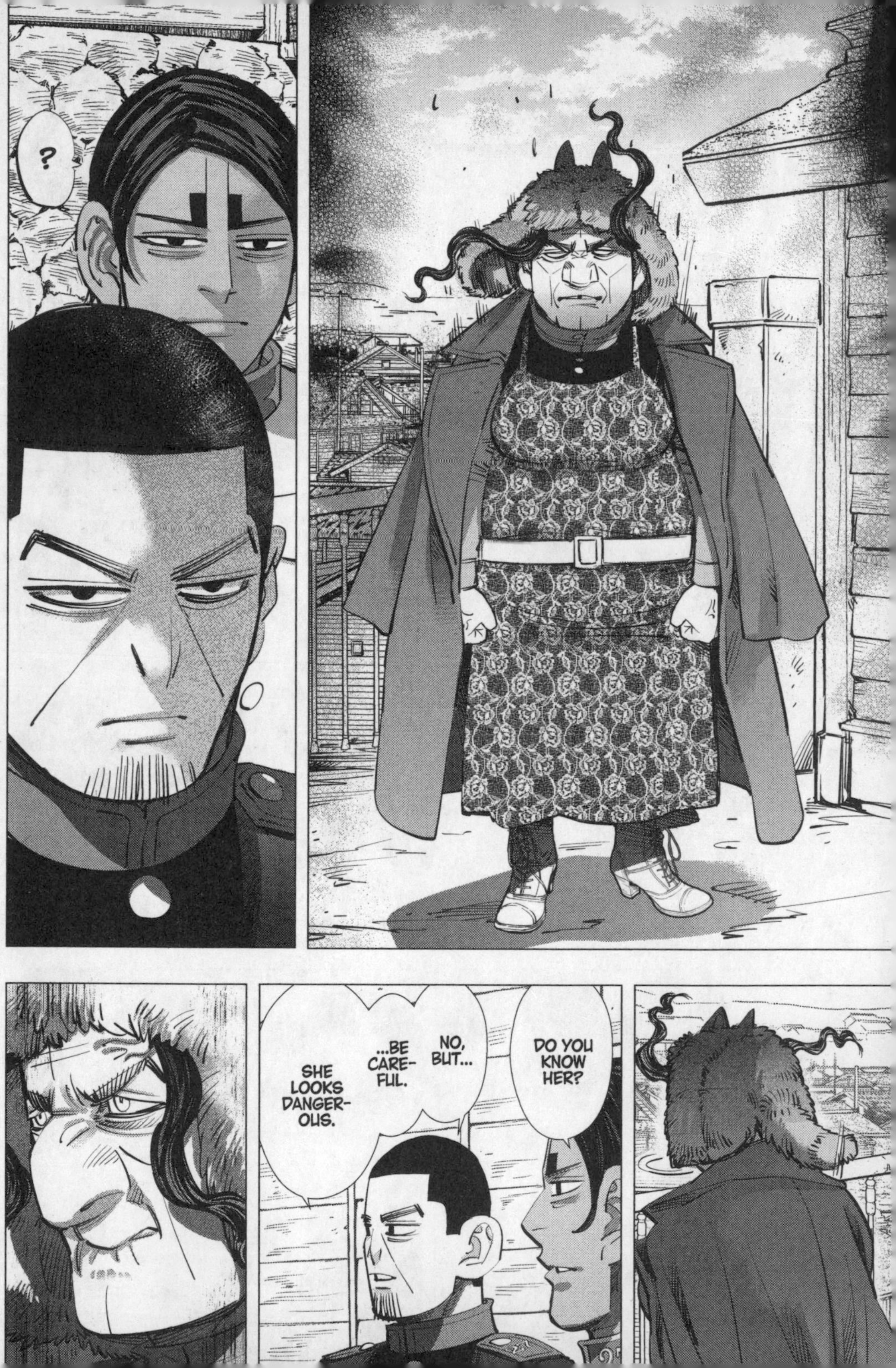
?
DO YOU KNOW HER?
NO, BUT...
...BE CARE-FUL.
SHE LOOKS DANGER-OUS.

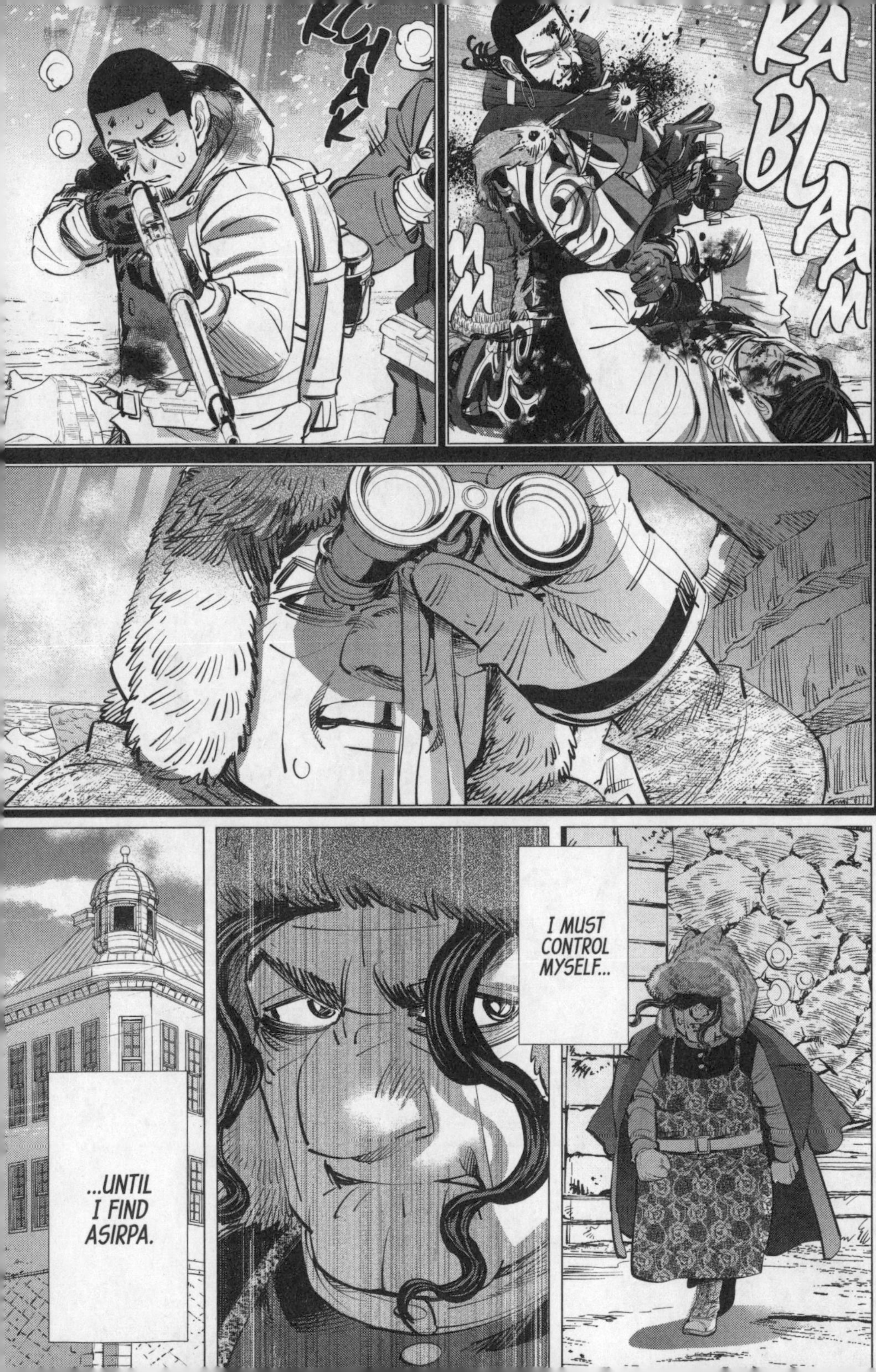
KA BLAAM
MM
KCHAK
I MUST CONTROL MYSELF...
...UNTIL I FIND ASIRPA.

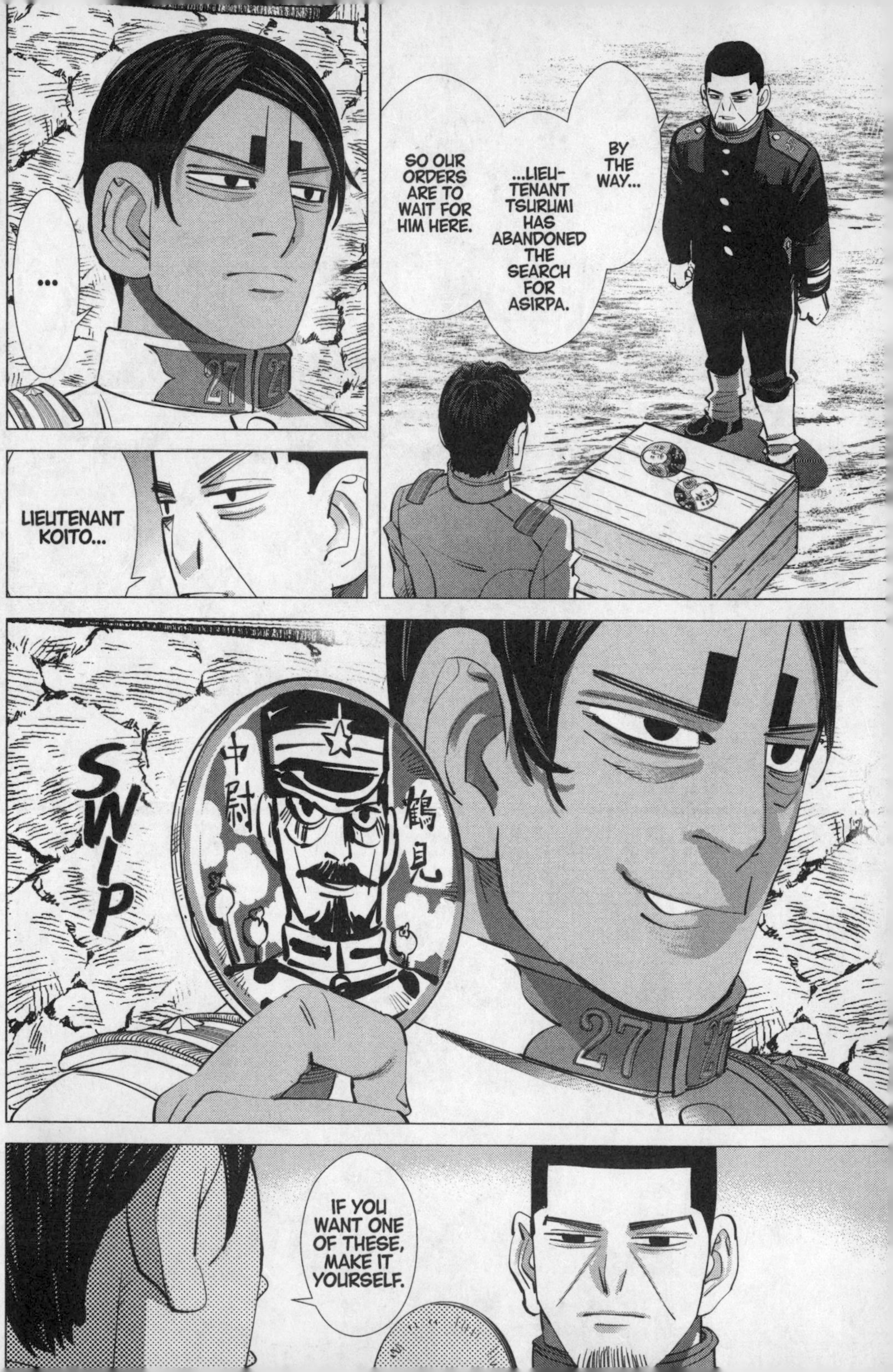
BY THE WAY...
...LIEU-TENANT TSURUMI HAS ABANDONED THE SEARCH FOR ASIRPA.
SO OUR ORDERS ARE TO WAIT FOR HIM HERE.
...
LIEUTENANT KOITO...
鶴見
中尉
SWIP
IF YOU WANT ONE OF THESE, MAKE IT YOURSELF.

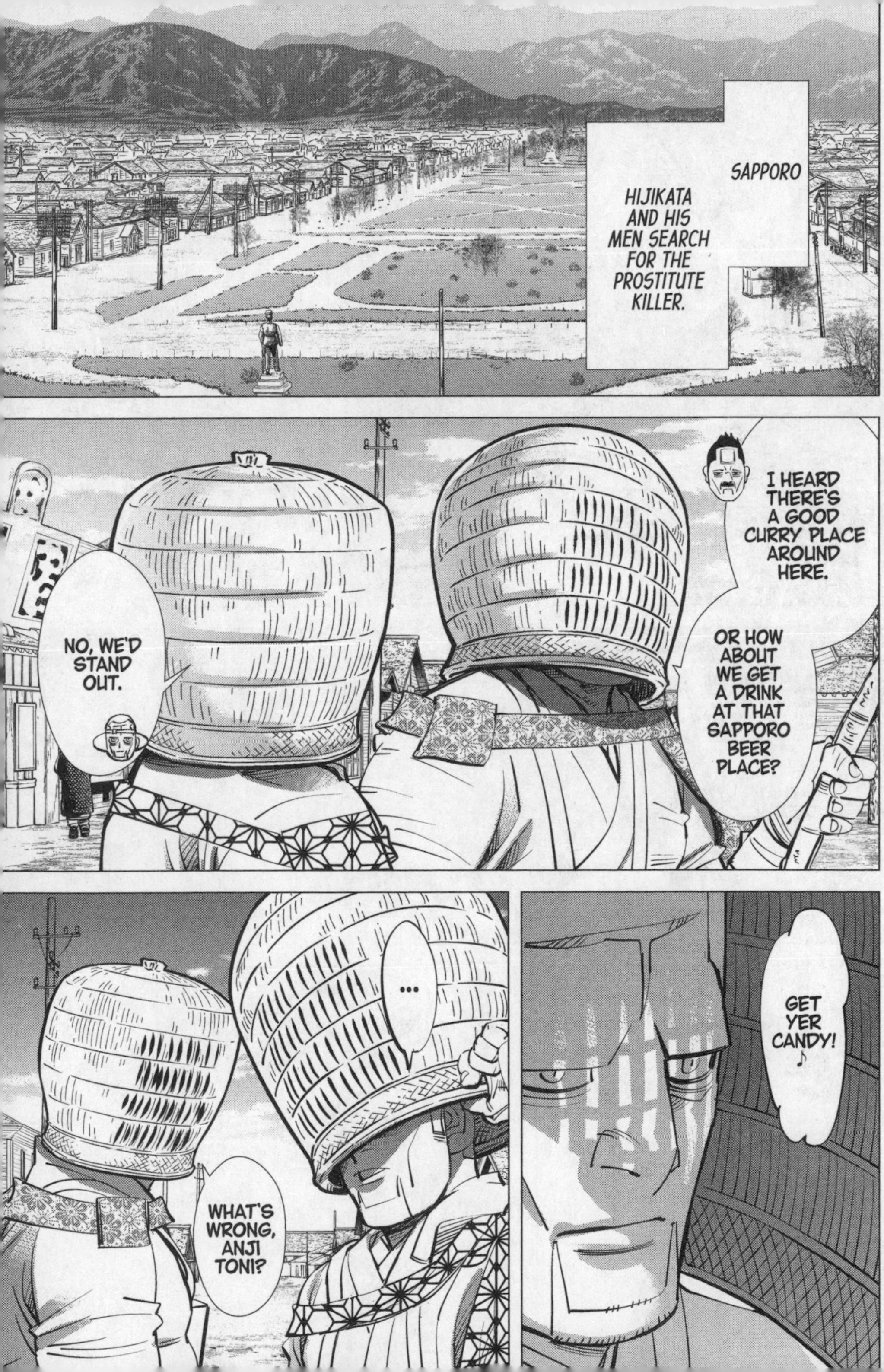
SAPPORO
HIJIKATA AND HIS MEN SEARCH FOR THE PROSTITUTE KILLER.
I HEARD THERE'S A GOOD CURRY PLACE AROUND HERE.
OR HOW ABOUT WE GET A DRINK AT THAT SAPPORO BEER PLACE?
NO, WE'D STAND OUT.
GET YER CANDY! ♪
...
WHAT'S WRONG, ANJI TONI?

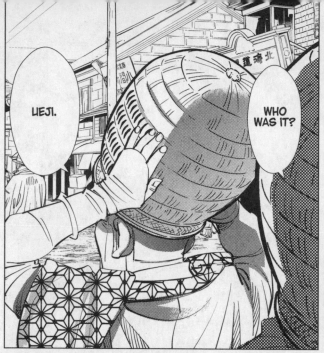

UEJI.

WHO WAS IT?

I HEARD A VOICE I RECOGNIZE.

THAT DEMON...

OH...HIM?

WHO'RE YOU LOOKING FOR?

TARO!

TARO!

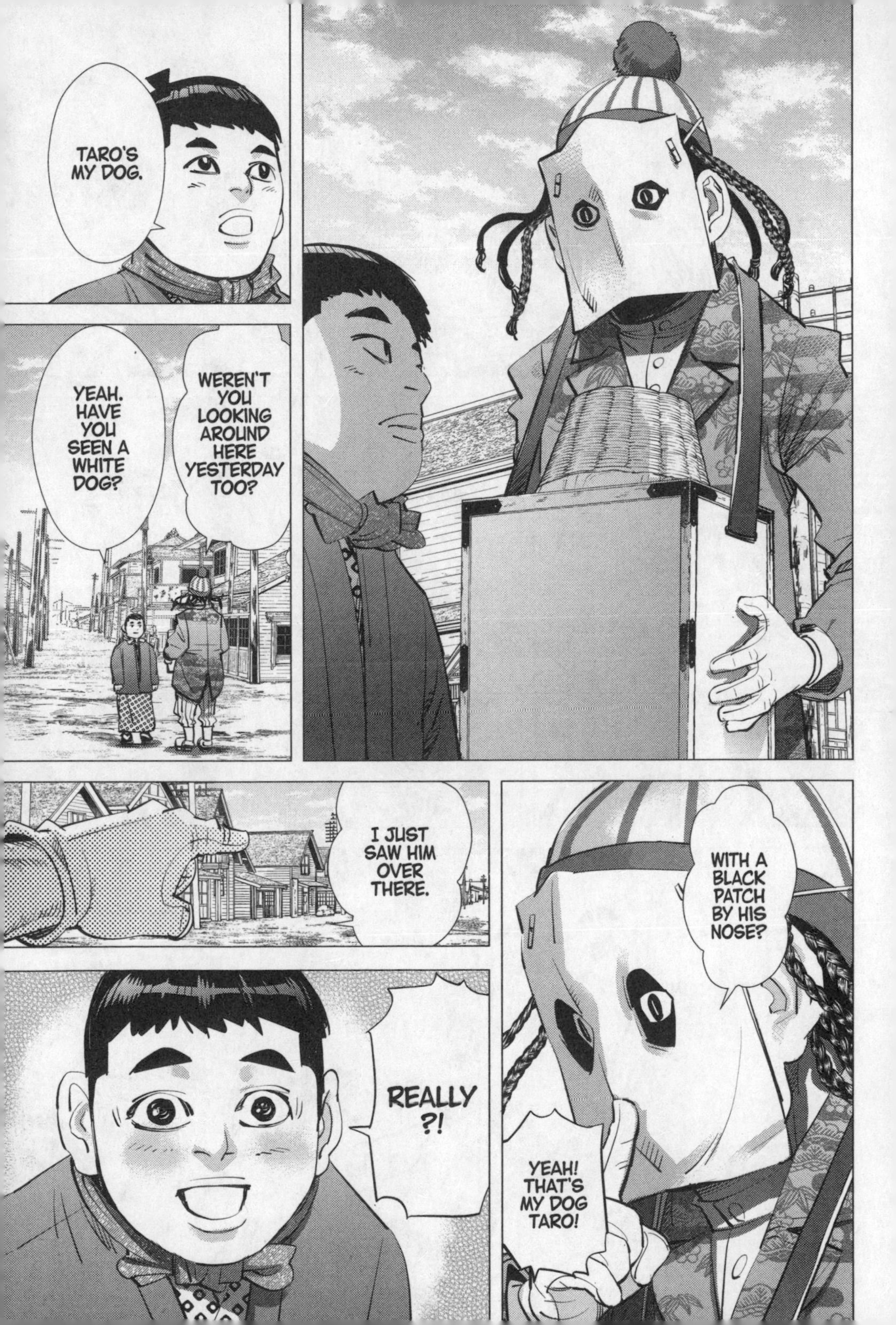

TARO'S MY DOG.
WEREN'T YOU LOOKING AROUND HERE YESTERDAY TOO?
YEAH. HAVE YOU SEEN A WHITE DOG?
WITH A BLACK PATCH BY HIS NOSE?
YEAH! THAT'S MY DOG TARO!
I JUST SAW HIM OVER THERE.
REALLY?!

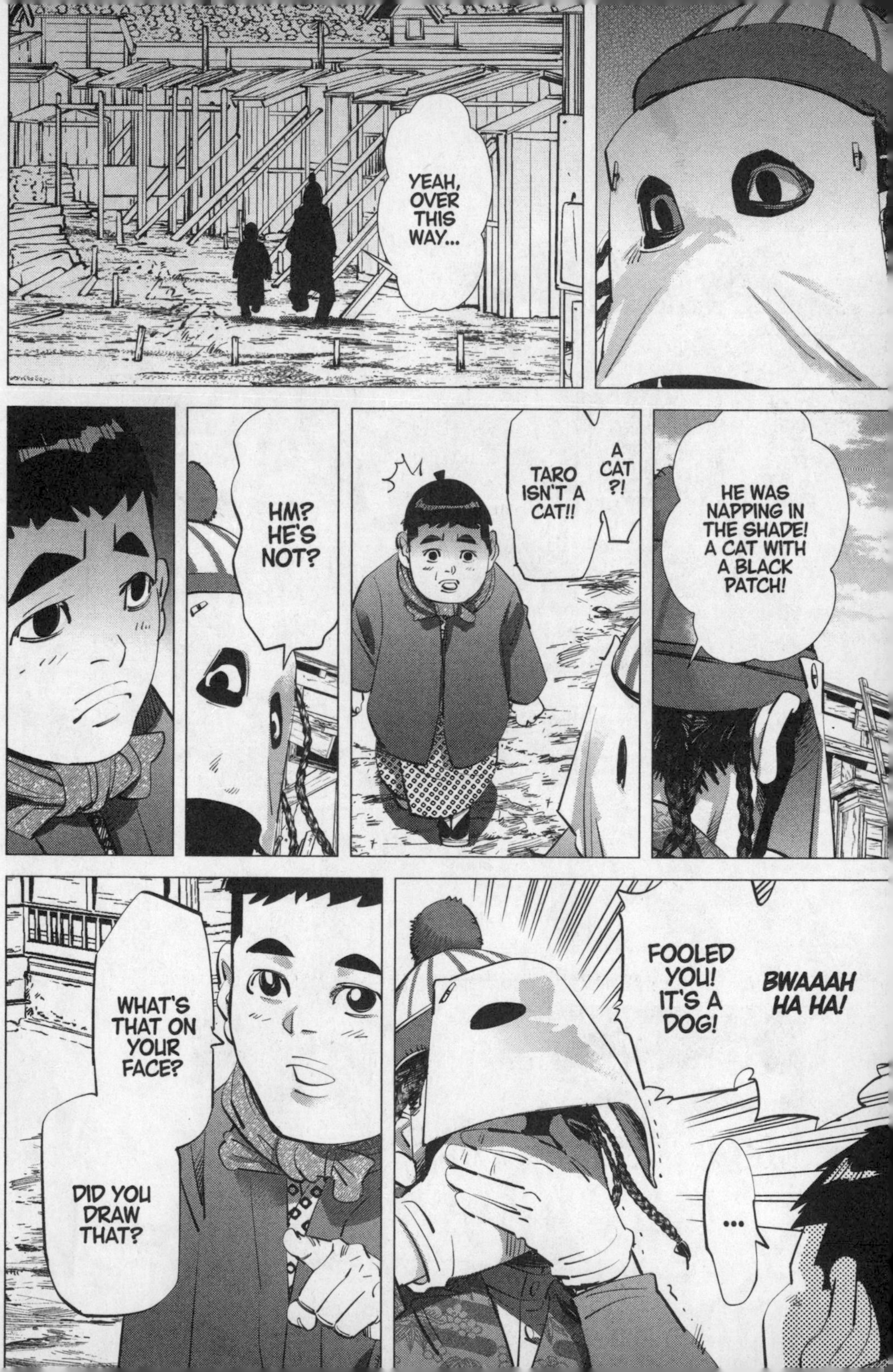
YEAH, OVER THIS WAY...
HE WAS NAPPING IN THE SHADE! A CAT WITH A BLACK PATCH!
A CAT ?!
TARO ISN'T A CAT!!
HM? HE'S NOT?
BWAAAH HA HA!
FOOLED YOU! IT'S A DOG!
...
WHAT'S THAT ON YOUR FACE?
DID YOU DRAW THAT?

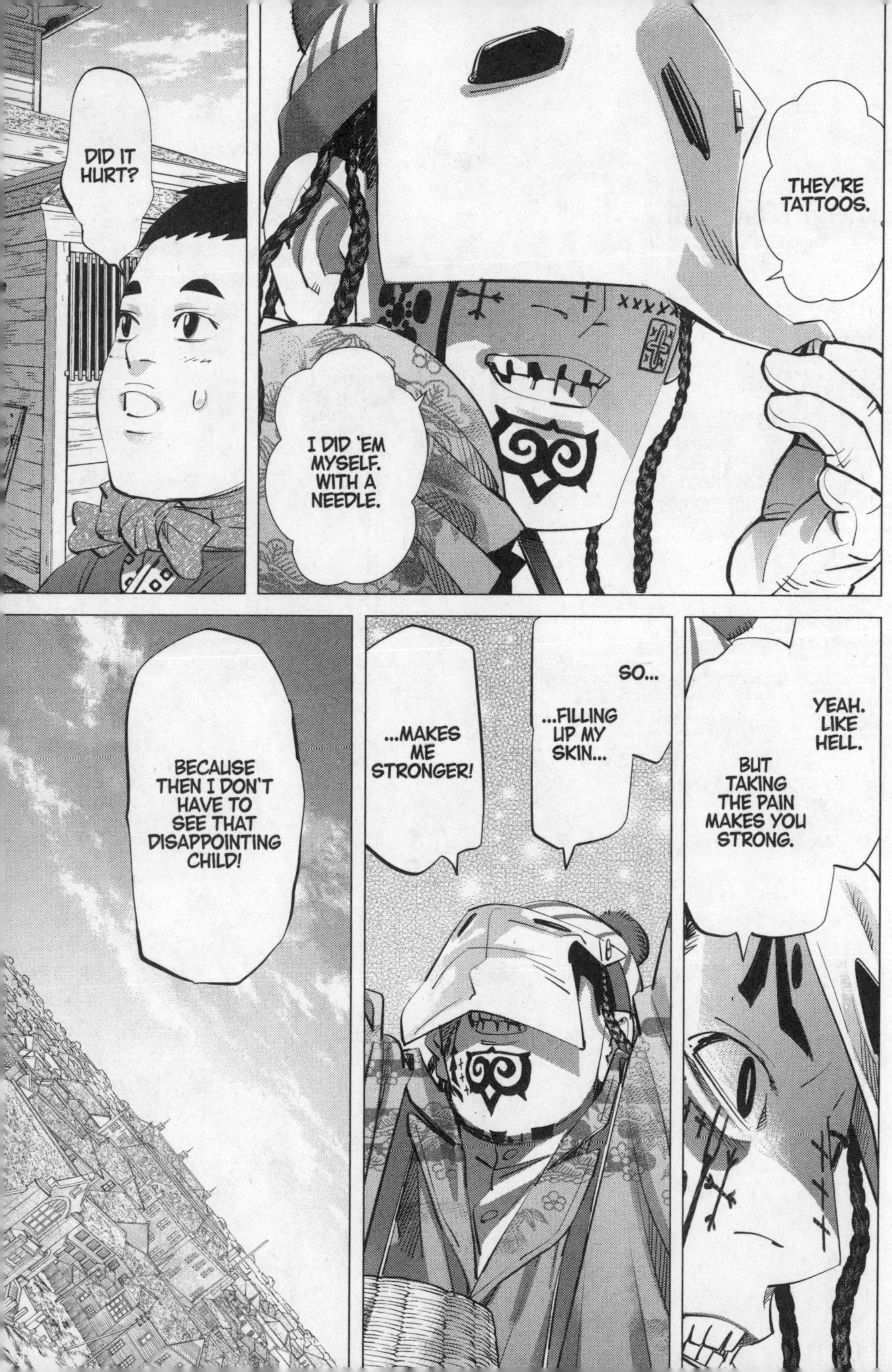
THEY'RE TATTOOS.
I DID 'EM MYSELF. WITH A NEEDLE.
DID IT HURT?
YEAH. LIKE HELL.
BUT TAKING THE PAIN MAKES YOU STRONG.
SO...
...FILLING UP MY SKIN...
...MAKES ME STRONGER!
BECAUSE THEN I DON'T HAVE TO SEE THAT DISAPPOINTING CHILD!

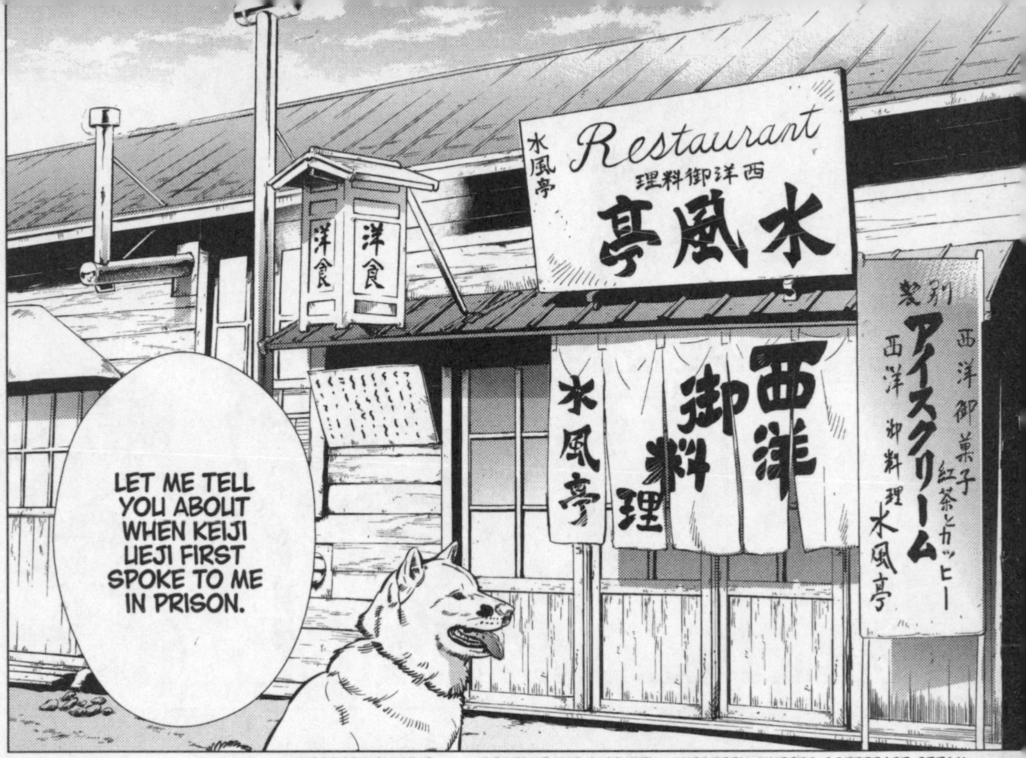
Restaurant
西洋御料理
水風亭
西洋御料理
水風亭
洋食
洋食
LET ME TELL YOU ABOUT WHEN KEIJI UEJI FIRST SPOKE TO ME IN PRISON.

*WESTERN CUISINE *RESTAURANT SUIFUTEI *WESTERN SWEETS COFFEE ICE CREAM

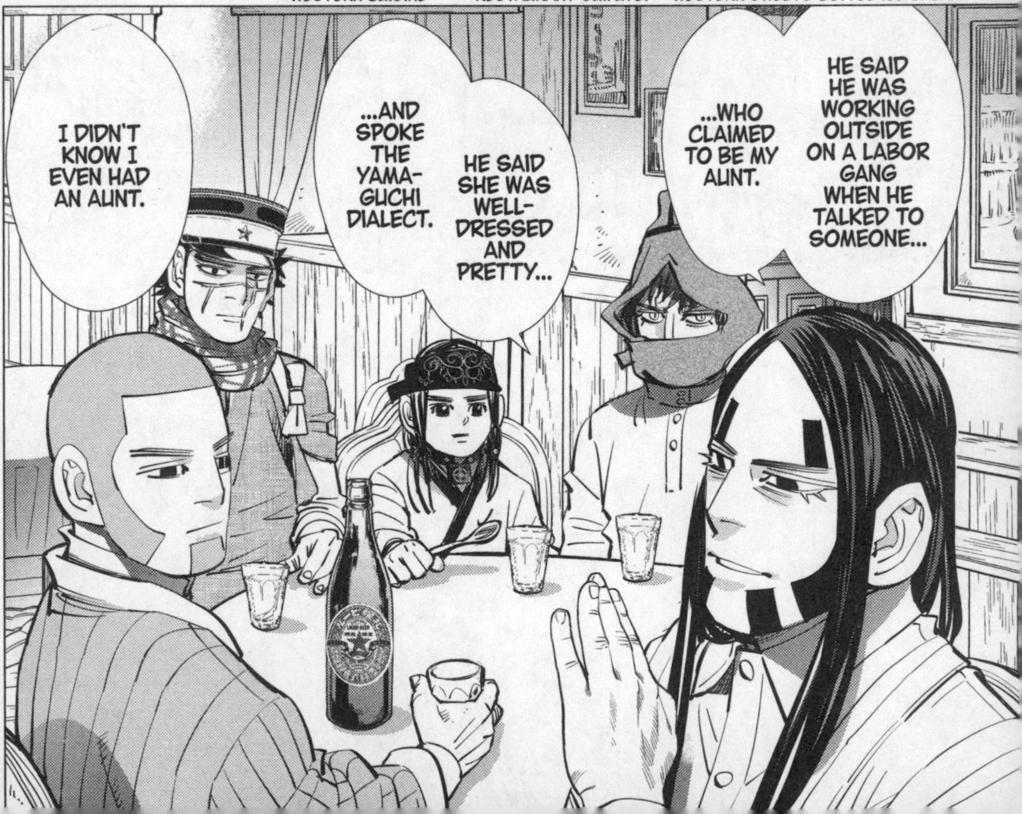
HE SAID HE WAS WORKING OUTSIDE ON A LABOR GANG WHEN HE TALKED TO SOMEONE...
...WHO CLAIMED TO BE MY AUNT.
HE SAID SHE WAS WELL-DRESSED AND PRETTY...
...AND SPOKE THE YAMA-GUCHI DIALECT.
I DIDN'T KNOW I EVEN HAD AN AUNT.

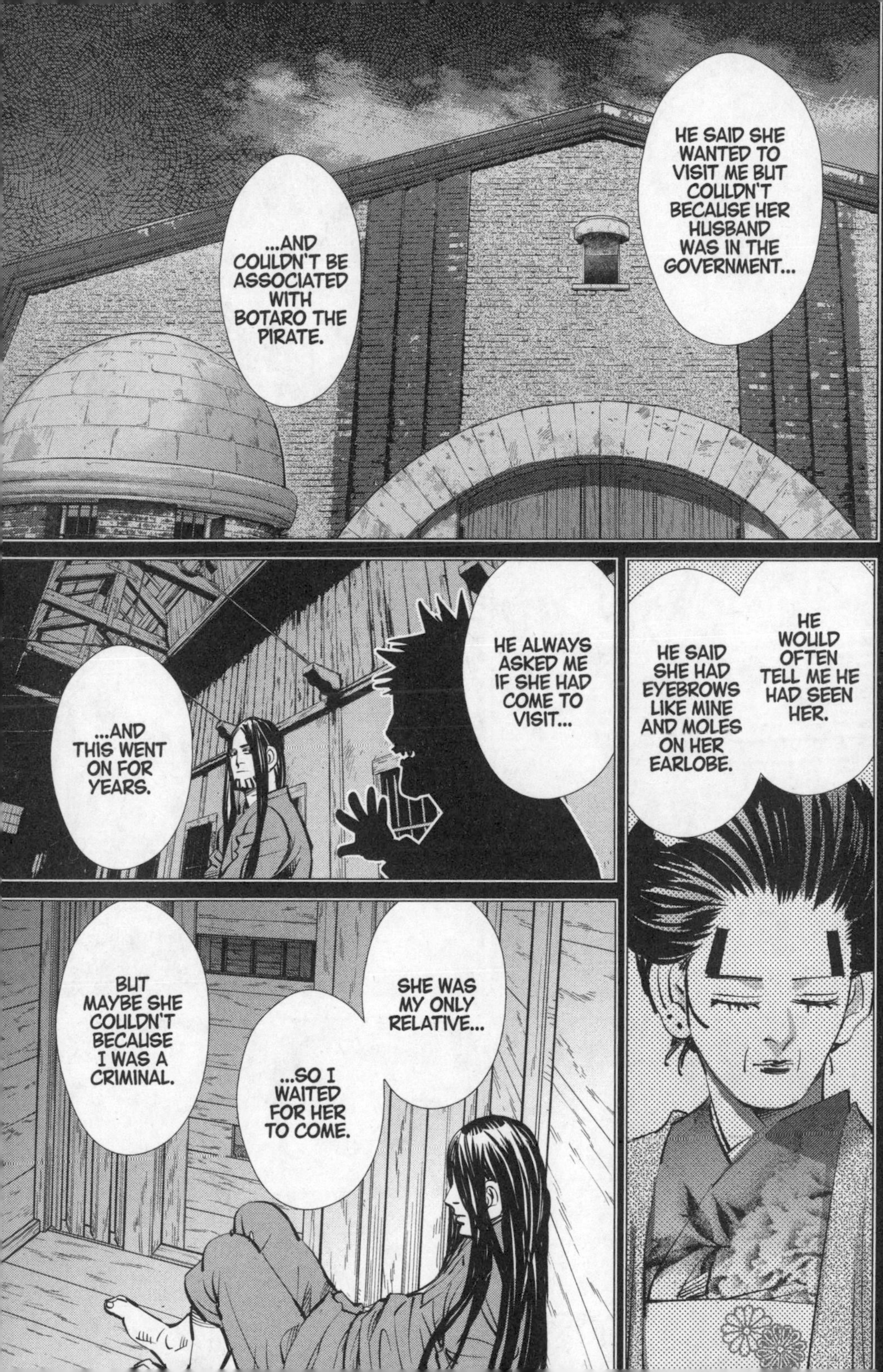
HE SAID SHE WANTED TO VISIT ME BUT COULDN'T BECAUSE HER HUSBAND WAS IN THE GOVERNMENT...
...AND COULDN'T BE ASSOCIATED WITH BOTARO THE PIRATE.
HE WOULD OFTEN TELL ME HE HAD SEEN HER.
HE SAID SHE HAD EYEBROWS LIKE MINE AND MOLES ON HER EARLOBE.
HE ALWAYS ASKED ME IF SHE HAD COME TO VISIT...
...AND THIS WENT ON FOR YEARS.
SHE WAS MY ONLY RELATIVE...
...SO I WAITED FOR HER TO COME.
BUT MAYBE SHE COULDN'T BECAUSE I WAS A CRIMINAL.

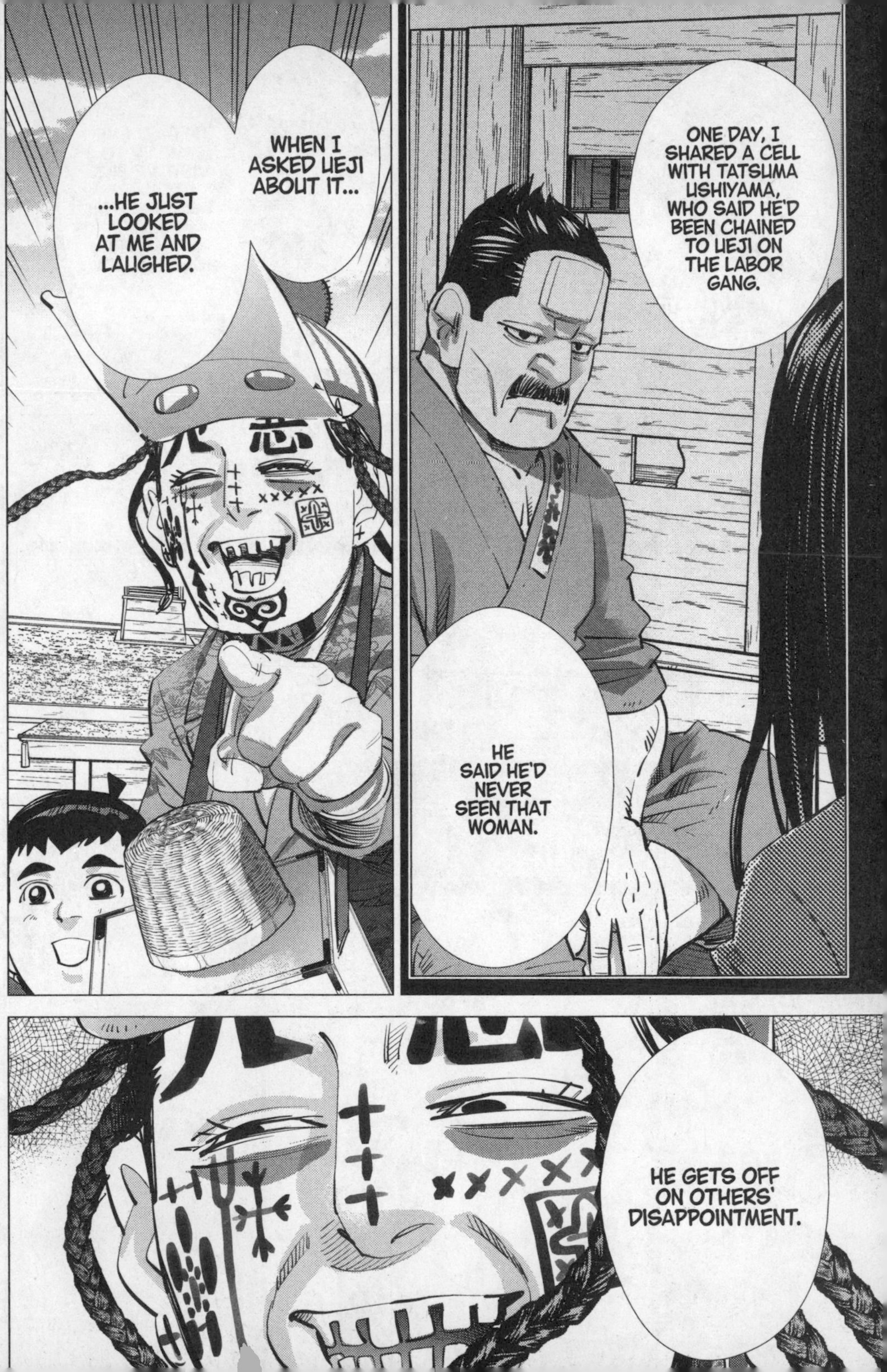
ONE DAY, I SHARED A CELL WITH TATSUMA USHIYAMA, WHO SAID HE'D BEEN CHAINED TO UEJI ON THE LABOR GANG.
HE SAID HE'D NEVER SEEN THAT WOMAN.
WHEN I ASKED UEJI ABOUT IT...
...HE JUST LOOKED AT ME AND LAUGHED.
HE GETS OFF ON OTHERS' DISAPPOINTMENT.

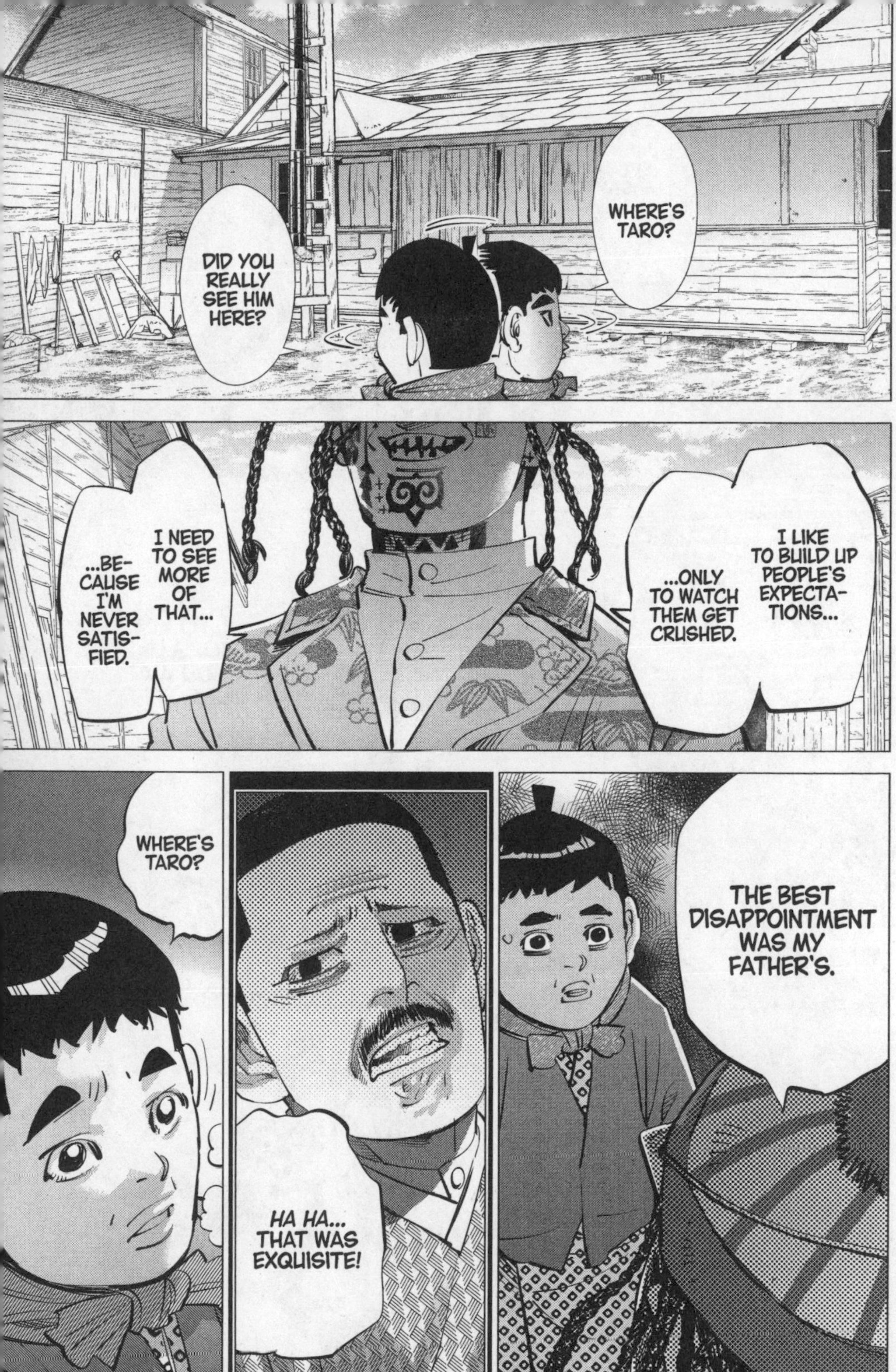
WHERE'S TARO?
DID YOU REALLY SEE HIM HERE?
I LIKE TO BUILD UP PEOPLE'S EXPECTATIONS...
...ONLY TO WATCH THEM GET CRUSHED.
I NEED TO SEE MORE OF THAT...
...BECAUSE I'M NEVER SATISFIED.
THE BEST DISAPPOINTMENT WAS MY FATHER'S.
HA HA... THAT WAS EXQUISITE!
WHERE'S TARO?

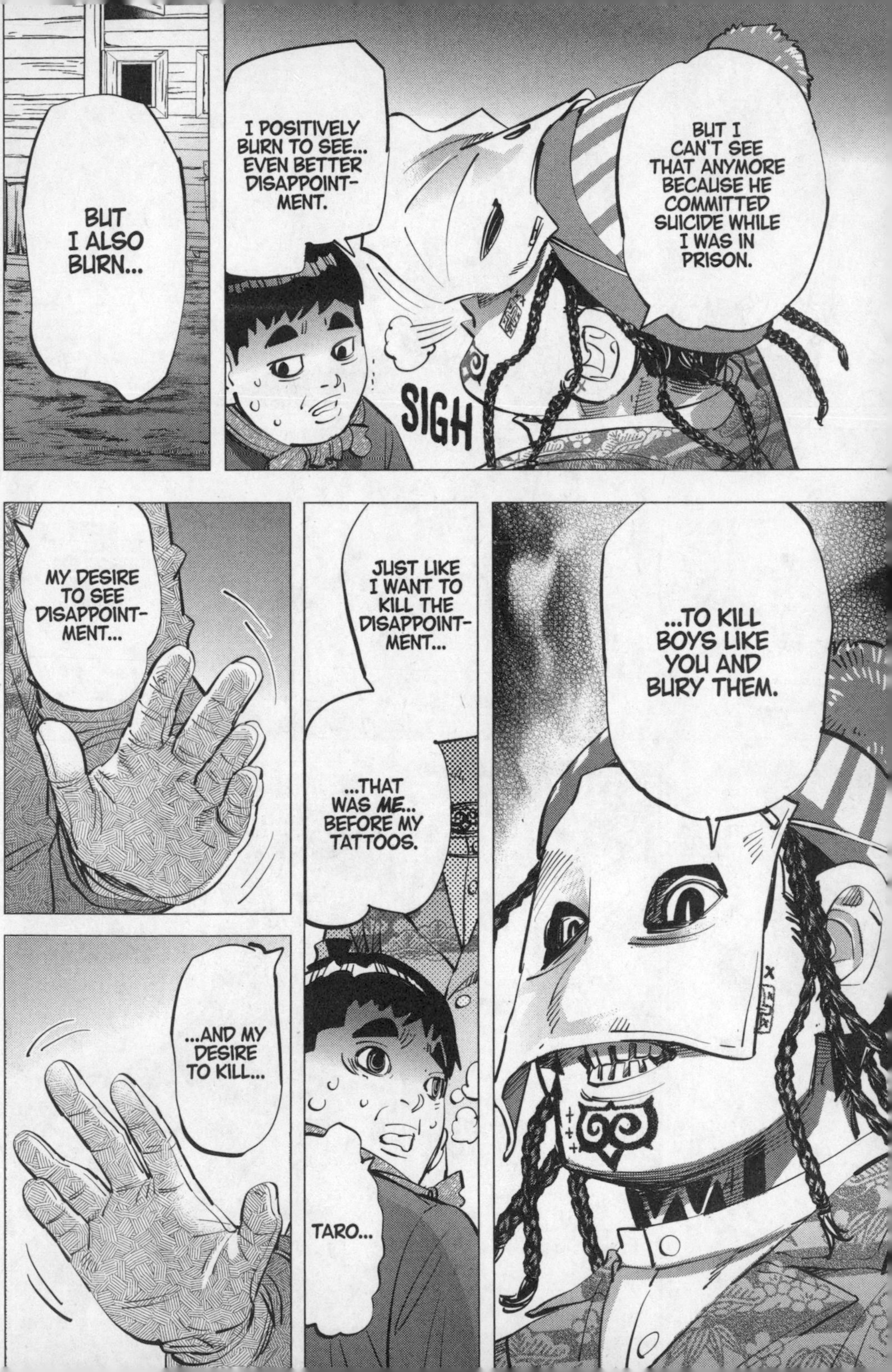
BUT I CAN'T SEE THAT ANYMORE BECAUSE HE COMMITTED SUICIDE WHILE I WAS IN PRISON.
I POSITIVELY BURN TO SEE... EVEN BETTER DISAPPOINT-MENT.
SIGH
BUT I ALSO BURN...
...TO KILL BOYS LIKE YOU AND BURY THEM.
JUST LIKE I WANT TO KILL THE DISAPPOINT-MENT...
...THAT WAS *ME*... BEFORE MY TATTOOS.
TARO...
MY DESIRE TO SEE DISAPPOINT-MENT...
...AND MY DESIRE TO KILL...

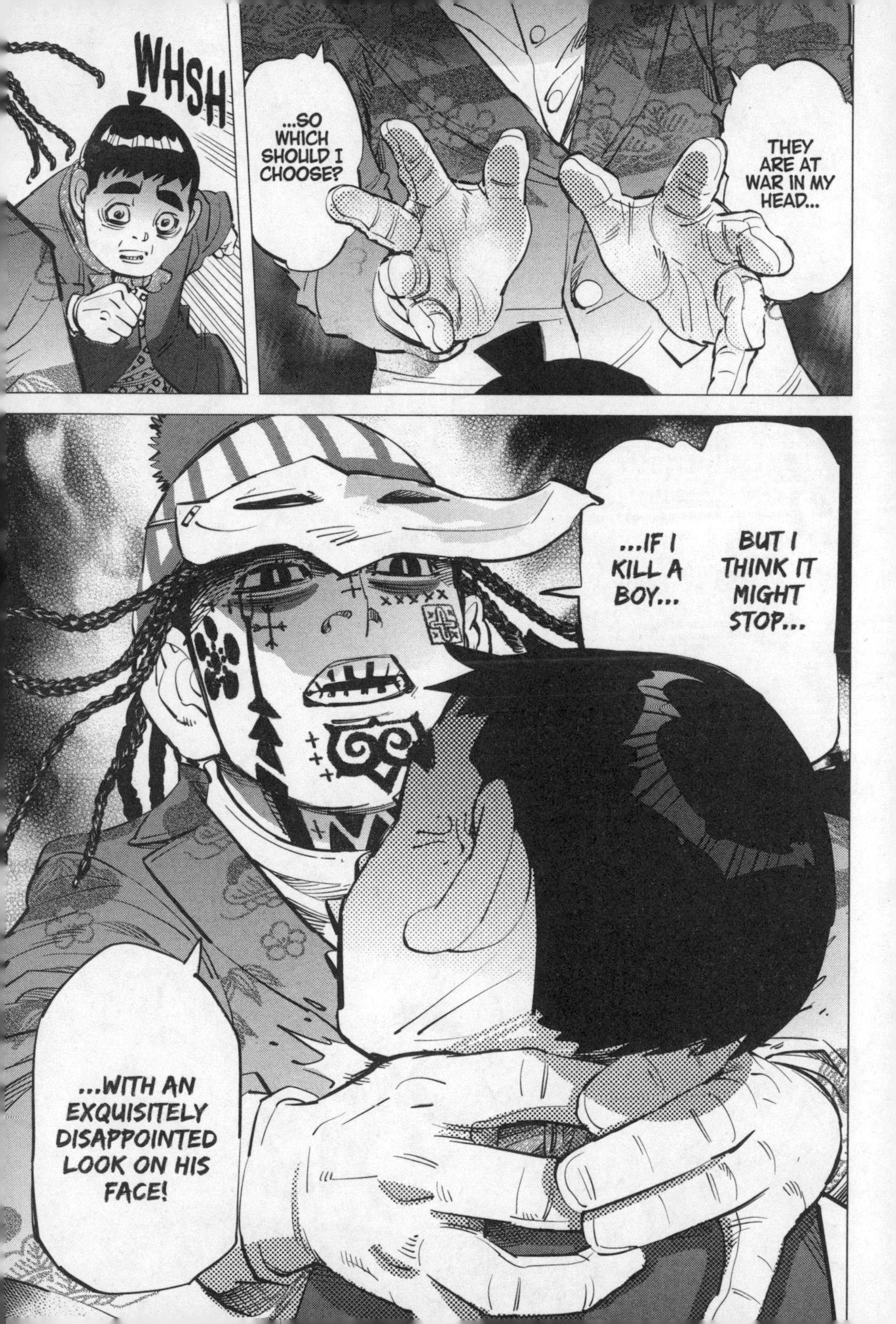
THEY ARE AT WAR IN MY HEAD...
...SO WHICH SHOULD I CHOOSE?
WHSH
BUT I THINK IT MIGHT STOP...
...IF I KILL A BOY...
...WITH AN EXQUISITELY DISAPPOINTED LOOK ON HIS FACE!

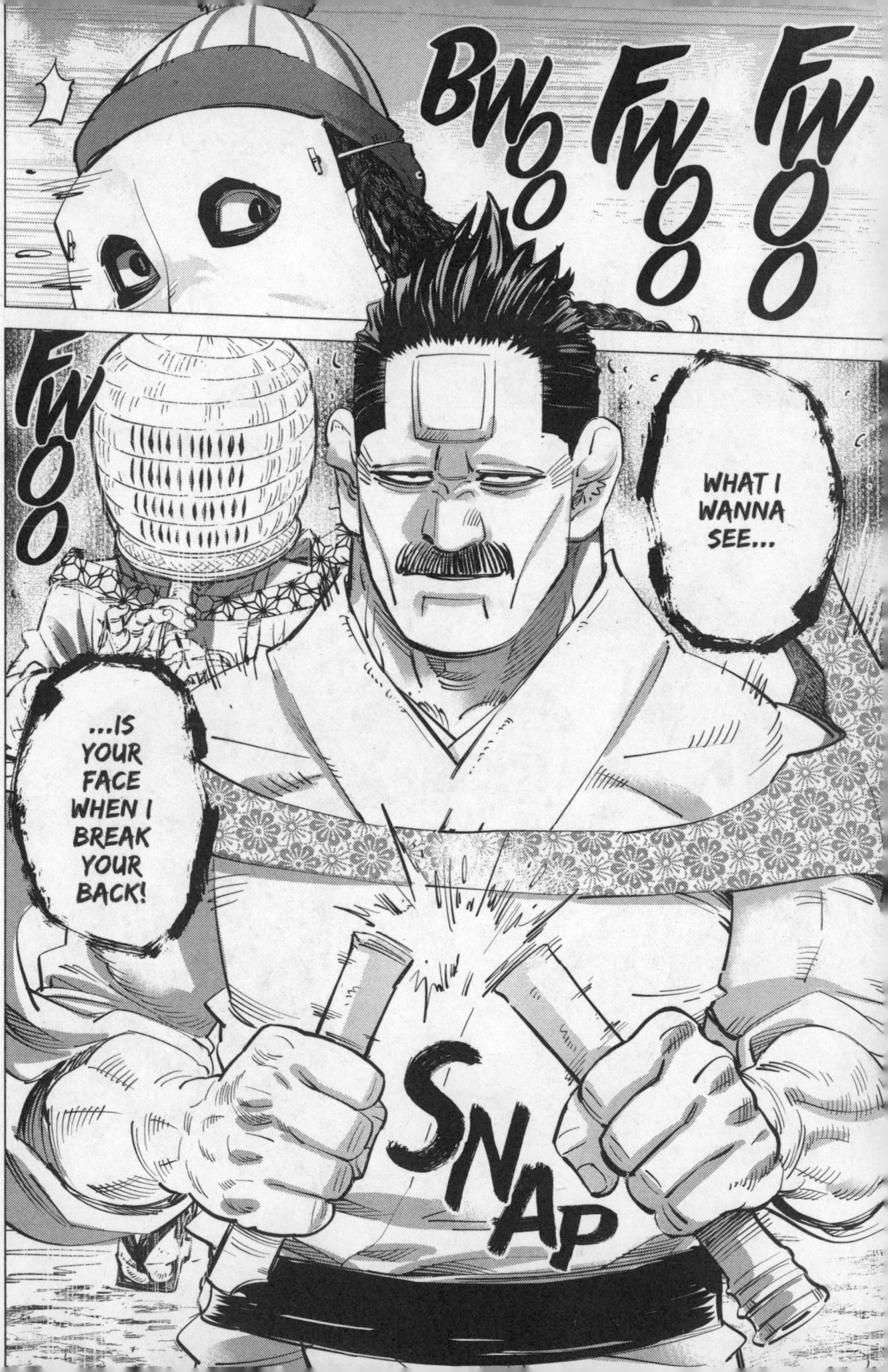
FWOOO
FWOOO
BWOO
WHAT I WANNA SEE...
FWOOO
...IS YOUR FACE WHEN I BREAK YOUR BACK!
SNAP

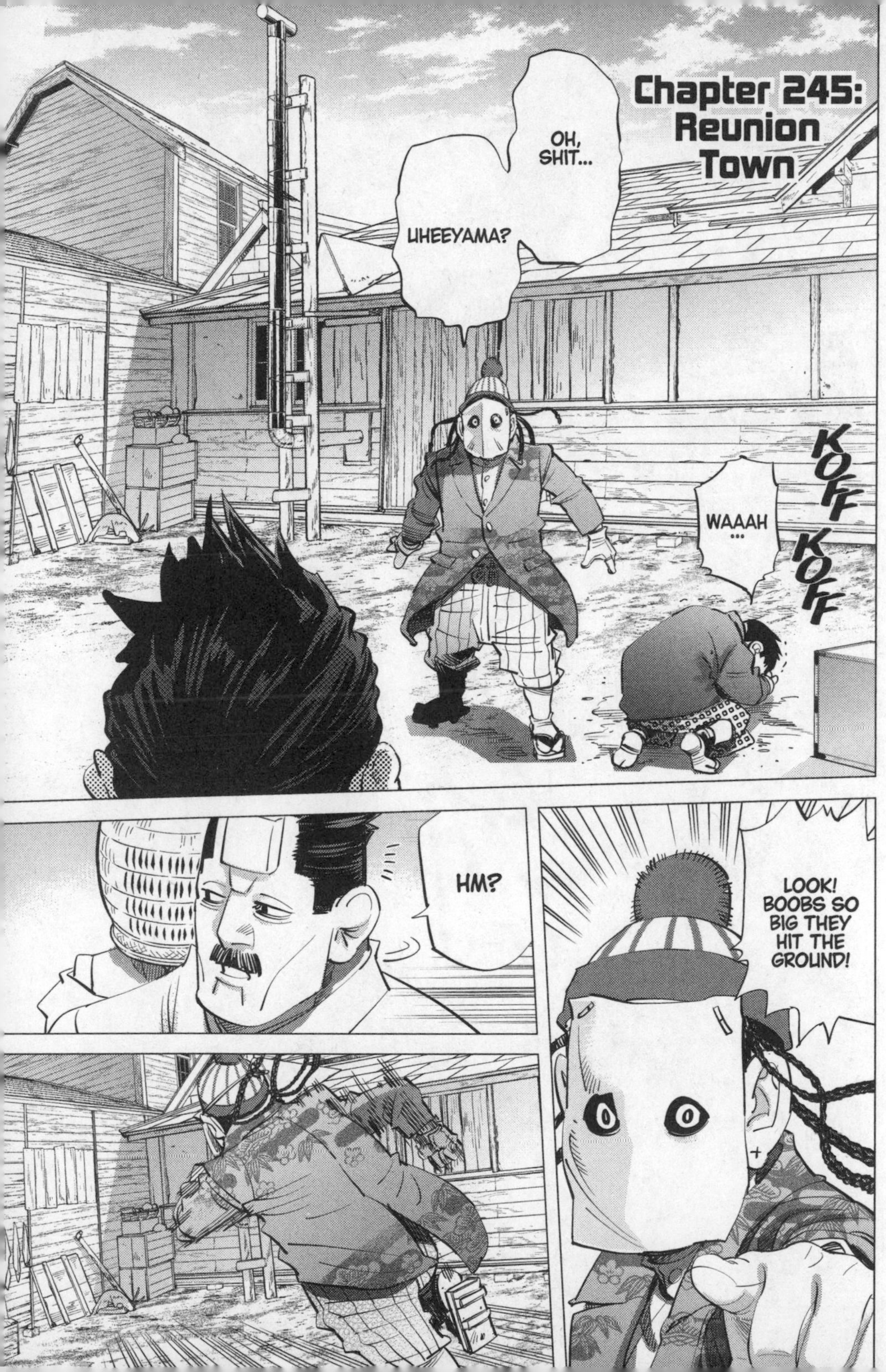
Chapter 245: Reunion Town
OH, SHIT...
UHEEYAMA?
WAAAH ...
KOFF KOFF KOFF
LOOK! BOOBS SO BIG THEY HIT THE GROUND!
HM?

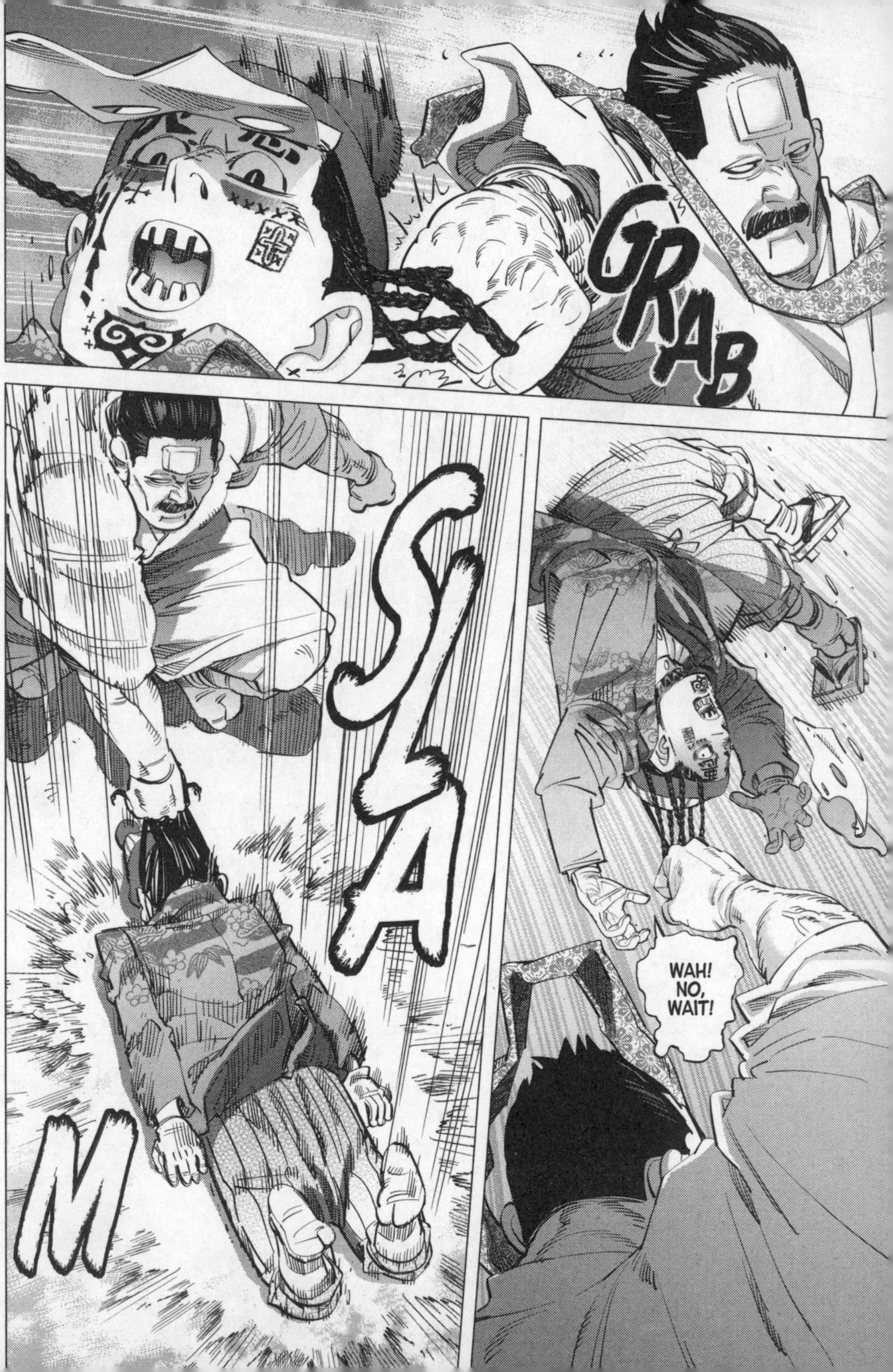
GRAB
WAH! NO, WAIT!
SLAM

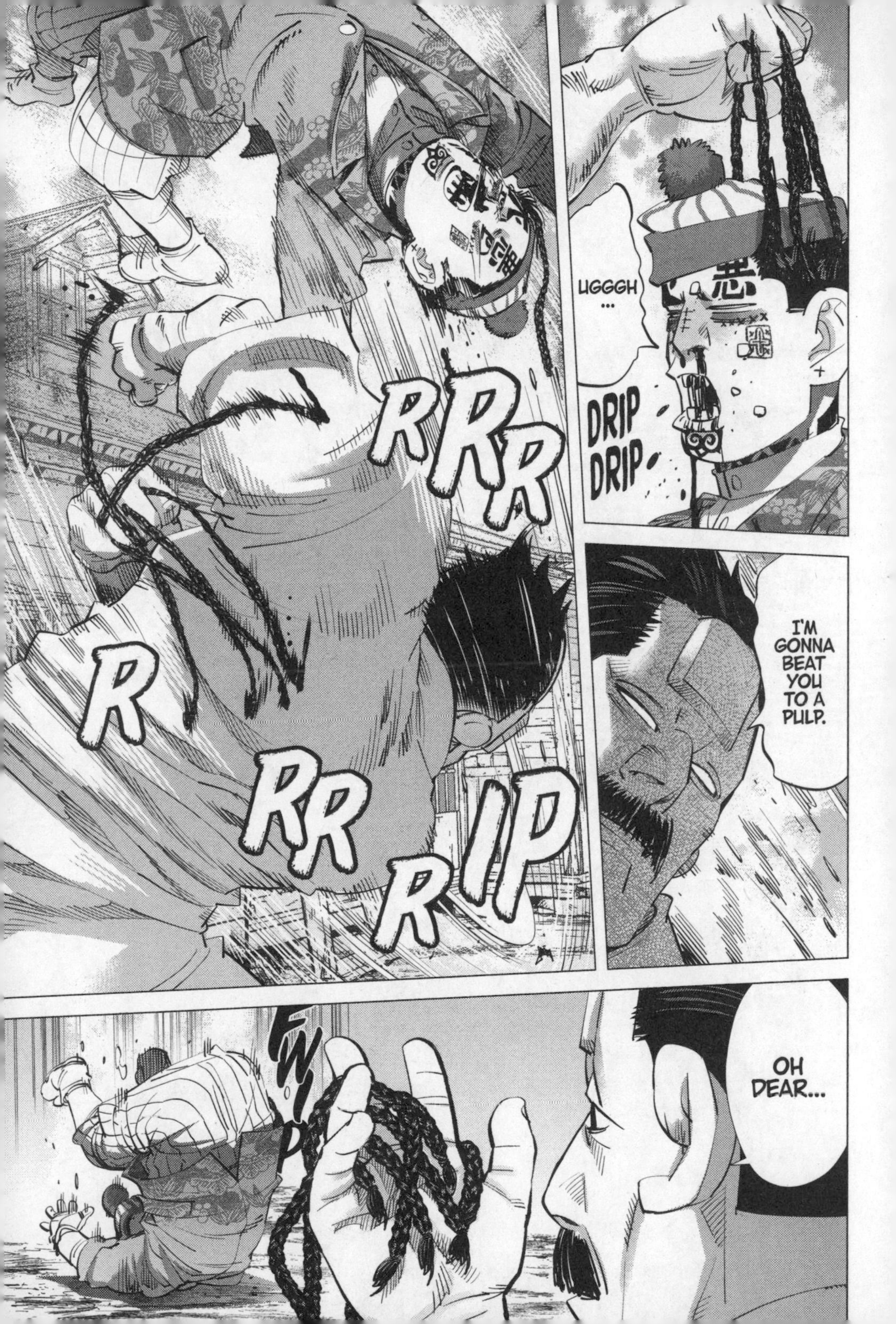
UGGGH...
悪
DRIP DRIP
I'M GONNA BEAT YOU TO A PULP.
RRRR
R
RR
RIP
OH DEAR...
FWIP

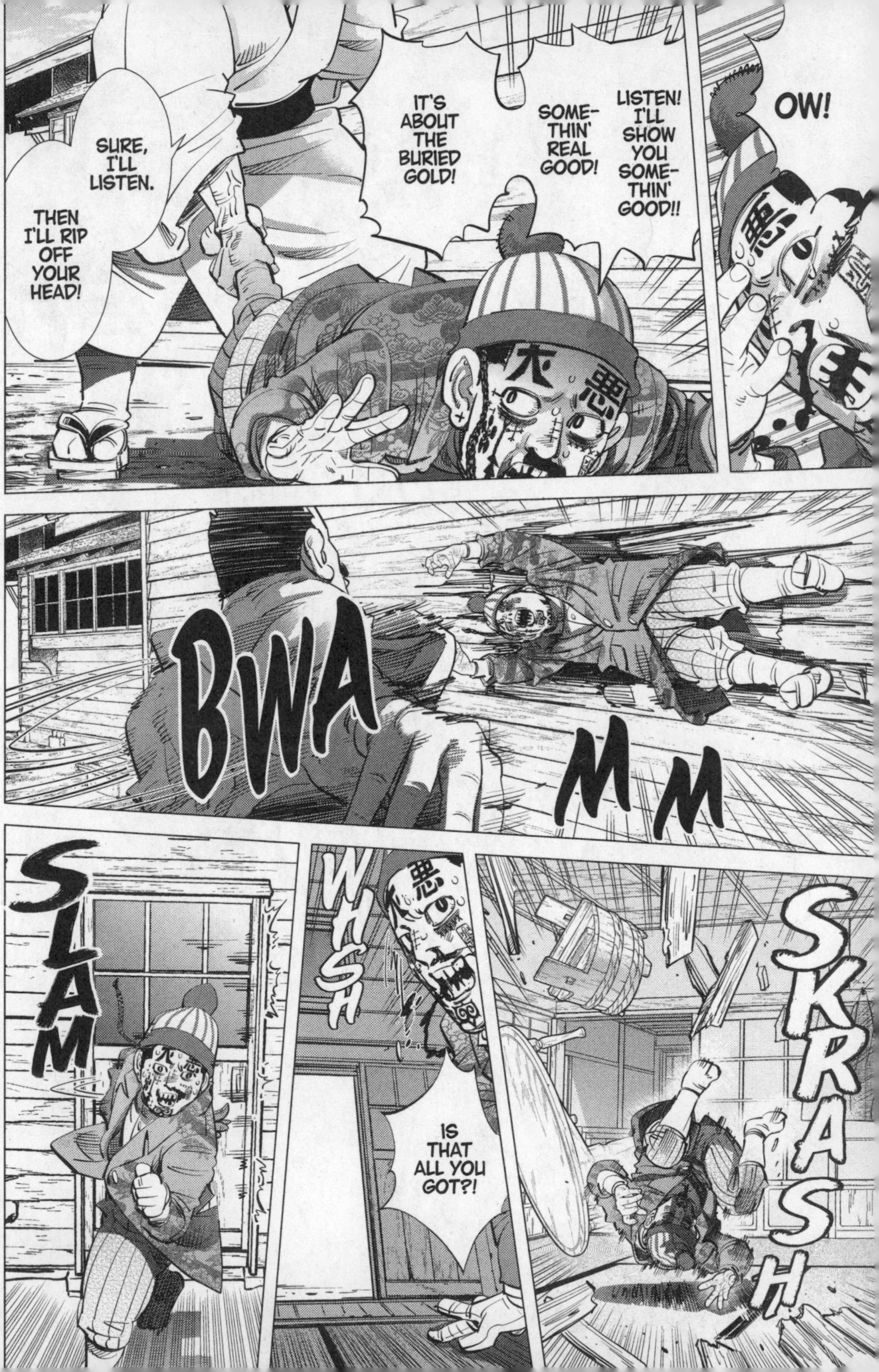
OW!
LISTEN! I'LL SHOW YOU SOME-THIN' GOOD!!
SOME-THIN' REAL GOOD!
IT'S ABOUT THE BURIED GOLD!
SURE, I'LL LISTEN.
THEN I'LL RIP OFF YOUR HEAD!
BWAMM
SKRASH
WHSH
IS THAT ALL YOU GOT?!
SLAM

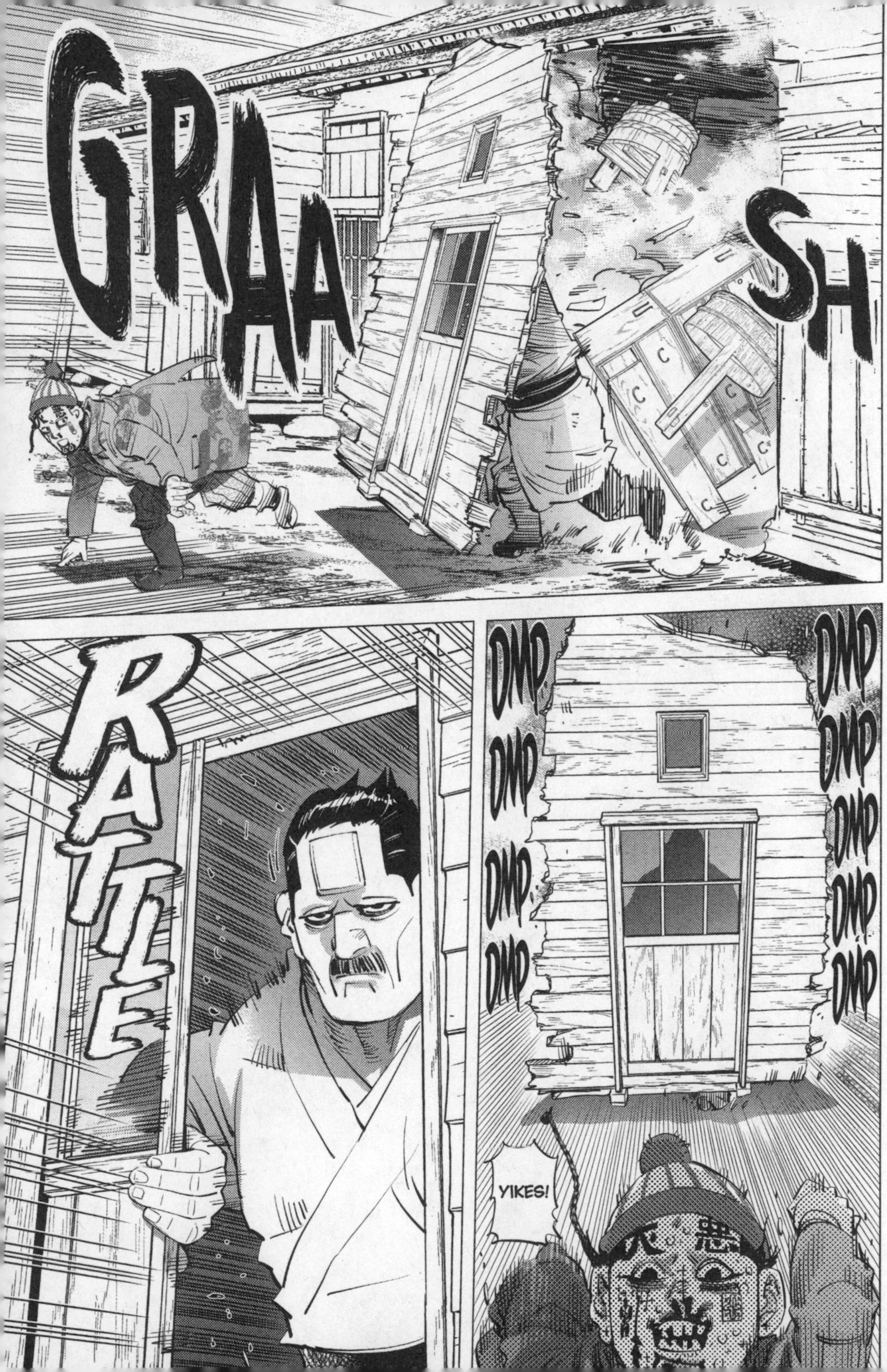
GRAASH
DMP DMP DMP DMP DMP DMP
DMP DMP DMP DMP
YIKES!
RATTLE

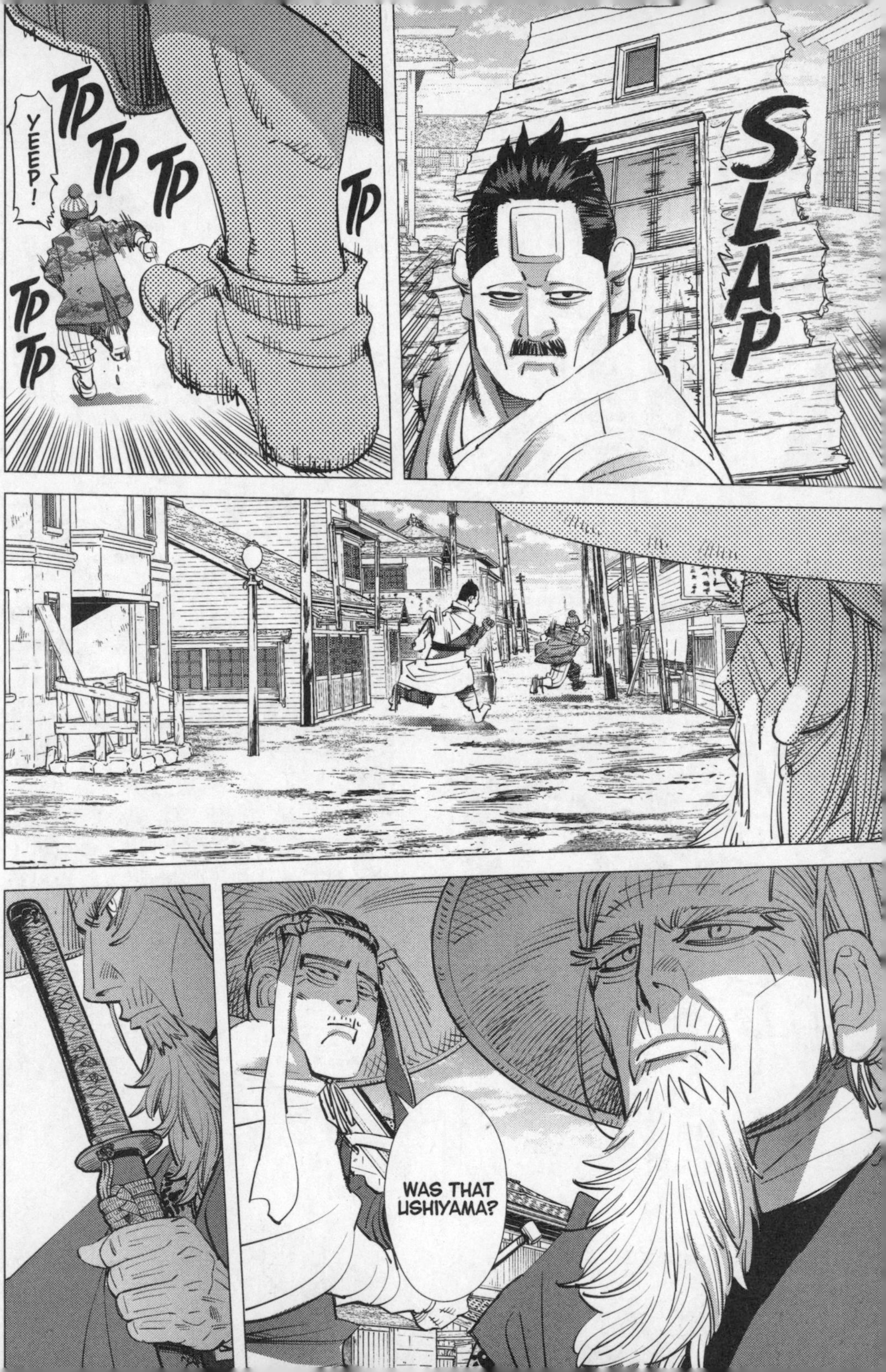
SLAP
TP
TP TP TP
YEEP!
TP TP
WAS THAT USHIYAMA?

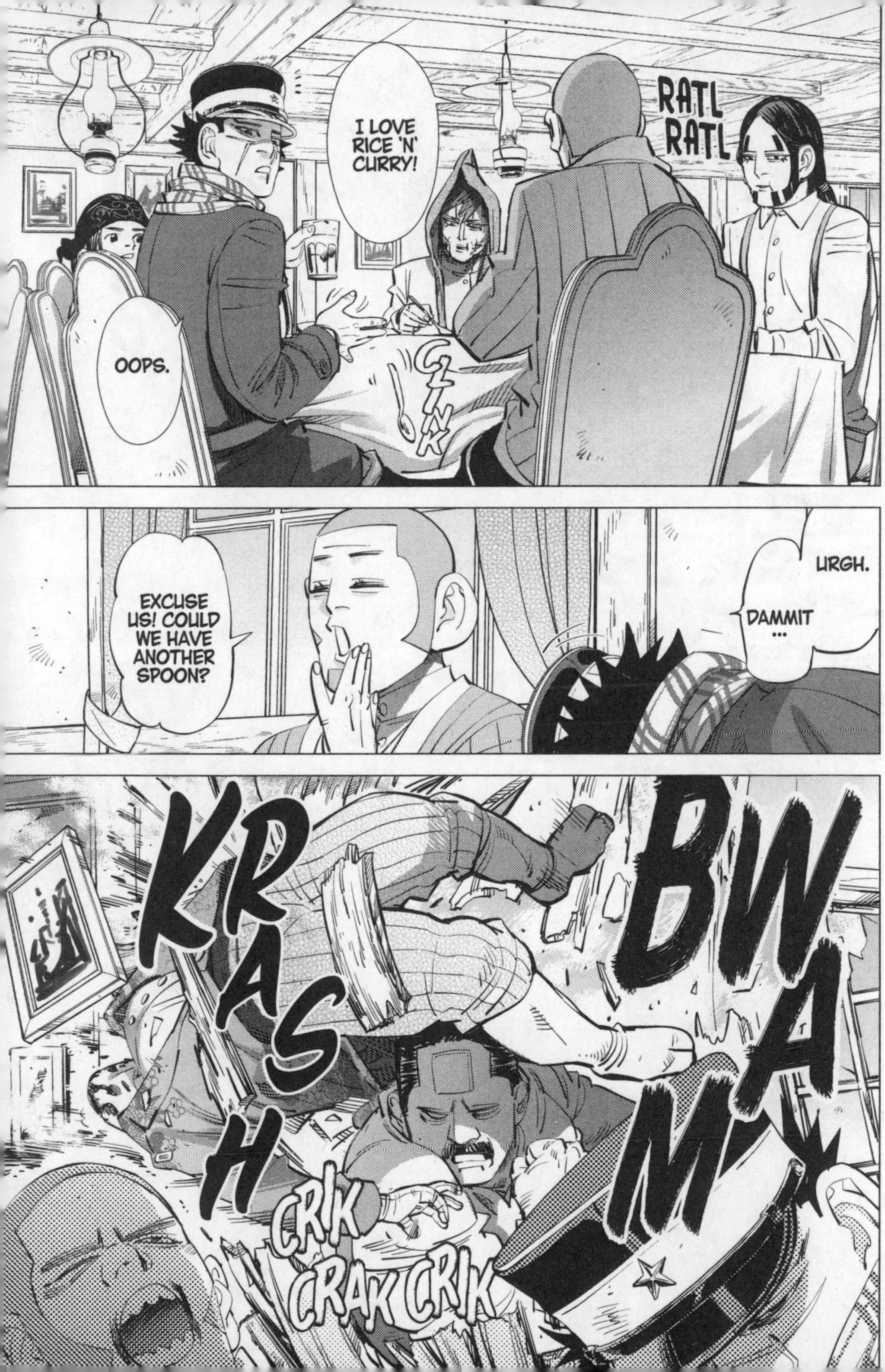
RATL RATL
I LOVE RICE 'N' CURRY!
CLINK
OOPS.
URGH.
DAMMIT ...
EXCUSE US! COULD WE HAVE ANOTHER SPOON?
BWAM
KRASH
CRIK CRAK CRIK

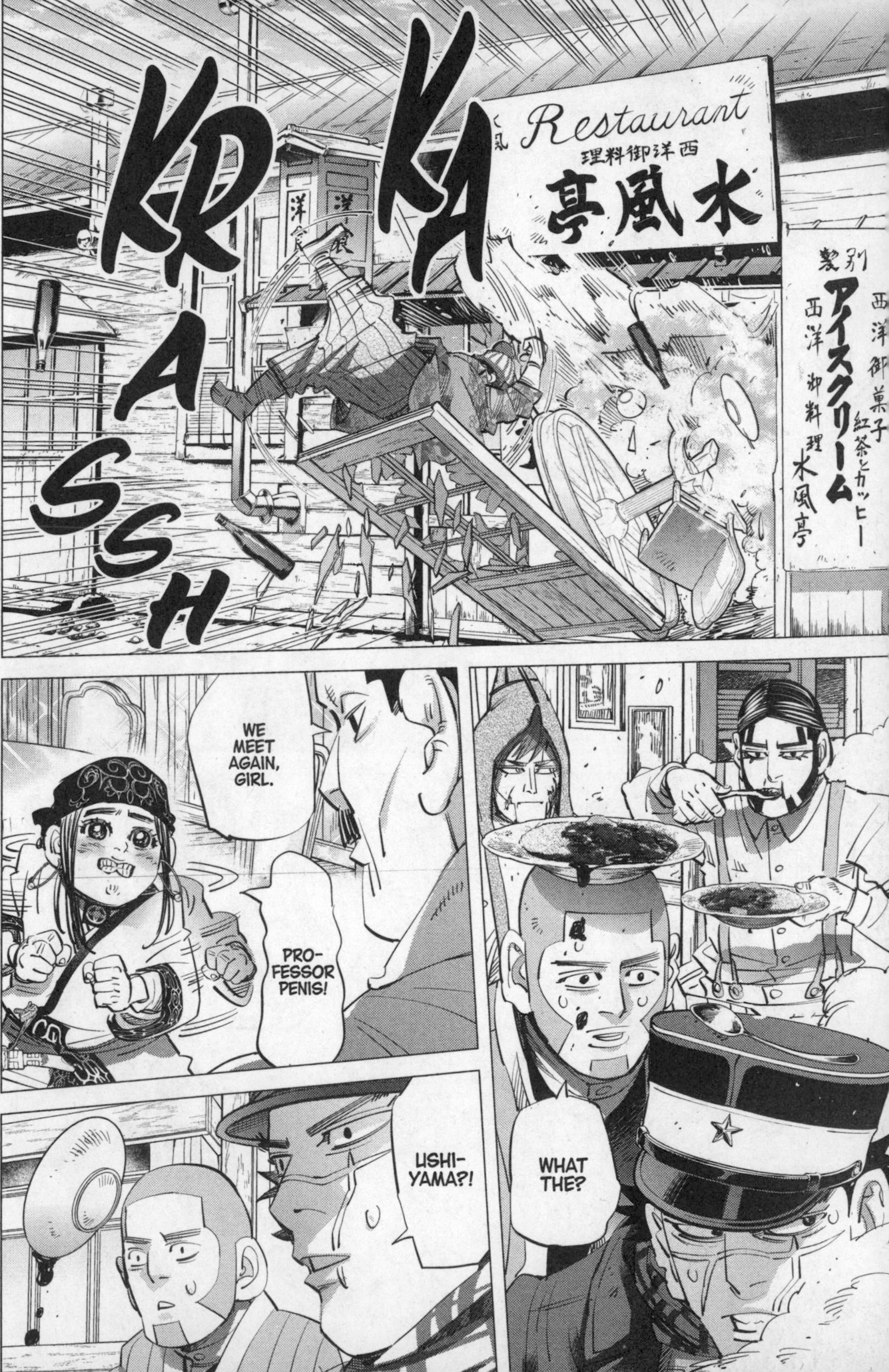
KA
KRASSH
Restaurant
西洋御料理
水風亭
洋食
洋食
西洋御菓子
紅茶とカッヒー
別製アイスクリーム
西洋御料理 水風亭
WE MEET AGAIN, GIRL.
PRO-FESSOR PENIS!
WHAT THE?
USHI-YAMA?!

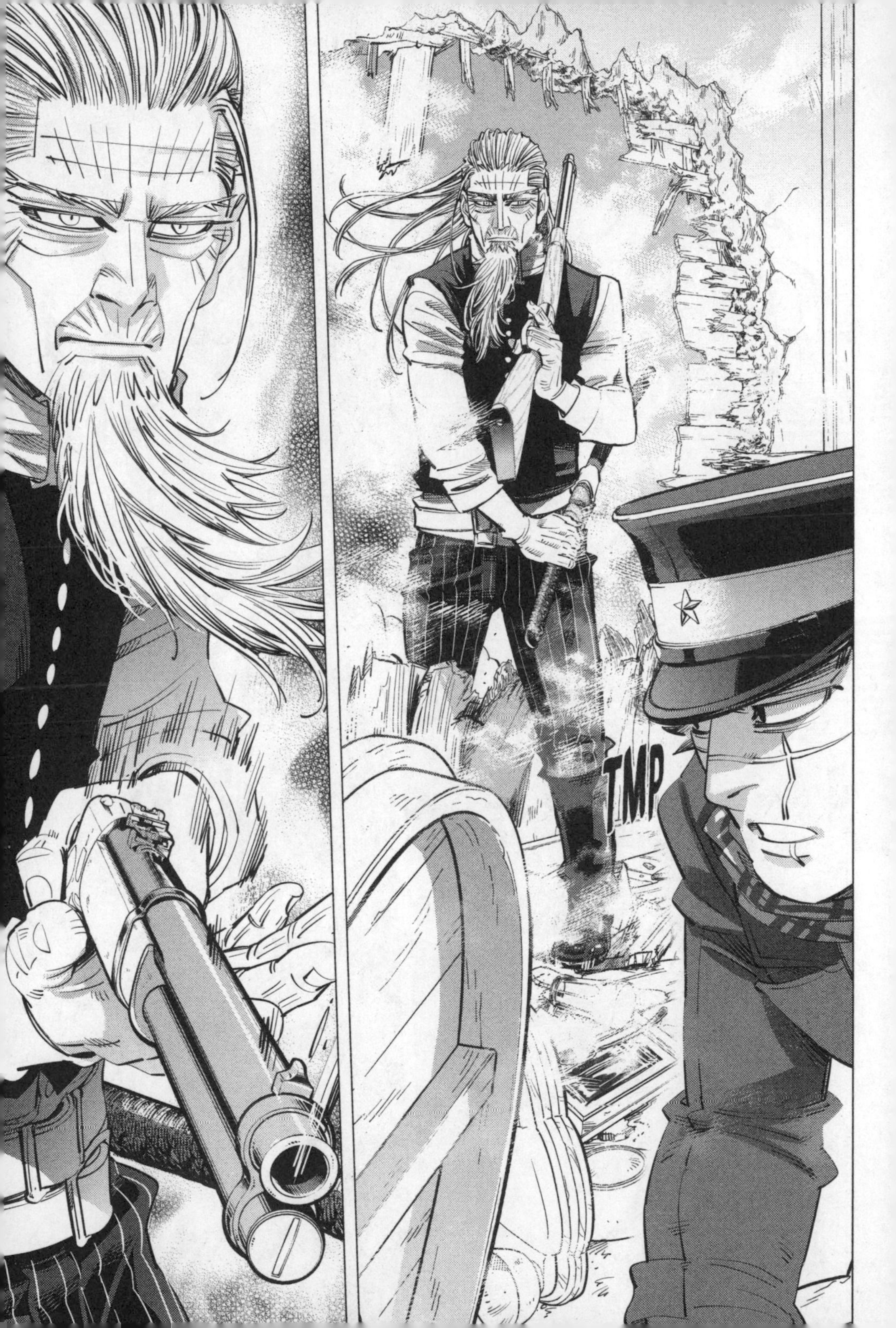
TMP

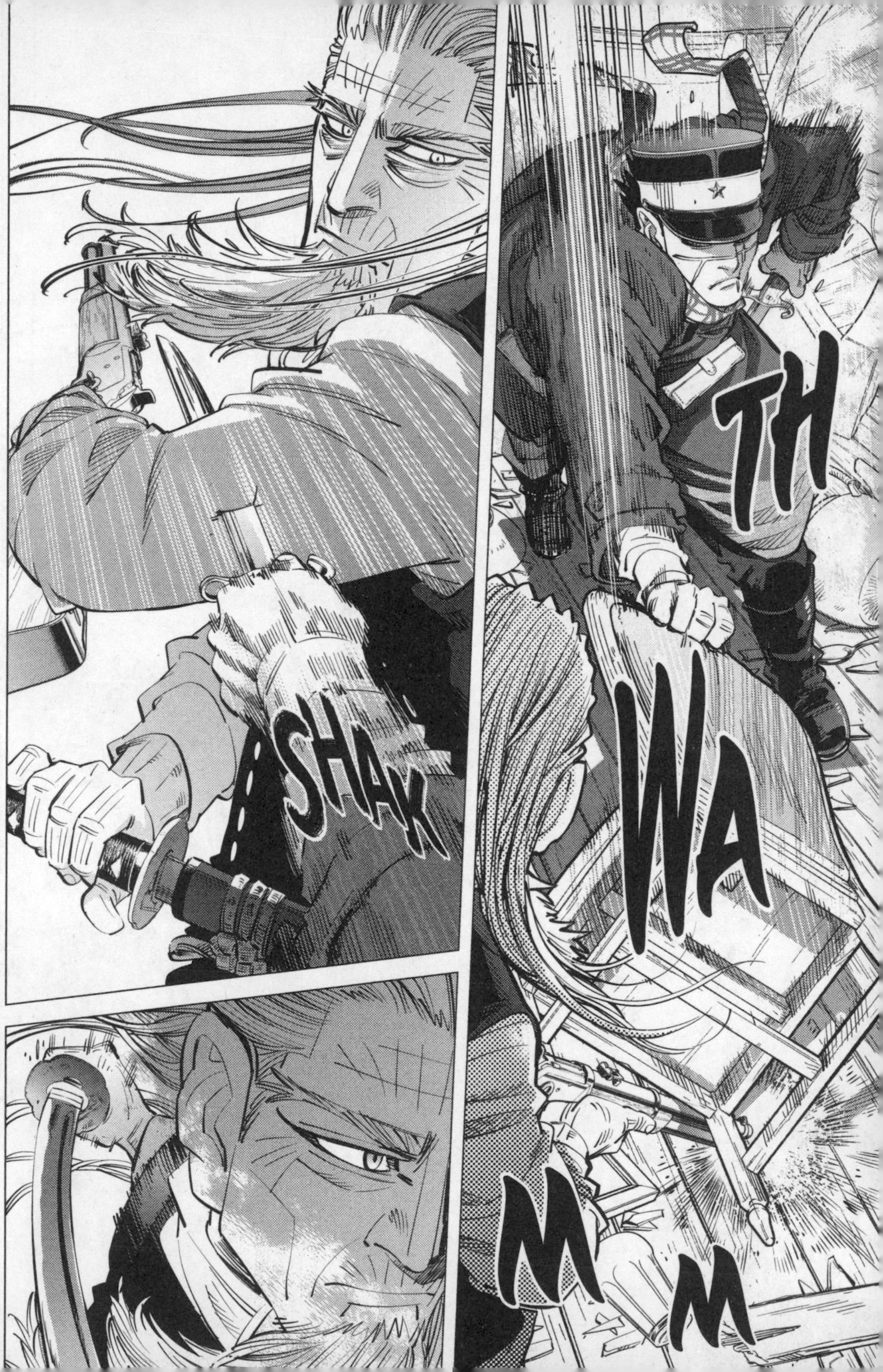
THWAMM
SHAK

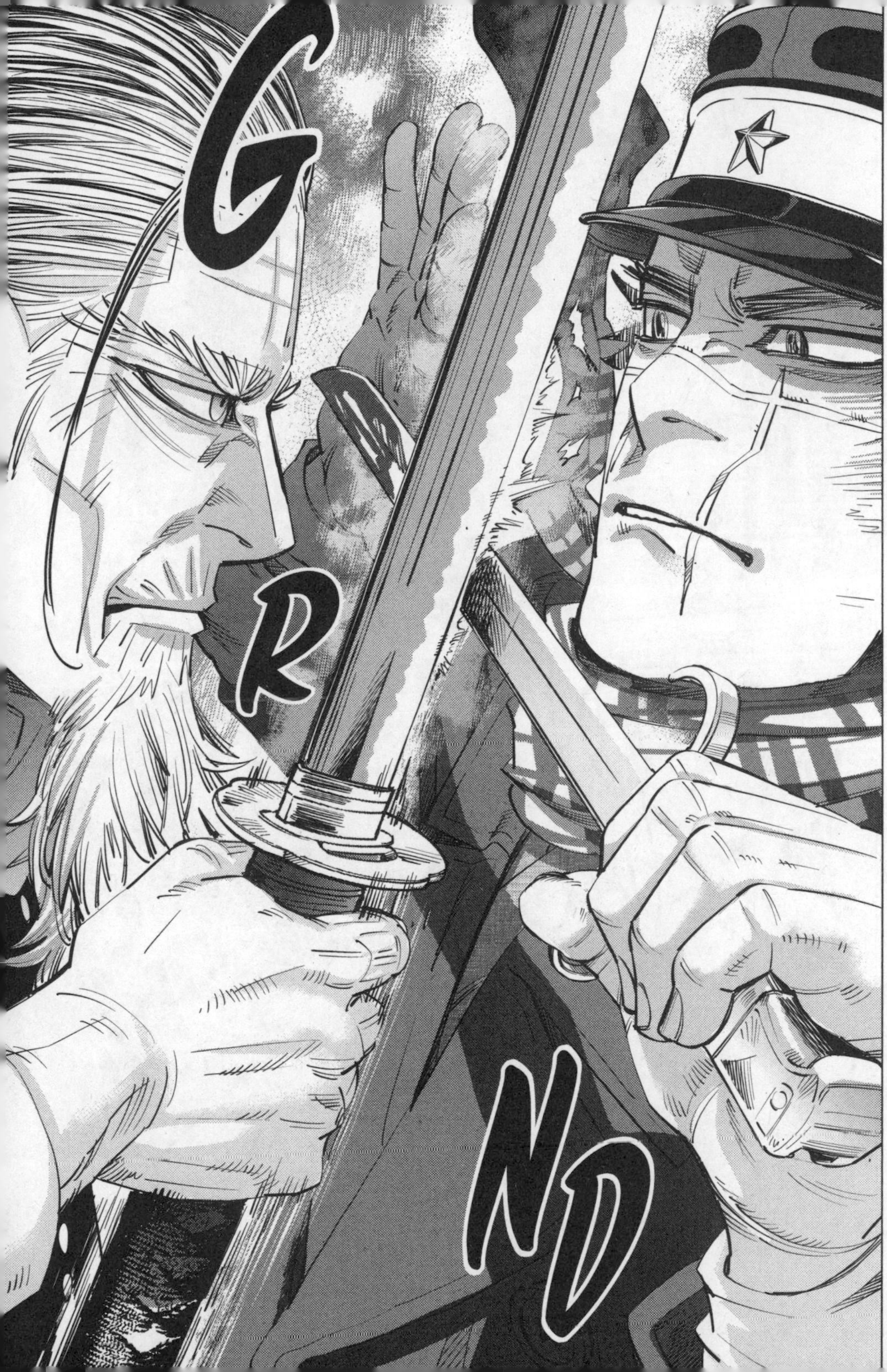
GRND

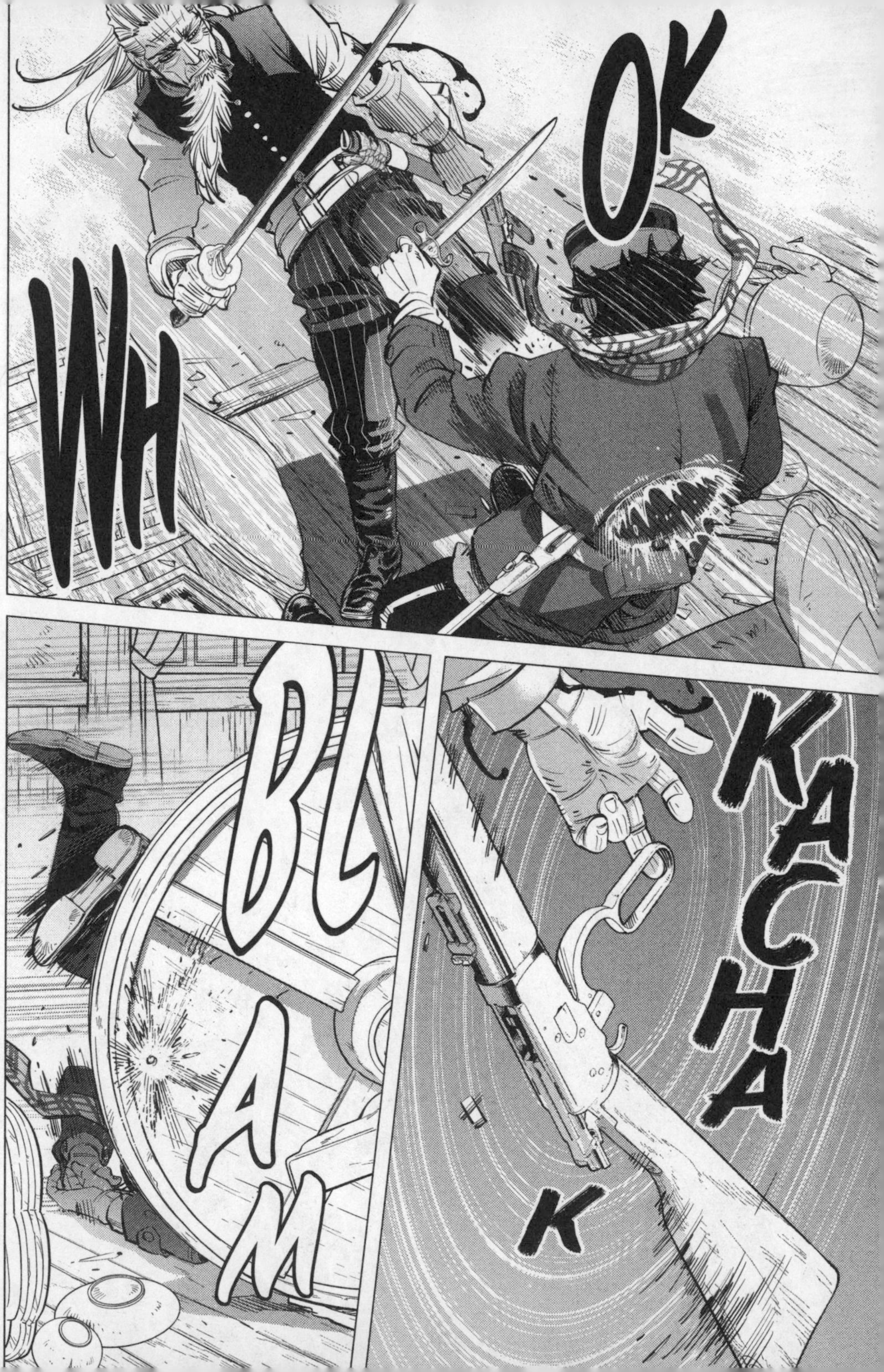
WH
OK
KACHA
K
BL
AM

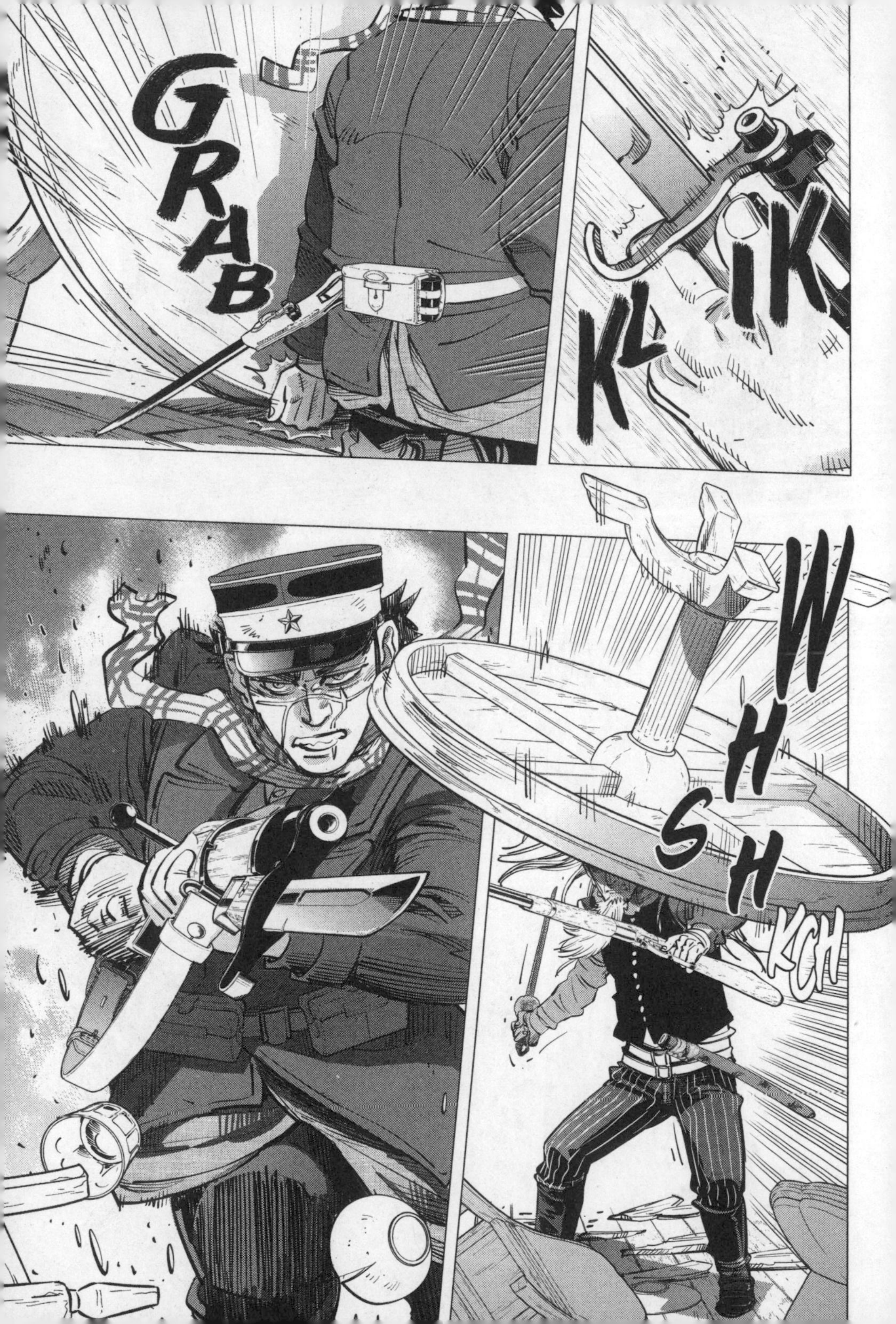
KLIK
GRAB
WHSH
KCH

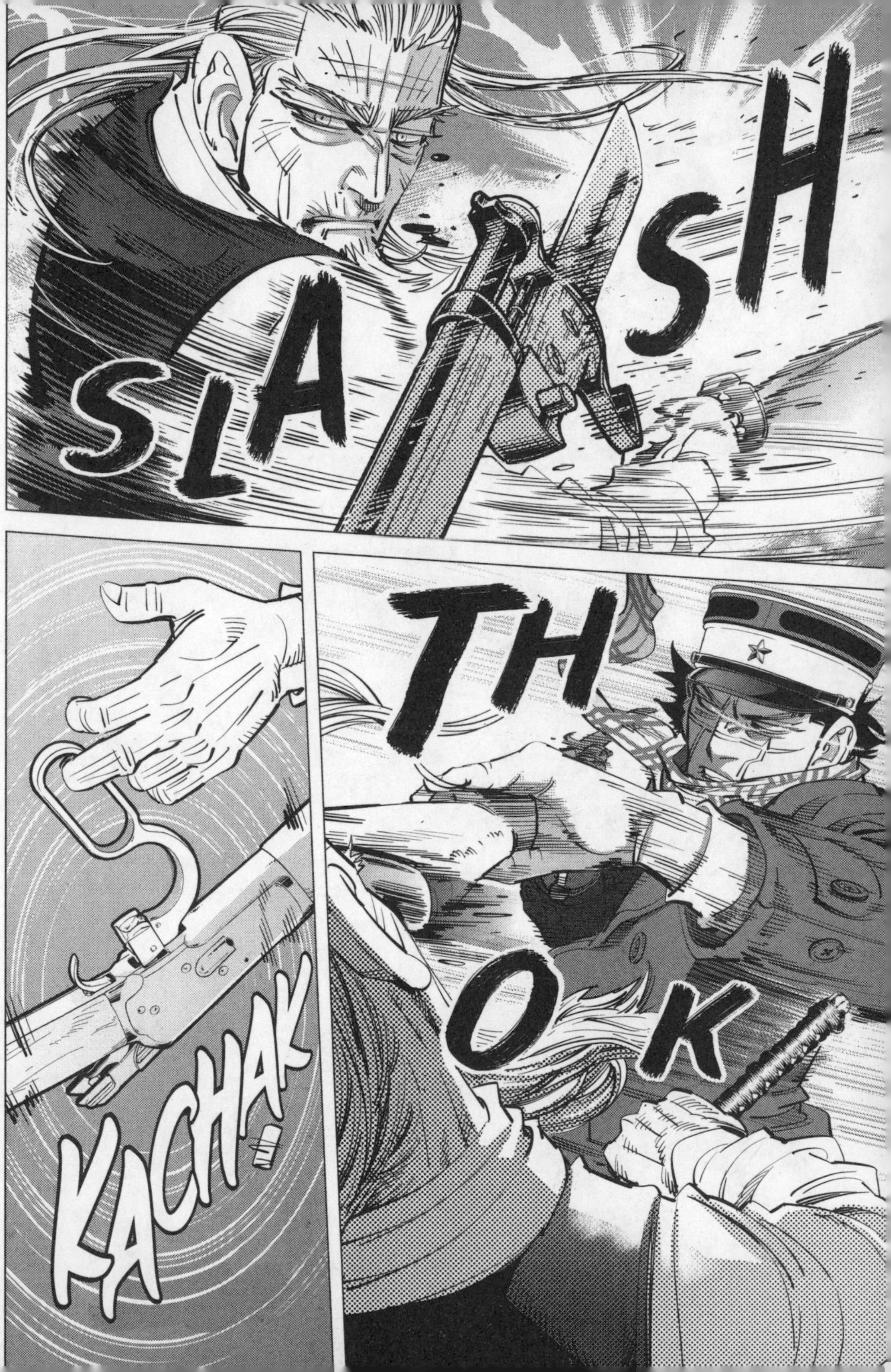
SLASH
THOK
KACHAK!

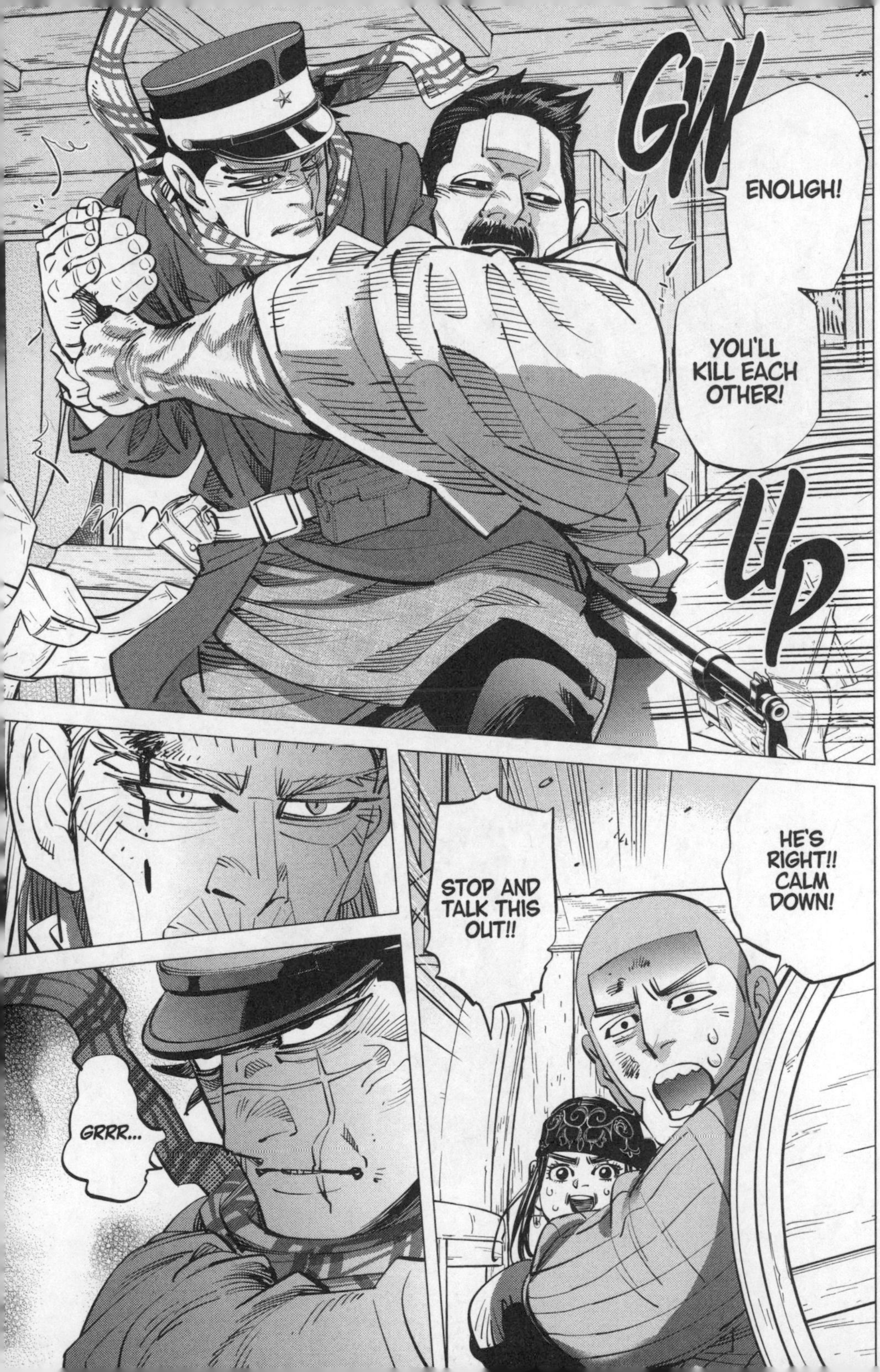
GW
ENOUGH!
YOU'LL KILL EACH OTHER!
UP
HE'S RIGHT!! CALM DOWN!
STOP AND TALK THIS OUT!!
GRRR...

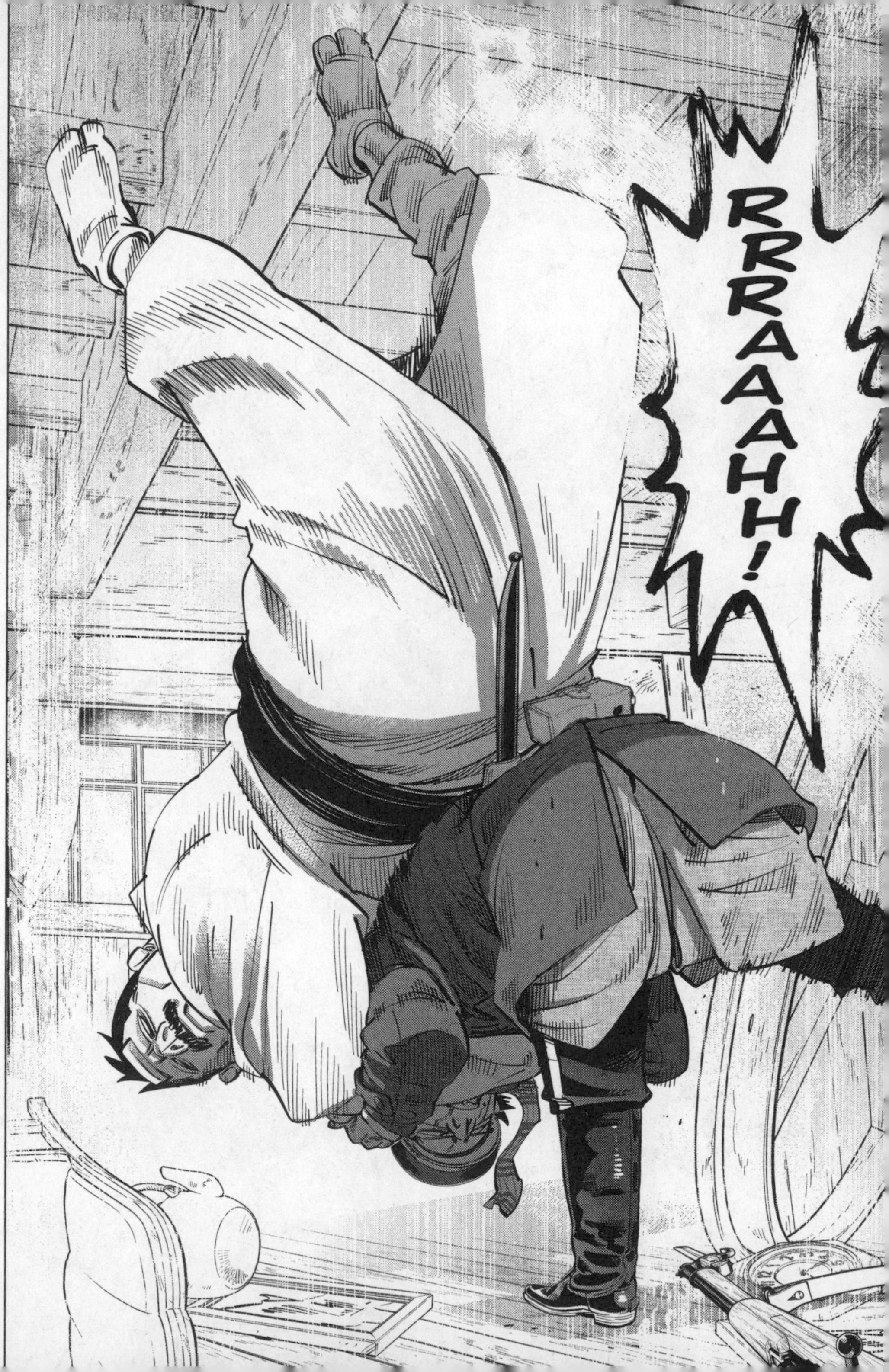
RRRAAAH!

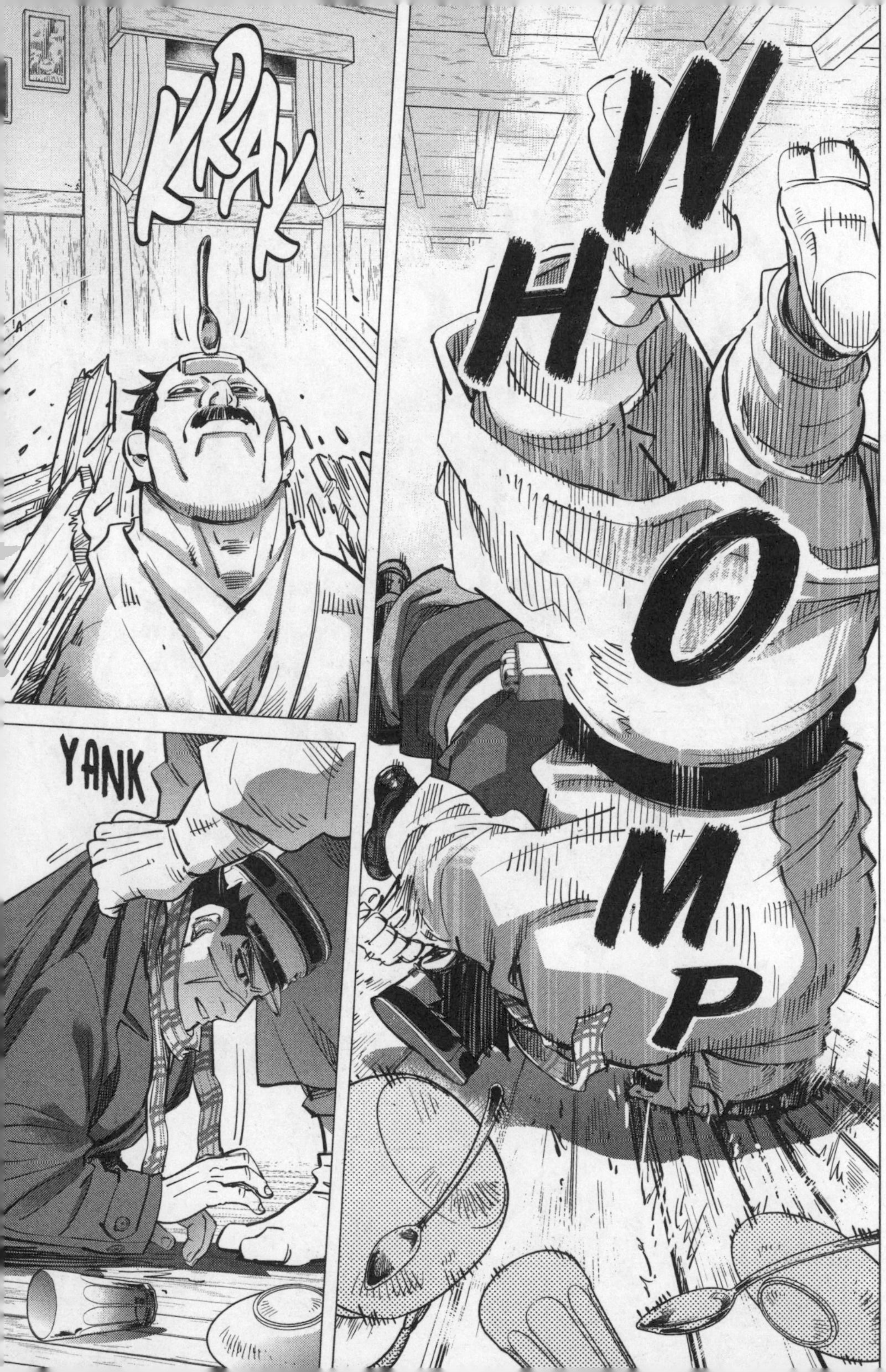
WHOMP
KRAK
YANK

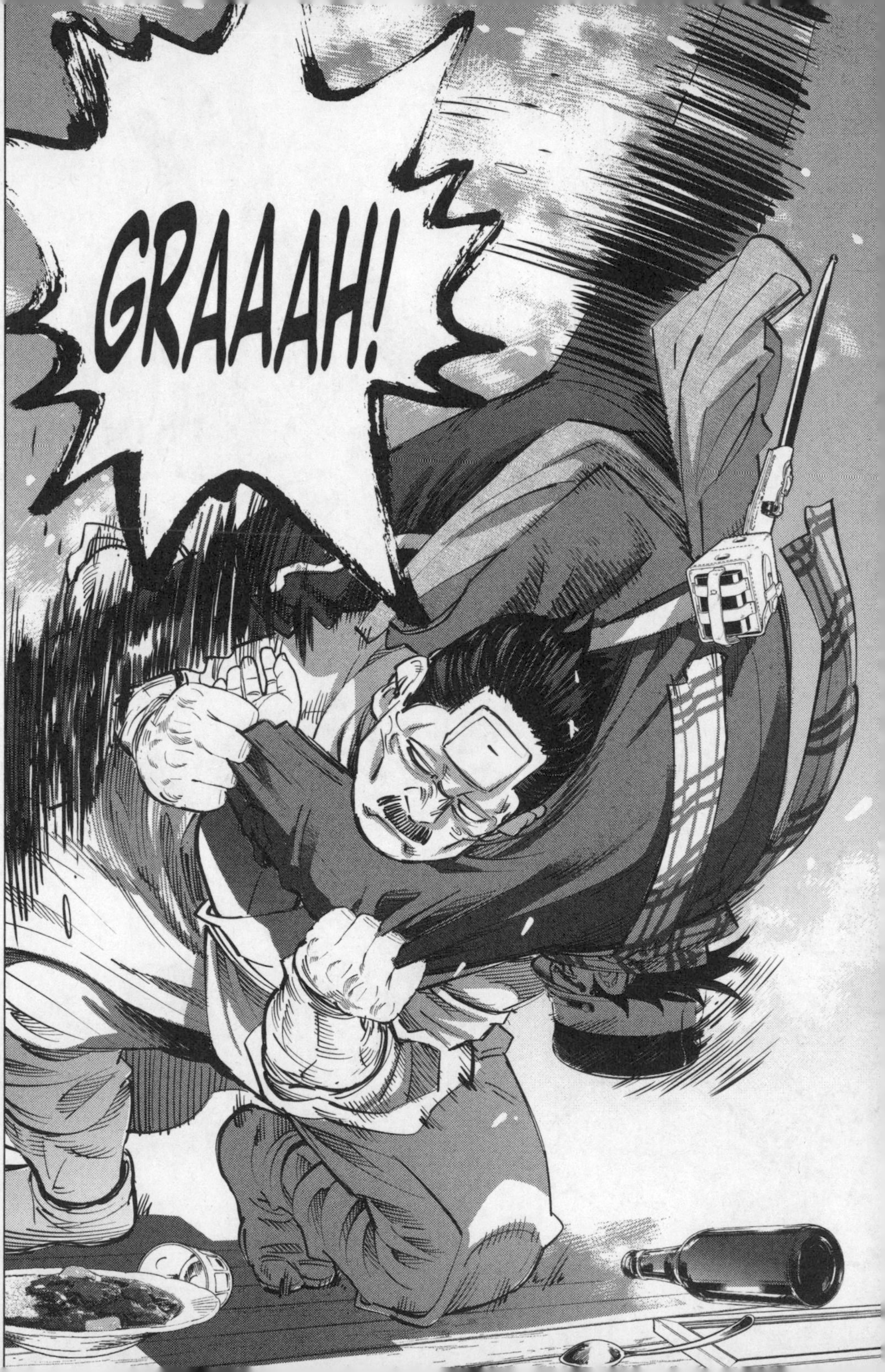
GRAAAH!

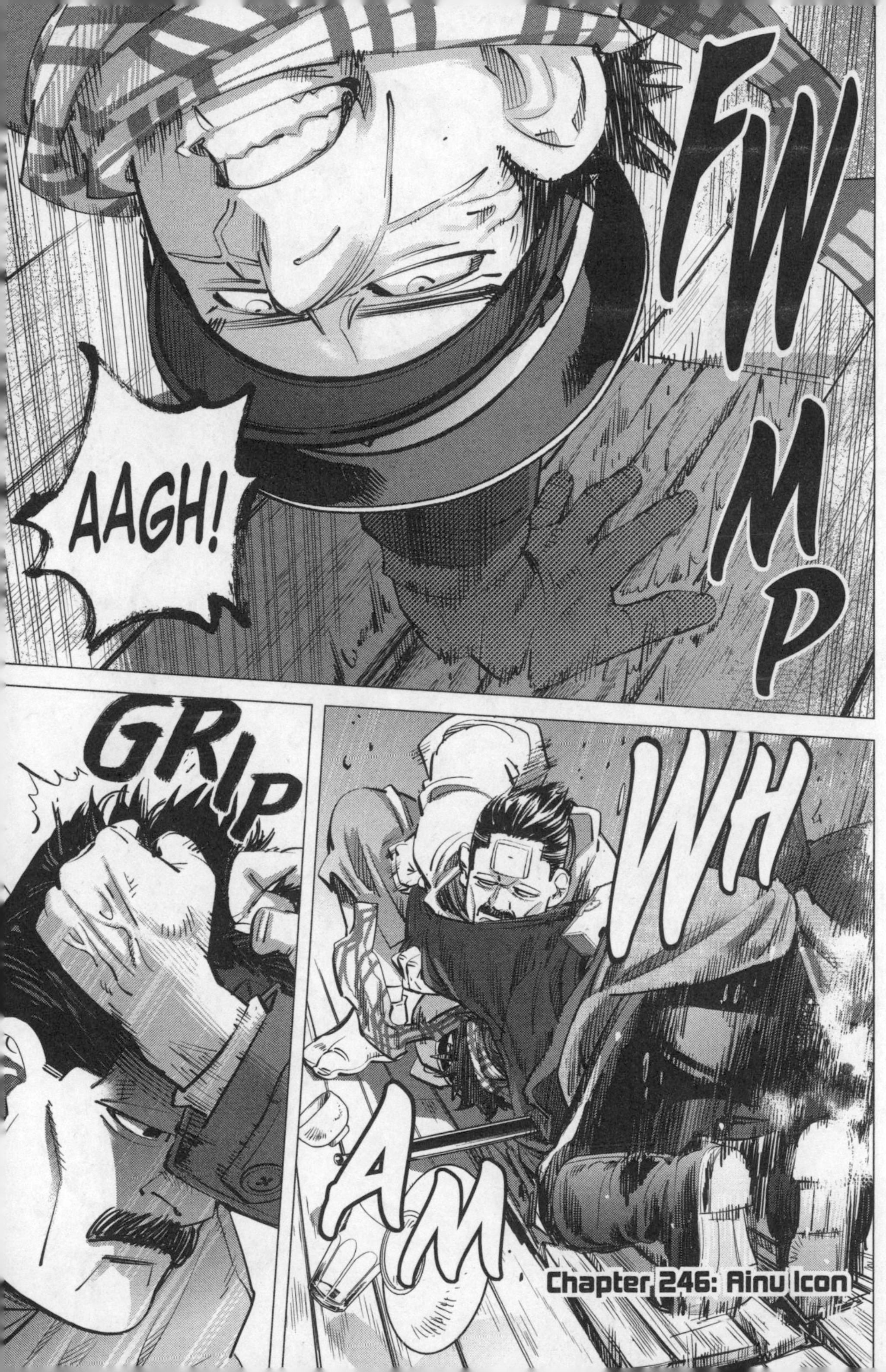
FWMP
AAGH!
WHAM
Chapter 246: Ainu Icon
GRIP

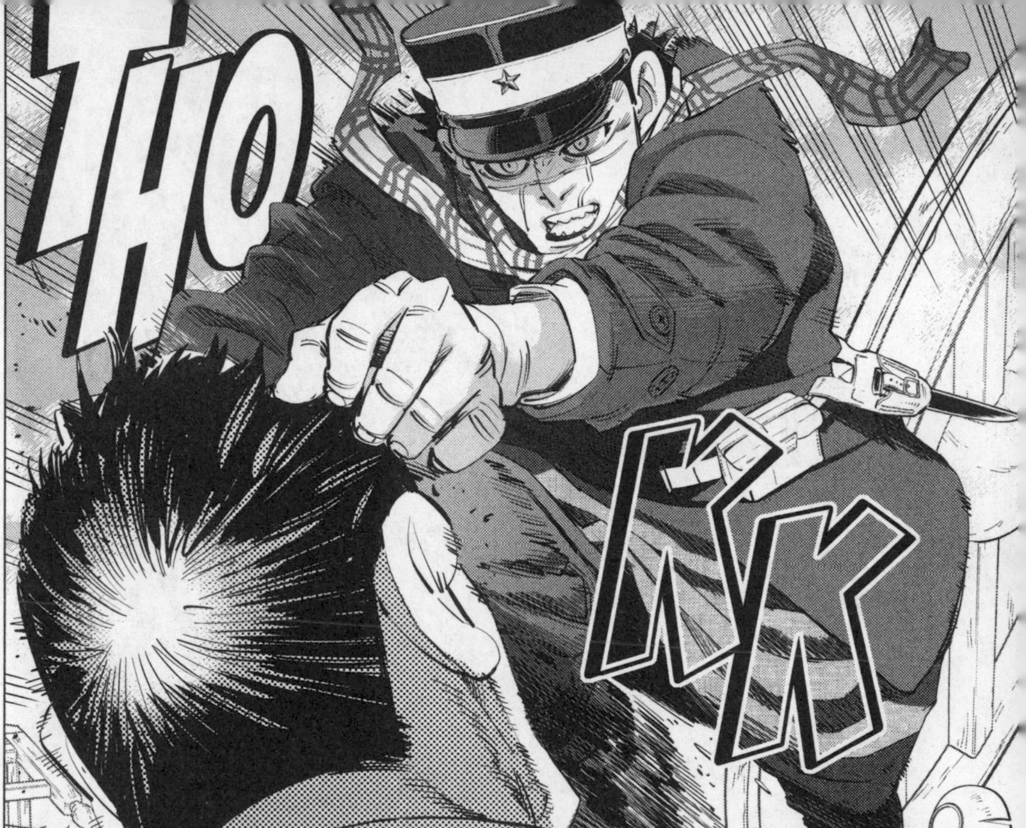
THO
KK

Chapter 246: Ainu Icon

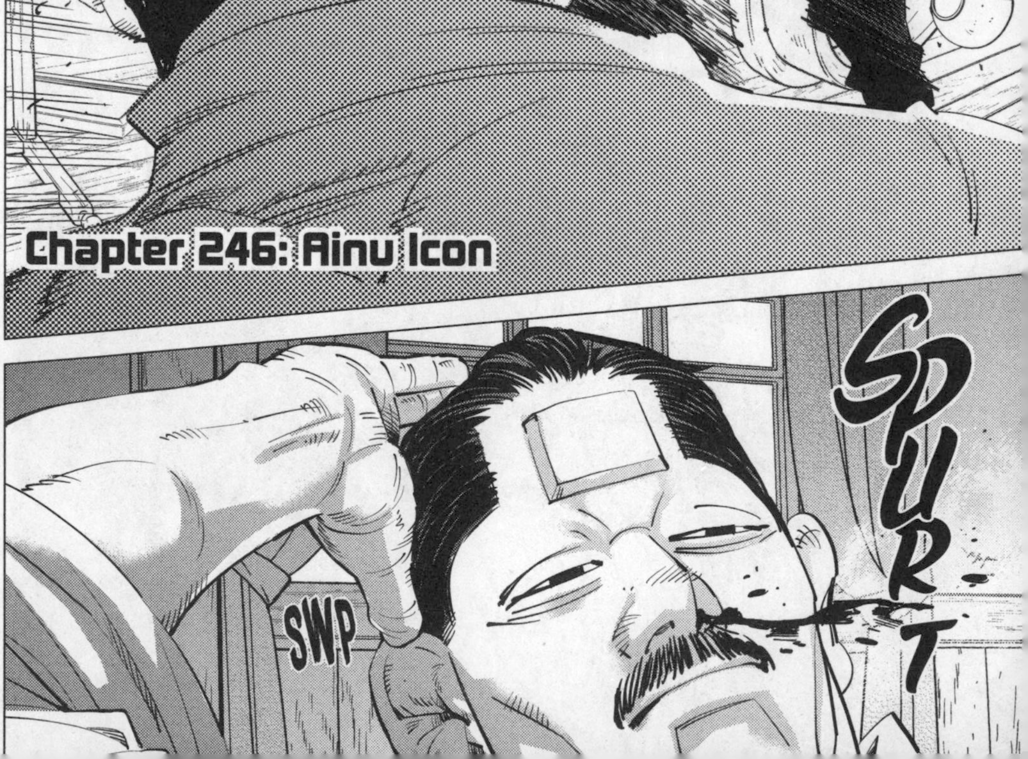
SPURT
SWP

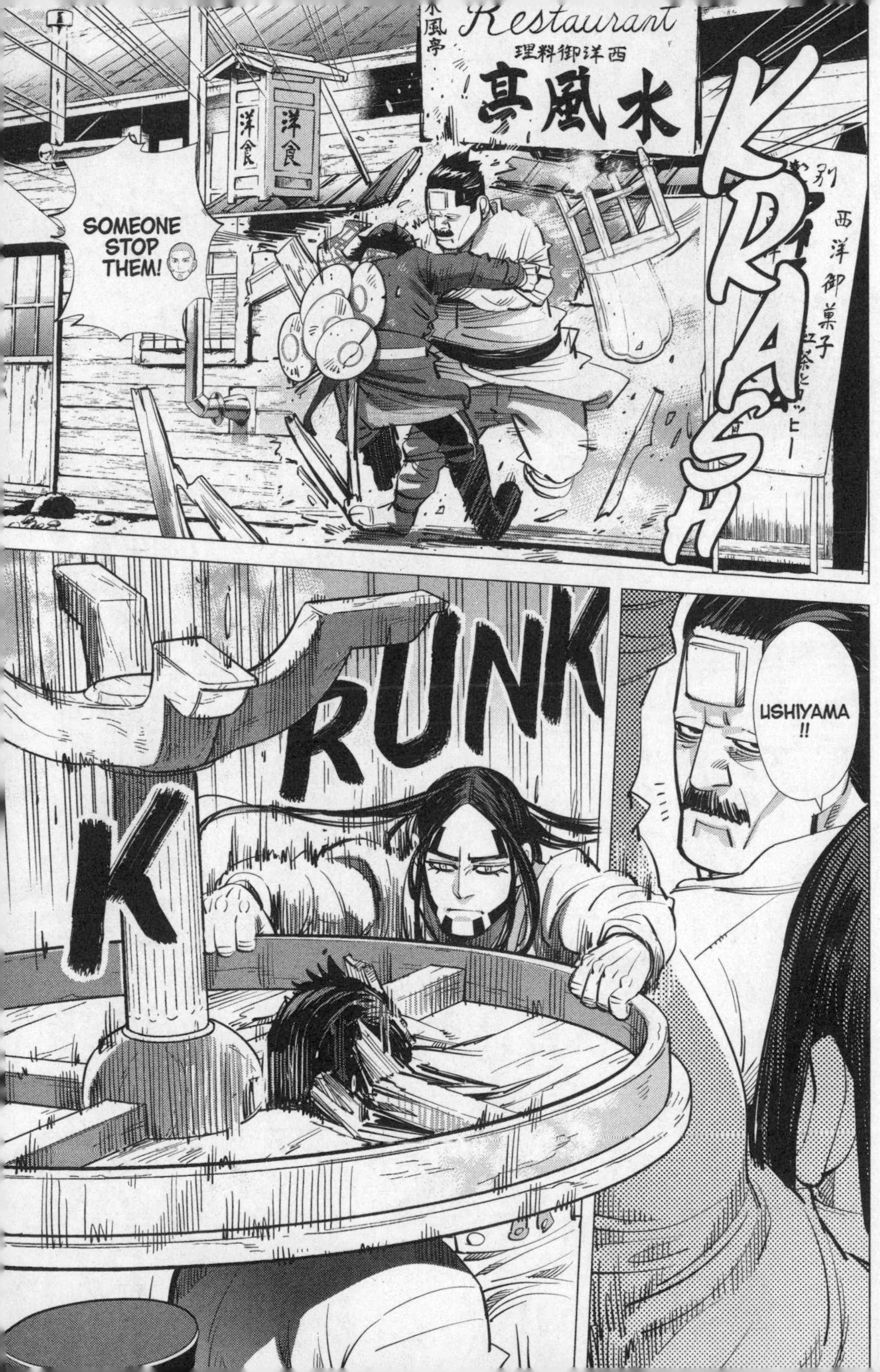
Restaurant
西洋御料理
水風亭
洋食
洋食
西洋御菓子
SOMEONE STOP THEM!
KRASH
USHIYAMA !!
KRUNK

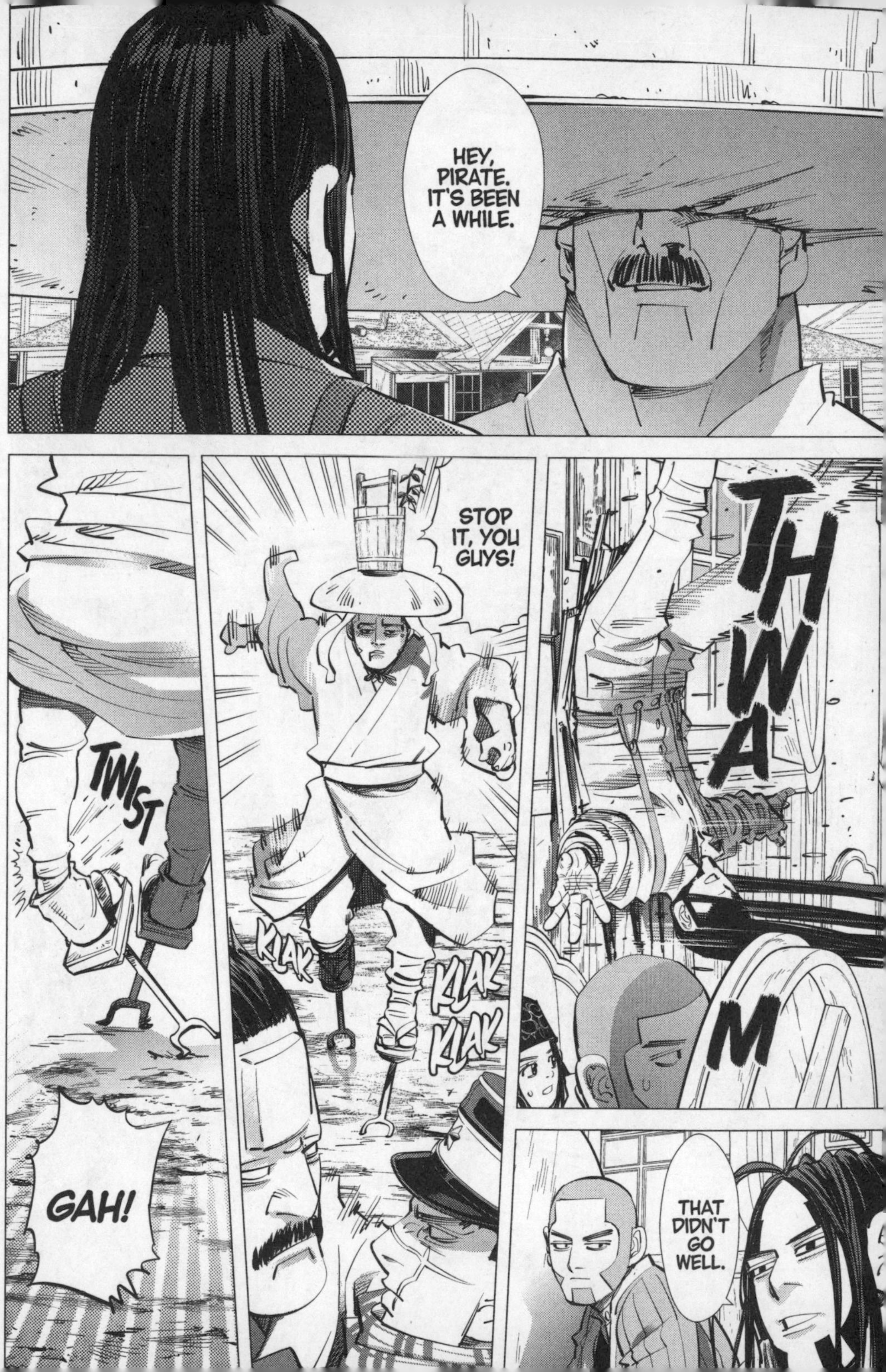
HEY, PIRATE. IT'S BEEN A WHILE.
THWAM
THAT DIDN'T GO WELL.
STOP IT, YOU GUYS!
KLAK
KLAK KLAK
TWIST
GAH!

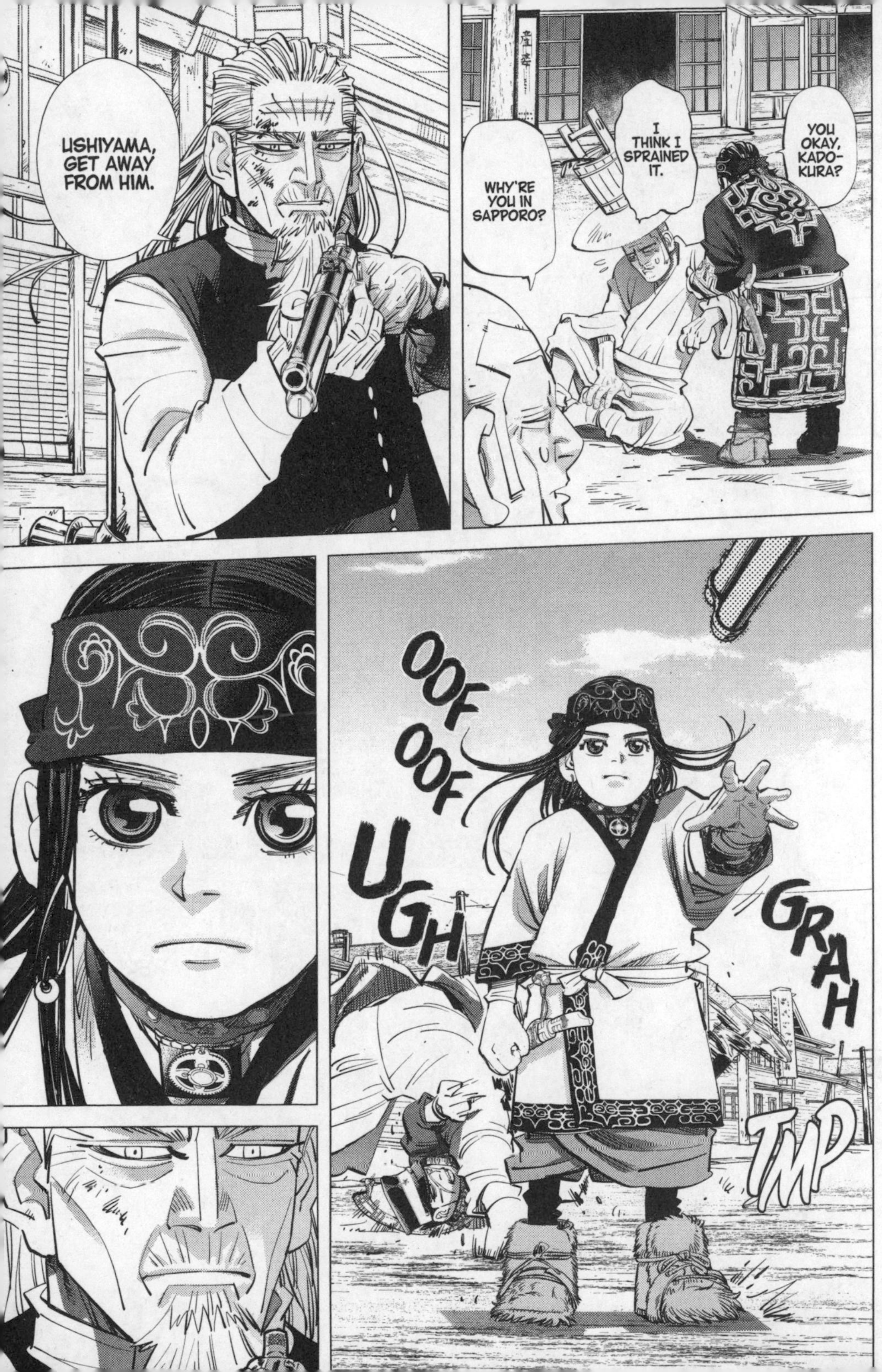
YOU OKAY, KADOKURA?
I THINK I SPRAINED IT.
WHY'RE YOU IN SAPPORO?
USHIYAMA, GET AWAY FROM HIM.
GRAH
OOF OOF
UGH
TMP

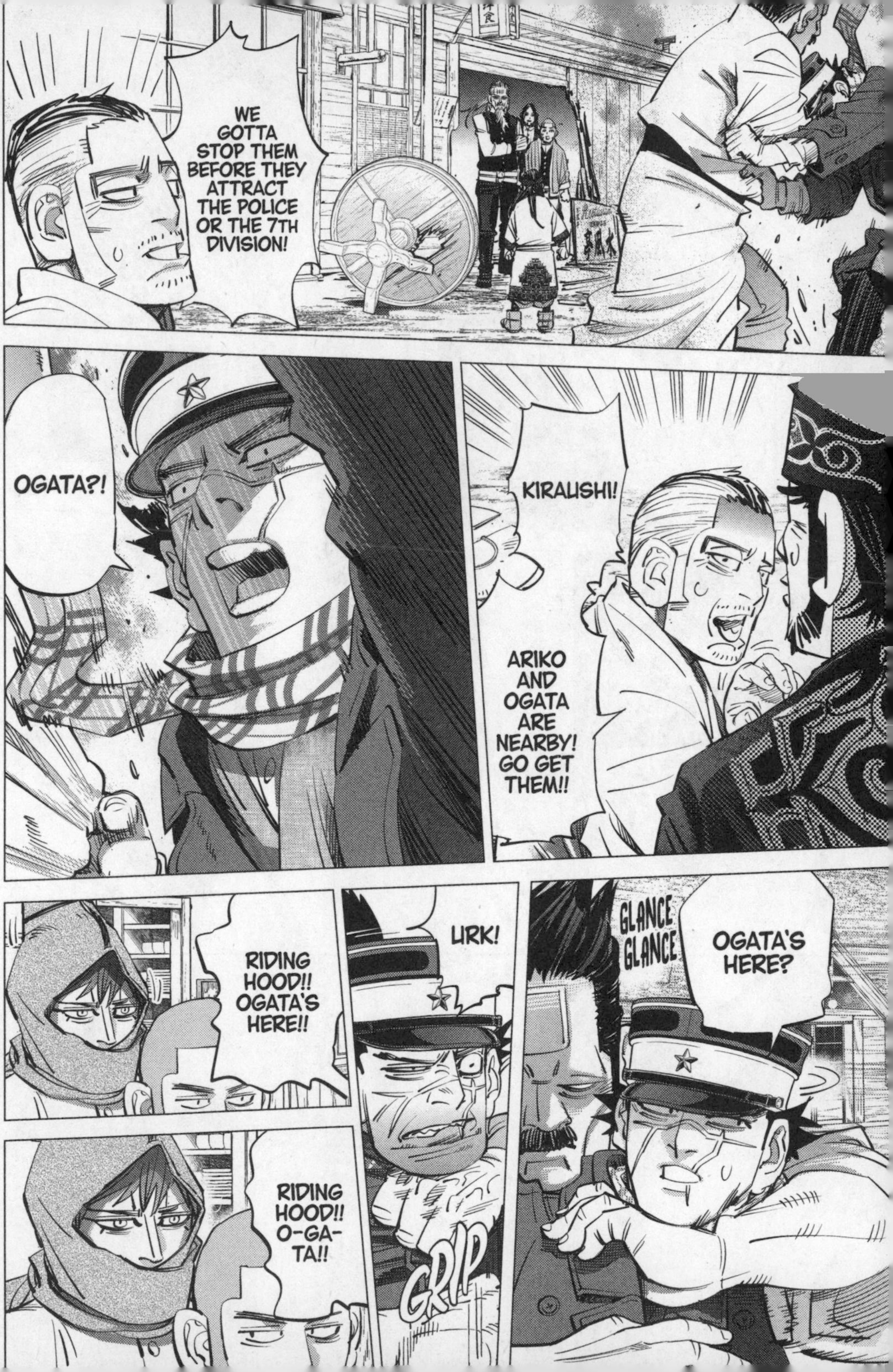
WE GOTTA STOP THEM BEFORE THEY ATTRACT THE POLICE OR THE 7TH DIVISION!
KIRAUSHI!
ARIKO AND OGATA ARE NEARBY! GO GET THEM!!
OGATA?!
GLANCE GLANCE
OGATA'S HERE?
URK!
GRIP
RIDING HOOD!! OGATA'S HERE!!
RIDING HOOD!! O-GA-TA!!

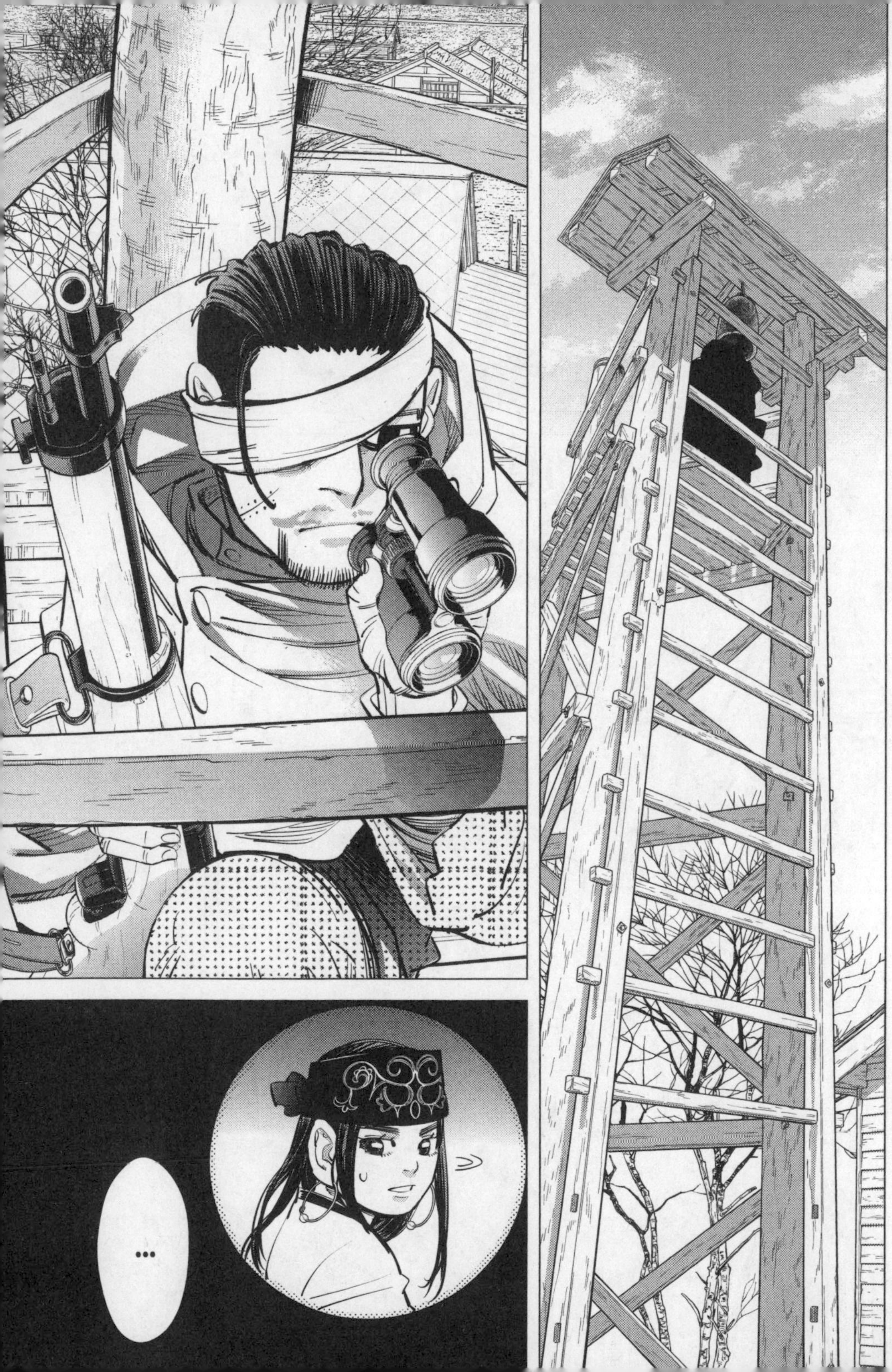
...

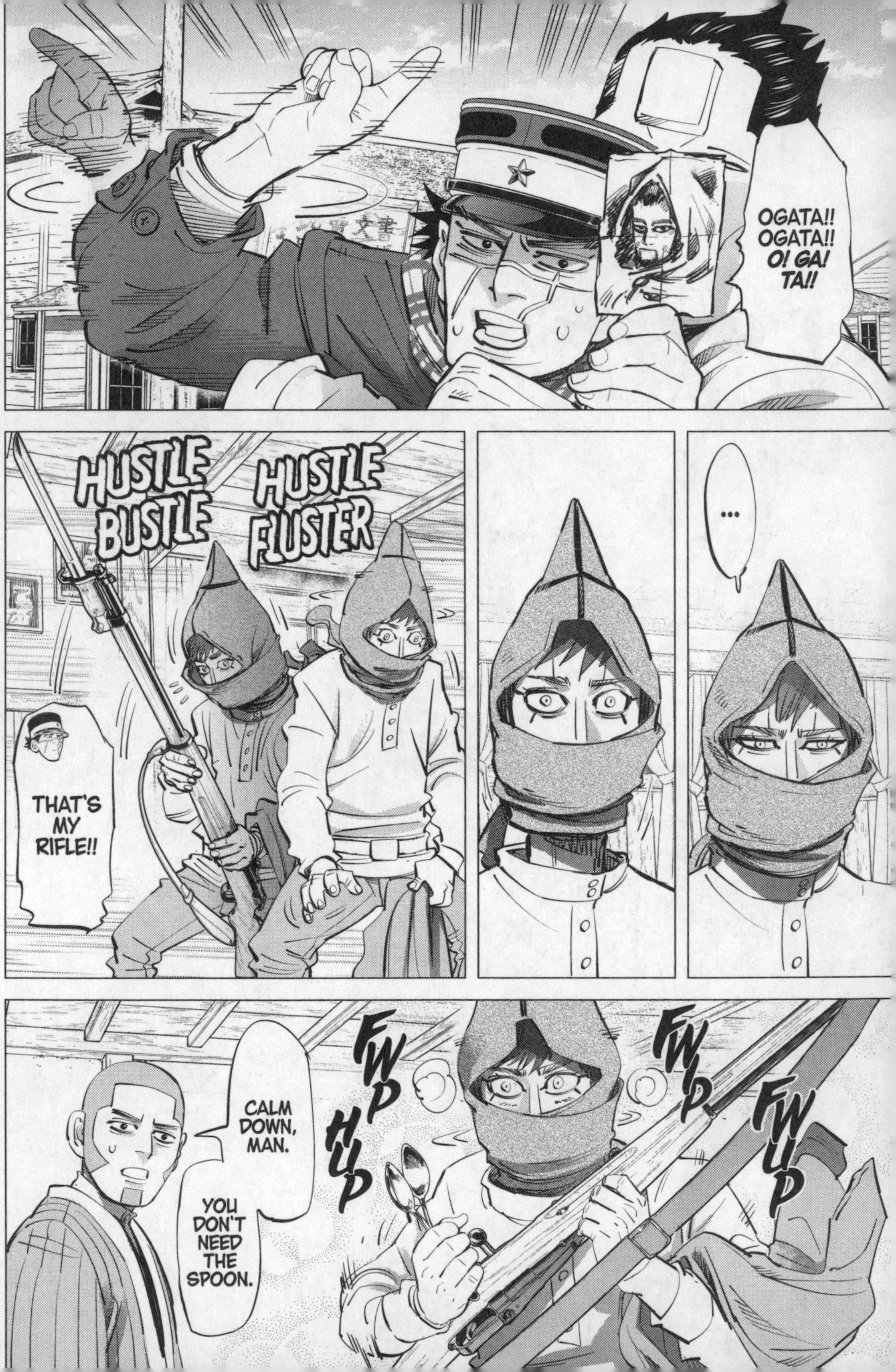
OGATA!! OGATA!! O! GA! TA!!
...
HUSTLE FLUSTER
HUSTLE BUSTLE
THAT'S MY RIFLE!!
FWUP
FWUP
FWP
HUP
CALM DOWN, MAN.
YOU DON'T NEED THE SPOON.

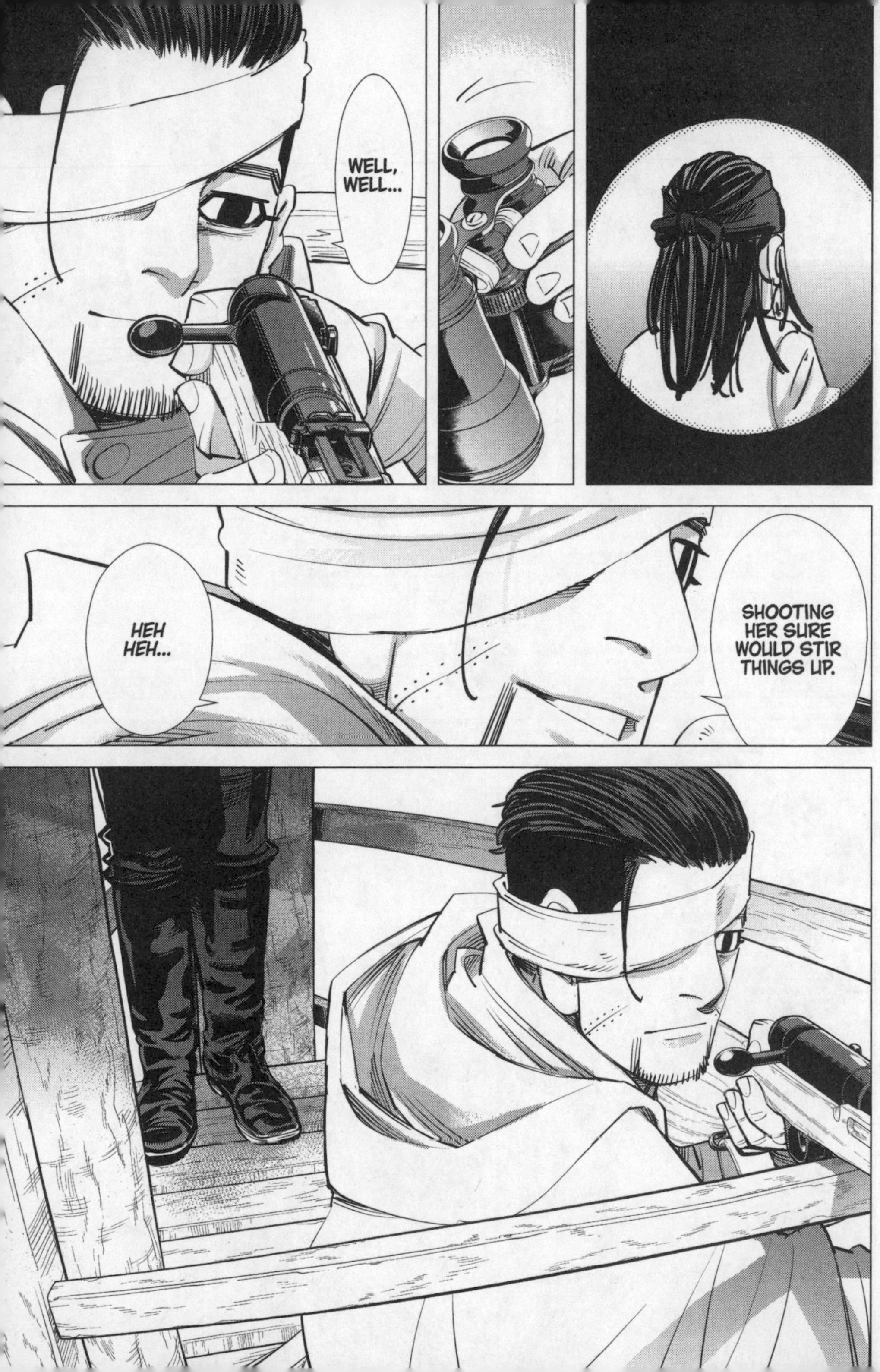
WELL, WELL...
SHOOTING HER SURE WOULD STIR THINGS UP.
HEH HEH...

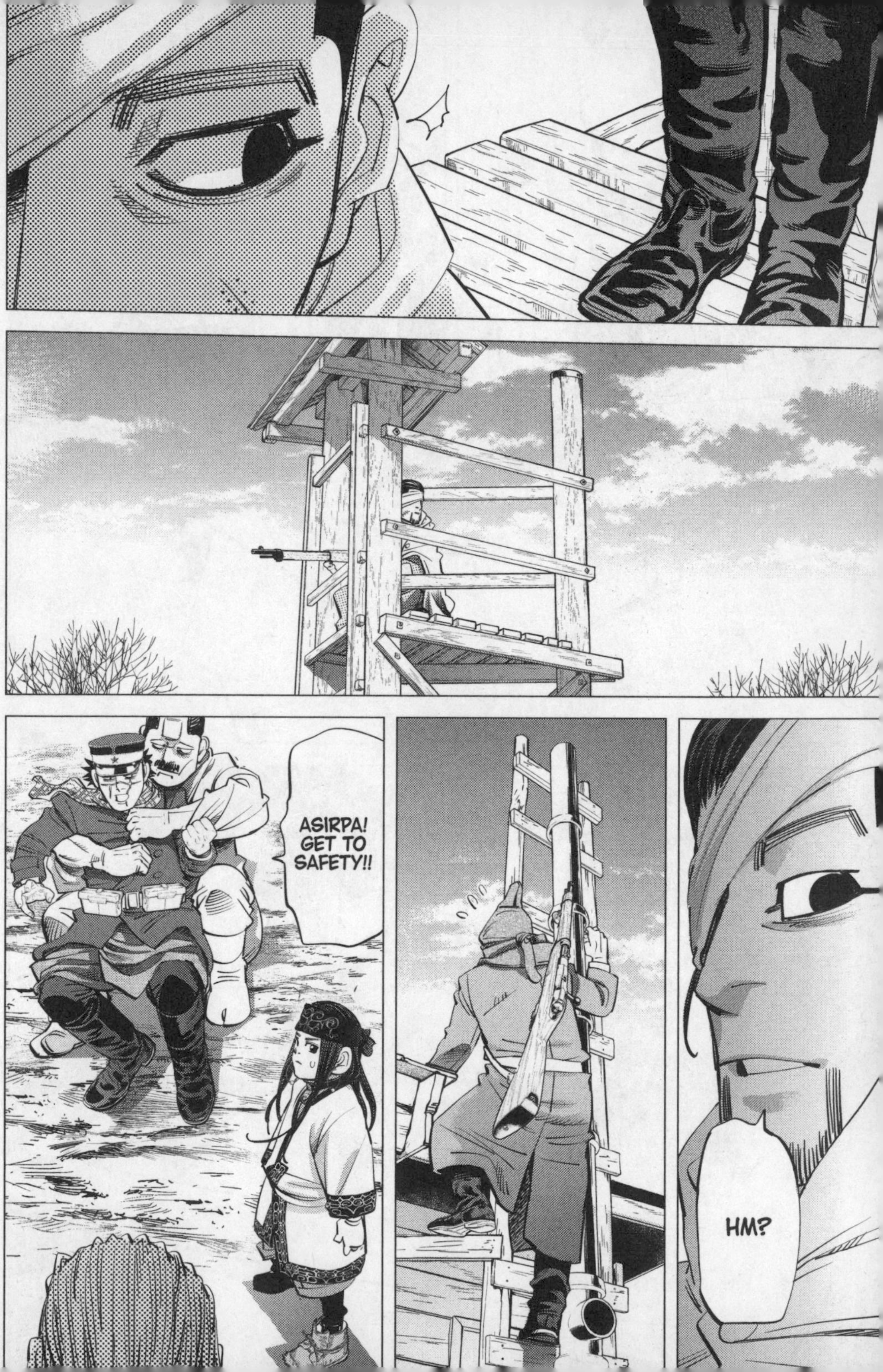
HM?
ASIRPA! GET TO SAFETY!!

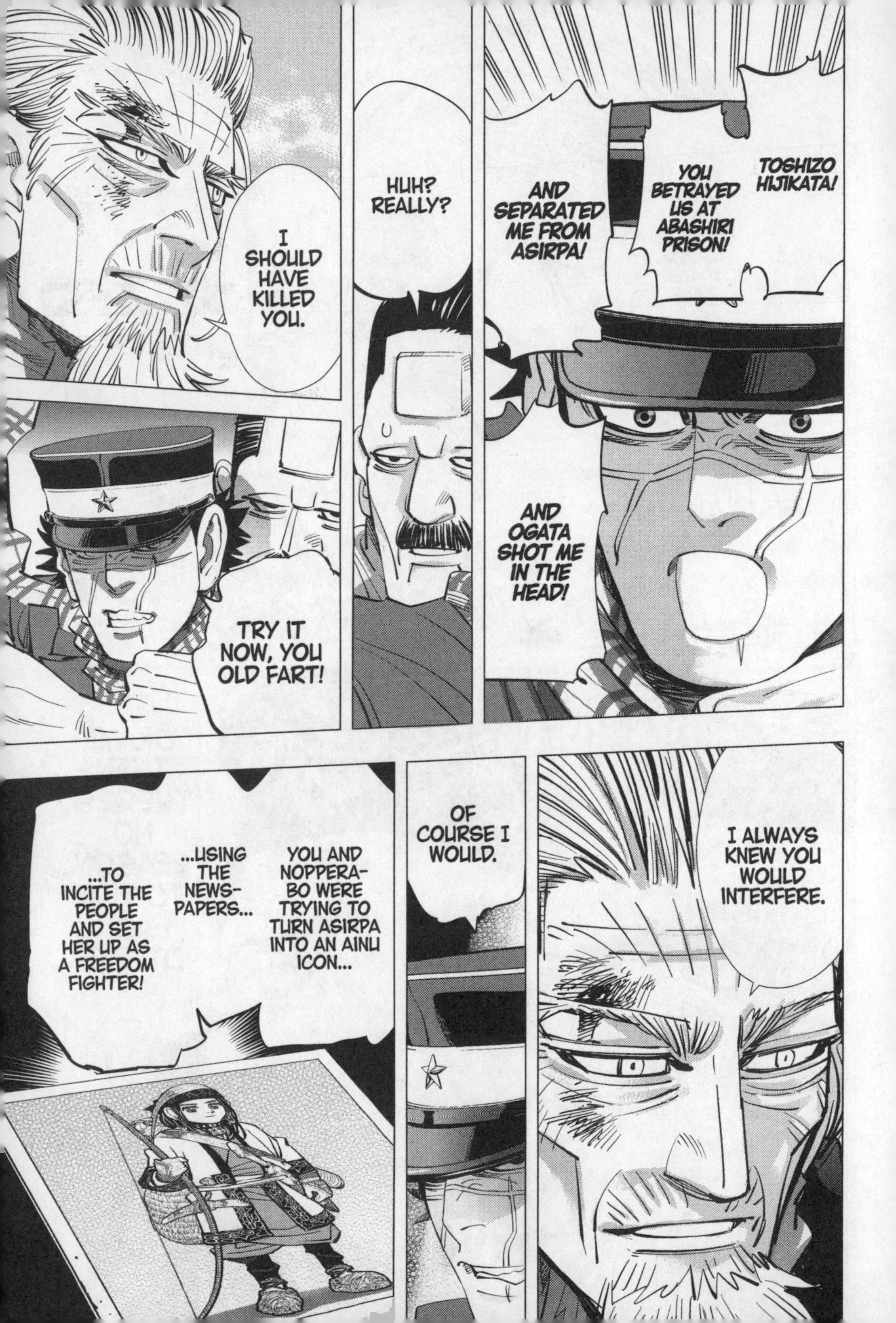
TOSHIZO HIJIKATA!
YOU BETRAYED US AT ABASHIRI PRISON!
AND SEPARATED ME FROM ASIRPA!
AND OGATA SHOT ME IN THE HEAD!
HUH? REALLY?
I SHOULD HAVE KILLED YOU.
TRY IT NOW, YOU OLD FART!
I ALWAYS KNEW YOU WOULD INTERFERE.
OF COURSE I WOULD.
YOU AND NOPPERA-BO WERE TRYING TO TURN ASIRPA INTO AN AINU ICON...
...USING THE NEWS-PAPERS...
...TO INCITE THE PEOPLE AND SET HER UP AS A FREEDOM FIGHTER!

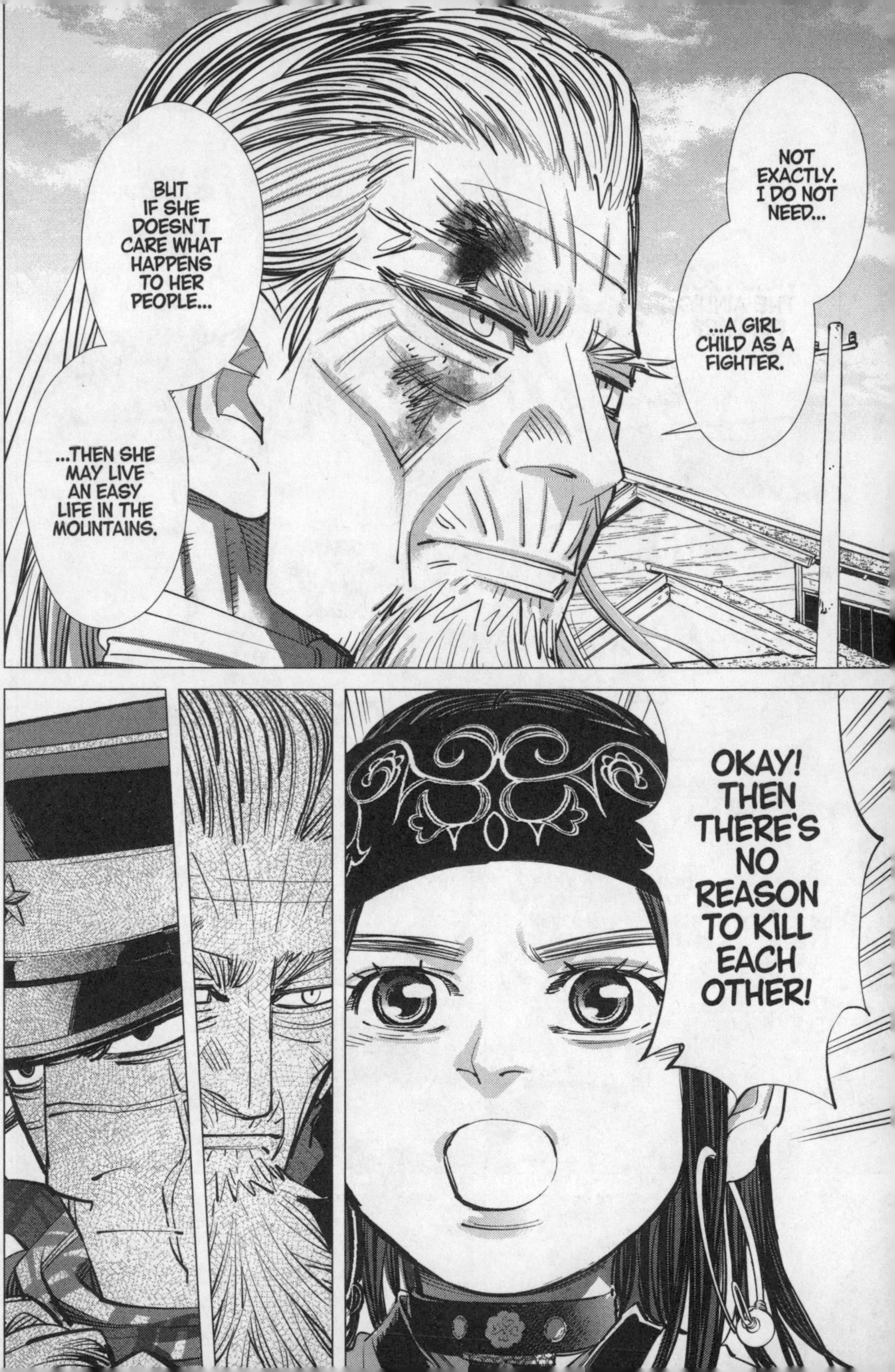
NOT EXACTLY. I DO NOT NEED...
...A GIRL CHILD AS A FIGHTER.
BUT IF SHE DOESN'T CARE WHAT HAPPENS TO HER PEOPLE...
...THEN SHE MAY LIVE AN EASY LIFE IN THE MOUNTAINS.
OKAY! THEN THERE'S NO REASON TO KILL EACH OTHER!

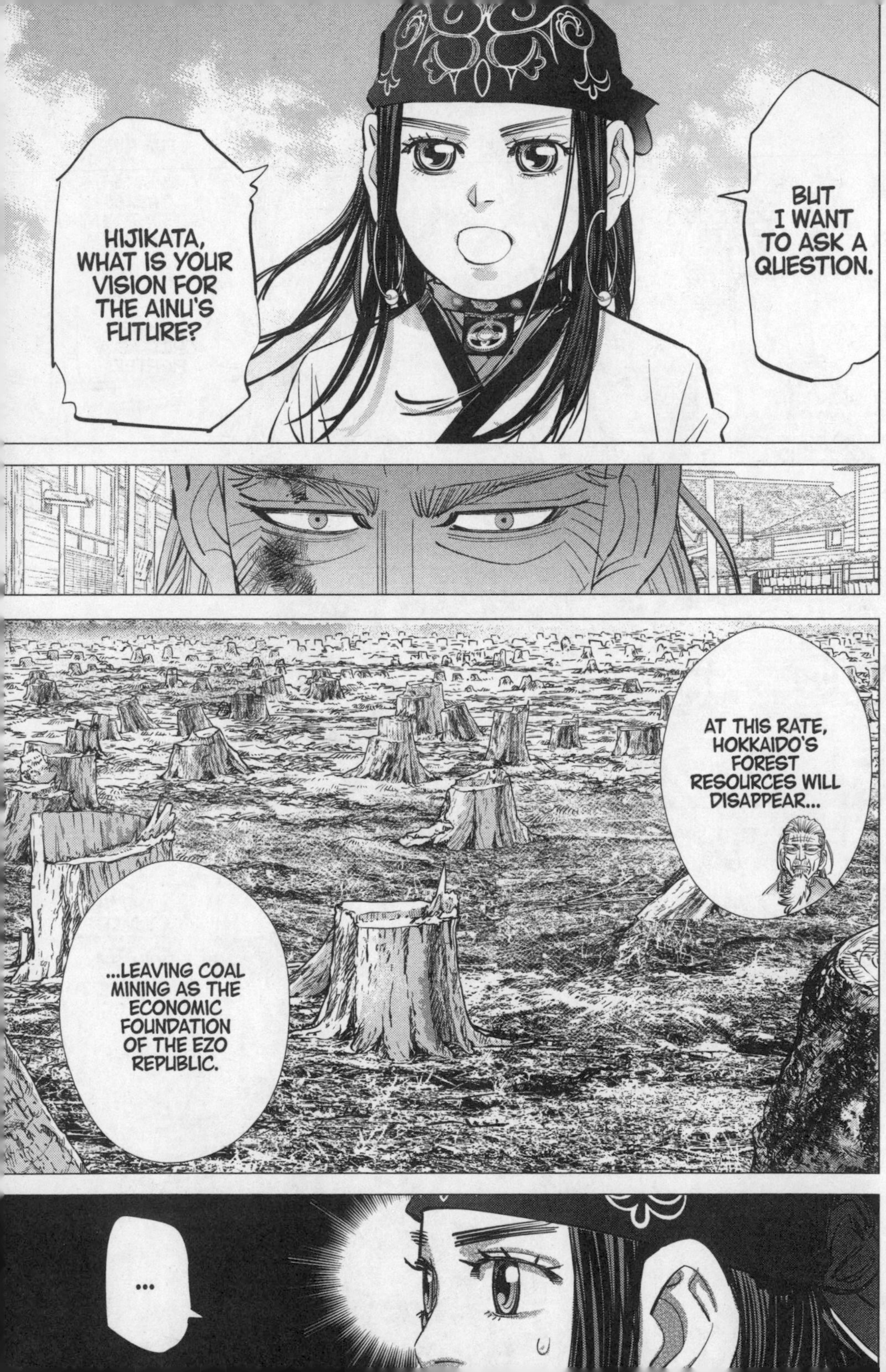
BUT I WANT TO ASK A QUESTION.
HIJIKATA, WHAT IS YOUR VISION FOR THE AINU'S FUTURE?
AT THIS RATE, HOKKAIDO'S FOREST RESOURCES WILL DISAPPEAR...
...LEAVING COAL MINING AS THE ECONOMIC FOUNDATION OF THE EZO REPUBLIC.
...

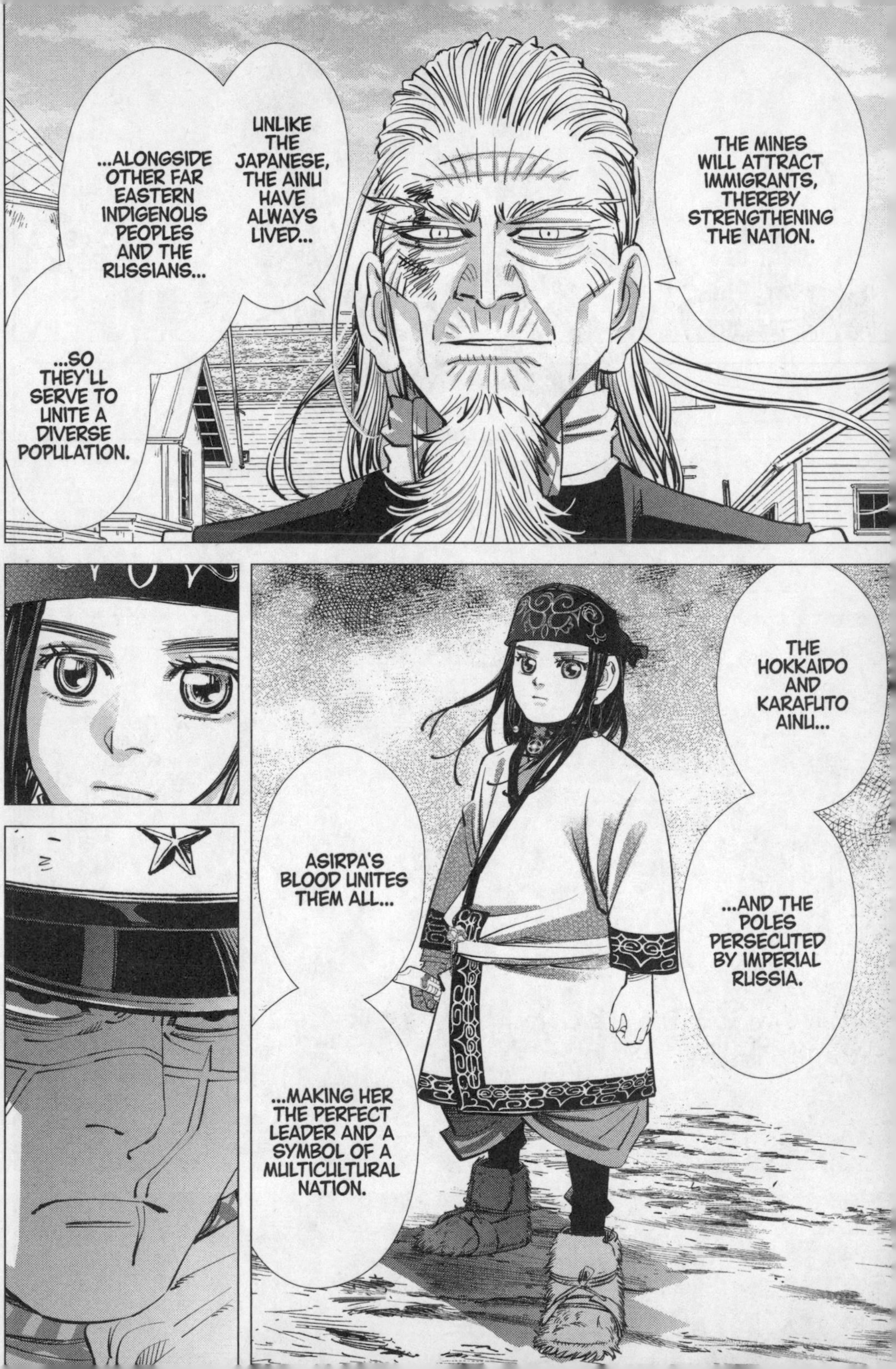
THE MINES WILL ATTRACT IMMIGRANTS, THEREBY STRENGTHENING THE NATION.
UNLIKE THE JAPANESE, THE AINU HAVE ALWAYS LIVED...
...ALONGSIDE OTHER FAR EASTERN INDIGENOUS PEOPLES AND THE RUSSIANS...
...SO THEY'LL SERVE TO UNITE A DIVERSE POPULATION.
THE HOKKAIDO AND KARAFUTO AINU...
...AND THE POLES PERSECUTED BY IMPERIAL RUSSIA.
ASIRPA'S BLOOD UNITES THEM ALL...
...MAKING HER THE PERFECT LEADER AND A SYMBOL OF A MULTICULTURAL NATION.

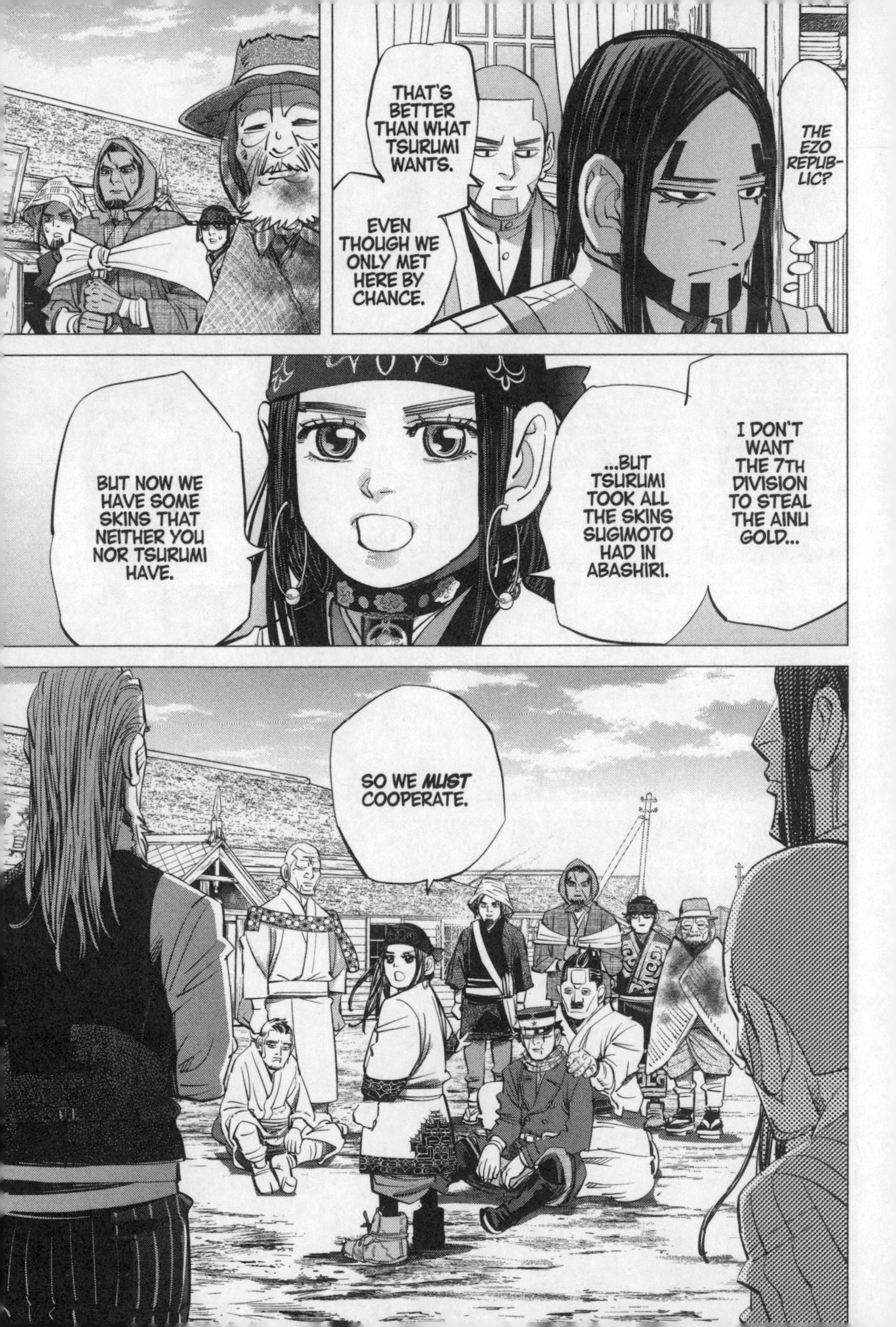
THE EZO REPUBLIC?
THAT'S BETTER THAN WHAT TSURUMI WANTS.
EVEN THOUGH WE ONLY MET HERE BY CHANCE.
I DON'T WANT THE 7TH DIVISION TO STEAL THE AINU GOLD...
...BUT TSURUMI TOOK ALL THE SKINS SUGIMOTO HAD IN ABASHIRI.
BUT NOW WE HAVE SOME SKINS THAT NEITHER YOU NOR TSURUMI HAVE.
SO WE *MUST* COOPERATE.

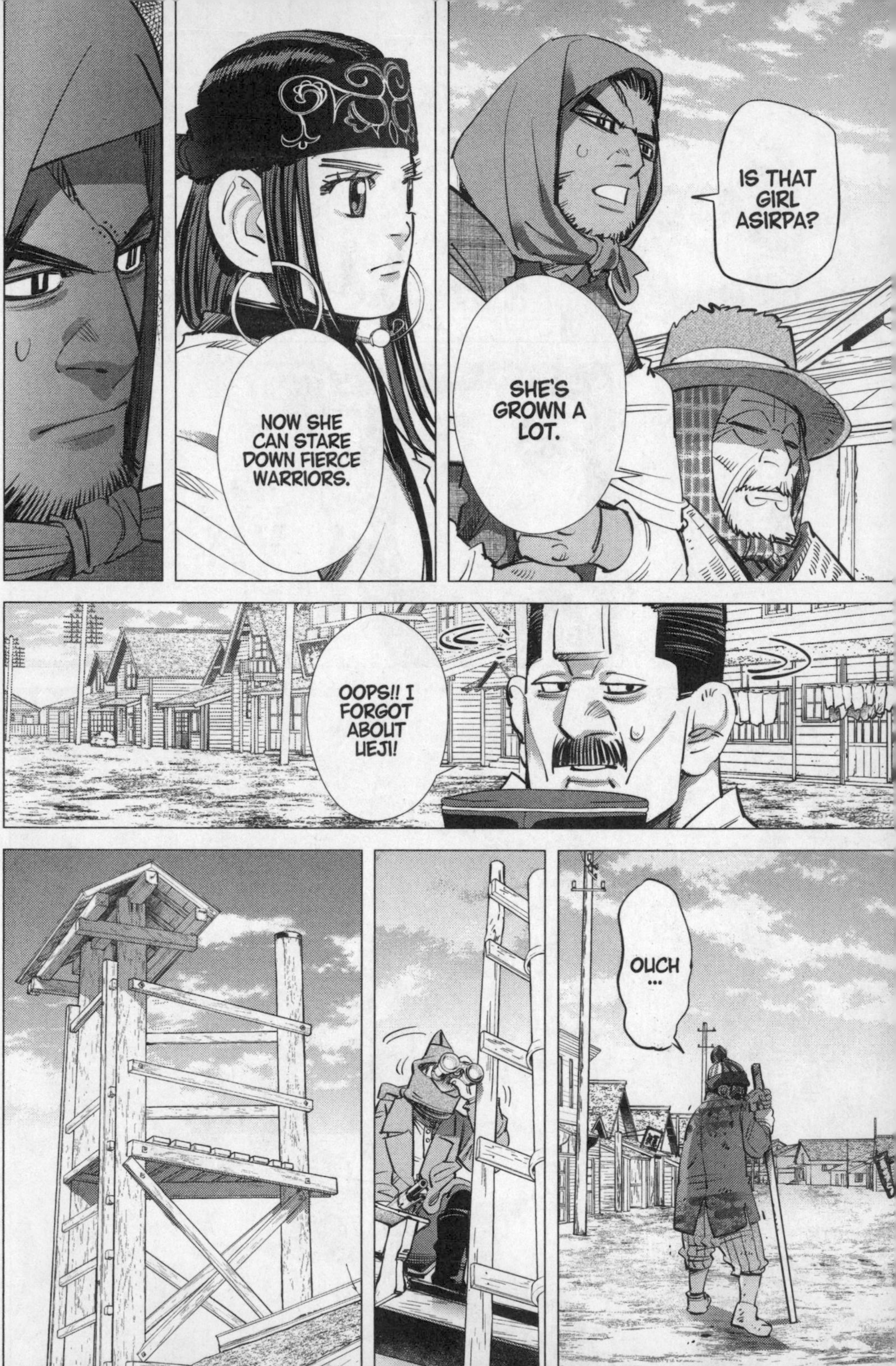
IS THAT GIRL ASIRPA?
SHE'S GROWN A LOT.
NOW SHE CAN STARE DOWN FIERCE WARRIORS.
OOPS!! I FORGOT ABOUT UEJI!
OUCH ...

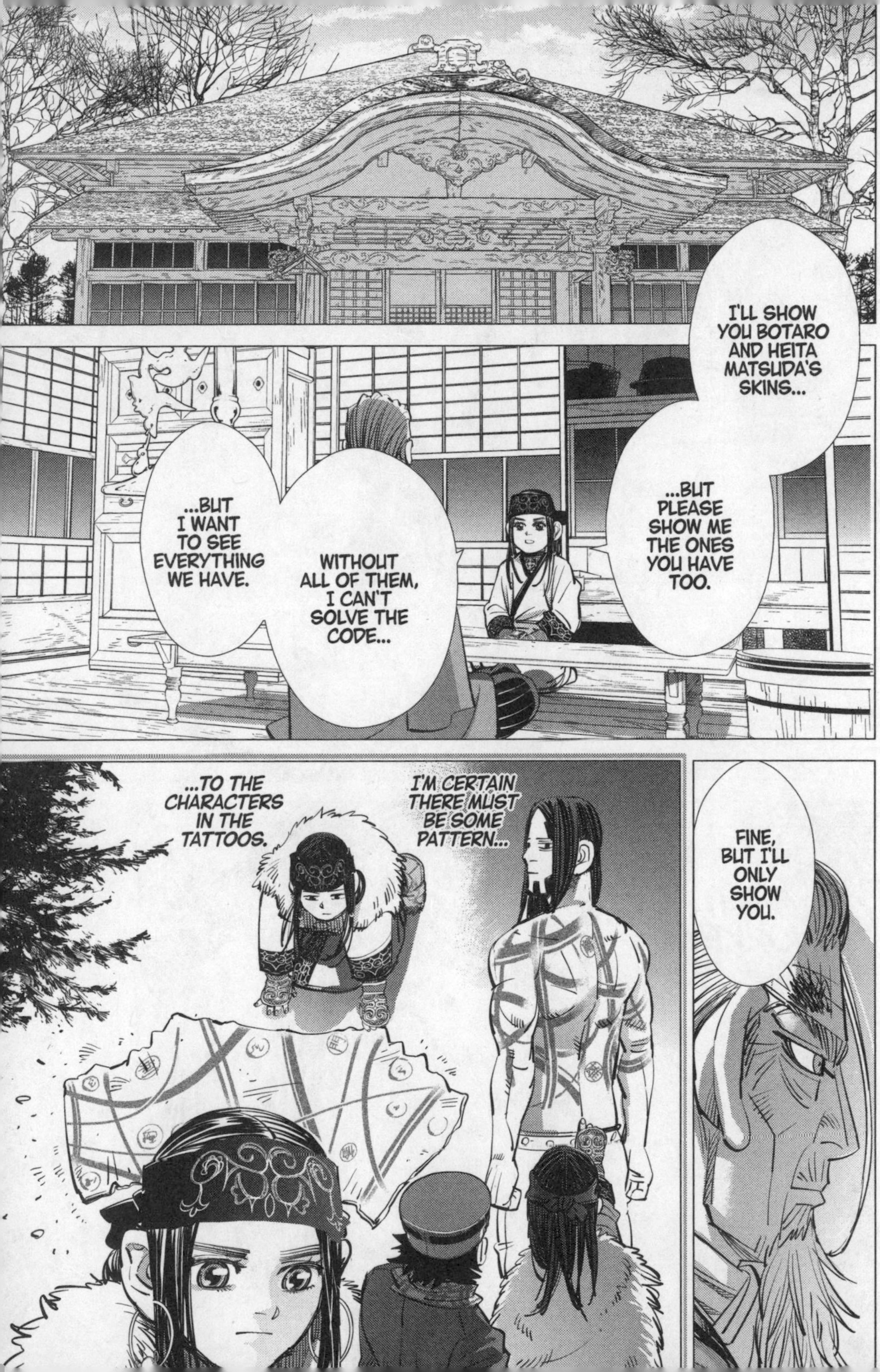
I'LL SHOW YOU BOTARO AND HEITA MATSUDA'S SKINS...
...BUT PLEASE SHOW ME THE ONES YOU HAVE TOO.
WITHOUT ALL OF THEM, I CAN'T SOLVE THE CODE...
...BUT I WANT TO SEE EVERYTHING WE HAVE.
FINE, BUT I'LL ONLY SHOW YOU.
I'M CERTAIN THERE MUST BE SOME PATTERN...
...TO THE CHARACTERS IN THE TATTOOS.

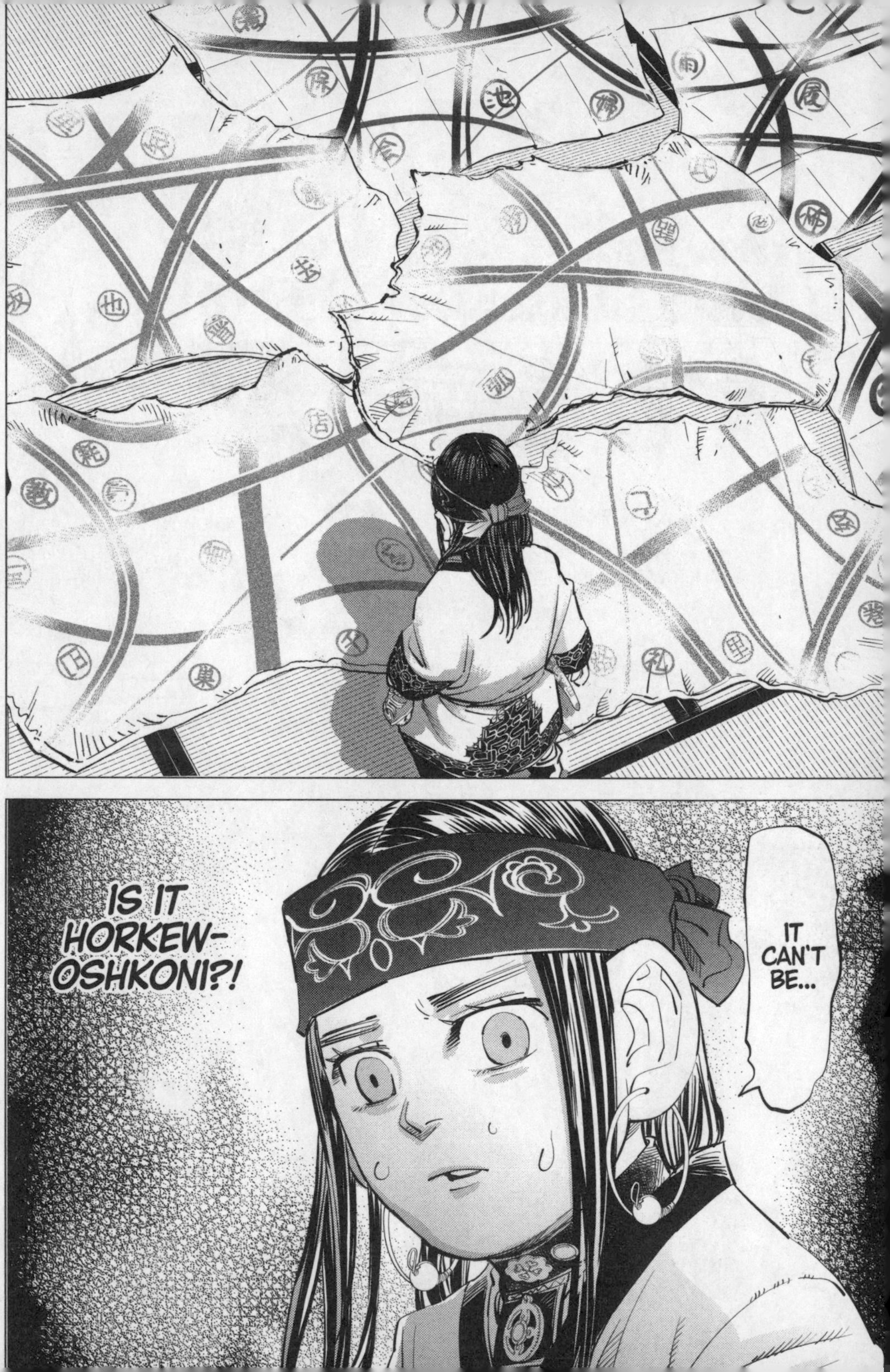
IT CAN'T BE...
IS IT HORKEW-OSHKONI?!

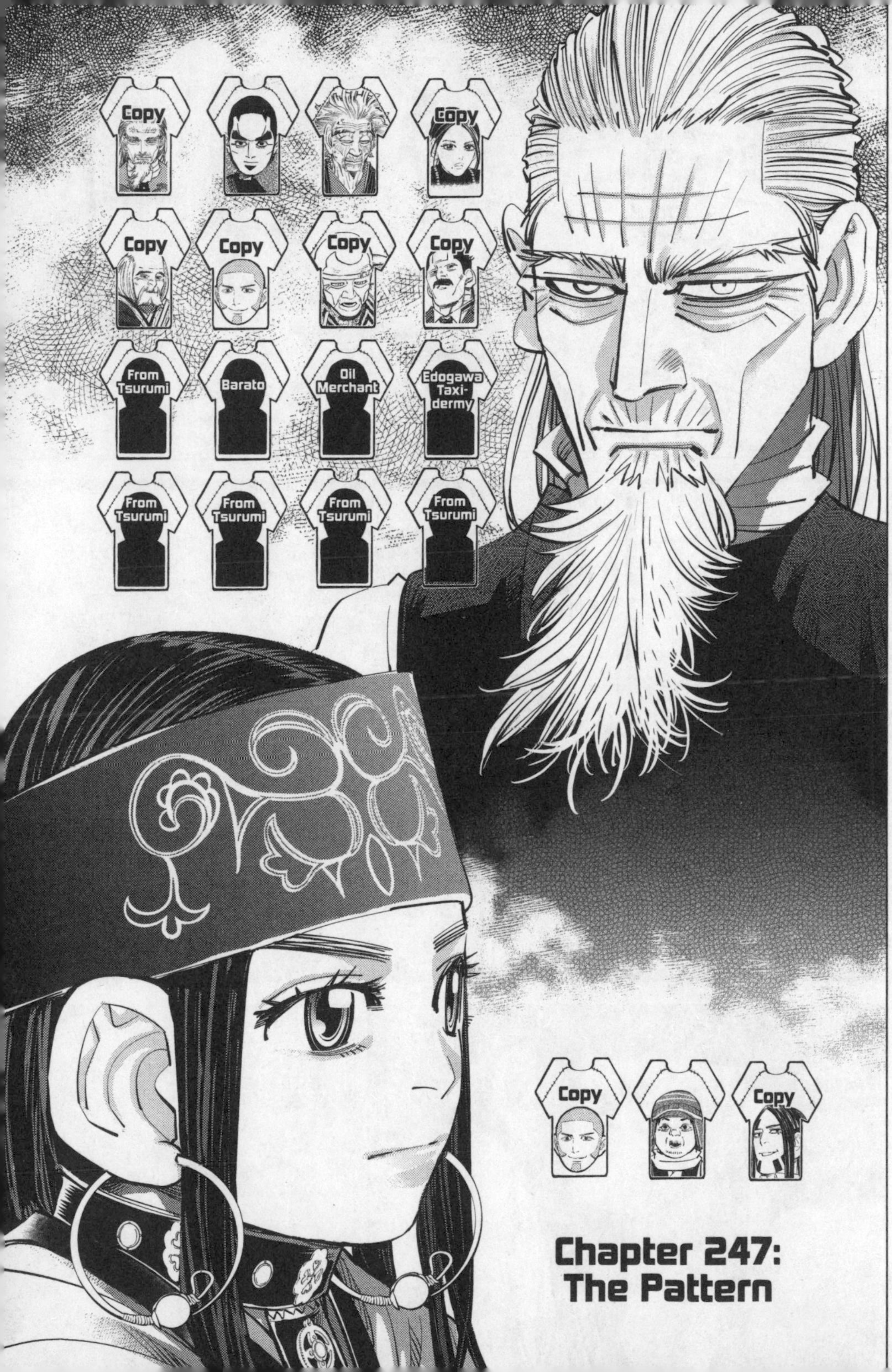
Copy
Copy
Copy
Copy
Copy
Copy
Edogawa Taxi-dermy
Oil Merchant
Barato
From Tsurumi
From Tsurumi
From Tsurumi
From Tsurumi
From Tsurumi
Copy
Copy

Chapter 247: The Pattern

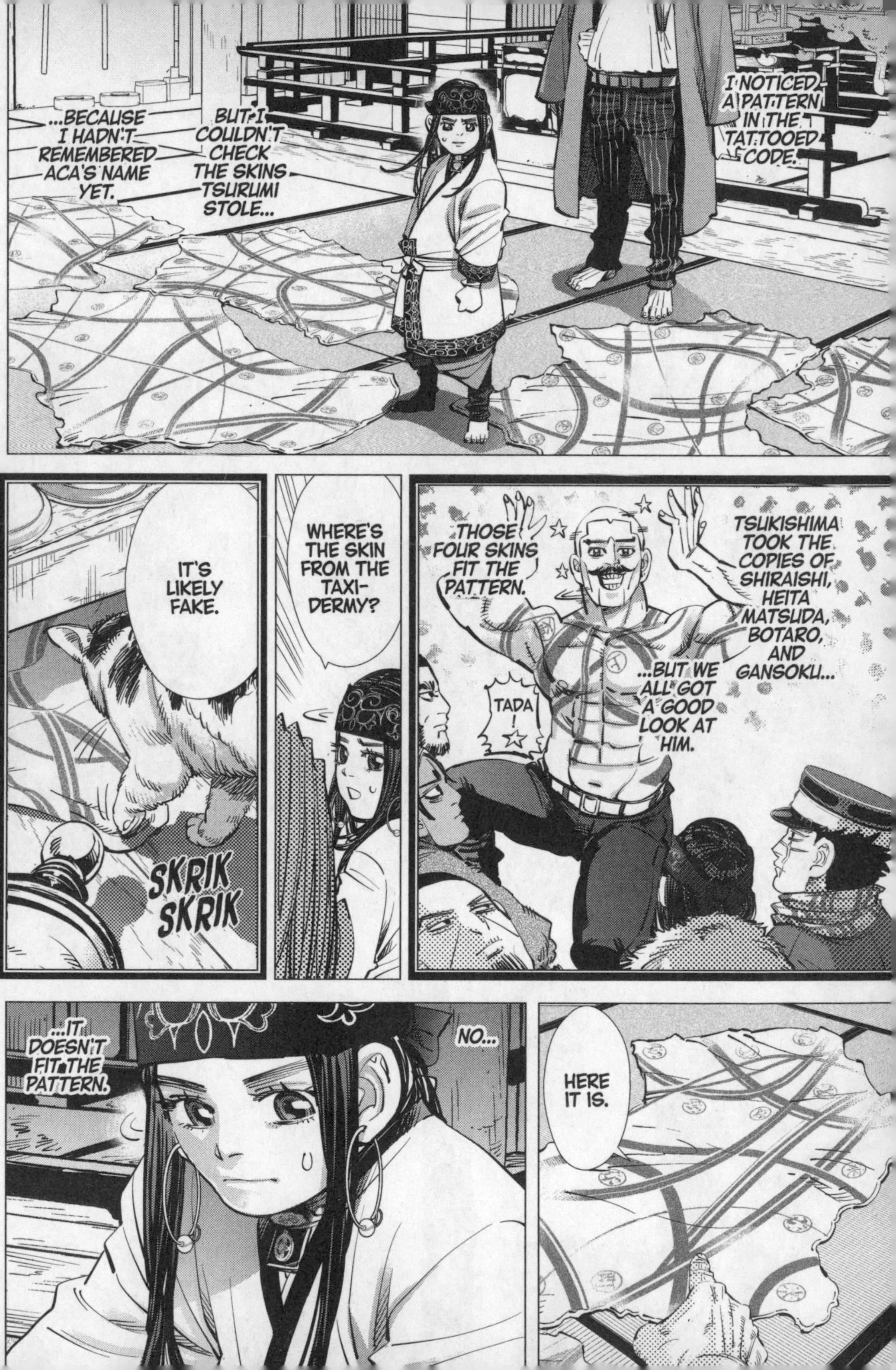
I NOTICED A PATTERN IN THE TATTOOED CODE.
BUT I COULDN'T CHECK THE SKINS TSURUMI STOLE...
...BECAUSE I HADN'T REMEMBERED ACA'S NAME YET.
TSUKISHIMA TOOK THE COPIES OF SHIRAISHI, HEITA MATSUDA, BOTARO, AND GANSOKU...
...BUT WE ALL GOT A GOOD LOOK AT HIM.
THOSE FOUR SKINS FIT THE PATTERN.
TADA!
WHERE'S THE SKIN FROM THE TAXI-DERMY?
IT'S LIKELY FAKE.
SKRIK SKRIK
HERE IT IS.
NO...
...IT DOESN'T FIT THE PATTERN.

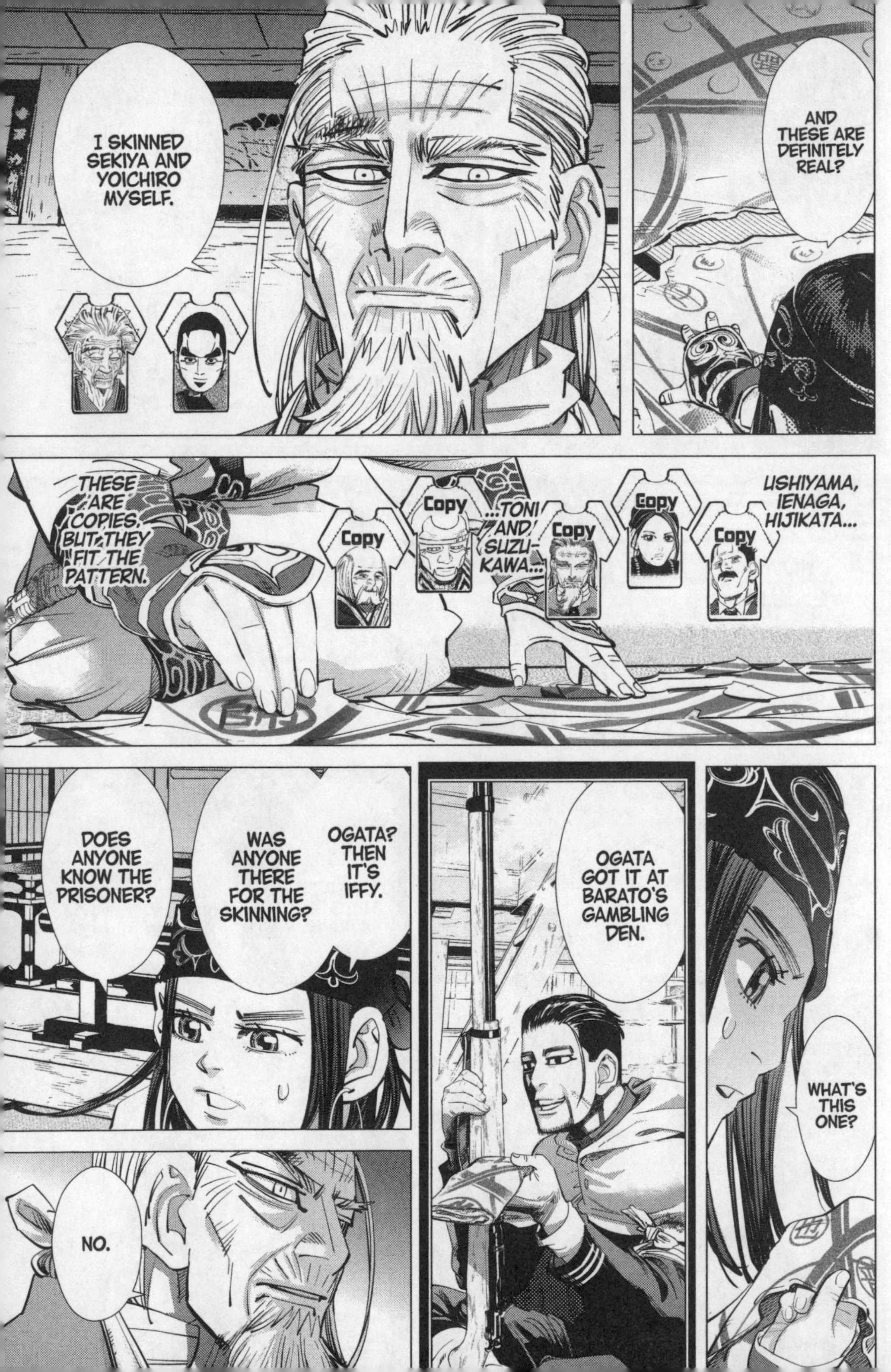
AND THESE ARE DEFINITELY REAL?
I SKINNED SEKIYA AND YOICHIRO MYSELF.
USHIYAMA, IENAGA, HIJIKATA...
Copy
Copy
Copy
...TONI AND SUZUKAWA...
Copy
Copy
THESE ARE COPIES. BUT THEY FIT THE PATTERN.
WHAT'S THIS ONE?
OGATA GOT IT AT BARATO'S GAMBLING DEN.
OGATA? THEN IT'S IFFY.
WAS ANYONE THERE FOR THE SKINNING?
DOES ANYONE KNOW THE PRISONER?
NO.

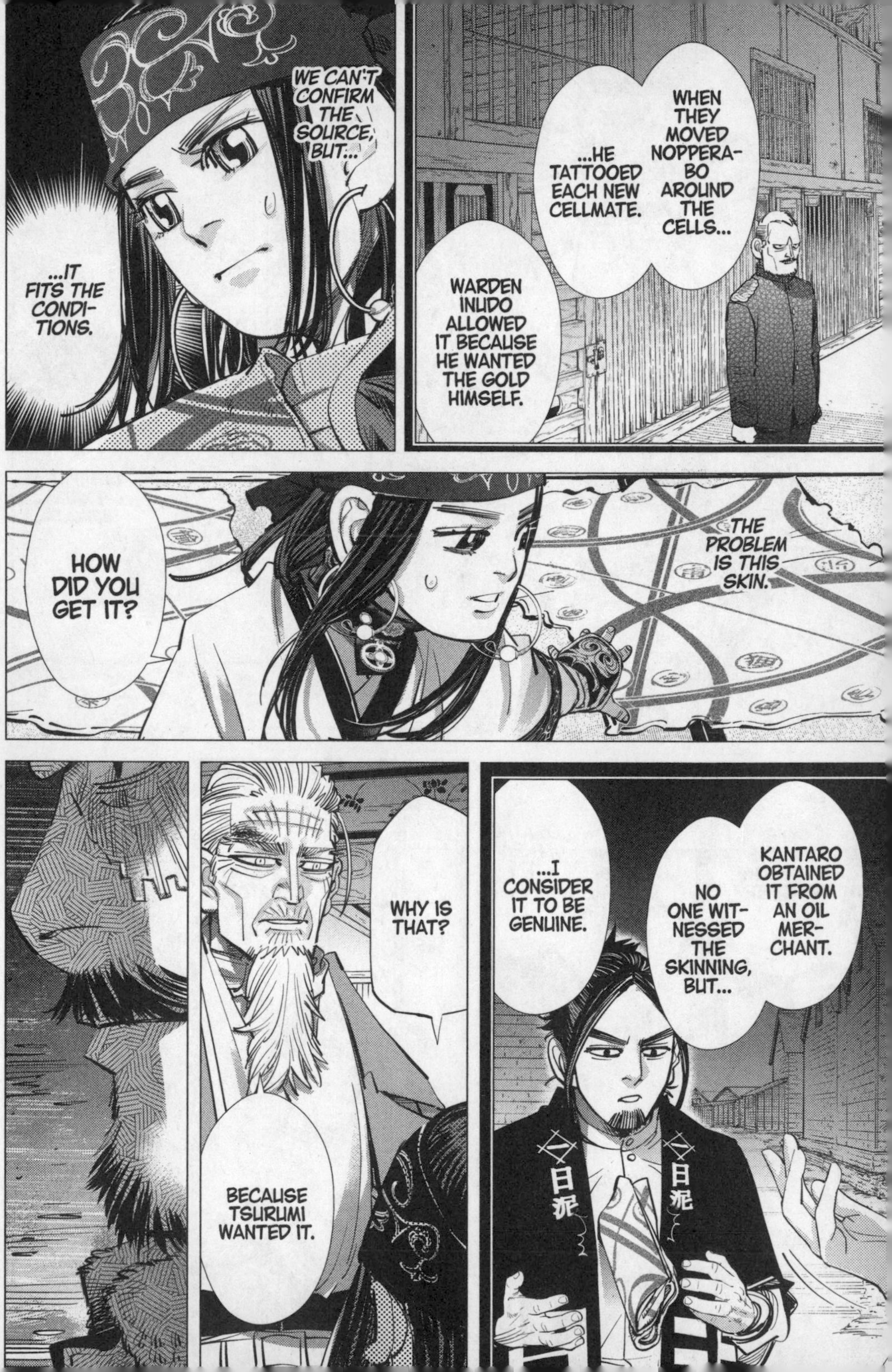
WHEN THEY MOVED NOPPERA-BO AROUND THE CELLS...
...HE TATTOOED EACH NEW CELLMATE.
WARDEN INUDO ALLOWED IT BECAUSE HE WANTED THE GOLD HIMSELF.
WE CAN'T CONFIRM THE SOURCE, BUT...
...IT FITS THE CONDITIONS.
THE PROBLEM IS THIS SKIN.
HOW DID YOU GET IT?
KANTARO OBTAINED IT FROM AN OIL MER-CHANT.
NO ONE WIT-NESSED THE SKINNING, BUT...
...I CONSIDER IT TO BE GENUINE.
WHY IS THAT?
BECAUSE TSURUMI WANTED IT.

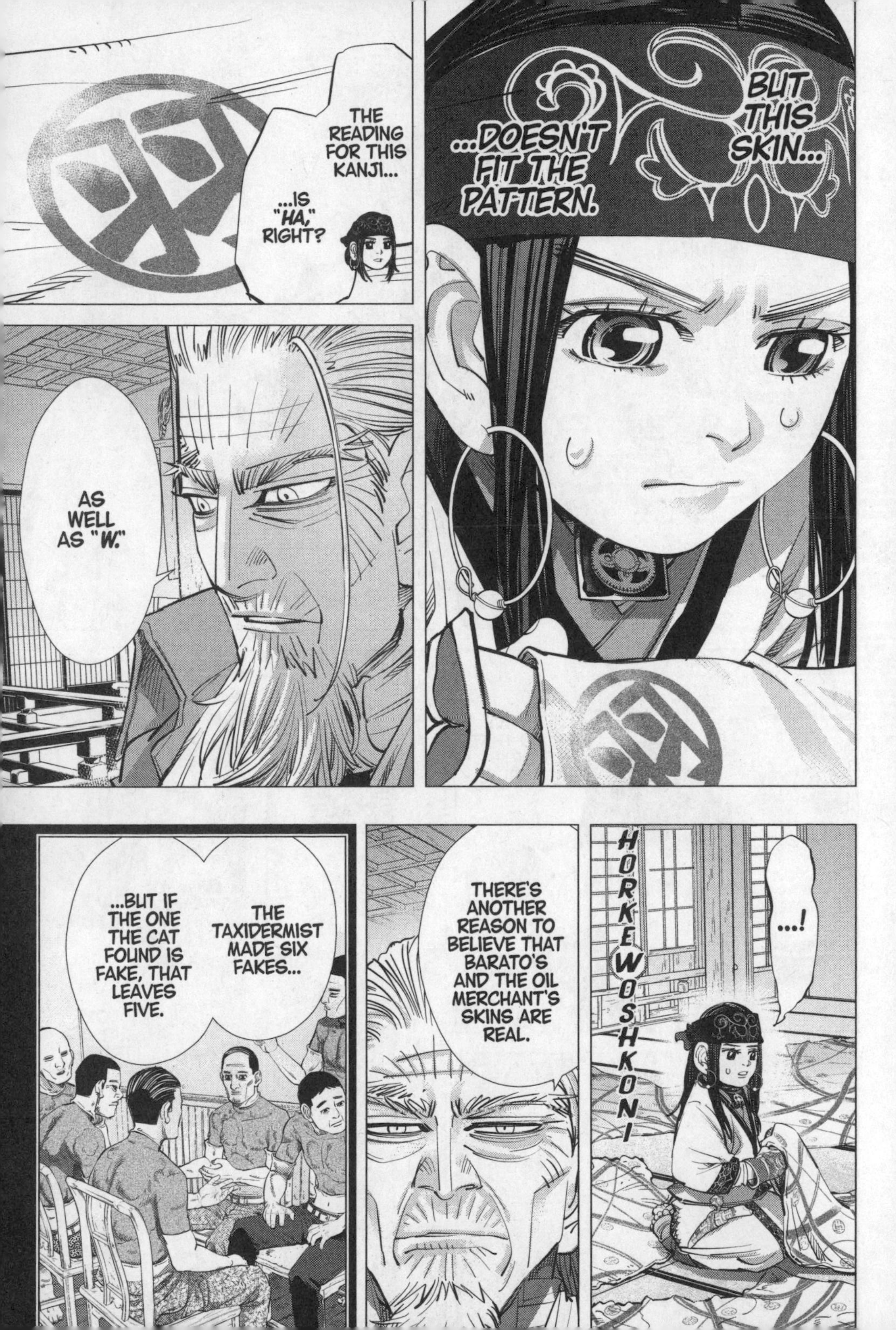
BUT THIS SKIN...
...DOESN'T FIT THE PATTERN.
THE READING FOR THIS KANJI...
...IS "HA," RIGHT?
AS WELL AS "W."
HORKEWOSHKONI
...!
THERE'S ANOTHER REASON TO BELIEVE THAT BARATO'S AND THE OIL MERCHANT'S SKINS ARE REAL.
THE TAXIDERMIST MADE SIX FAKES...
...BUT IF THE ONE THE CAT FOUND IS FAKE, THAT LEAVES FIVE.

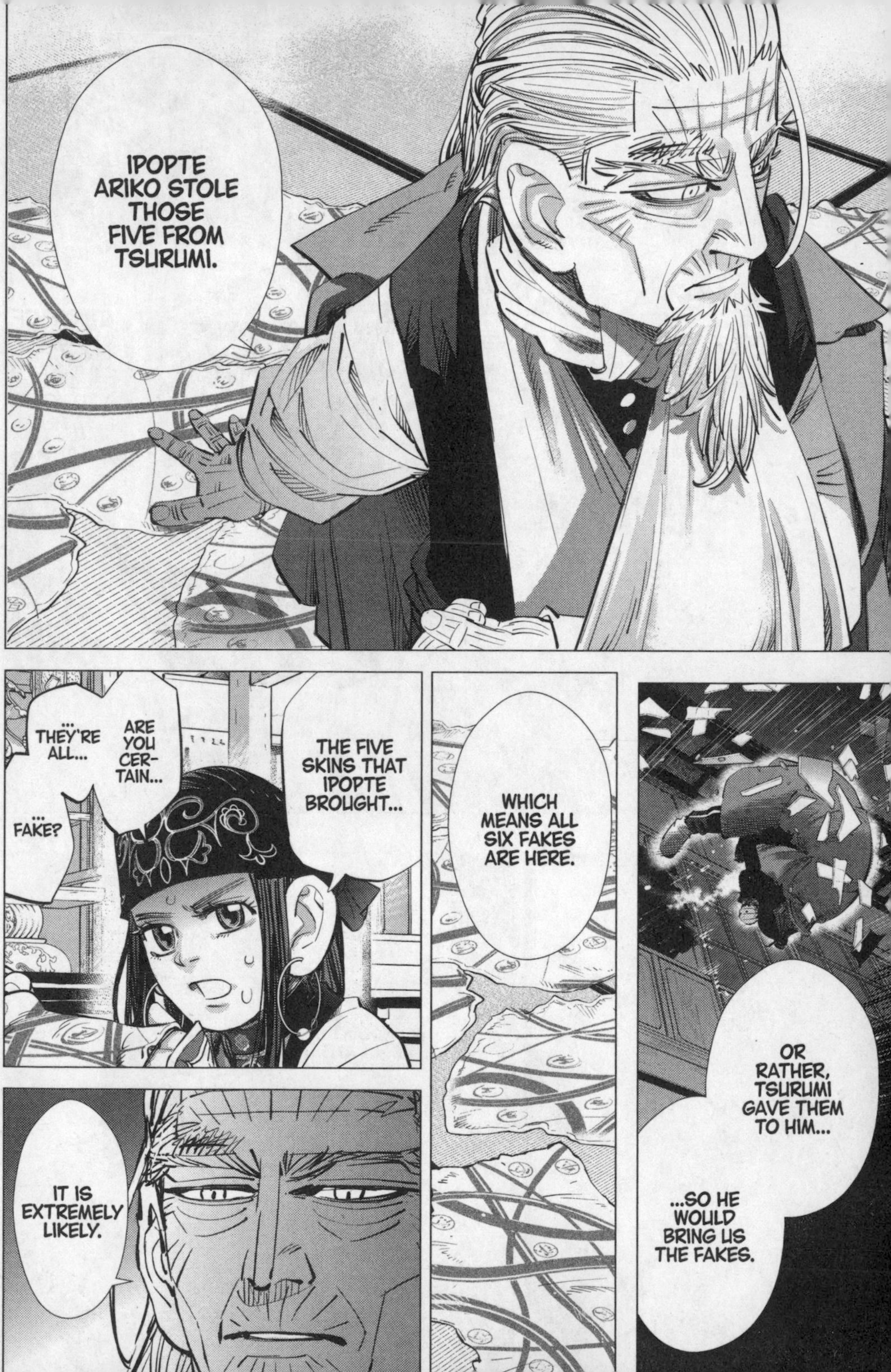
IPOPTE ARIKO STOLE THOSE FIVE FROM TSURUMI.
OR RATHER, TSURUMI GAVE THEM TO HIM...
...SO HE WOULD BRING US THE FAKES.
WHICH MEANS ALL SIX FAKES ARE HERE.
THE FIVE SKINS THAT IPOPTE BROUGHT...
ARE YOU CERTAIN...
...THEY'RE ALL...
...FAKE?
IT IS EXTREMELY LIKELY.

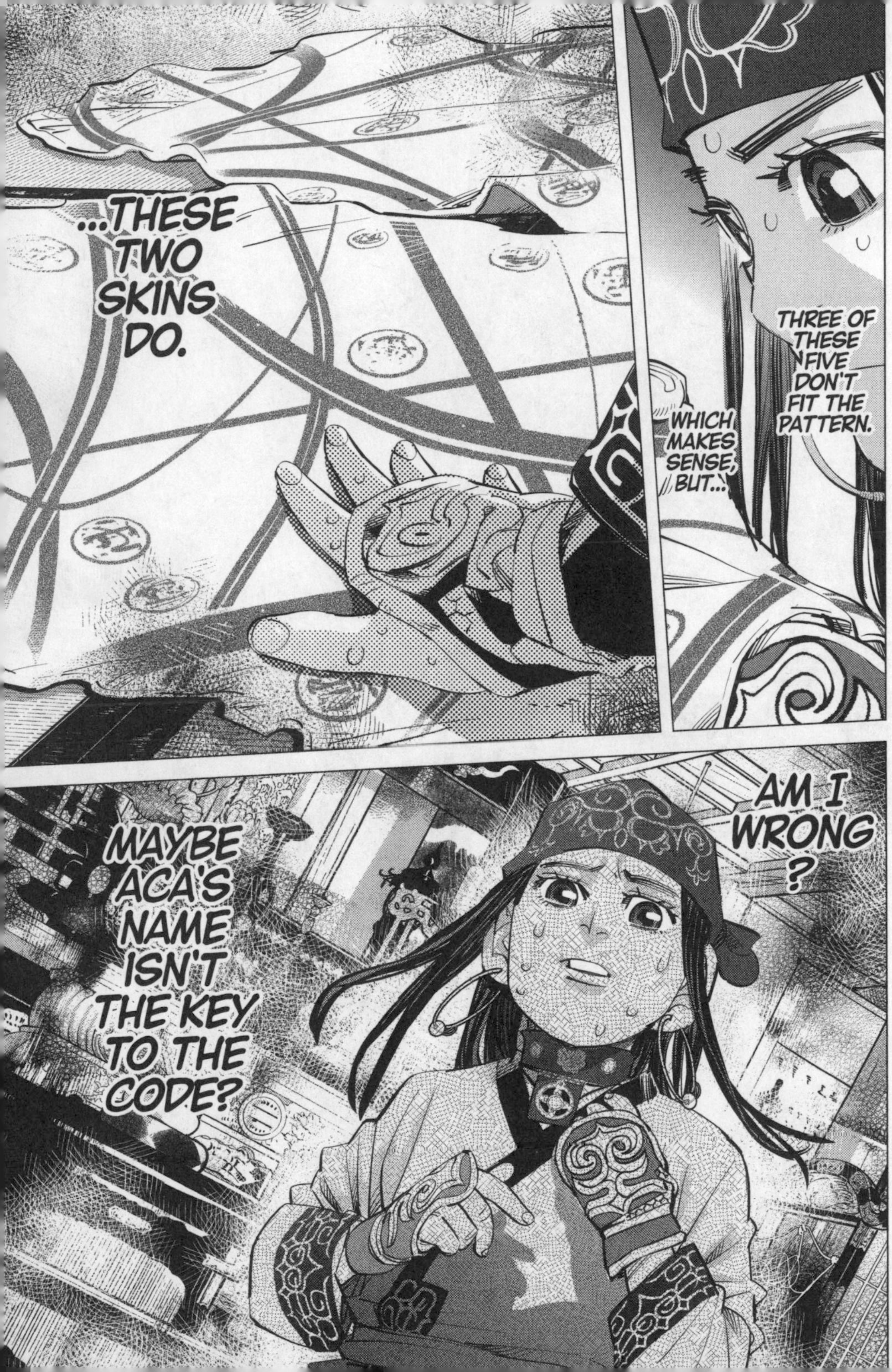
THREE OF THESE FIVE DON'T FIT THE PATTERN.
WHICH MAKES SENSE, BUT...
...THESE TWO SKINS DO.
AM I WRONG?
MAYBE ACA'S NAME ISN'T THE KEY TO THE CODE?

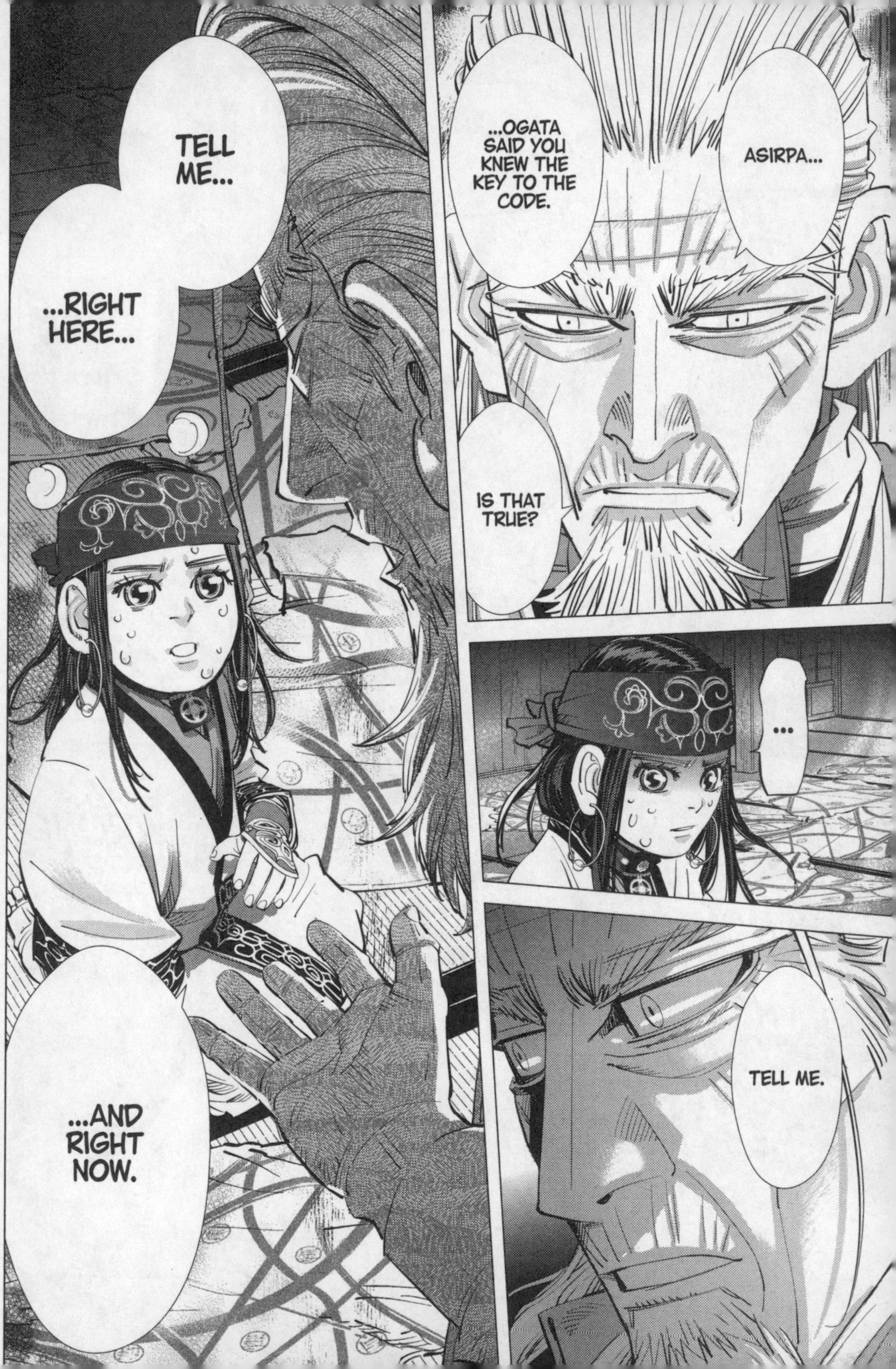
ASIRPA...
...OGATA SAID YOU KNEW THE KEY TO THE CODE.
IS THAT TRUE?
...
TELL ME.
TELL ME...
...RIGHT HERE...
...AND RIGHT NOW.

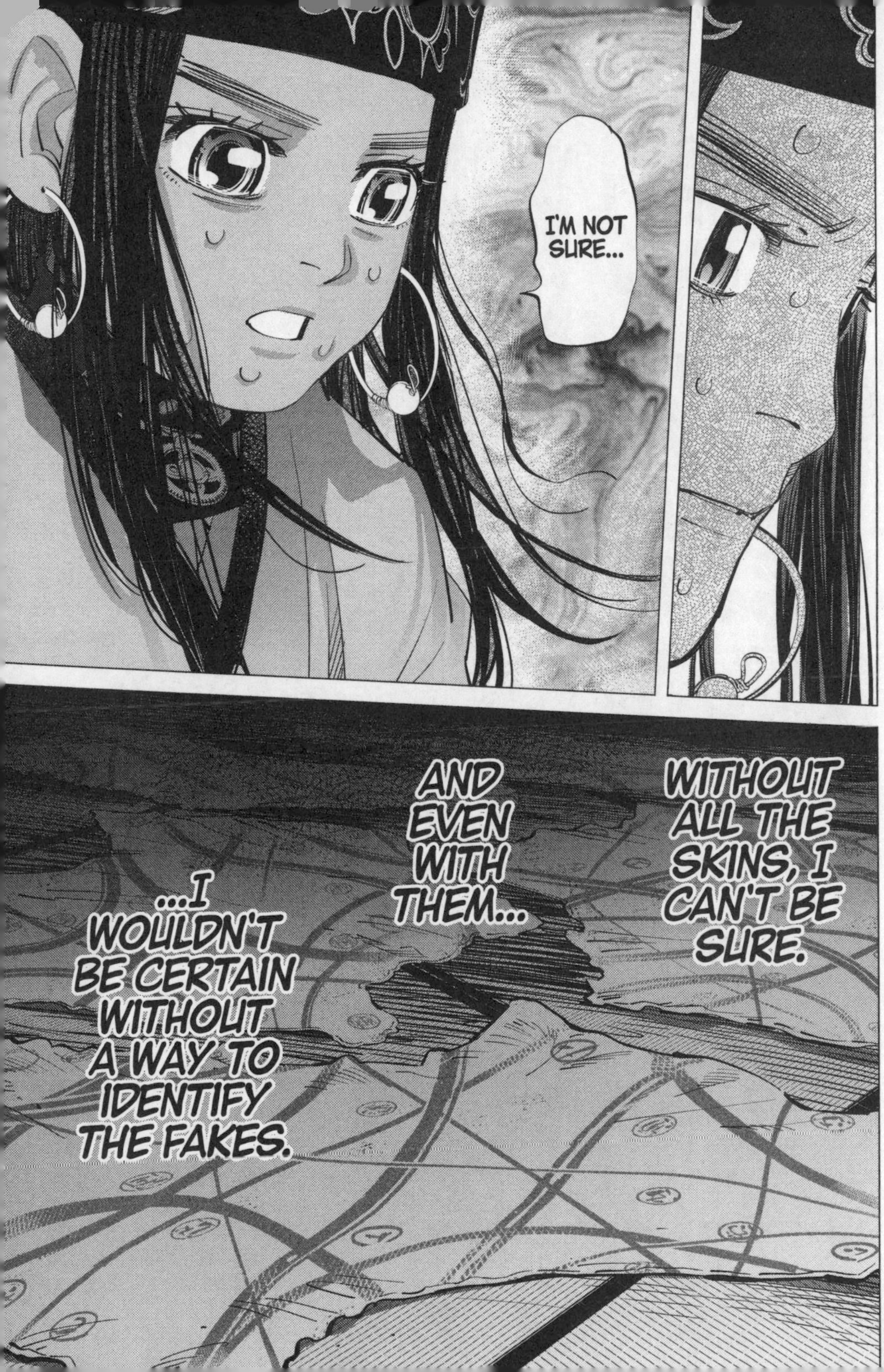
I'M NOT SURE...
WITHOUT ALL THE SKINS, I CAN'T BE SURE.
AND EVEN WITH THEM...
...I WOULDN'T BE CERTAIN WITHOUT A WAY TO IDENTIFY THE FAKES.

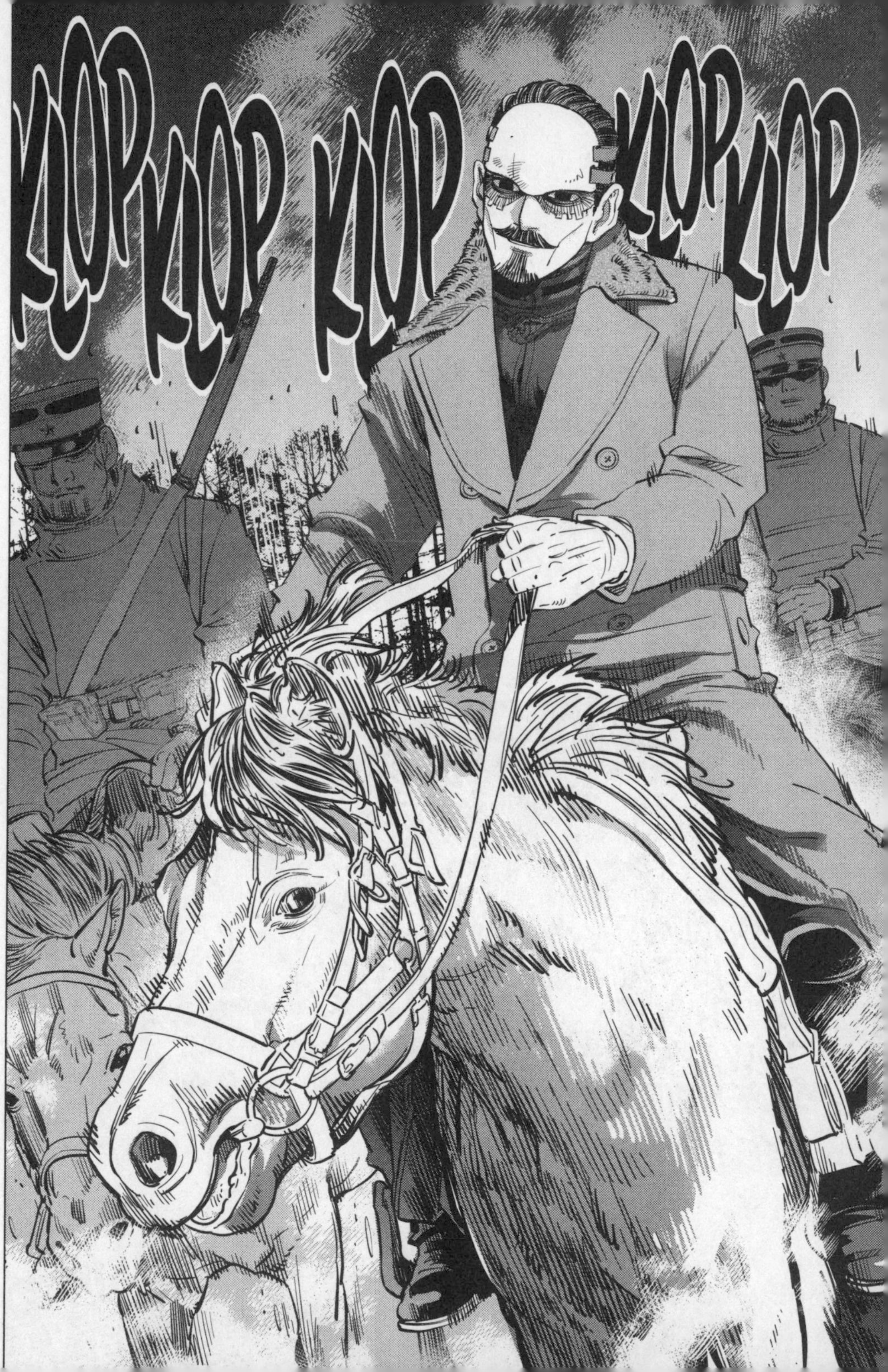
KLOP
KLOP
KLOP
KLOP
KLOP

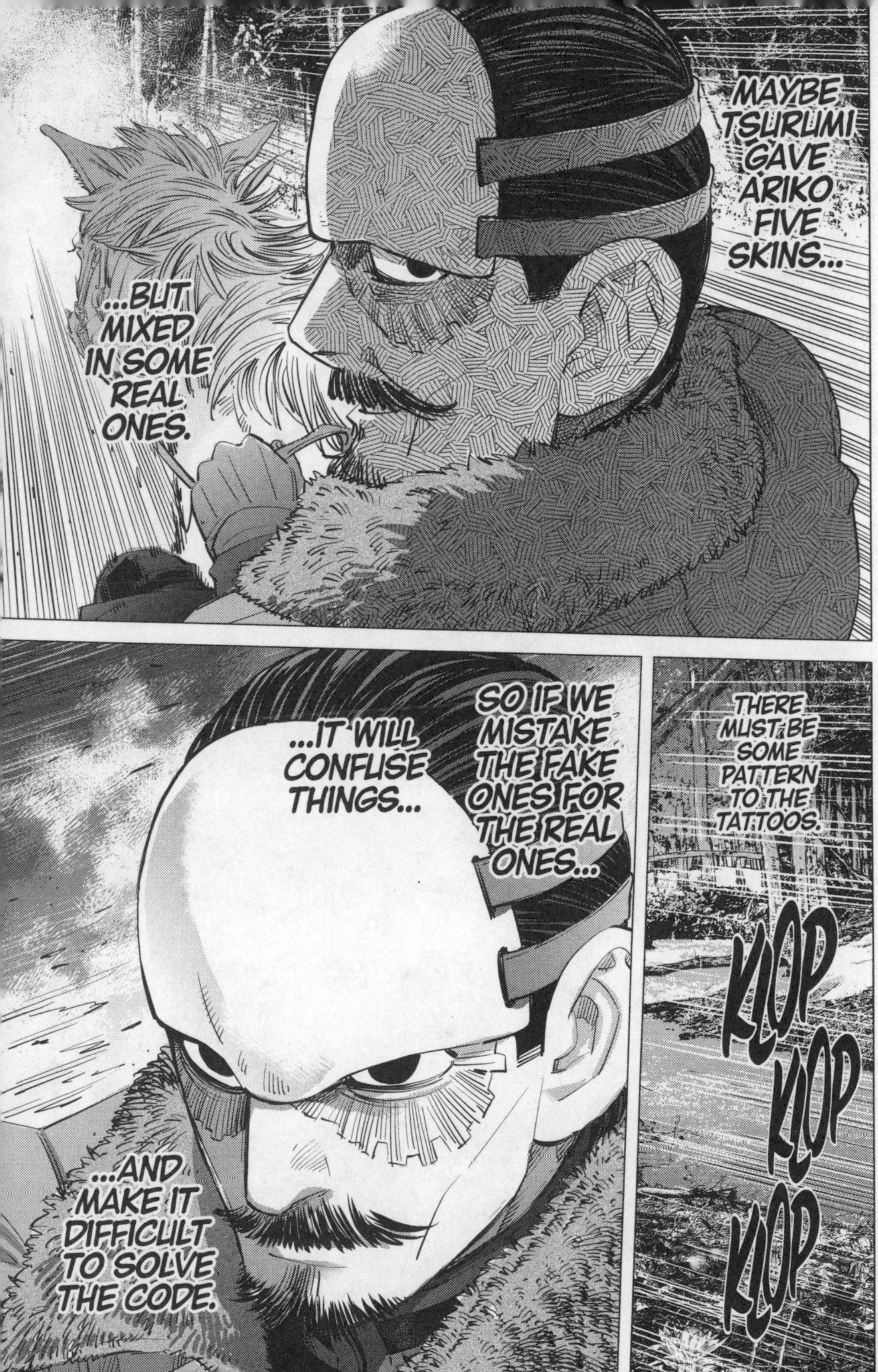
MAYBE TSURUMI GAVE ARIKO FIVE SKINS...
...BUT MIXED IN SOME REAL ONES.
THERE MUST BE SOME PATTERN TO THE TATTOOS.
KLOP
KLOP
KLOP
SO IF WE MISTAKE THE FAKE ONES FOR THE REAL ONES...
...IT WILL CONFUSE THINGS...
...AND MAKE IT DIFFICULT TO SOLVE THE CODE.

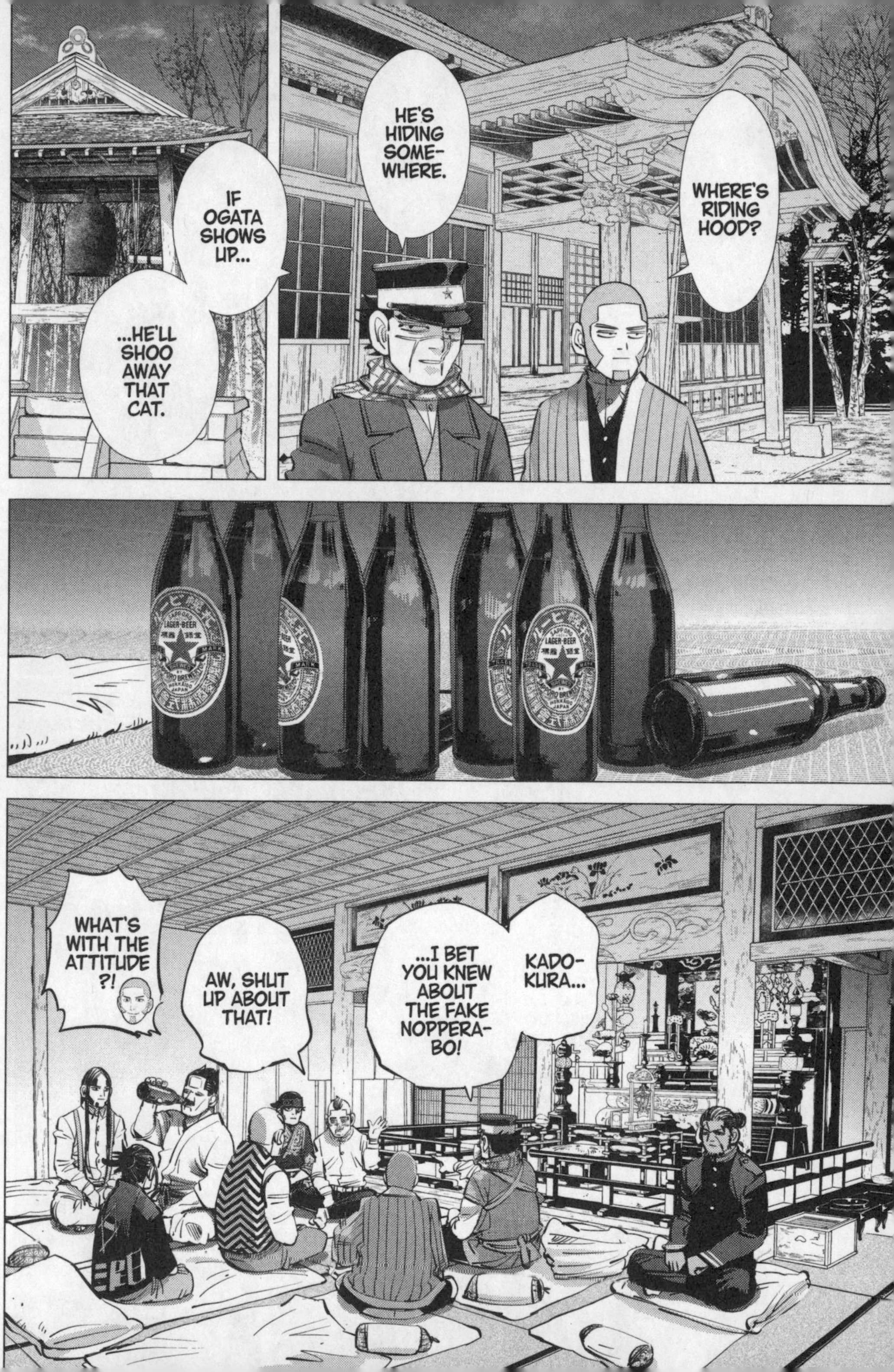
WHERE'S RIDING HOOD?
HE'S HIDING SOME-WHERE.
IF OGATA SHOWS UP...
...HE'LL SHOO AWAY THAT CAT.
LAGER-BEER
KADO-KURA...
...I BET YOU KNEW ABOUT THE FAKE NOPPERA-BO!
AW, SHUT UP ABOUT THAT!
WHAT'S WITH THE ATTITUDE?!

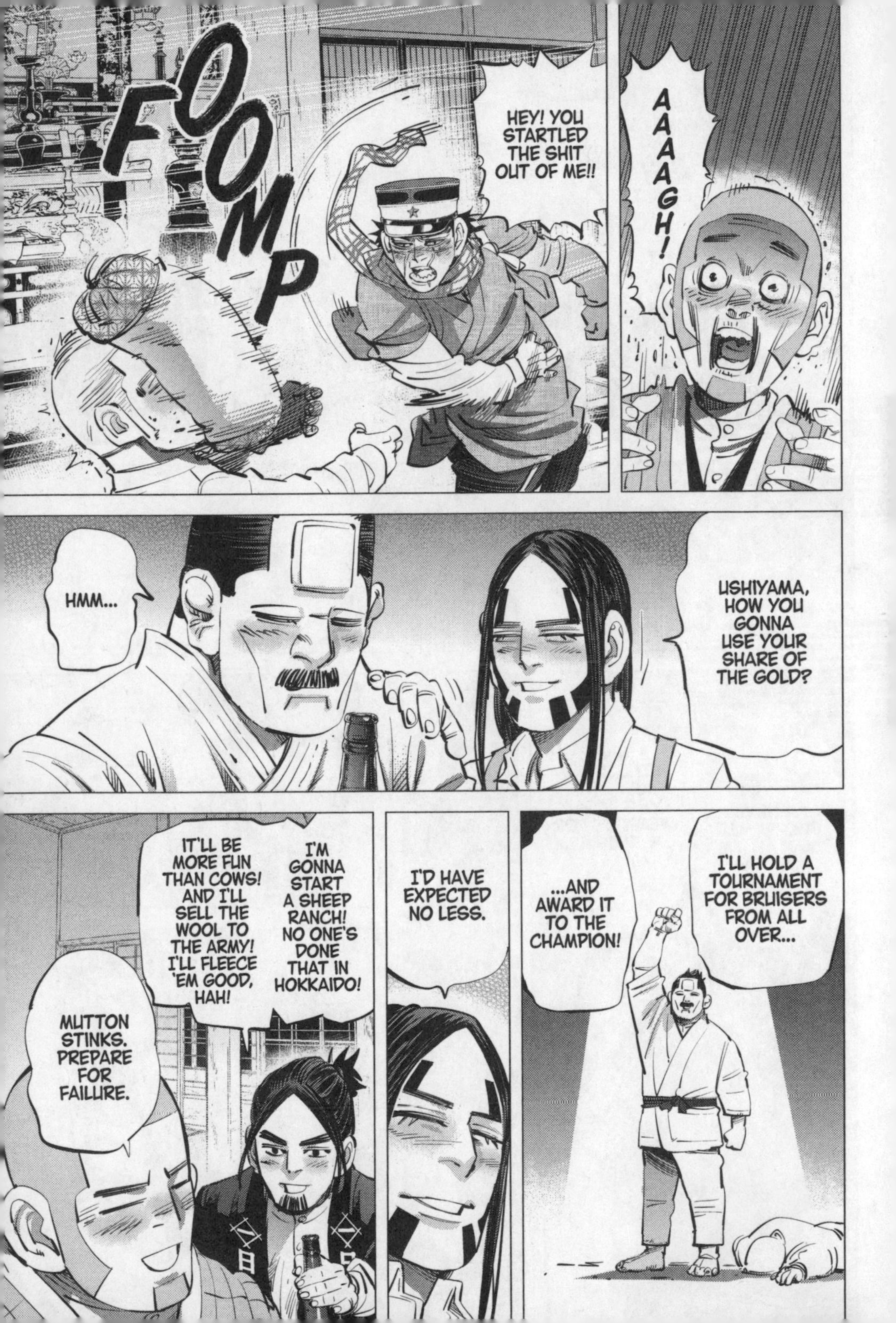
AAAAGH!
HEY! YOU STARTLED THE SHIT OUT OF ME!!
FOOMP
USHIYAMA, HOW YOU GONNA USE YOUR SHARE OF THE GOLD?
HMM...
I'LL HOLD A TOURNAMENT FOR BRUISERS FROM ALL OVER...
...AND AWARD IT TO THE CHAMPION!
I'D HAVE EXPECTED NO LESS.
I'M GONNA START A SHEEP RANCH! NO ONE'S DONE THAT IN HOKKAIDO!
IT'LL BE MORE FUN THAN COWS! AND I'LL SELL THE WOOL TO THE ARMY! I'LL FLEECE 'EM GOOD, HAH!
MUTTON STINKS. PREPARE FOR FAILURE.

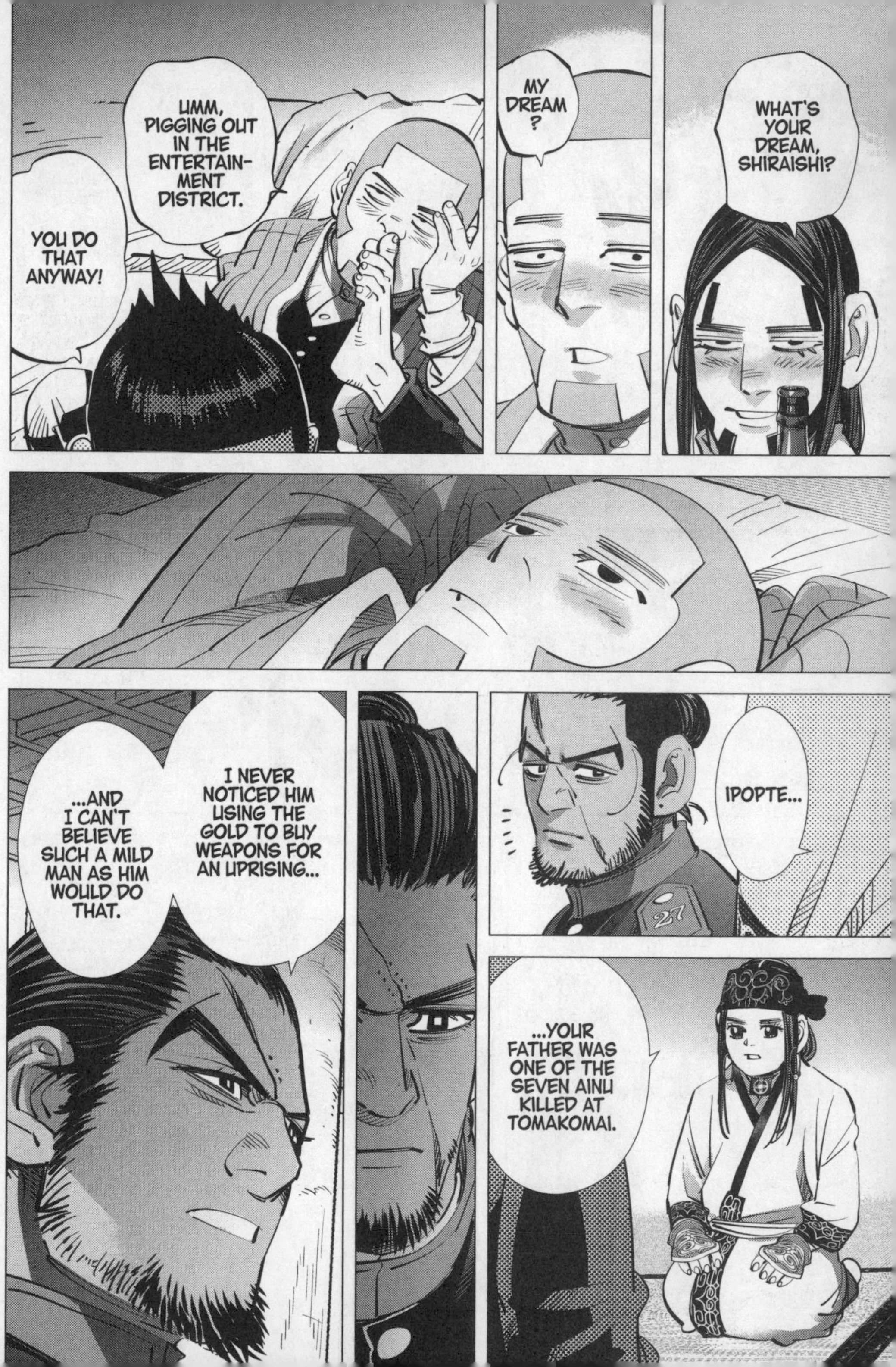
WHAT'S YOUR DREAM, SHIRAISHI?
MY DREAM?
UMM, PIGGING OUT IN THE ENTERTAINMENT DISTRICT.
YOU DO THAT ANYWAY!
IPOPTE...
...YOUR FATHER WAS ONE OF THE SEVEN AINU KILLED AT TOMAKOMAI.
I NEVER NOTICED HIM USING THE GOLD TO BUY WEAPONS FOR AN UPRISING...
...AND I CAN'T BELIEVE SUCH A MILD MAN AS HIM WOULD DO THAT.

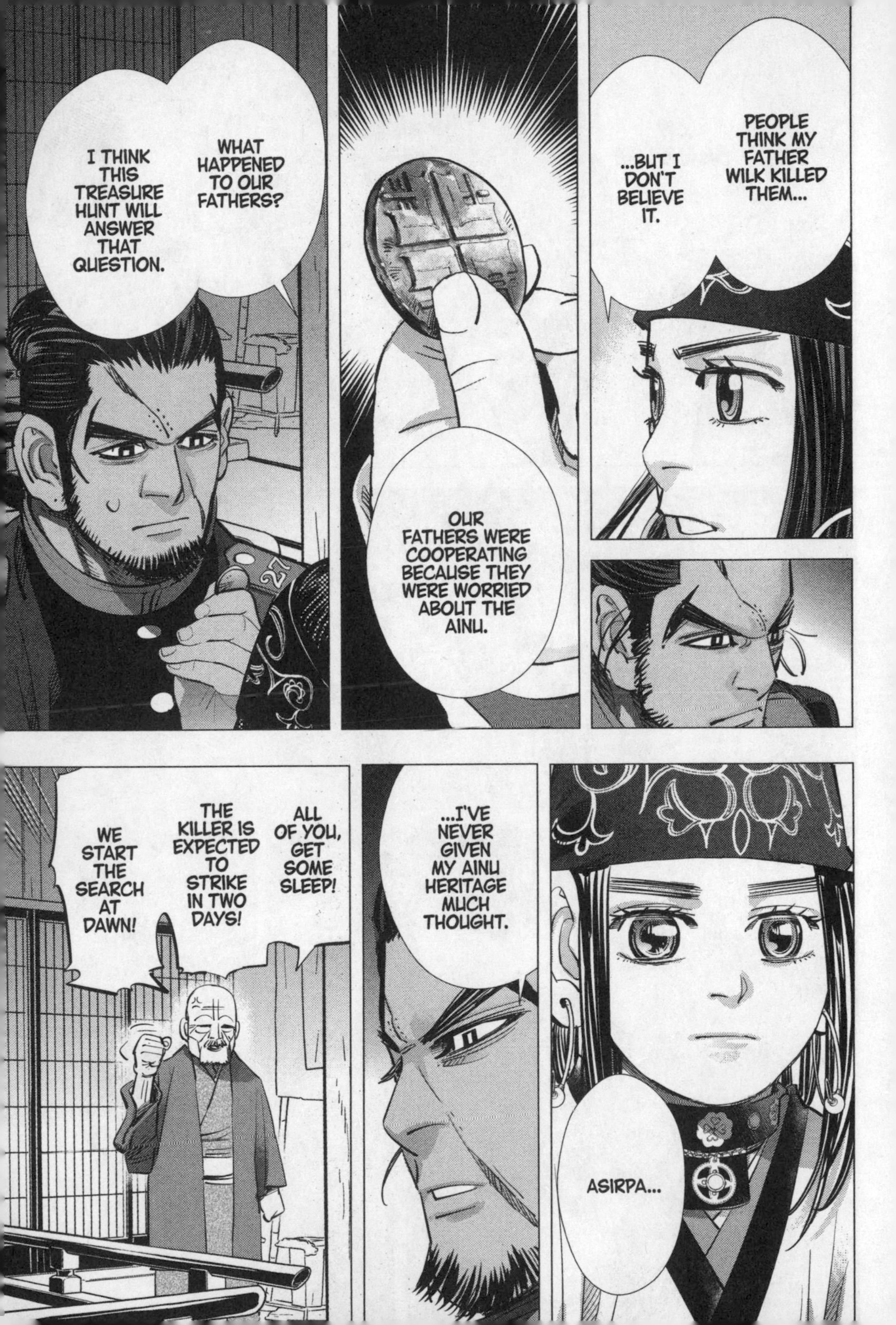
PEOPLE THINK MY FATHER WILK KILLED THEM...
...BUT I DON'T BELIEVE IT.
OUR FATHERS WERE COOPERATING BECAUSE THEY WERE WORRIED ABOUT THE AINU.
WHAT HAPPENED TO OUR FATHERS?
I THINK THIS TREASURE HUNT WILL ANSWER THAT QUESTION.
ASIRPA...
...I'VE NEVER GIVEN MY AINU HERITAGE MUCH THOUGHT.
ALL OF YOU, GET SOME SLEEP!
THE KILLER IS EXPECTED TO STRIKE IN TWO DAYS!
WE START THE SEARCH AT DAWN!

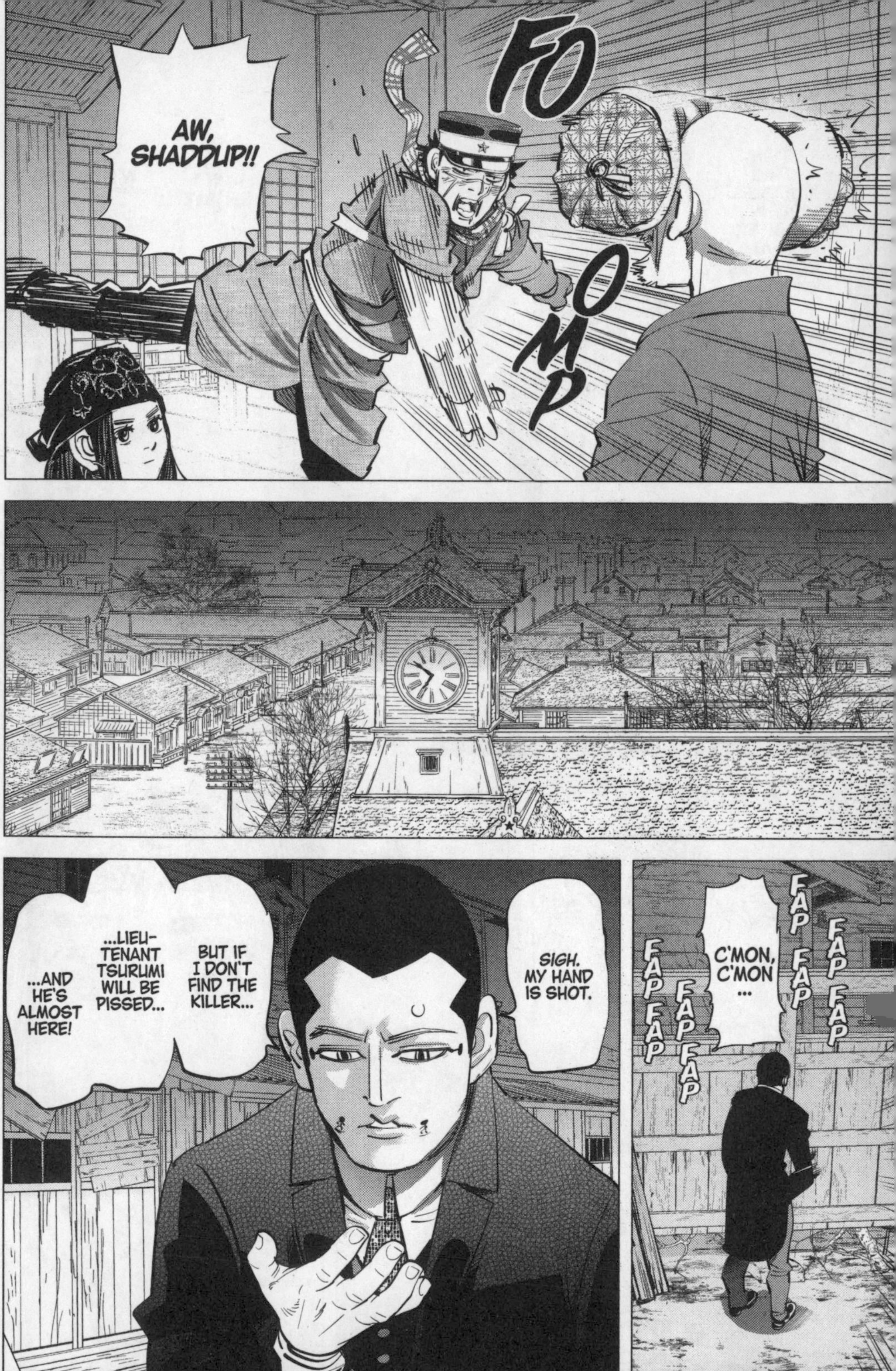
AW, SHADDUP!!
FOOMP
FAP FAP FAP FAP FAP FAP FAP FAP FAP FAP FAP
C'MON, C'MON ...
SIGH. MY HAND IS SHOT.
BUT IF I DON'T FIND THE KILLER...
...LIEU-TENANT TSURUMI WILL BE PISSED...
...AND HE'S ALMOST HERE!

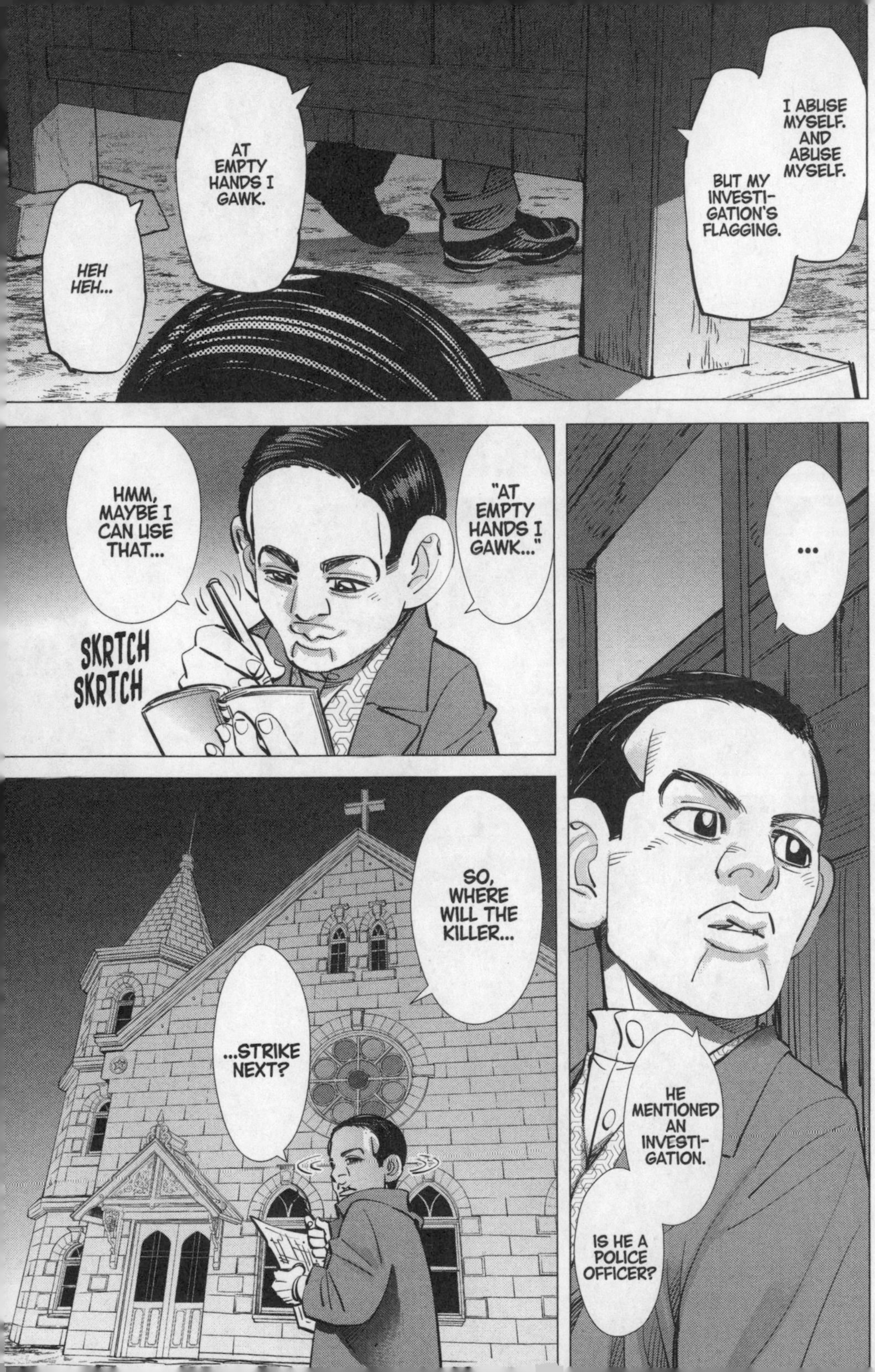
I ABUSE MYSELF. AND ABUSE MYSELF.
BUT MY INVESTIGATION'S FLAGGING.
AT EMPTY HANDS I GAWK.
HEH HEH...
...
HE MENTIONED AN INVESTIGATION.
IS HE A POLICE OFFICER?
"AT EMPTY HANDS I GAWK..."
HMM, MAYBE I CAN USE THAT...
SKRTCH SKRTCH
SO, WHERE WILL THE KILLER...
...STRIKE NEXT?

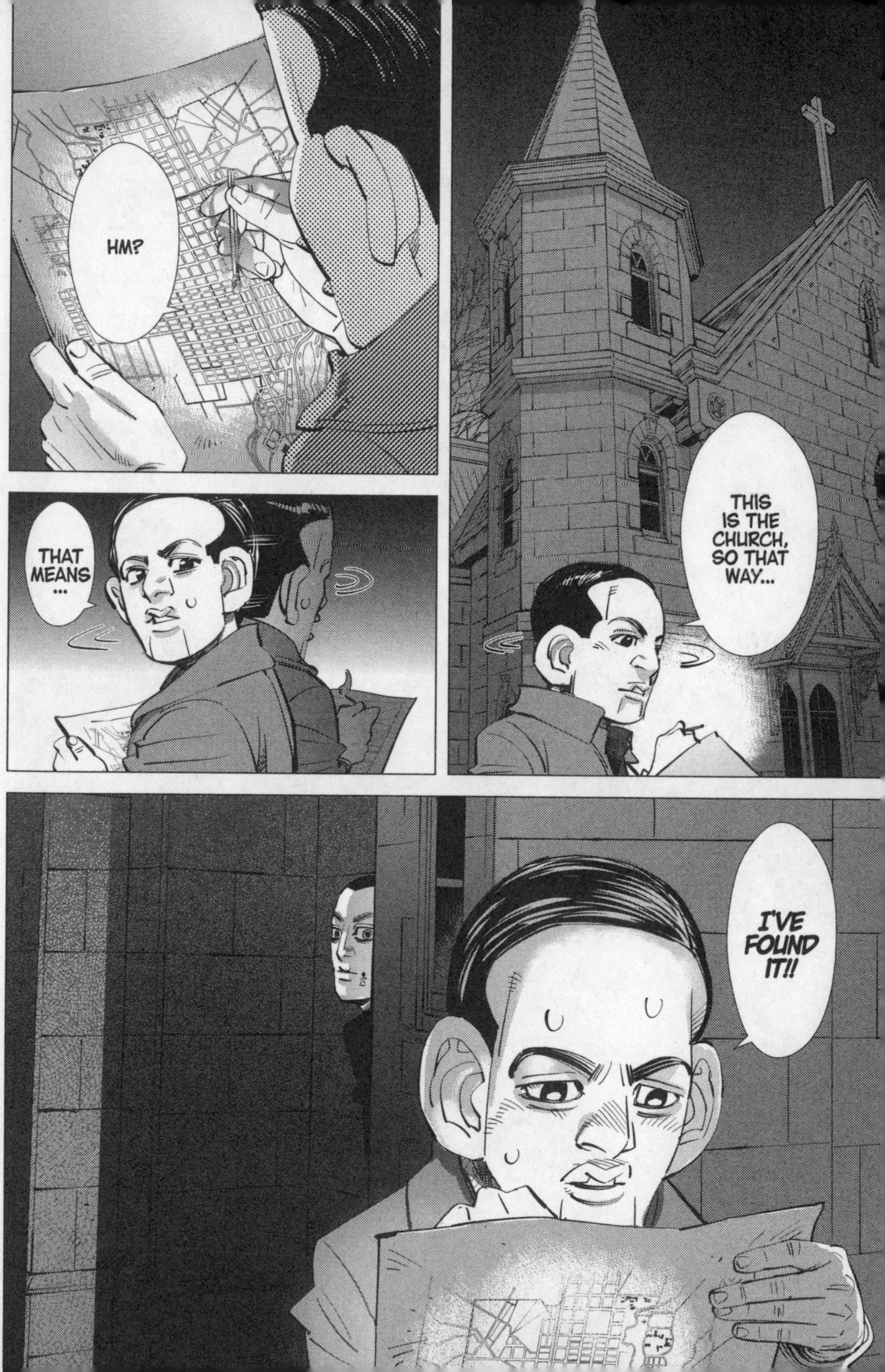
THIS IS THE CHURCH, SO THAT WAY...
HM?
THAT MEANS ...
I'VE FOUND IT!!

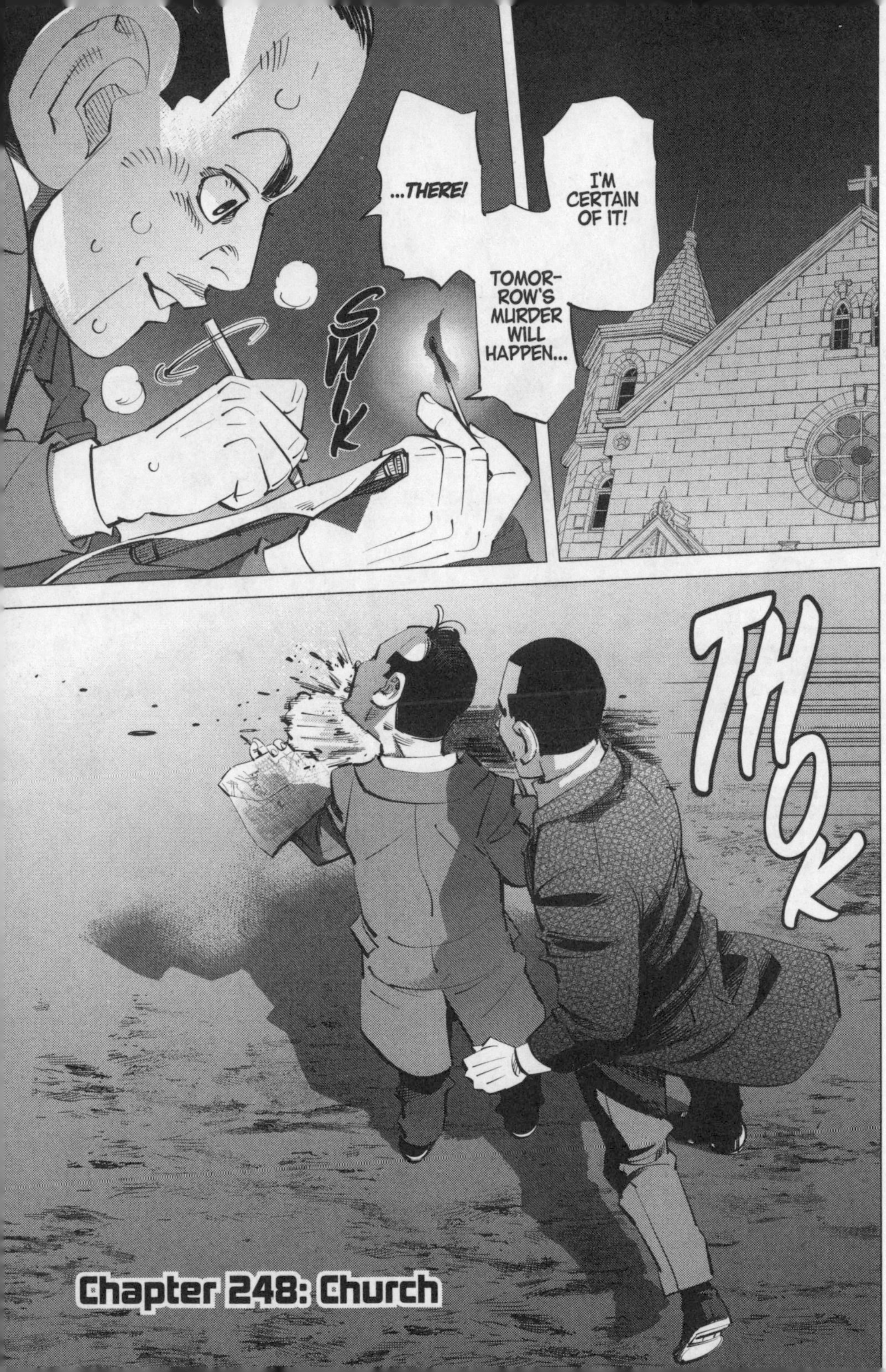
I'M CERTAIN OF IT!
TOMOR-ROW'S MURDER WILL HAPPEN...
...THERE!
SWIK
THOK

Chapter 248: Church

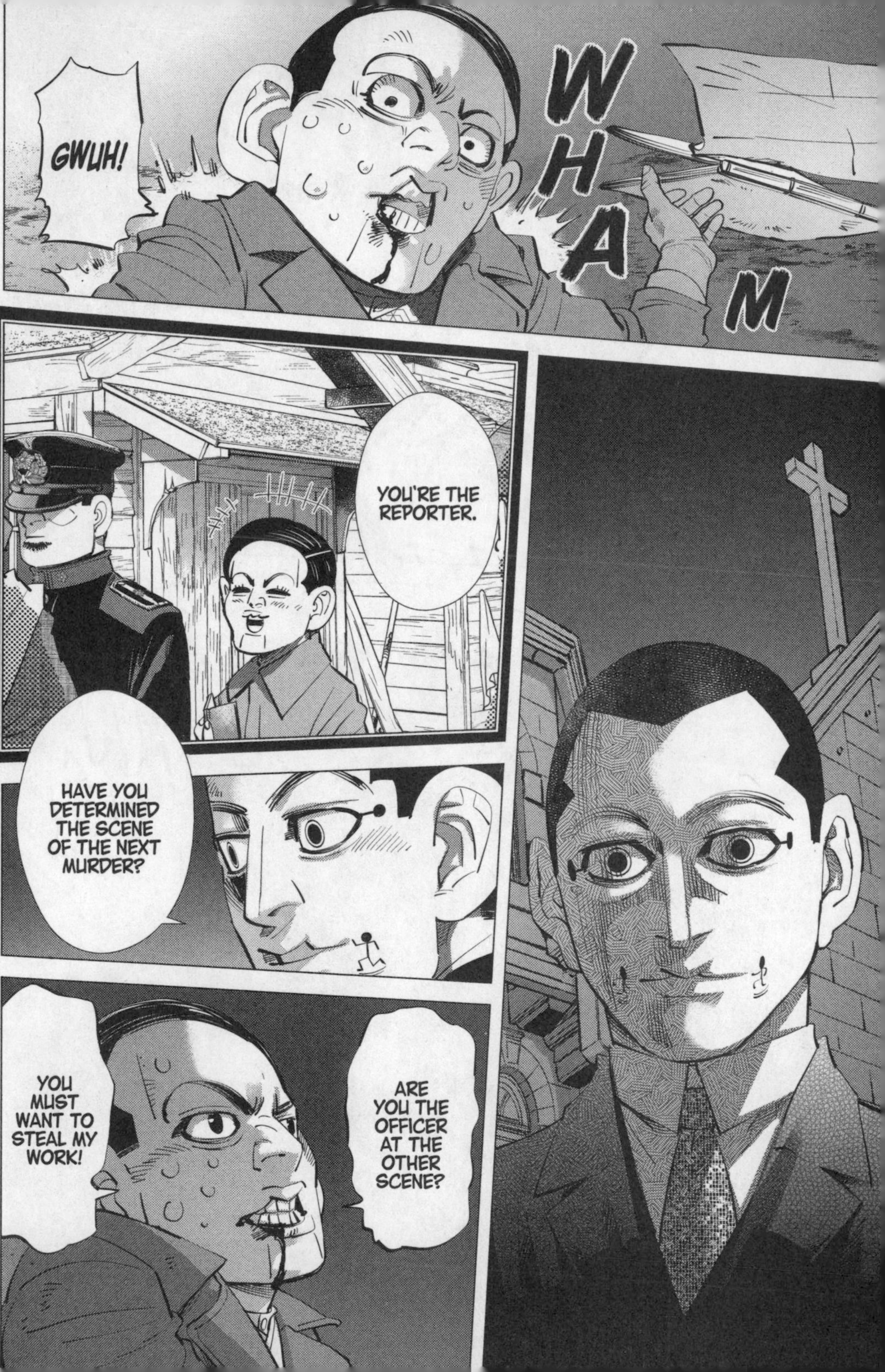
WHAM
GWUH!
YOU'RE THE REPORTER.
HAVE YOU DETERMINED THE SCENE OF THE NEXT MURDER?
ARE YOU THE OFFICER AT THE OTHER SCENE?
YOU MUST WANT TO STEAL MY WORK!

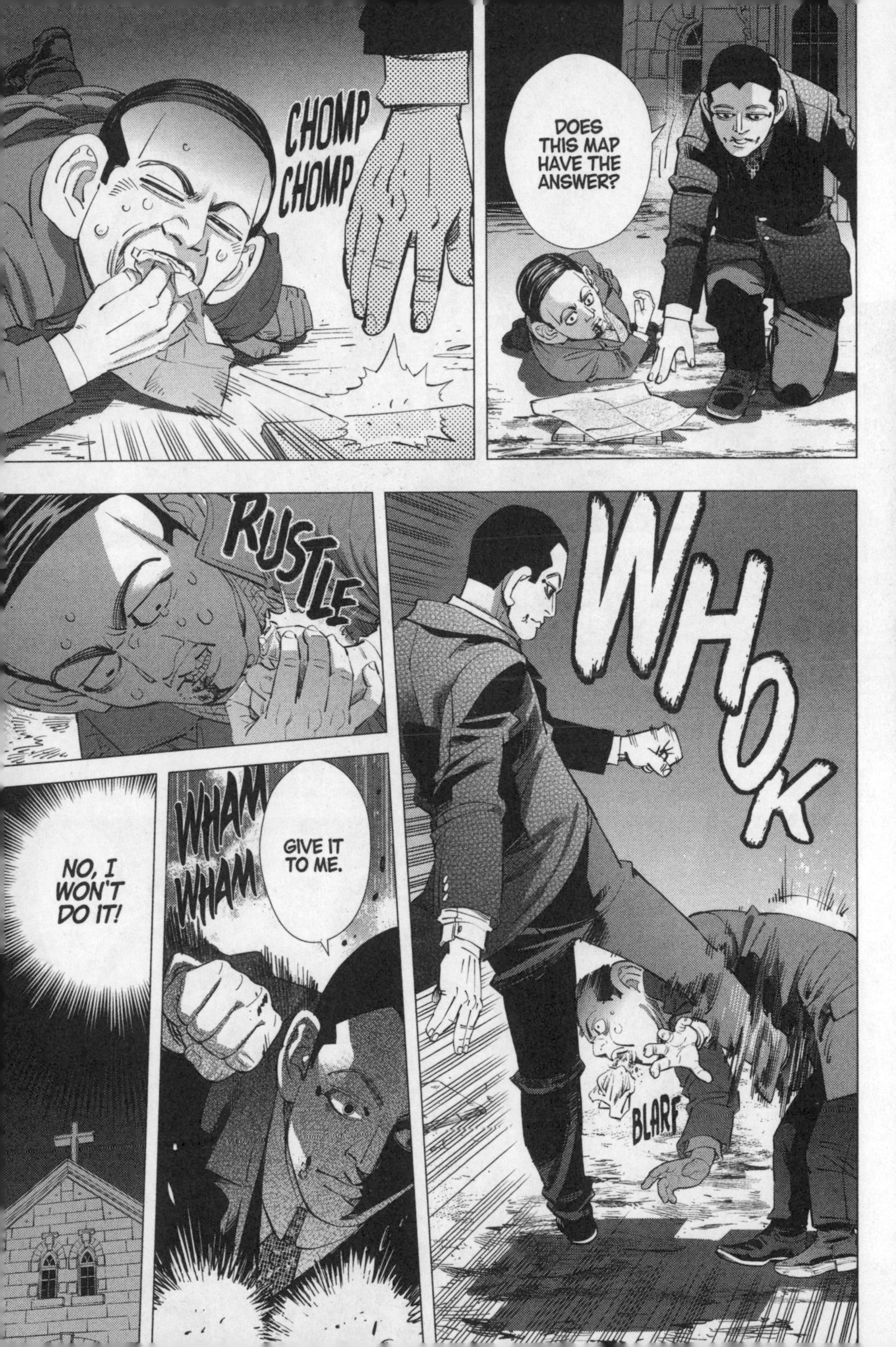
DOES THIS MAP HAVE THE ANSWER?
CHOMP CHOMP
WHOK
BLARF
RUSTLE
WHAM WHAM
GIVE IT TO ME.
NO, I WON'T DO IT!

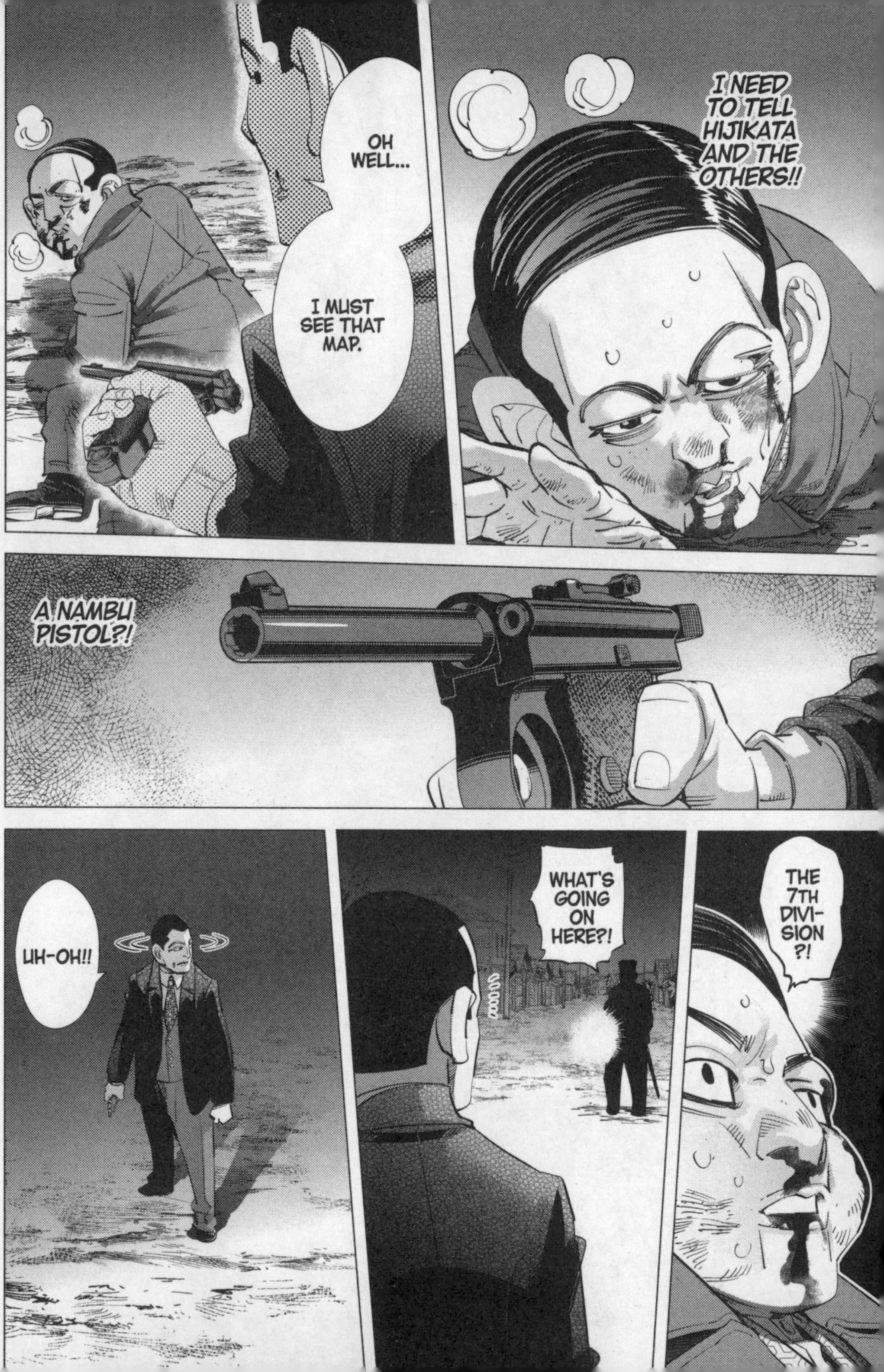
I NEED TO TELL HIJIKATA AND THE OTHERS!!
OH WELL...
I MUST SEE THAT MAP.
A NAMBU PISTOL?!
THE 7TH DIVI-SION ?!
WHAT'S GOING ON HERE?!
UH-OH!!

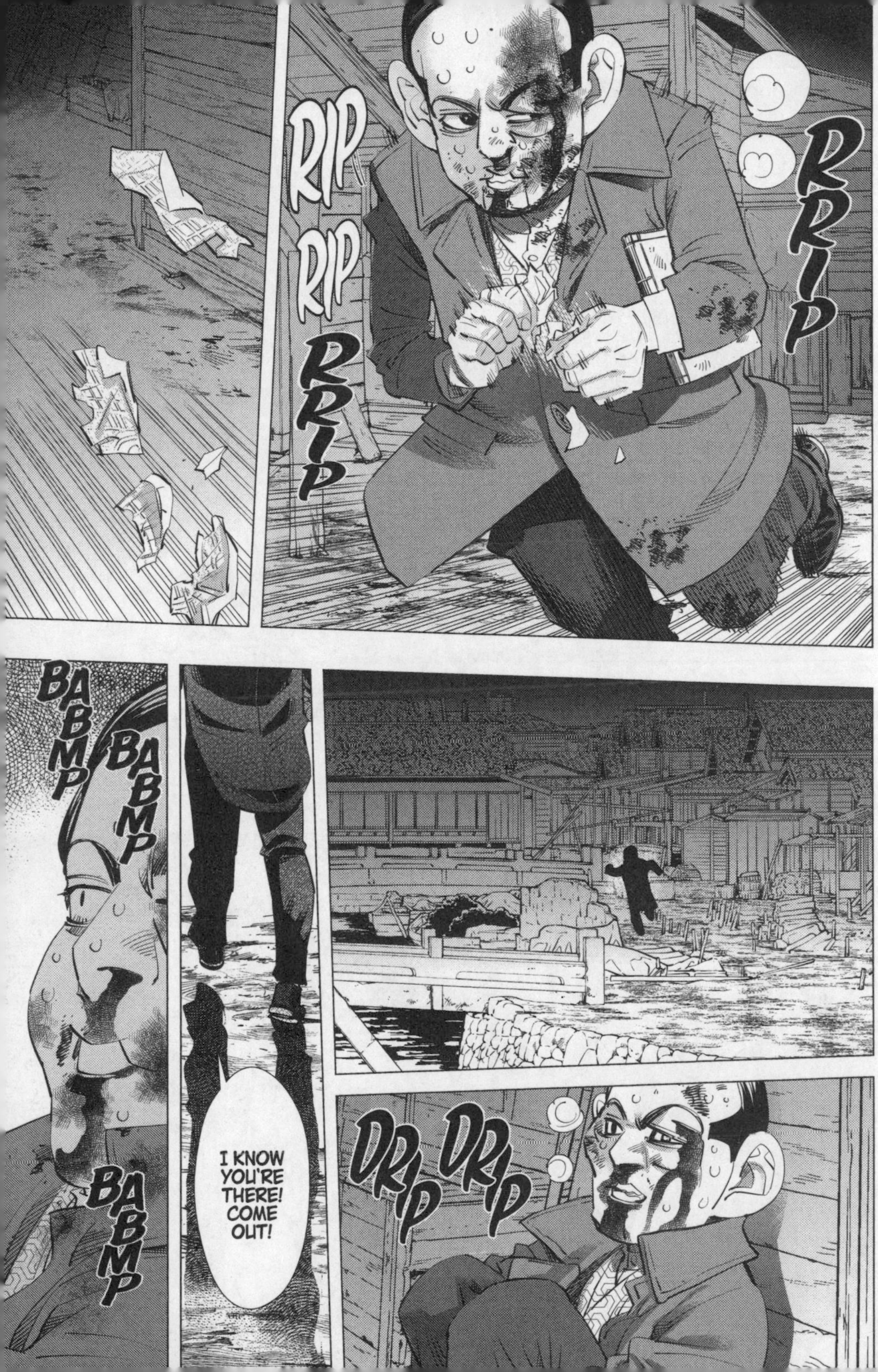
RRIP
RIP
RIP
RRIP
DRIP
DRIP
I KNOW YOU'RE THERE! COME OUT!
BABMP
BABMP
BABMP

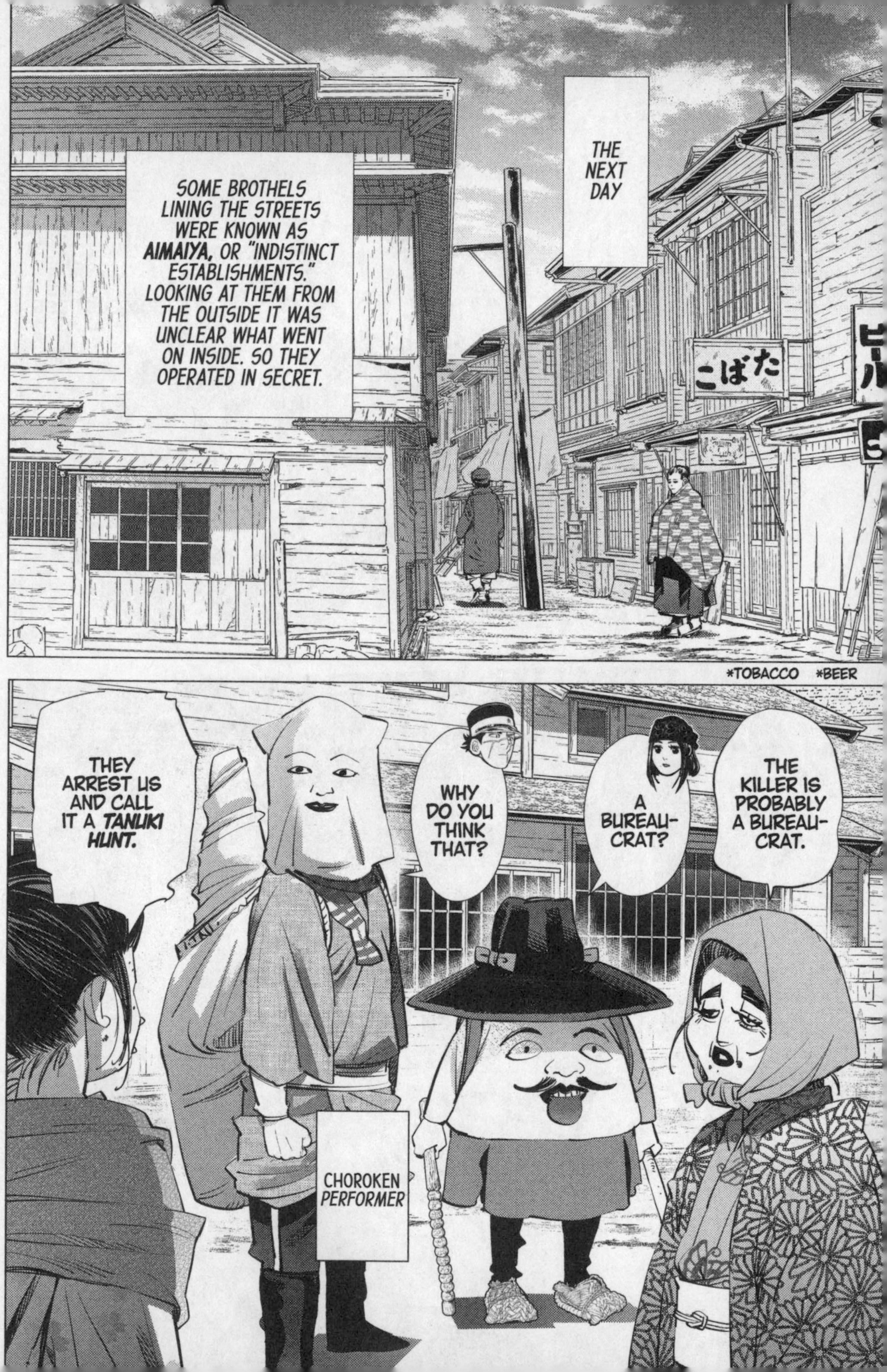
THE NEXT DAY
SOME BROTHELS LINING THE STREETS WERE KNOWN AS AIMAIYA, OR "INDISTINCT ESTABLISHMENTS." LOOKING AT THEM FROM THE OUTSIDE IT WAS UNCLEAR WHAT WENT ON INSIDE. SO THEY OPERATED IN SECRET.
こばた
*TOBACCO *BEER
THE KILLER IS PROBABLY A BUREAU-CRAT.
A BUREAU-CRAT?
WHY DO YOU THINK THAT?
THEY ARREST US AND CALL IT A TANUKI HUNT.
CHOROKEN PERFORMER

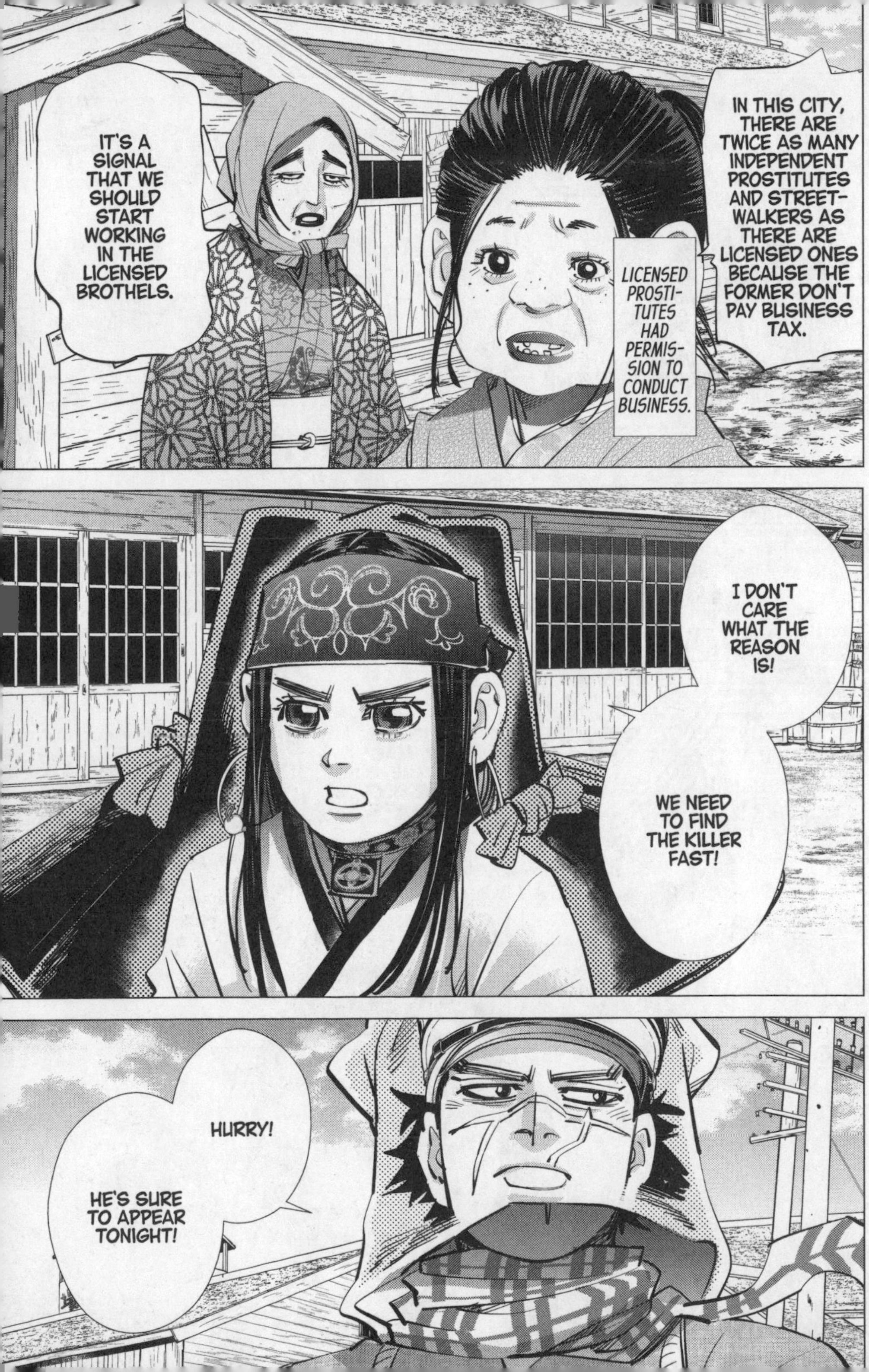
IN THIS CITY, THERE ARE TWICE AS MANY INDEPENDENT PROSTITUTES AND STREET-WALKERS AS THERE ARE LICENSED ONES BECAUSE THE FORMER DON'T PAY BUSINESS TAX.
LICENSED PROSTI-TUTES HAD PERMIS-SION TO CONDUCT BUSINESS.
IT'S A SIGNAL THAT WE SHOULD START WORKING IN THE LICENSED BROTHELS.
I DON'T CARE WHAT THE REASON IS!
WE NEED TO FIND THE KILLER FAST!
HURRY!
HE'S SURE TO APPEAR TONIGHT!

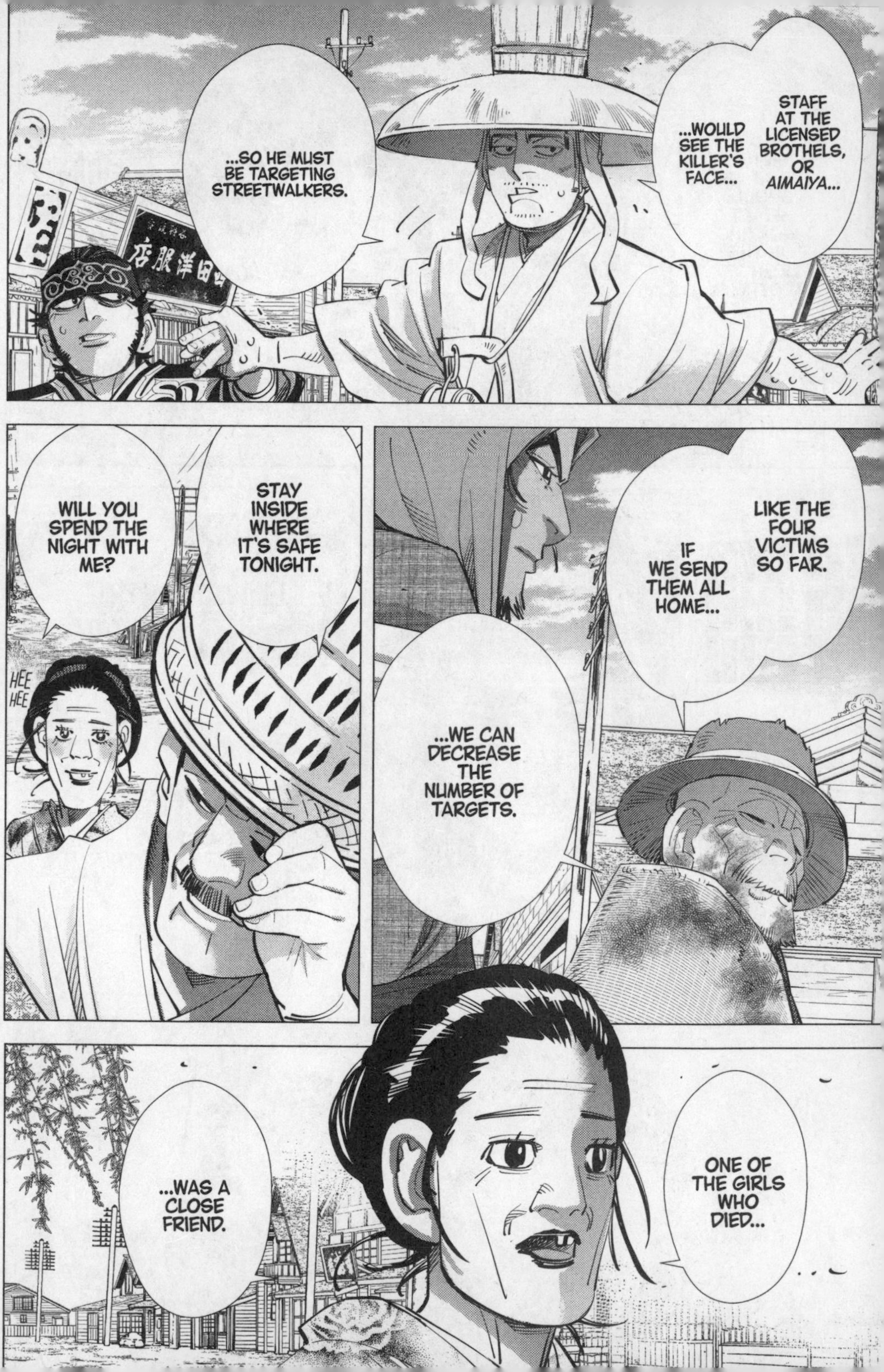
STAFF AT THE LICENSED BROTHELS, OR AIMAIYA...
...WOULD SEE THE KILLER'S FACE...
...SO HE MUST BE TARGETING STREETWALKERS.
山田洋服店
LIKE THE FOUR VICTIMS SO FAR.
IF WE SEND THEM ALL HOME...
...WE CAN DECREASE THE NUMBER OF TARGETS.
STAY INSIDE WHERE IT'S SAFE TONIGHT.
WILL YOU SPEND THE NIGHT WITH ME?
HEE HEE
ONE OF THE GIRLS WHO DIED...
...WAS A CLOSE FRIEND.

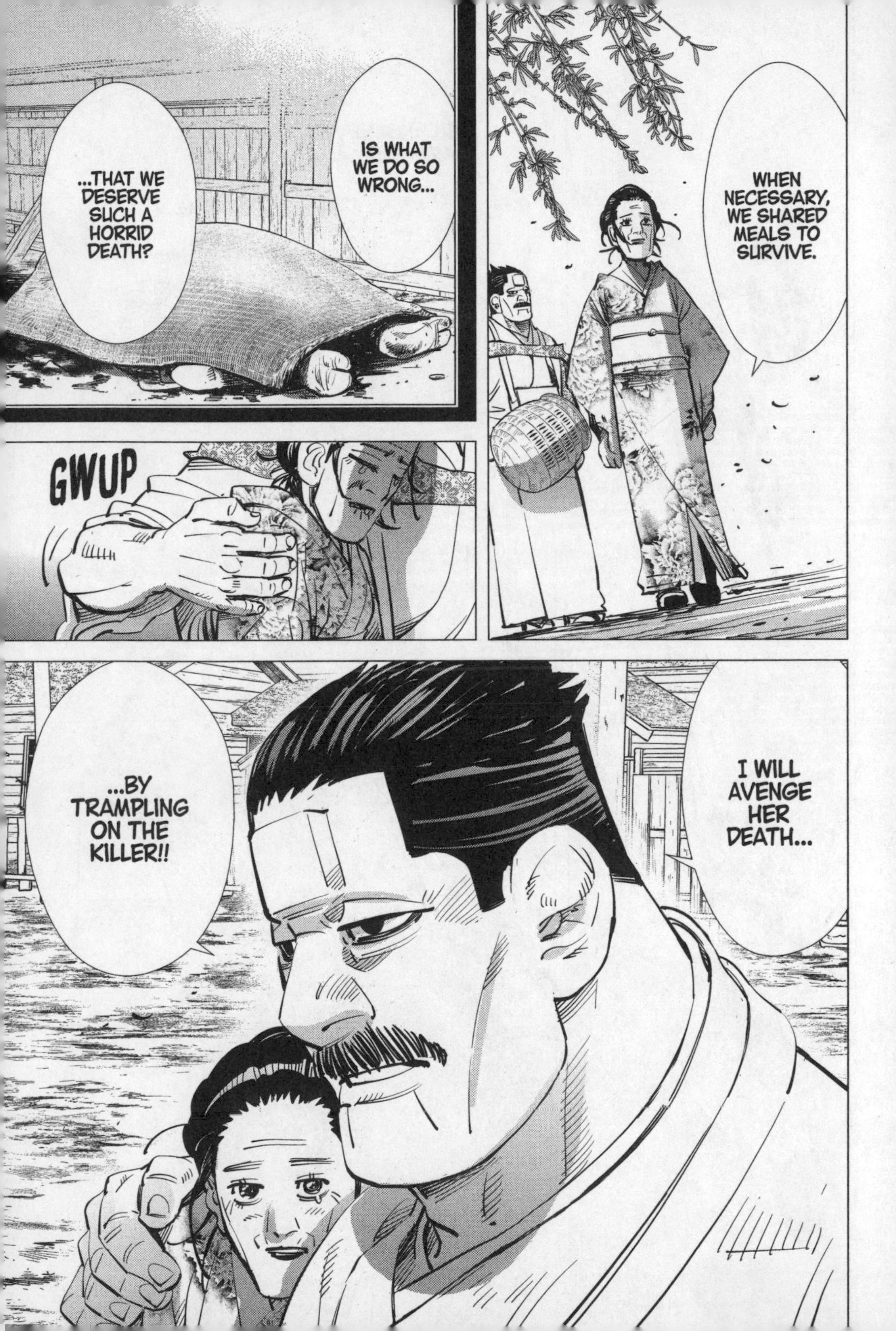
WHEN NECESSARY, WE SHARED MEALS TO SURVIVE.
IS WHAT WE DO SO WRONG...
...THAT WE DESERVE SUCH A HORRID DEATH?
GWUP
I WILL AVENGE HER DEATH...
...BY TRAMPLING ON THE KILLER!!

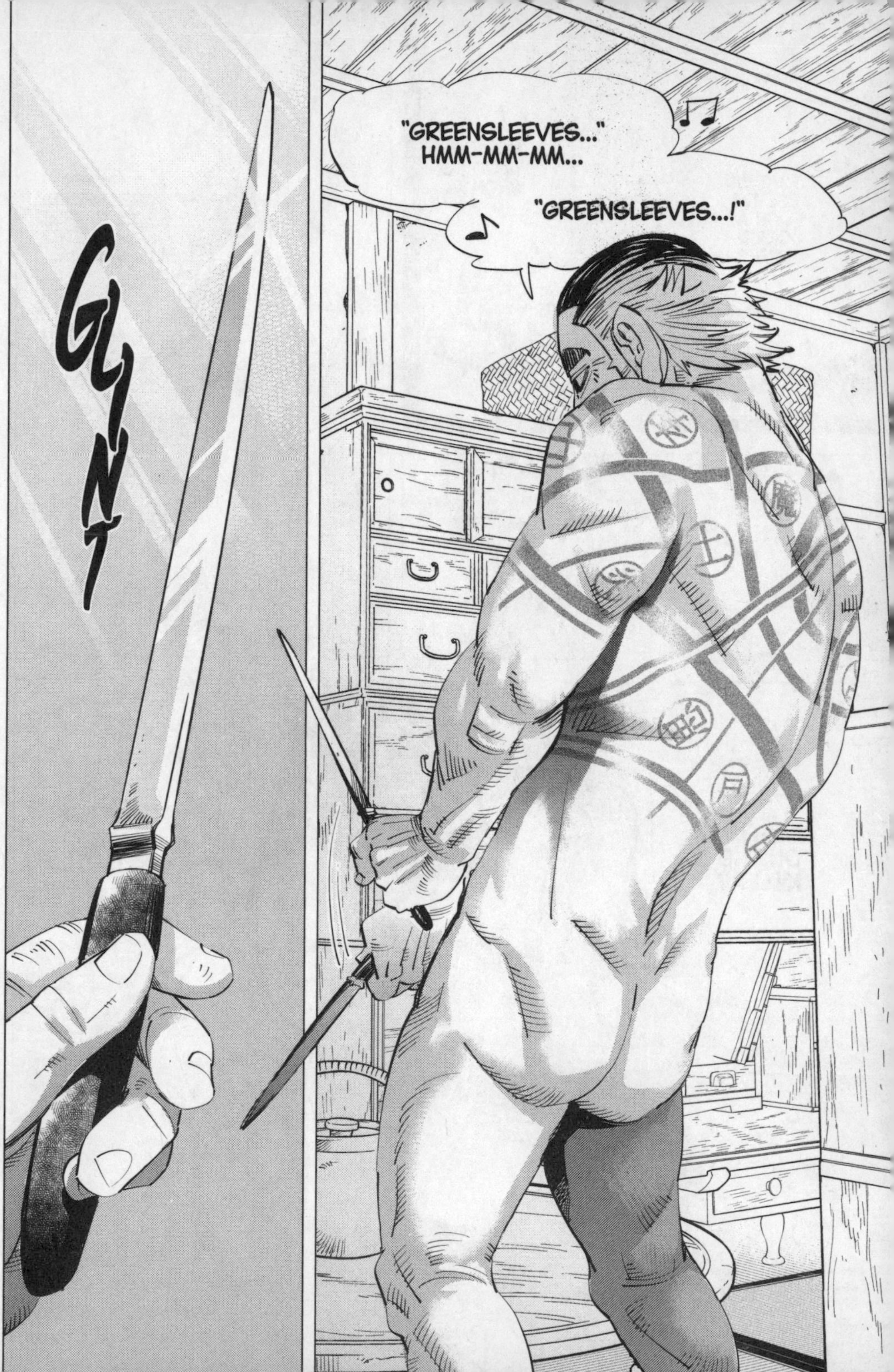
"GREENSLEEVES..." HMM-MM-MM... "GREENSLEEVES...!"
GLINT

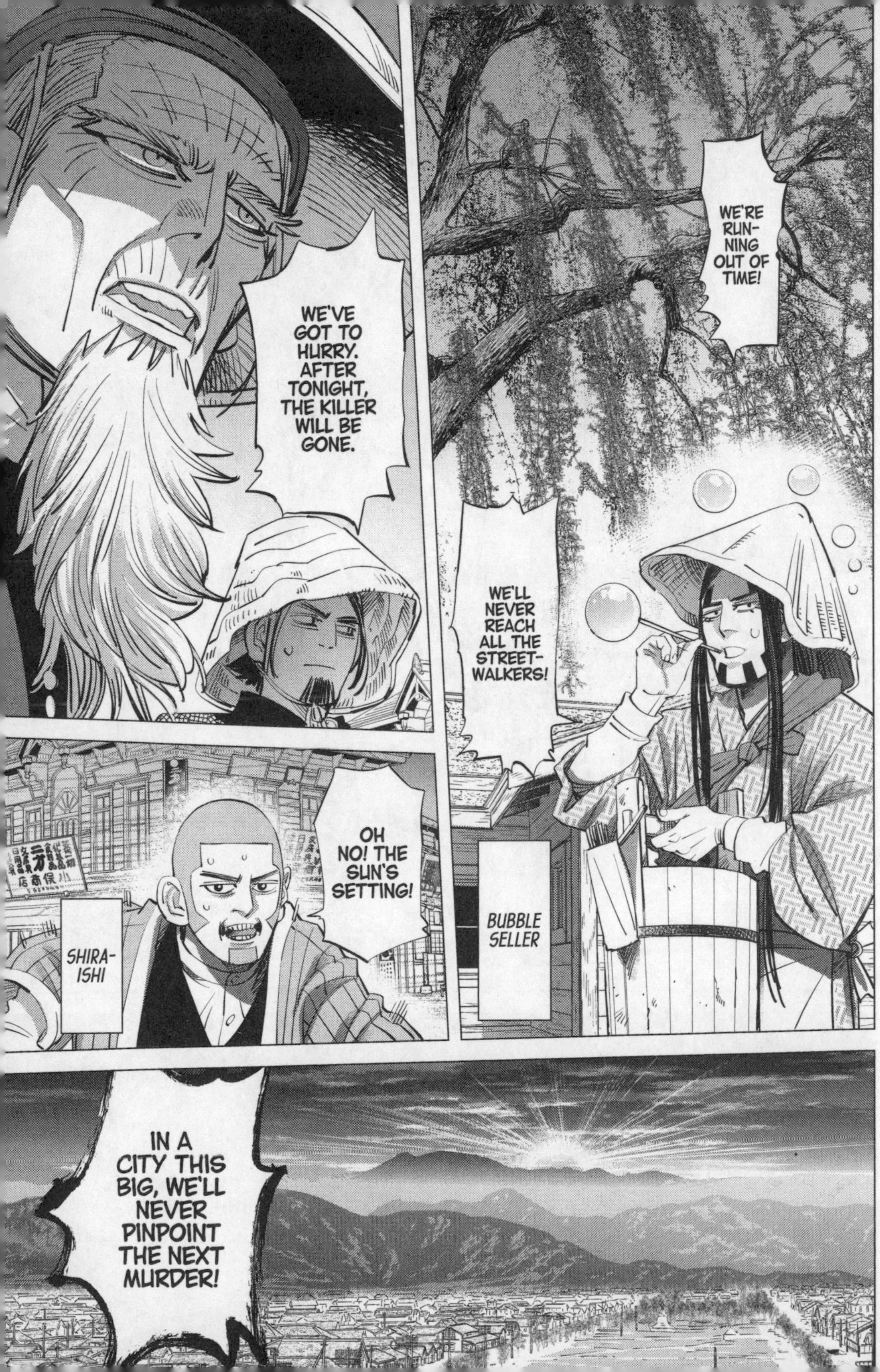
WE'RE RUNNING OUT OF TIME!
WE'LL NEVER REACH ALL THE STREETWALKERS!
BUBBLE SELLER
WE'VE GOT TO HURRY. AFTER TONIGHT, THE KILLER WILL BE GONE.
OH NO! THE SUN'S SETTING!
SHIRAISHI
IN A CITY THIS BIG, WE'LL NEVER PINPOINT THE NEXT MURDER!

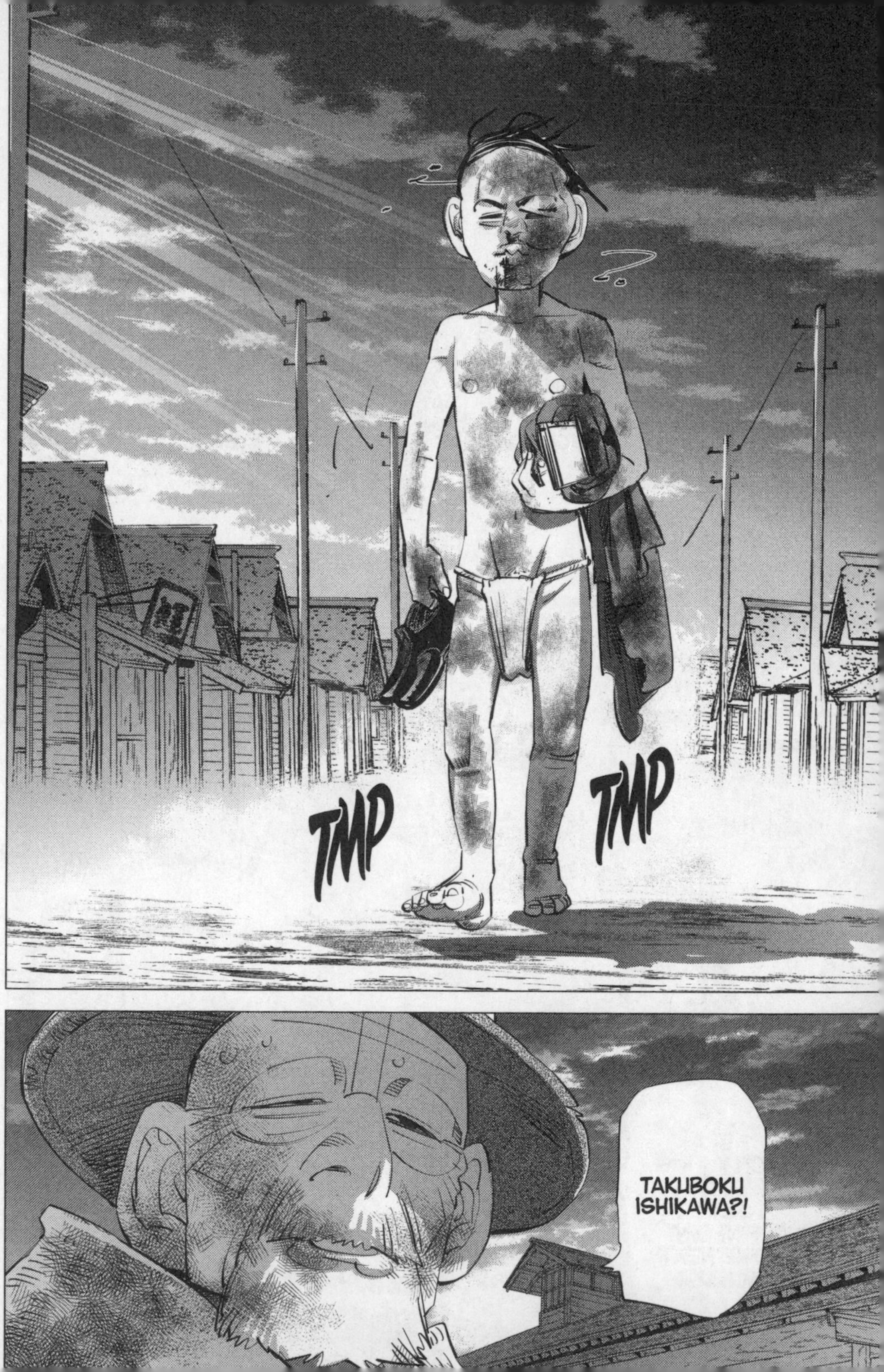
TMP
TMP
TAKUBOKU ISHIKAWA?!

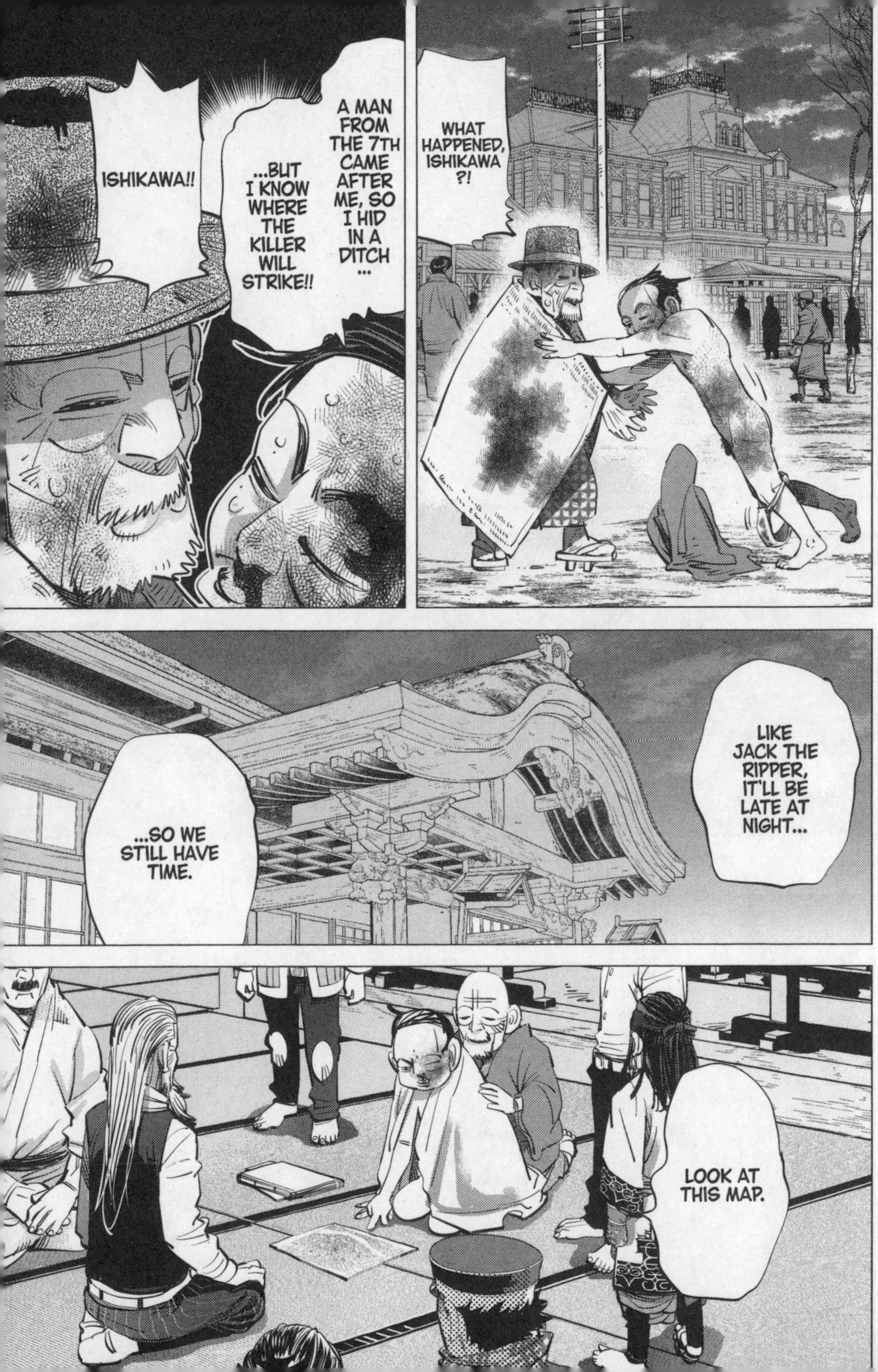
WHAT HAPPENED, ISHIKAWA?!
A MAN FROM THE 7TH CAME AFTER ME, SO I HID IN A DITCH...
...BUT I KNOW WHERE THE KILLER WILL STRIKE!!
ISHIKAWA!!
LIKE JACK THE RIPPER, IT'LL BE LATE AT NIGHT...
...SO WE STILL HAVE TIME.
LOOK AT THIS MAP.

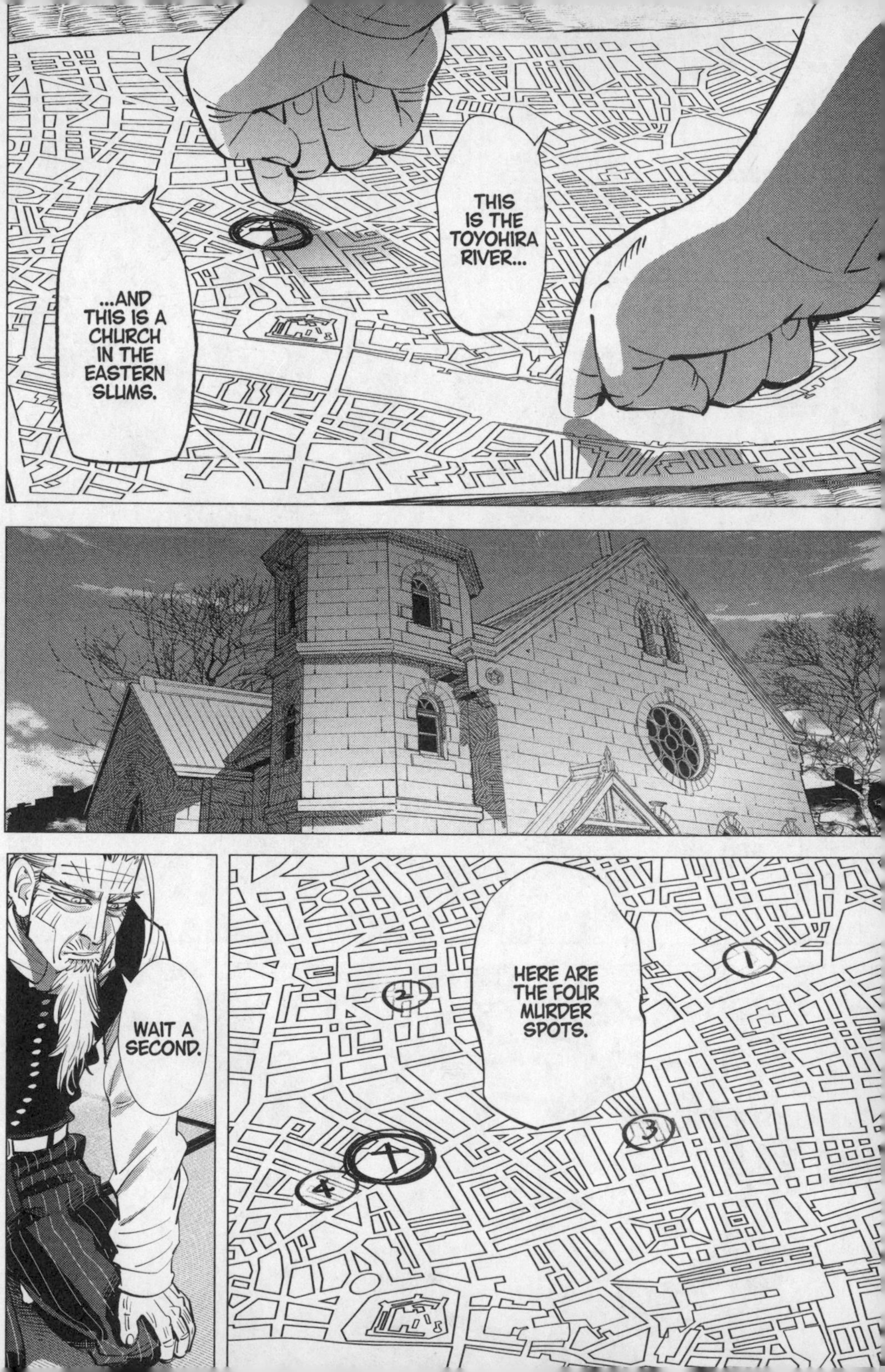
THIS IS THE TOYOHIRA RIVER...
...AND THIS IS A CHURCH IN THE EASTERN SLUMS.
HERE ARE THE FOUR MURDER SPOTS.
WAIT A SECOND.

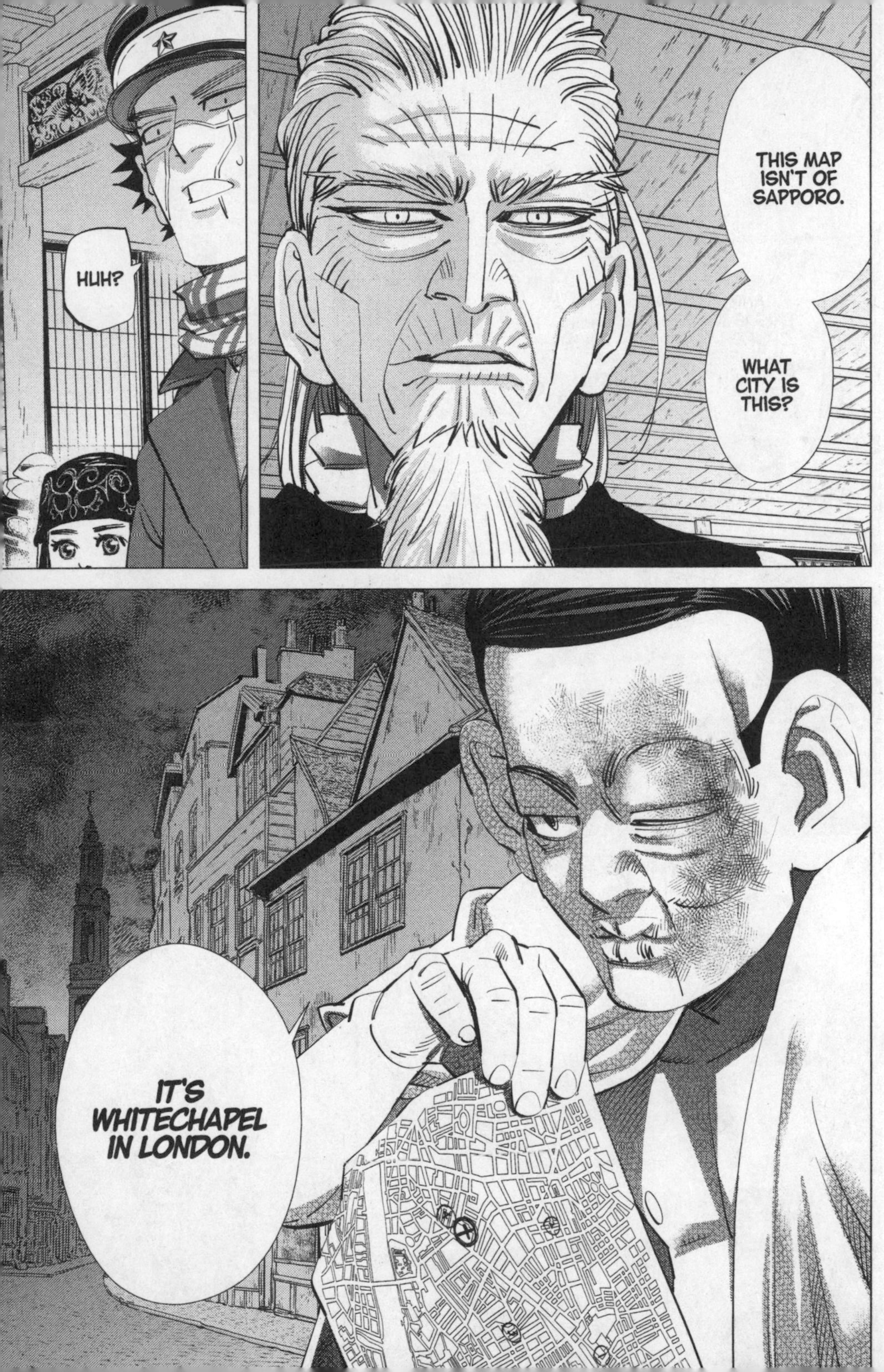
THIS MAP ISN'T OF SAPPORO.
WHAT CITY IS THIS?
HUH?
IT'S WHITECHAPEL IN LONDON.

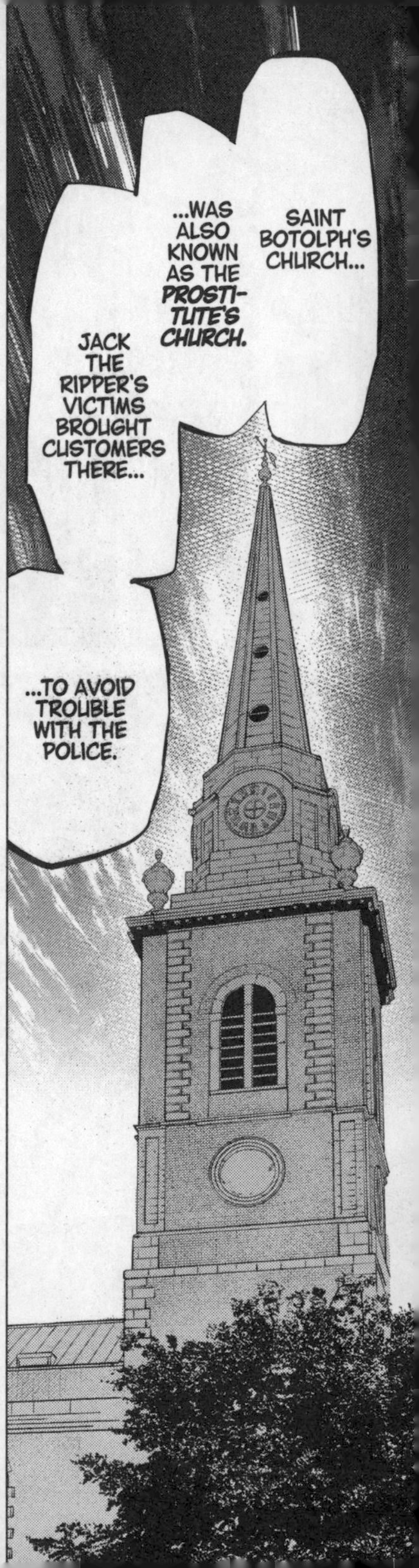
SAINT BOTOLPH'S CHURCH...
...WAS ALSO KNOWN AS THE PROSTITUTE'S CHURCH.
JACK THE RIPPER'S VICTIMS BROUGHT CUSTOMERS THERE...
...TO AVOID TROUBLE WITH THE POLICE.
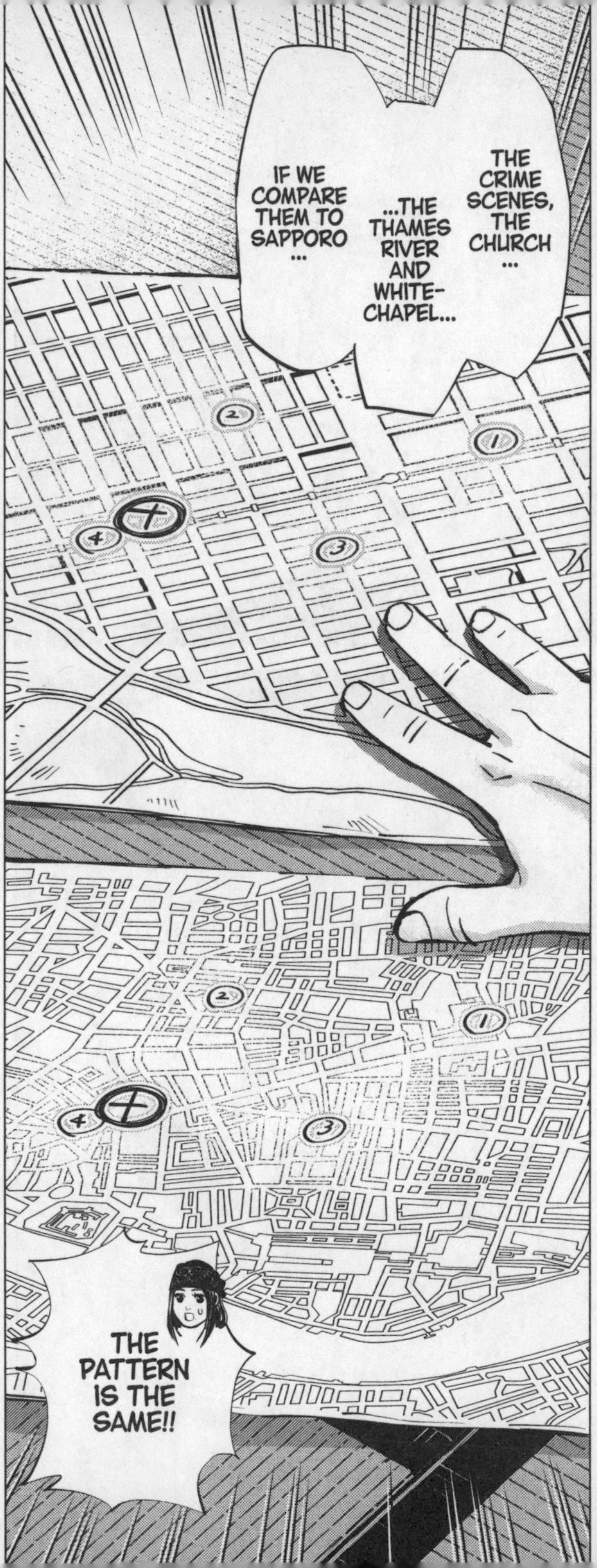
THE CRIME SCENES, THE CHURCH...
...THE THAMES RIVER AND WHITE-CHAPEL...
IF WE COMPARE THEM TO SAPPORO...
THE PATTERN IS THE SAME!!

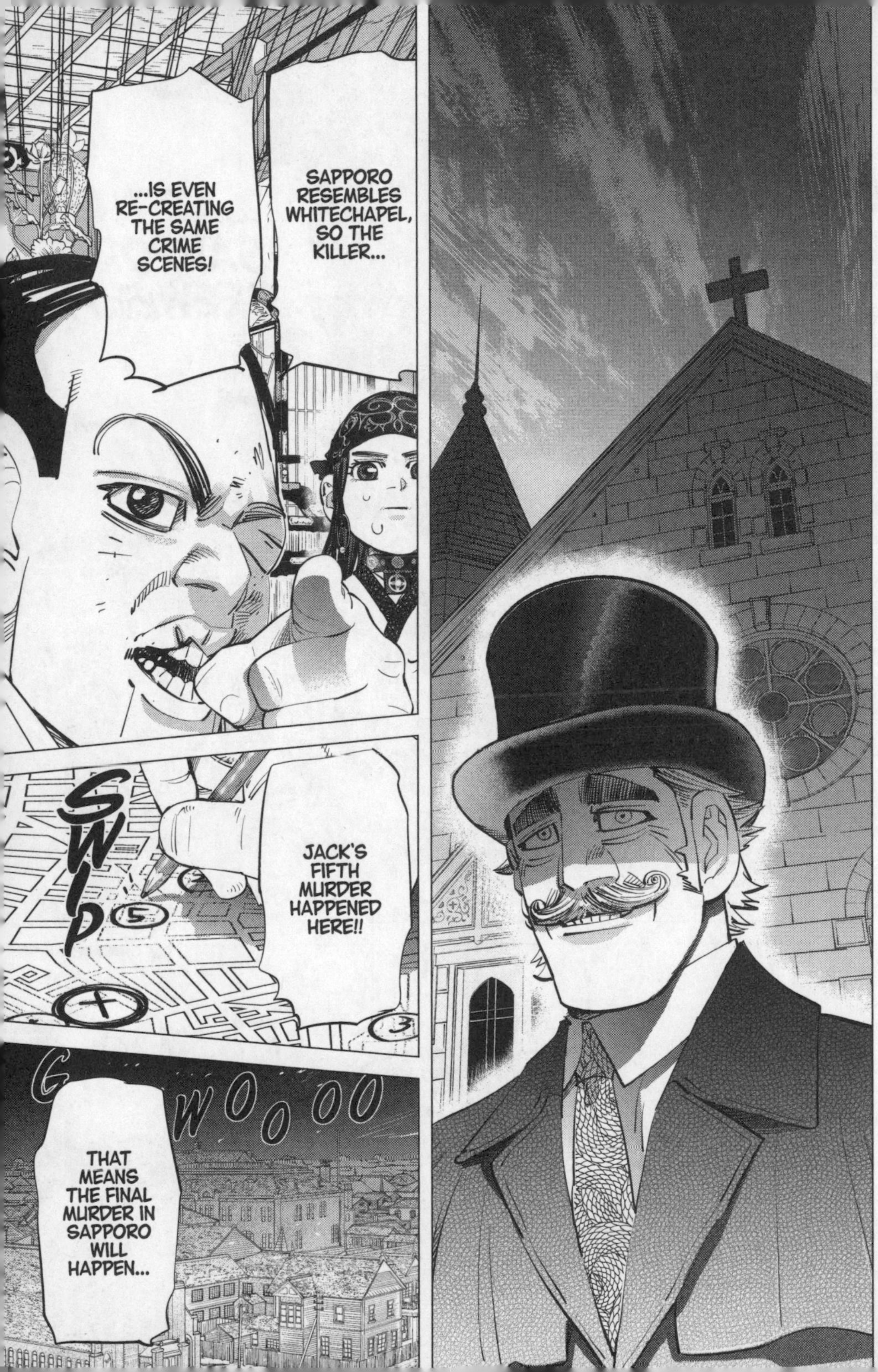
SAPPORO RESEMBLES WHITECHAPEL, SO THE KILLER...
...IS EVEN RE-CREATING THE SAME CRIME SCENES!
SWIP
JACK'S FIFTH MURDER HAPPENED HERE!!
GWOOOOO
THAT MEANS THE FINAL MURDER IN SAPPORO WILL HAPPEN...

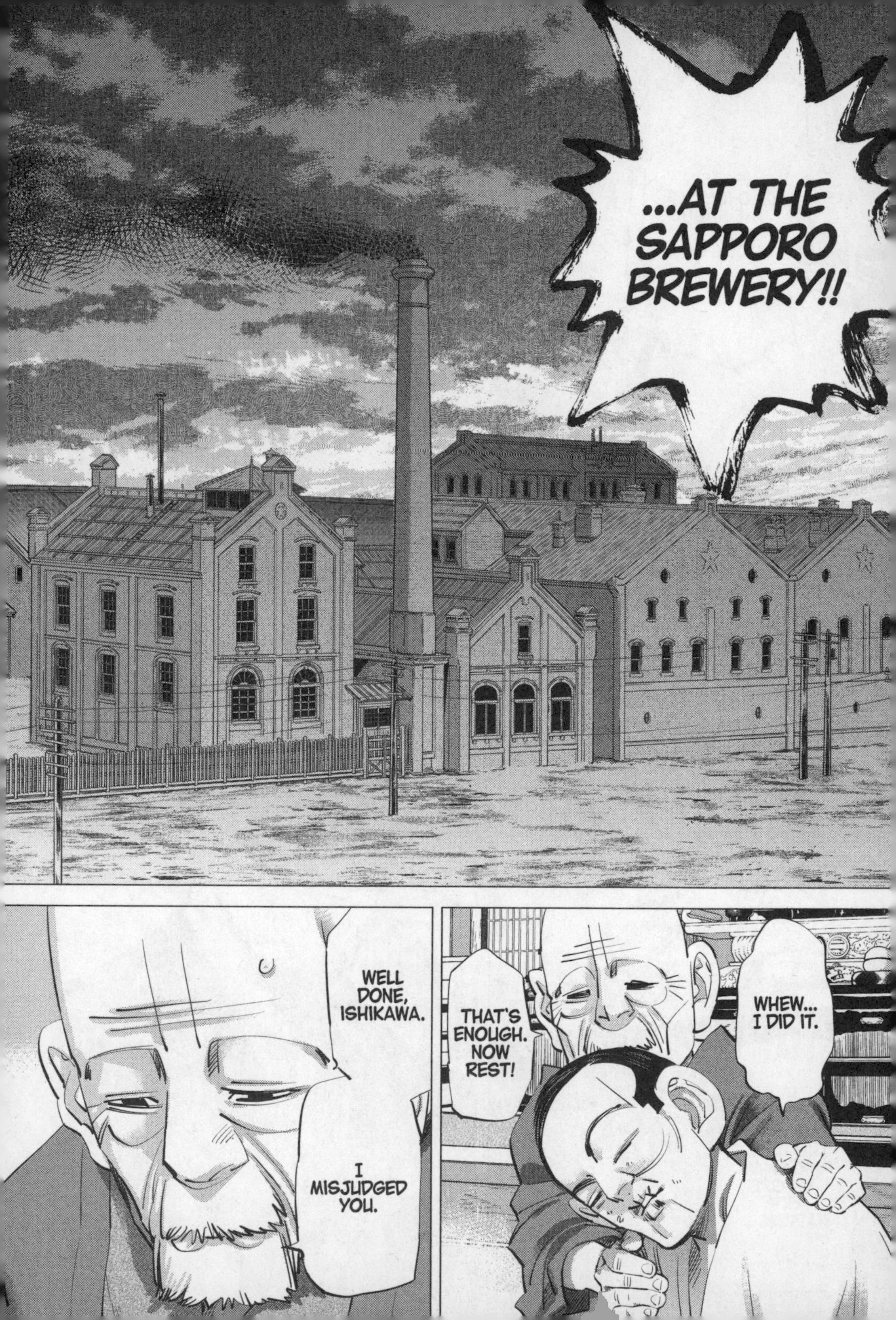
...AT THE SAPPORO BREWERY!!
WHEW... I DID IT.
THAT'S ENOUGH. NOW REST!
WELL DONE, ISHIKAWA.
I MISJUDGED YOU.

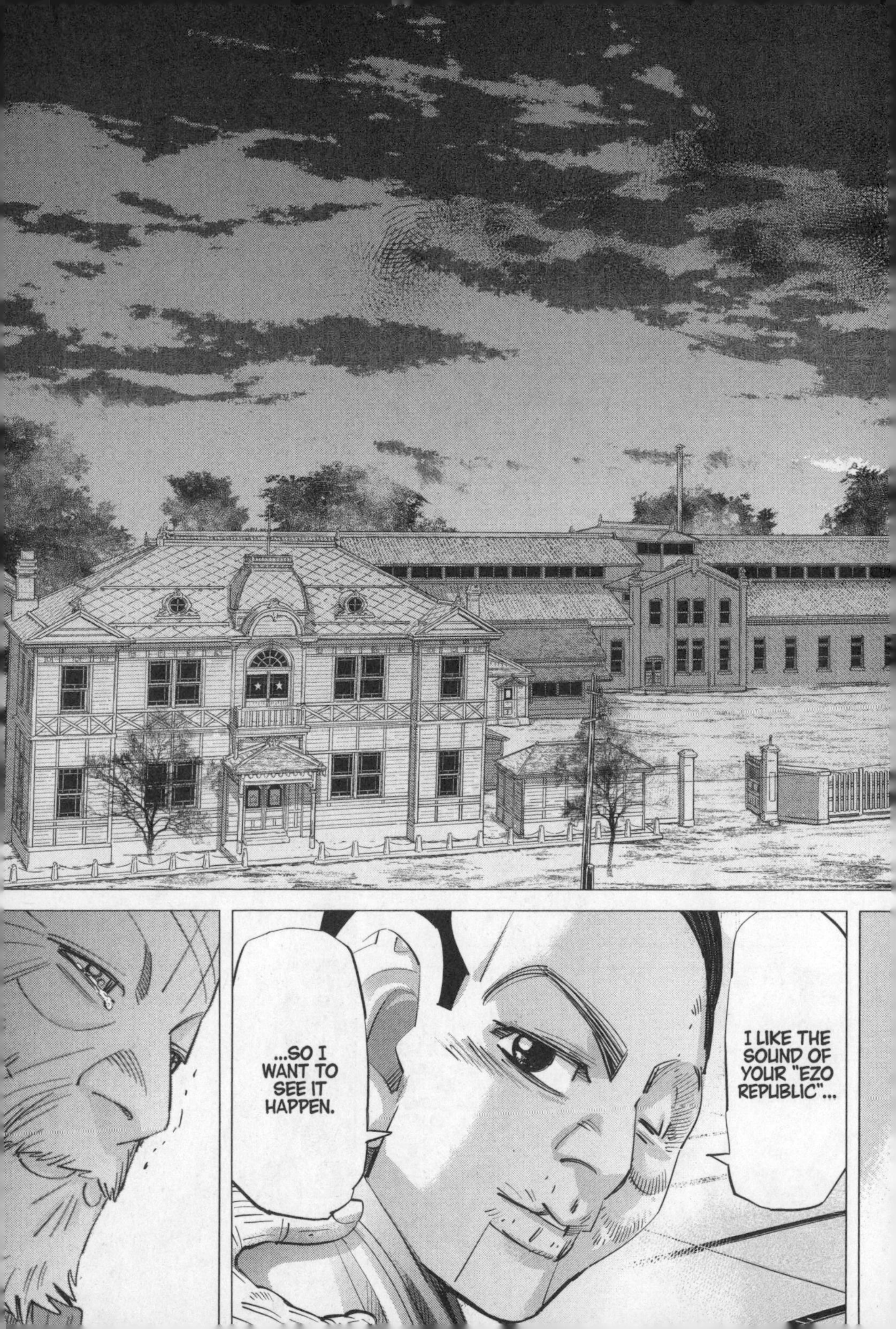
I LIKE THE SOUND OF YOUR "EZO REPUBLIC"...
...SO I WANT TO SEE IT HAPPEN.

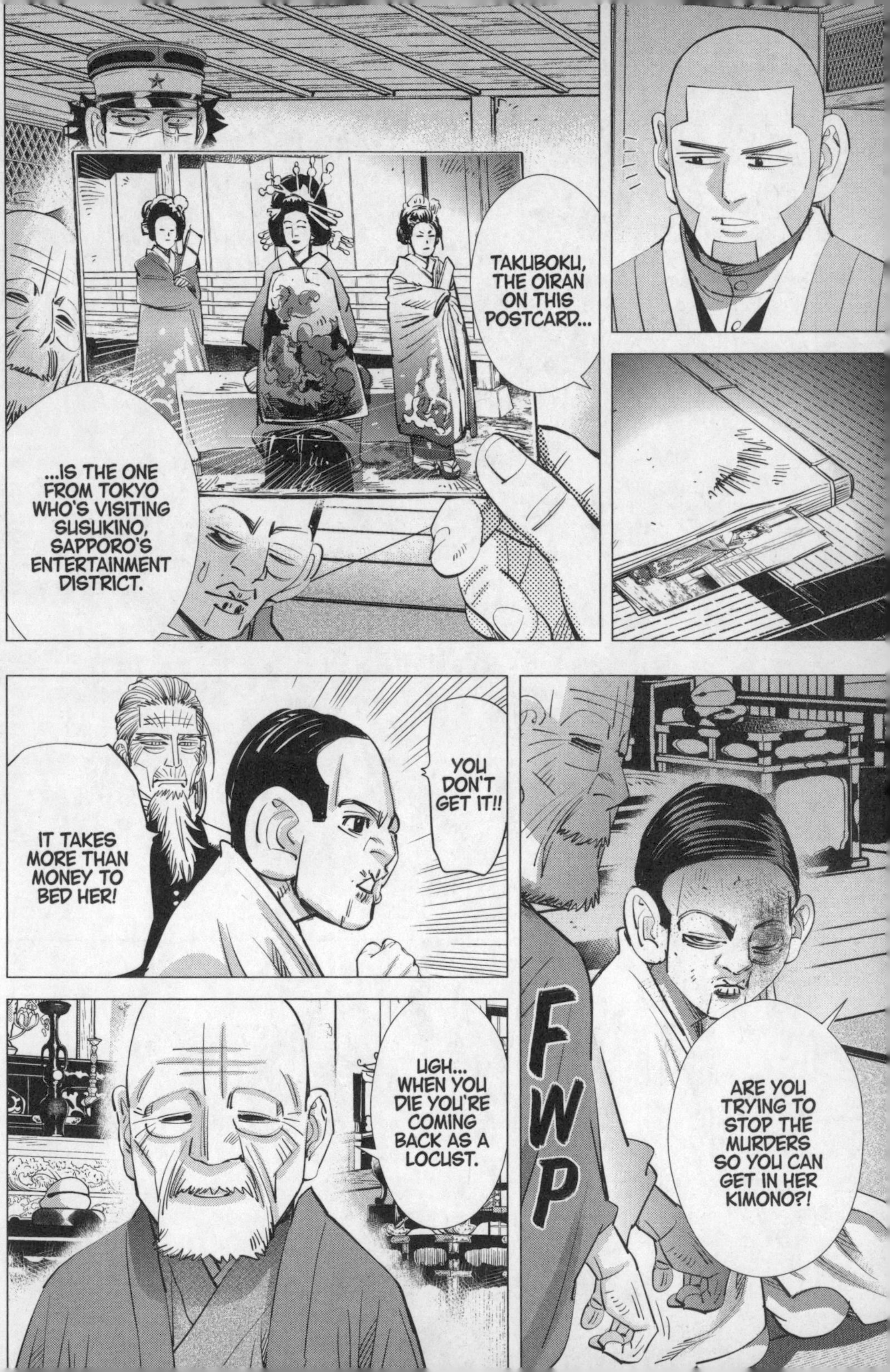
TAKUBOKU, THE OIRAN ON THIS POSTCARD...
...IS THE ONE FROM TOKYO WHO'S VISITING SUSUKINO, SAPPORO'S ENTERTAINMENT DISTRICT.
FWP
ARE YOU TRYING TO STOP THE MURDERS SO YOU CAN GET IN HER KIMONO?!
YOU DON'T GET IT!!
IT TAKES MORE THAN MONEY TO BED HER!
UGH... WHEN YOU DIE YOU'RE COMING BACK AS A LOCUST.

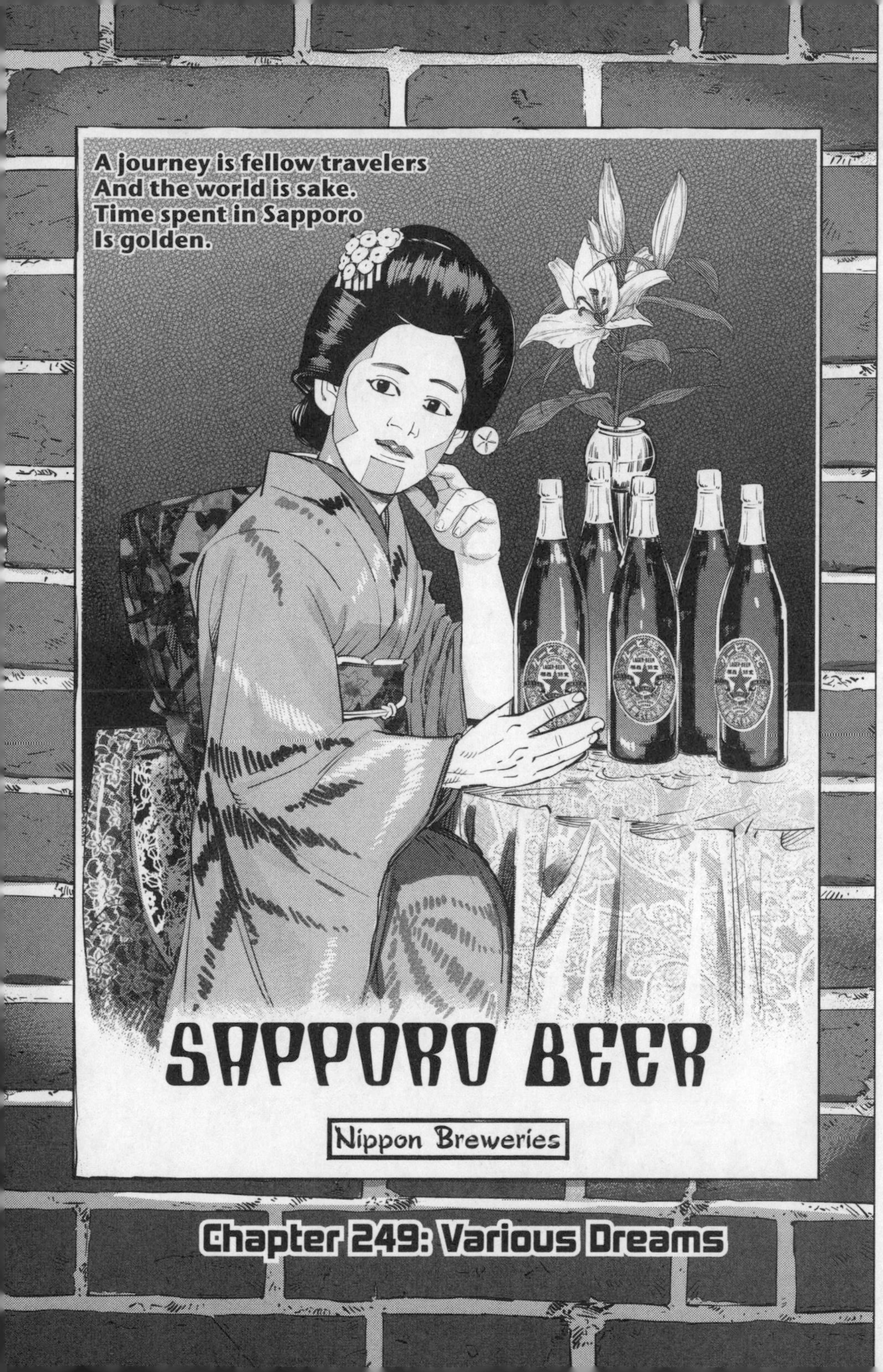

Chapter 249: Various Dreams

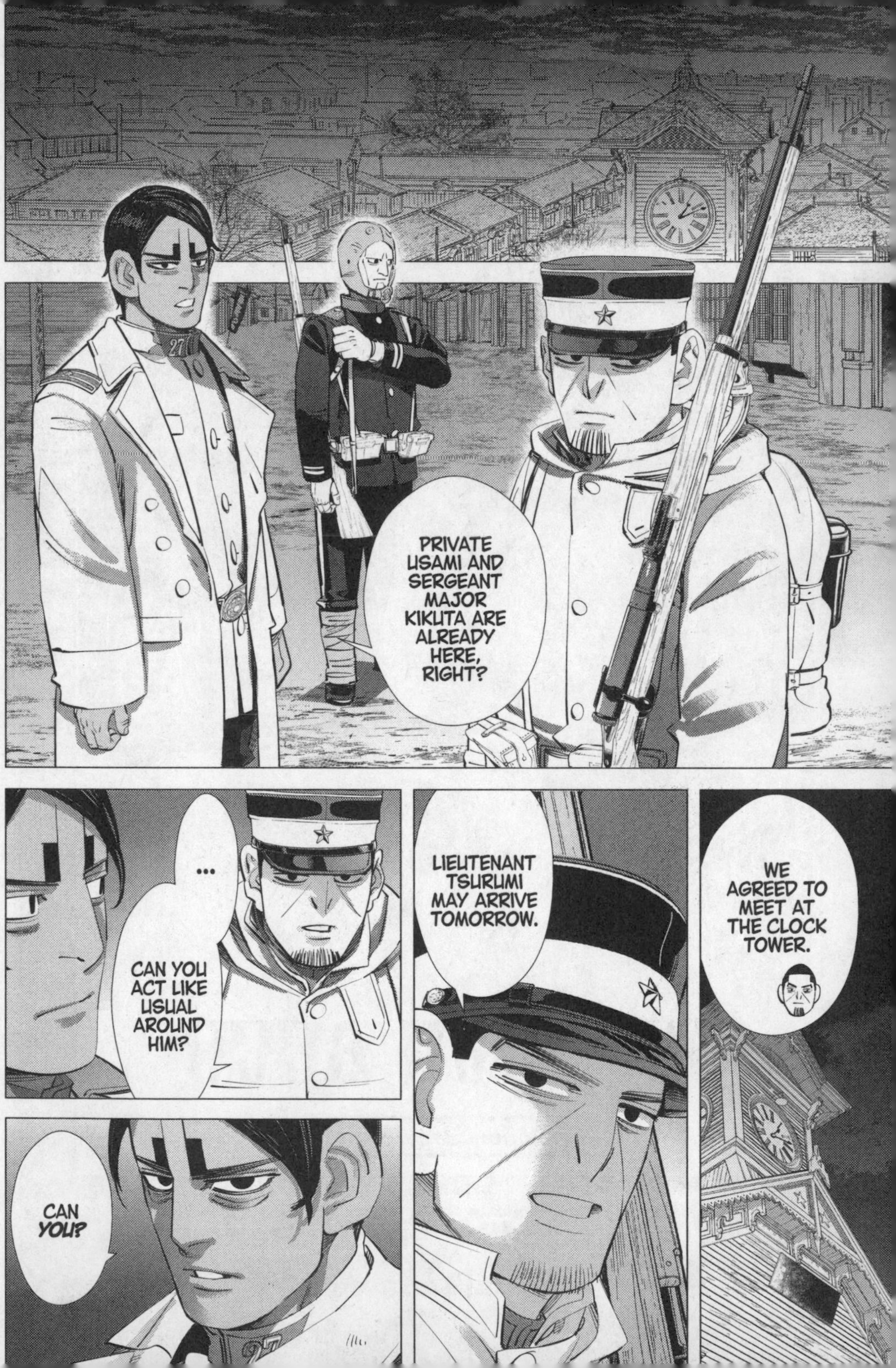
PRIVATE USAMI AND SERGEANT MAJOR KIKUTA ARE ALREADY HERE, RIGHT?
WE AGREED TO MEET AT THE CLOCK TOWER.
LIEUTENANT TSURUMI MAY ARRIVE TOMORROW.
...
CAN YOU ACT LIKE USUAL AROUND HIM?
CAN *YOU?*

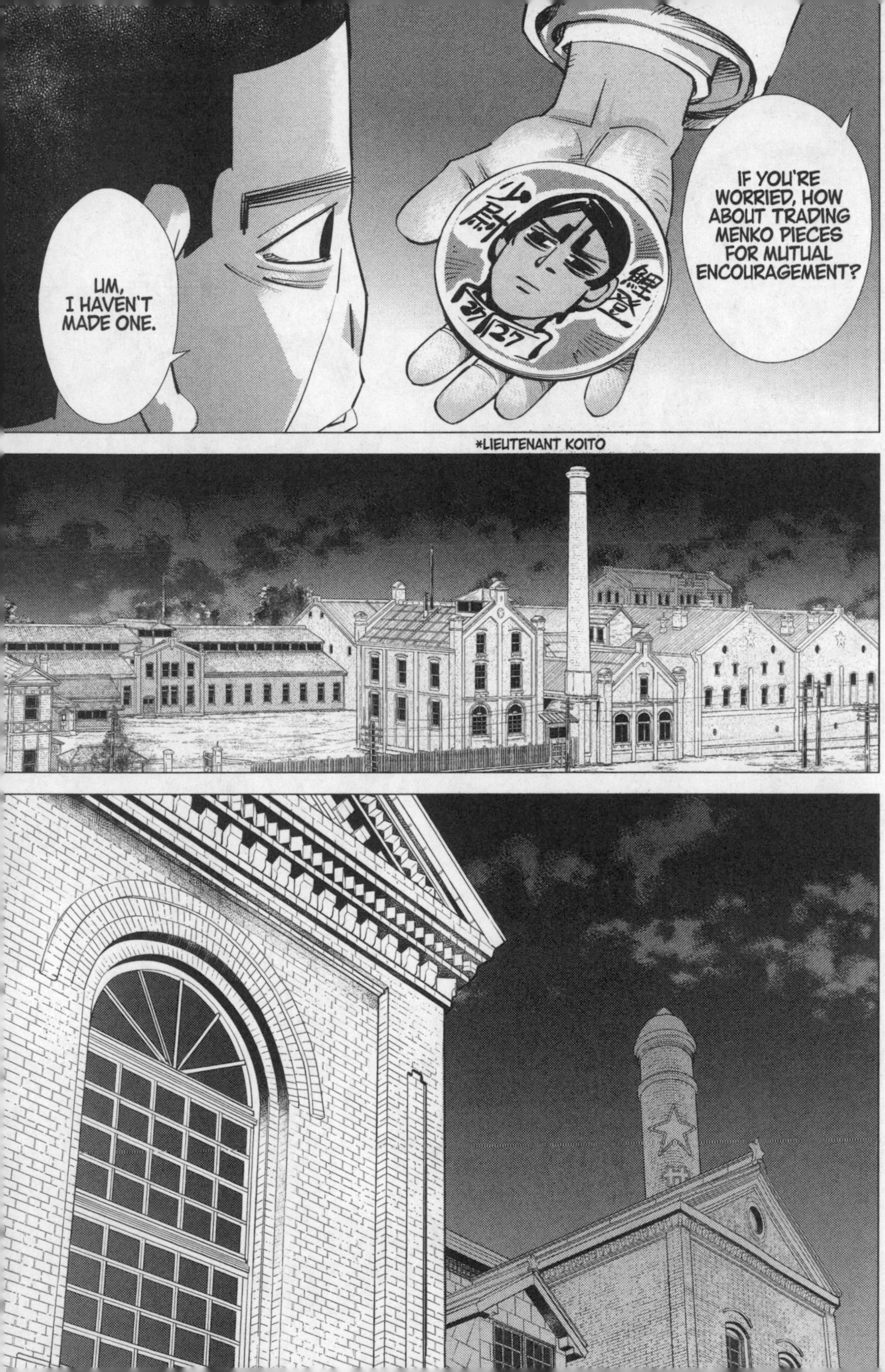
IF YOU'RE WORRIED, HOW ABOUT TRADING MENKO PIECES FOR MUTUAL ENCOURAGEMENT?
UM, I HAVEN'T MADE ONE.
*LIEUTENANT KOITO

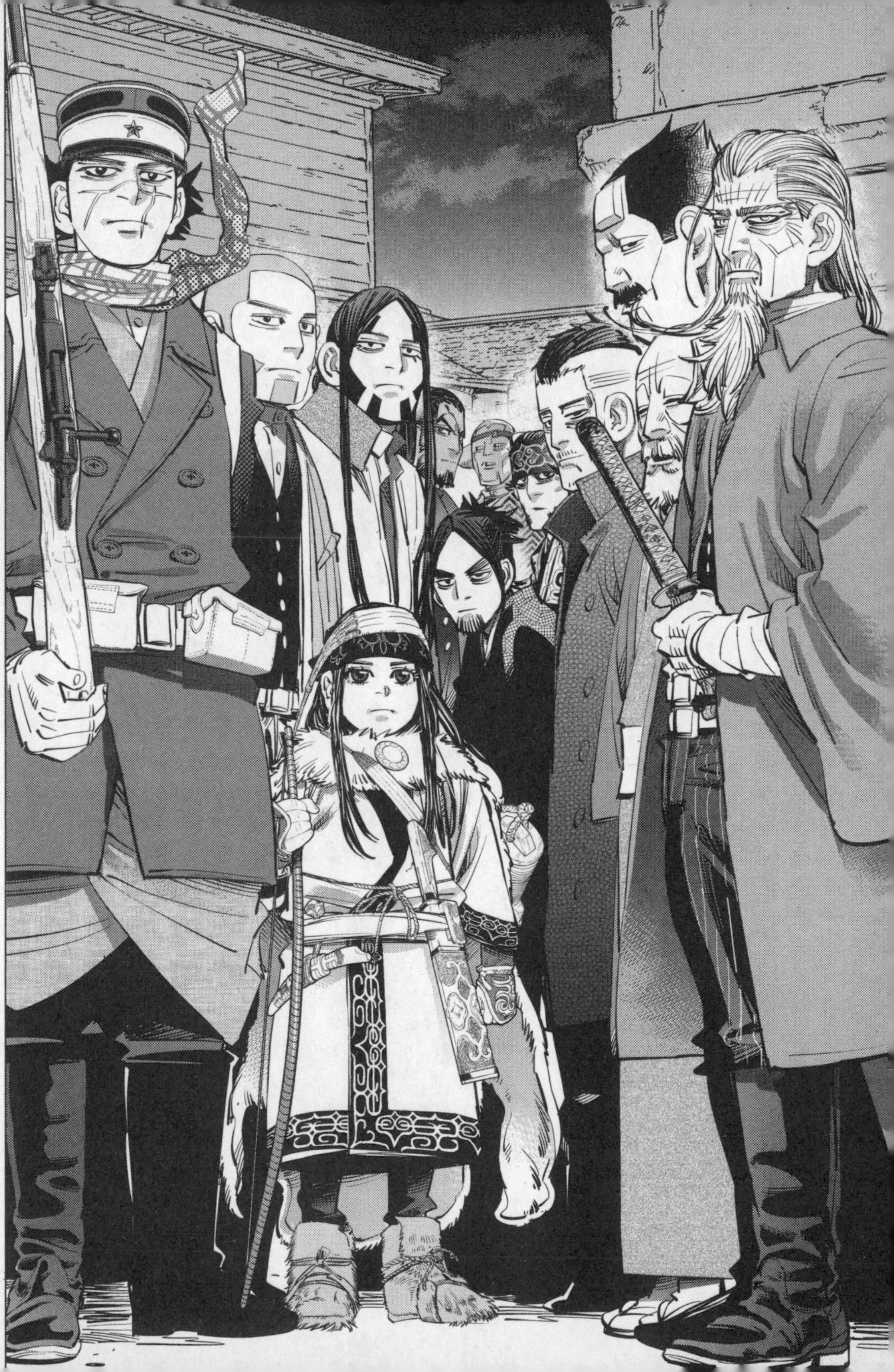

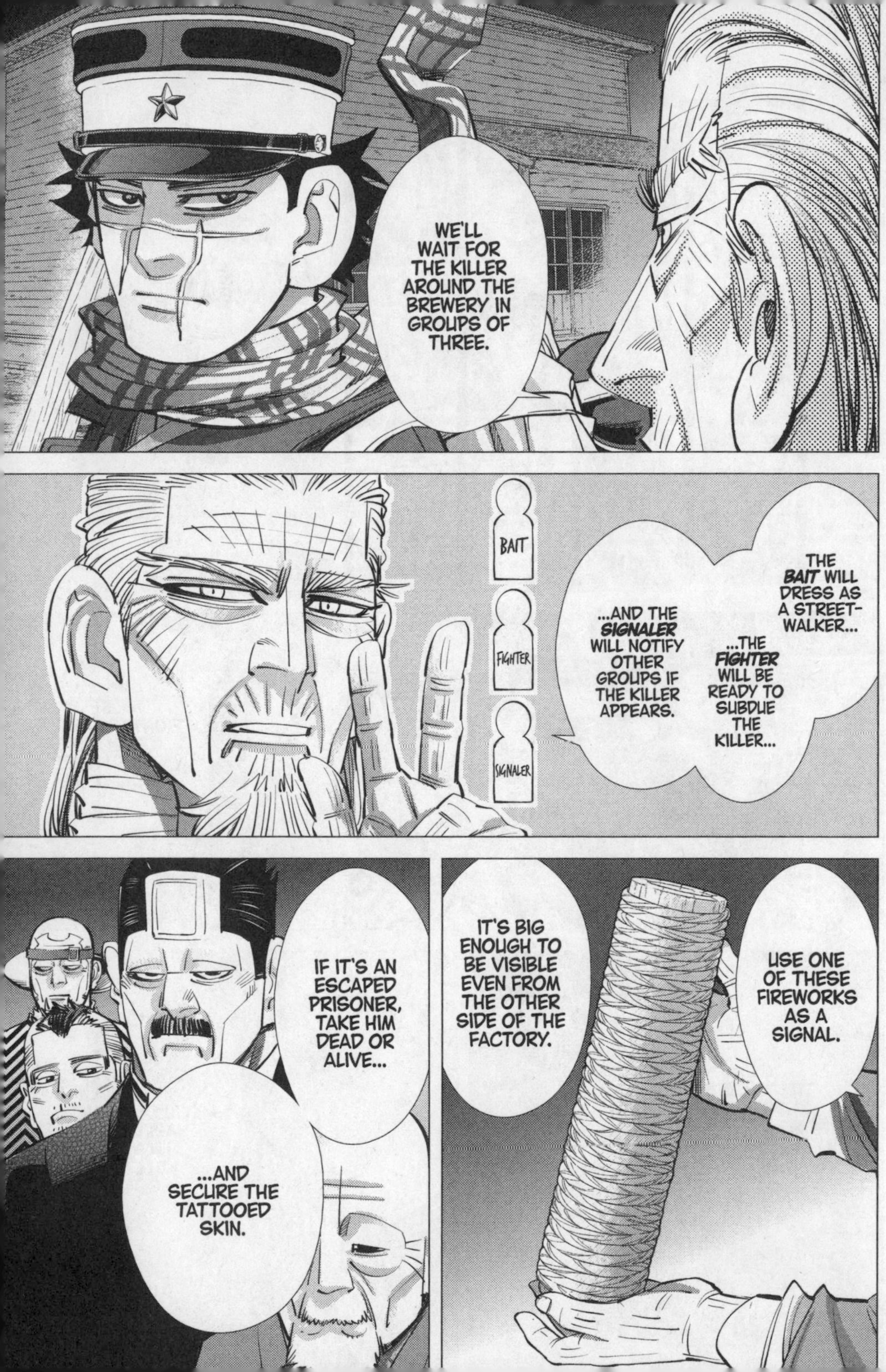
WE'LL WAIT FOR THE KILLER AROUND THE BREWERY IN GROUPS OF THREE.
THE BAIT WILL DRESS AS A STREET-WALKER...
...THE FIGHTER WILL BE READY TO SUBDUE THE KILLER...
...AND THE SIGNALER WILL NOTIFY OTHER GROUPS IF THE KILLER APPEARS.
BAIT
FIGHTER
SIGNALER
USE ONE OF THESE FIREWORKS AS A SIGNAL.
IT'S BIG ENOUGH TO BE VISIBLE EVEN FROM THE OTHER SIDE OF THE FACTORY.
IF IT'S AN ESCAPED PRISONER, TAKE HIM DEAD OR ALIVE...
...AND SECURE THE TATTOOED SKIN.

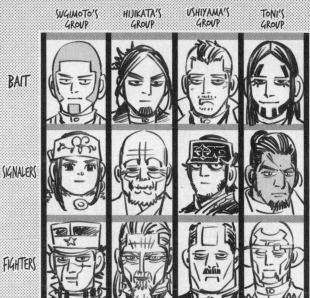

	SUGIMOTO'S GROUP	HIJIKATA'S GROUP	USHIYAMA'S GROUP	TONI'S GROUP
BAIT				
SIGNALERS				
FIGHTERS				

KANTARO, SHIRAISHI, KADOKURA, AND THE PIRATE ARE THE STREET-WALKERS.

NAGAKURA, ASIRPA, KIRAUSHI, AND ARIKO ARE THE SIGNALERS.

AND SUGIMOTO, ANJI TONI, USHIYAMA, AND I ARE THE FIGHTERS.

THOSE FIGHTERS ARE TOUGH. DO WE EVEN NEED SIGNALERS?

ALL THAT'S LEFT IS TO SEND HOME ANY REAL STREETWALKERS.

I HOPE THIS GOES WELL, BUT SOMETHING UNFORESEEN COULD ALWAYS HAPPEN AND ALLOW THE KILLER TO ESCAPE.

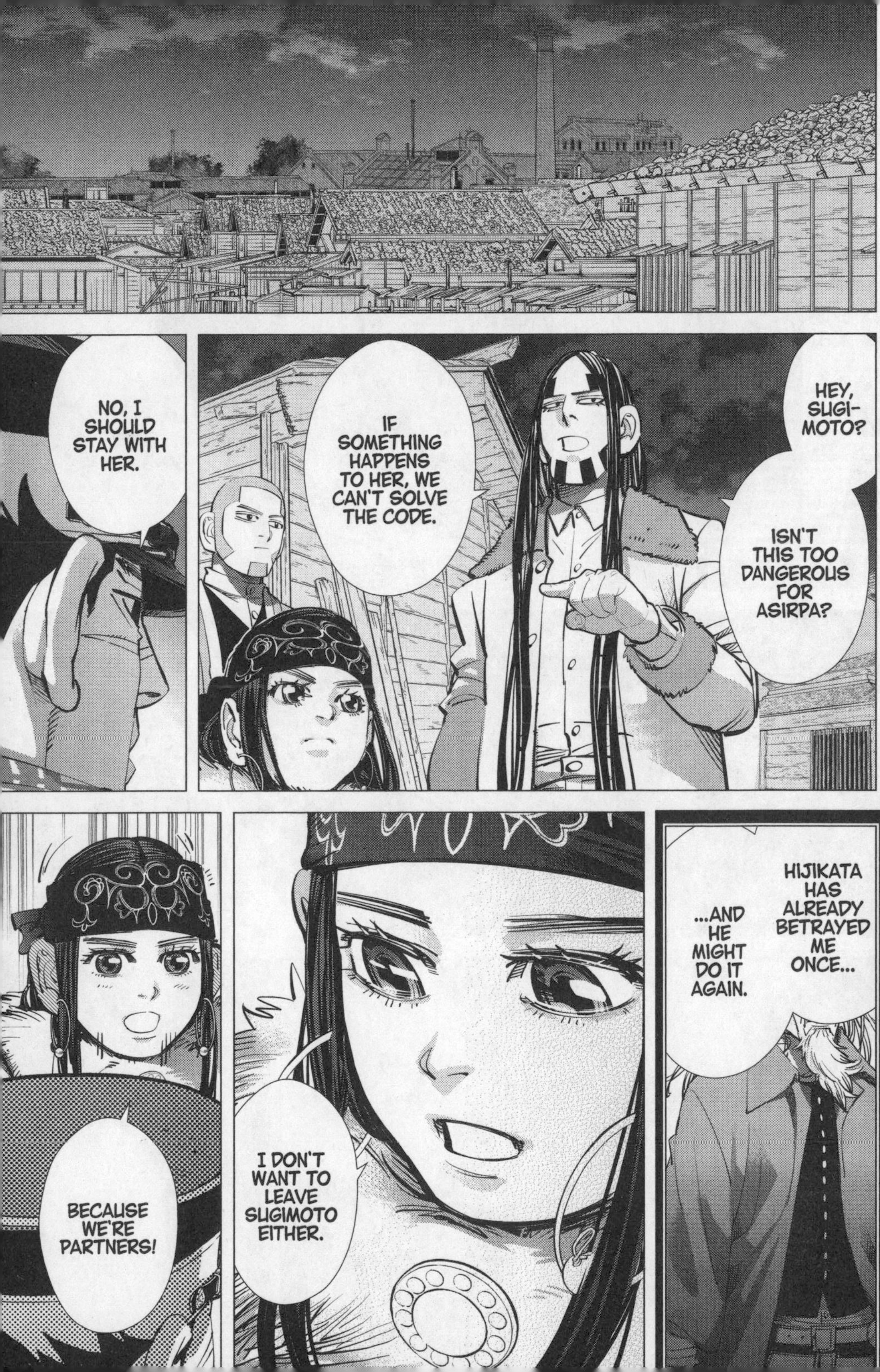
HEY, SUGI-MOTO?
ISN'T THIS TOO DANGEROUS FOR ASIRPA?
IF SOMETHING HAPPENS TO HER, WE CAN'T SOLVE THE CODE.
NO, I SHOULD STAY WITH HER.
HIJIKATA HAS ALREADY BETRAYED ME ONCE...
...AND HE MIGHT DO IT AGAIN.
I DON'T WANT TO LEAVE SUGIMOTO EITHER.
BECAUSE WE'RE PARTNERS!

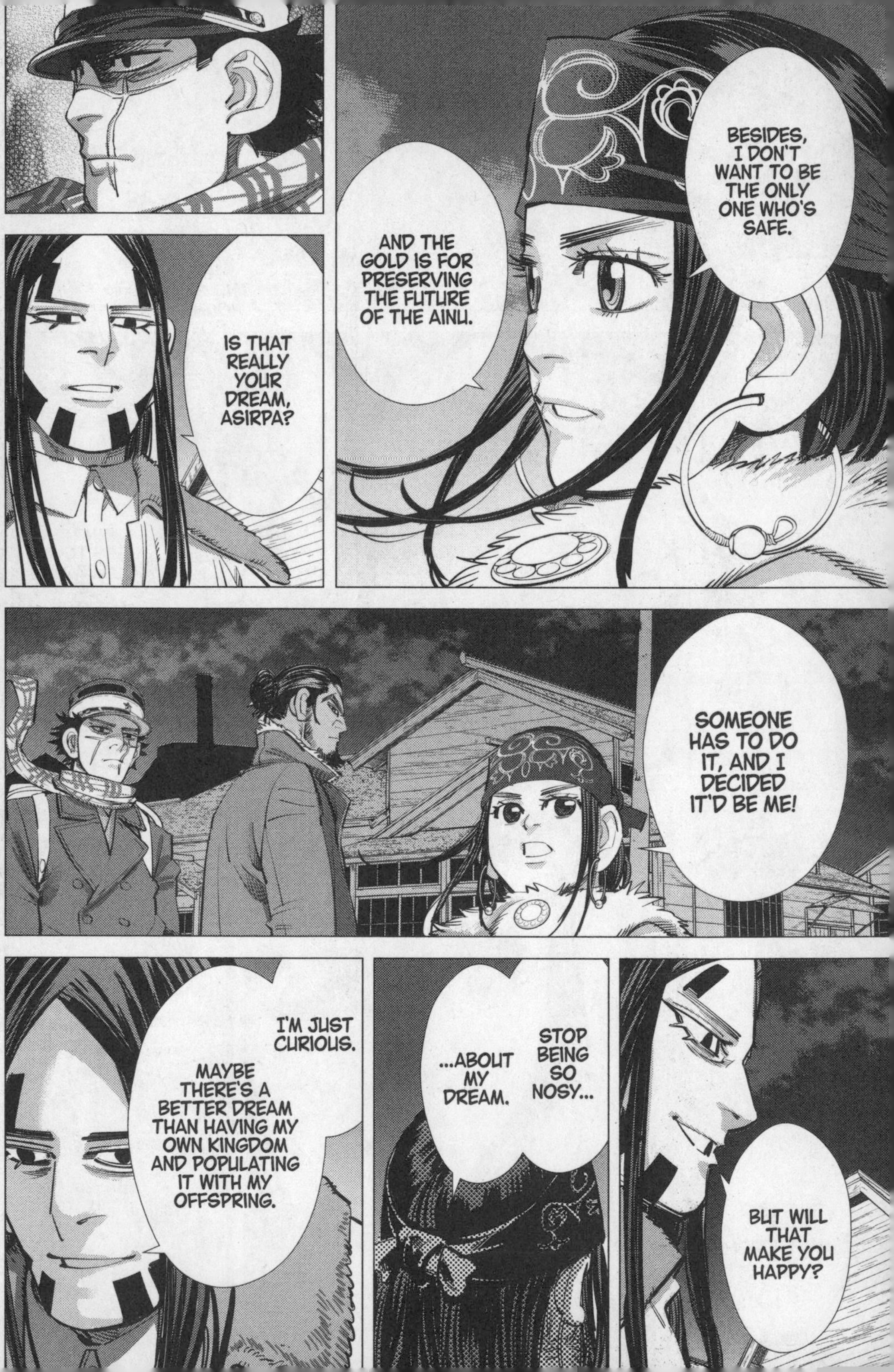
BESIDES, I DON'T WANT TO BE THE ONLY ONE WHO'S SAFE.
AND THE GOLD IS FOR PRESERVING THE FUTURE OF THE AINU.
IS THAT REALLY YOUR DREAM, ASIRPA?
SOMEONE HAS TO DO IT, AND I DECIDED IT'D BE ME!
BUT WILL THAT MAKE YOU HAPPY?
STOP BEING SO NOSY...
...ABOUT MY DREAM.
I'M JUST CURIOUS.
MAYBE THERE'S A BETTER DREAM THAN HAVING MY OWN KINGDOM AND POPULATING IT WITH MY OFFSPRING.

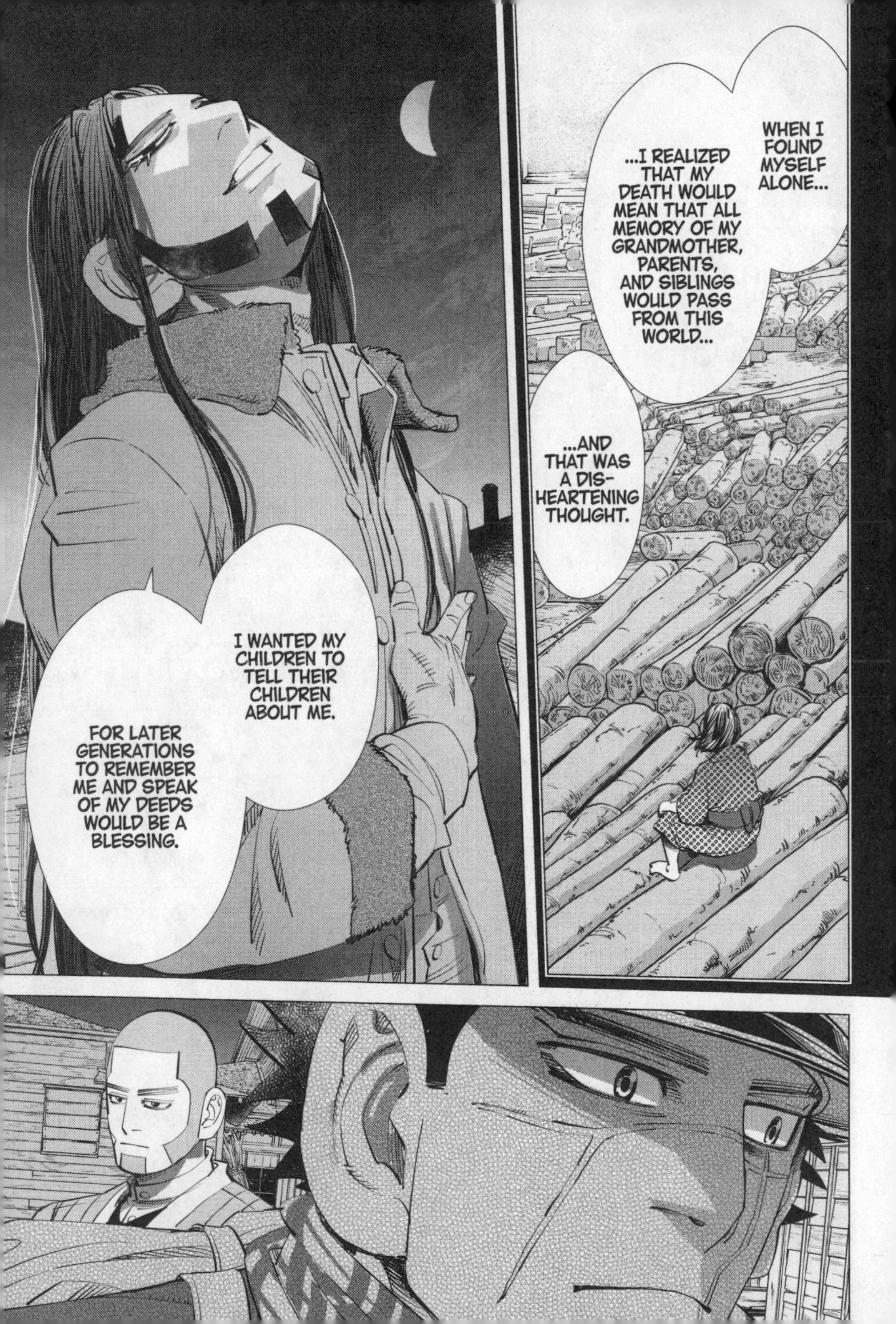
WHEN I FOUND MYSELF ALONE...
...I REALIZED THAT MY DEATH WOULD MEAN THAT ALL MEMORY OF MY GRANDMOTHER, PARENTS, AND SIBLINGS WOULD PASS FROM THIS WORLD...
...AND THAT WAS A DIS-HEARTENING THOUGHT.
I WANTED MY CHILDREN TO TELL THEIR CHILDREN ABOUT ME.
FOR LATER GENERATIONS TO REMEMBER ME AND SPEAK OF MY DEEDS WOULD BE A BLESSING.

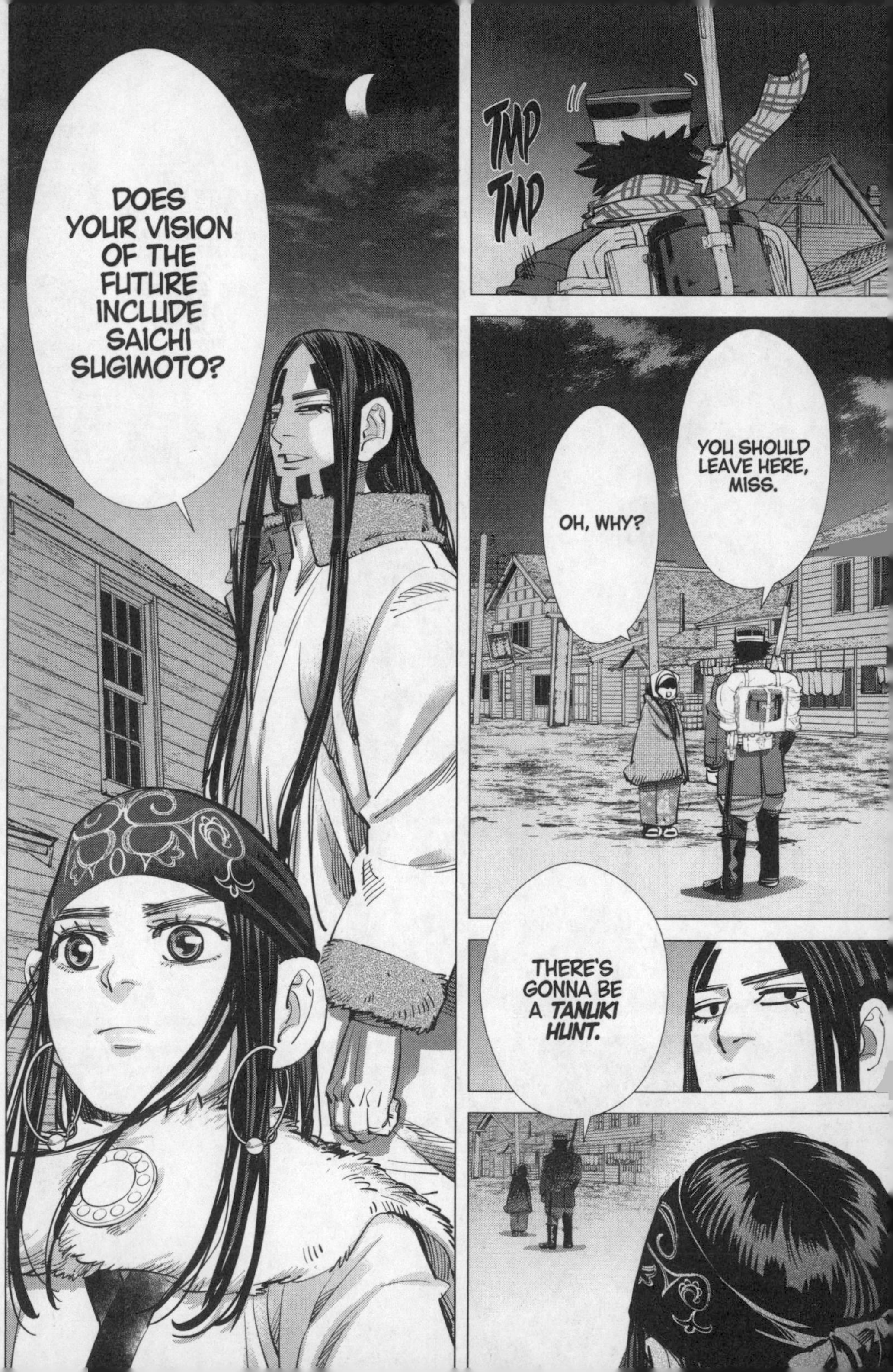
TMP TMP
YOU SHOULD LEAVE HERE, MISS.
OH, WHY?
THERE'S GONNA BE A *TANUKI HUNT.*
DOES YOUR VISION OF THE FUTURE INCLUDE SAICHI SUGIMOTO?

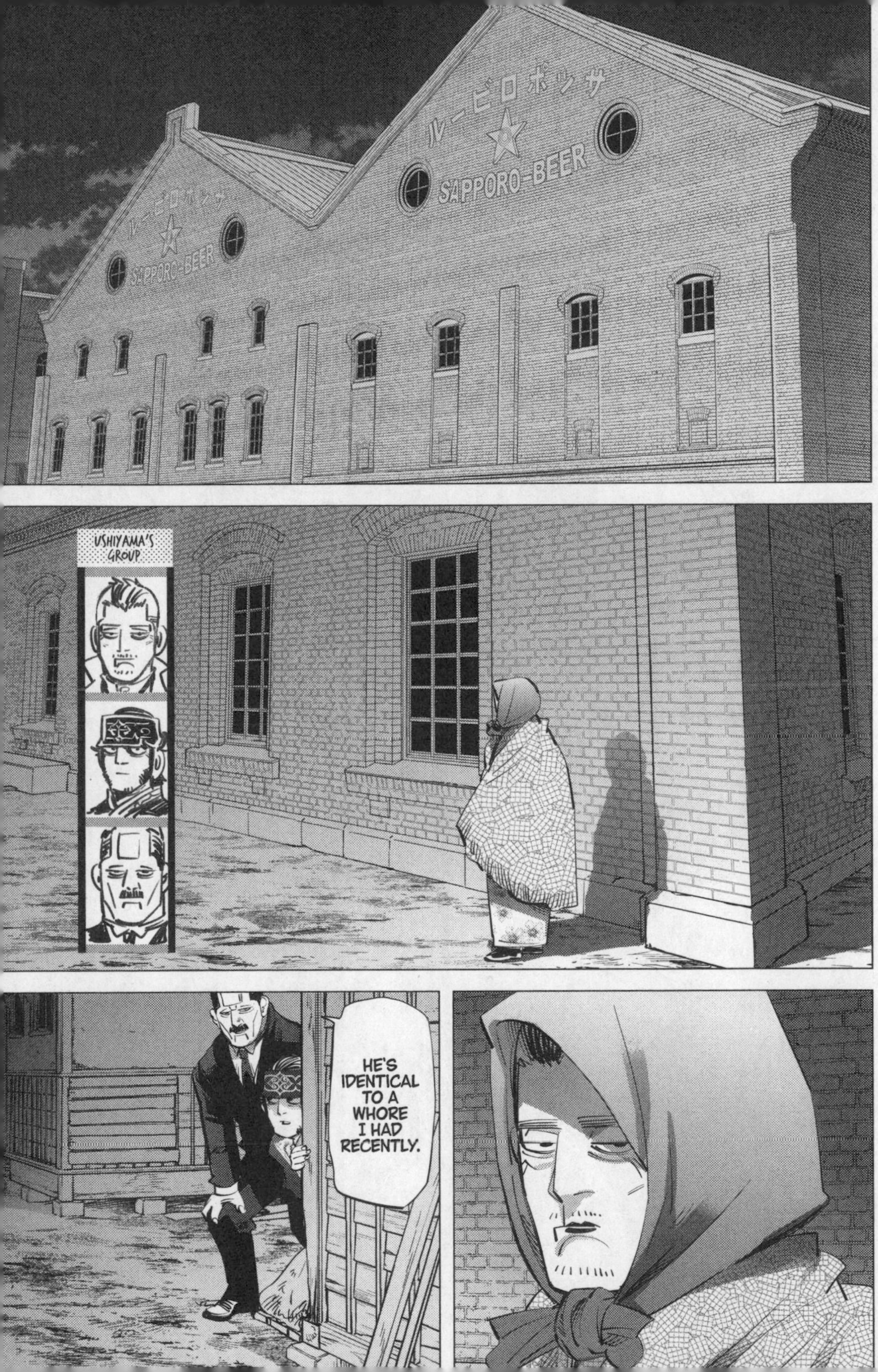
サッポロビール
SAPPORO-BEER
サッポロビール
SAPPORO-BEER
USHIYAMA'S GROUP
HE'S IDENTICAL TO A WHORE I HAD RECENTLY.

HIJIKATA'S GROUP

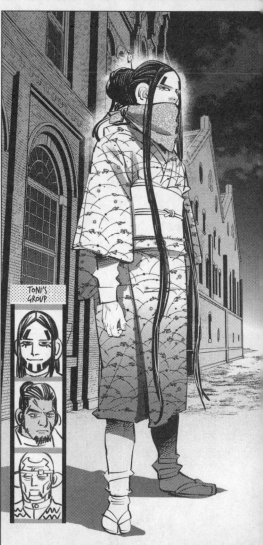

THAT'S A LANKY WOMAN.

YEAH, YOU'D'VE BEEN BETTER.

SUGIMOTO'S GROUP

TONI'S GROUP

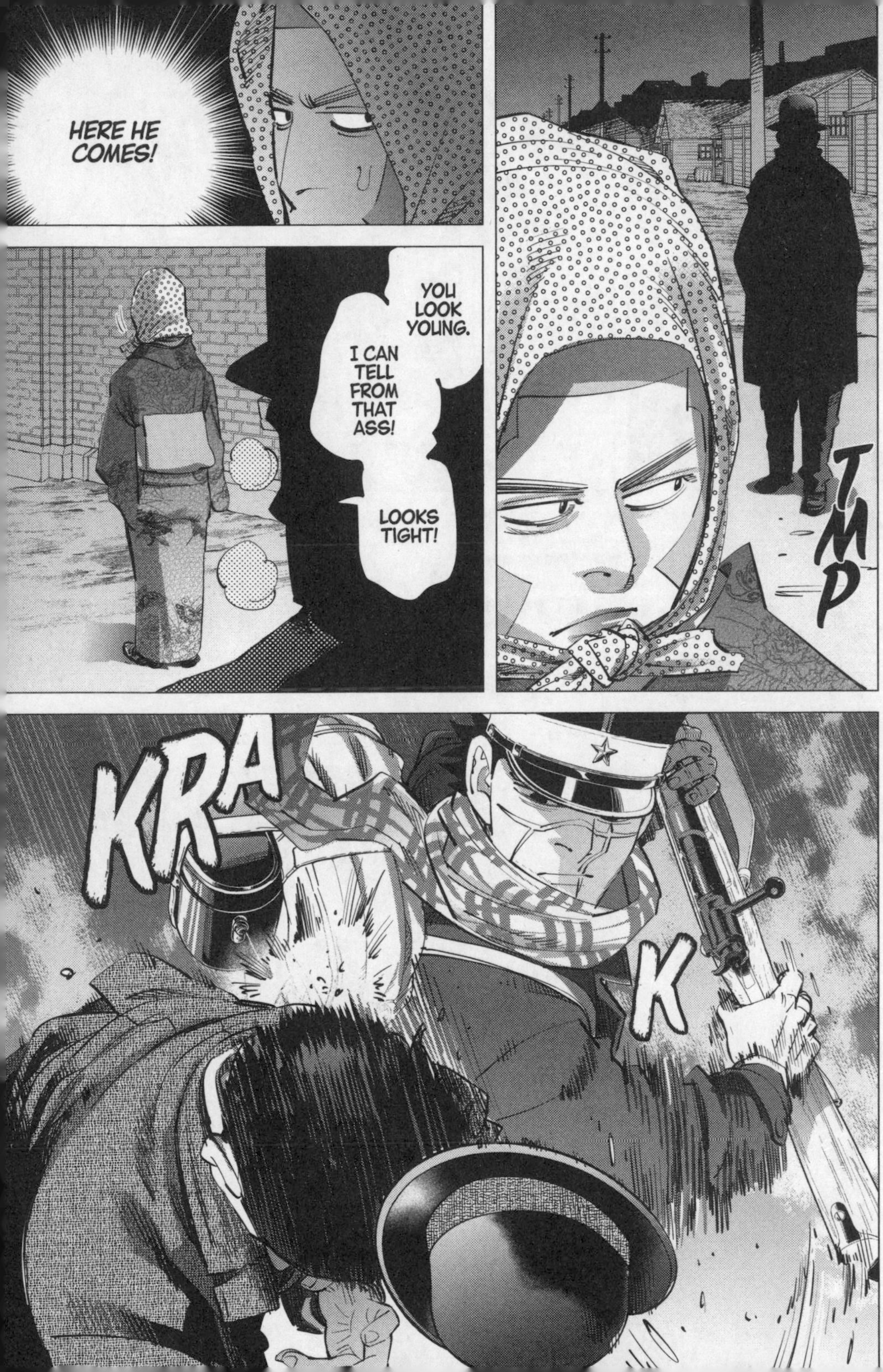
TMP
HERE HE COMES!
YOU LOOK YOUNG. I CAN TELL FROM THAT ASS!
LOOKS TIGHT!
KRAK

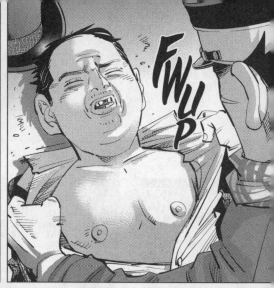

FWUP

GOOD EVENING.

HIJIKATA'S GROUP.

TMP

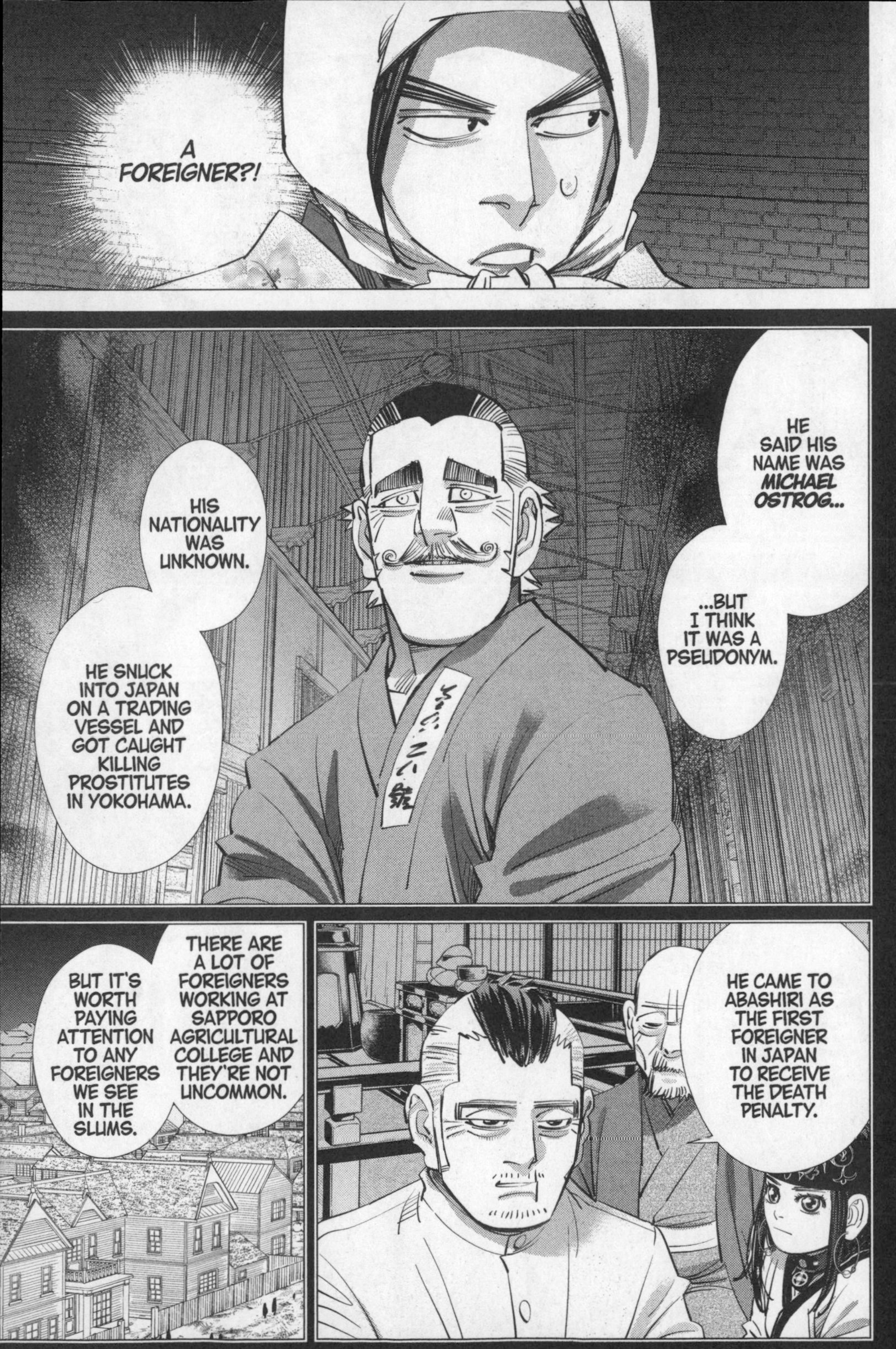
A FOREIGNER?!
HE SAID HIS NAME WAS MICHAEL OSTROG...
...BUT I THINK IT WAS A PSEUDONYM.
HIS NATIONALITY WAS UNKNOWN.
HE SNUCK INTO JAPAN ON A TRADING VESSEL AND GOT CAUGHT KILLING PROSTITUTES IN YOKOHAMA.
HE CAME TO ABASHIRI AS THE FIRST FOREIGNER IN JAPAN TO RECEIVE THE DEATH PENALTY.
THERE ARE A LOT OF FOREIGNERS WORKING AT SAPPORO AGRICULTURAL COLLEGE AND THEY'RE NOT UNCOMMON.
BUT IT'S WORTH PAYING ATTENTION TO ANY FOREIGNERS WE SEE IN THE SLUMS.

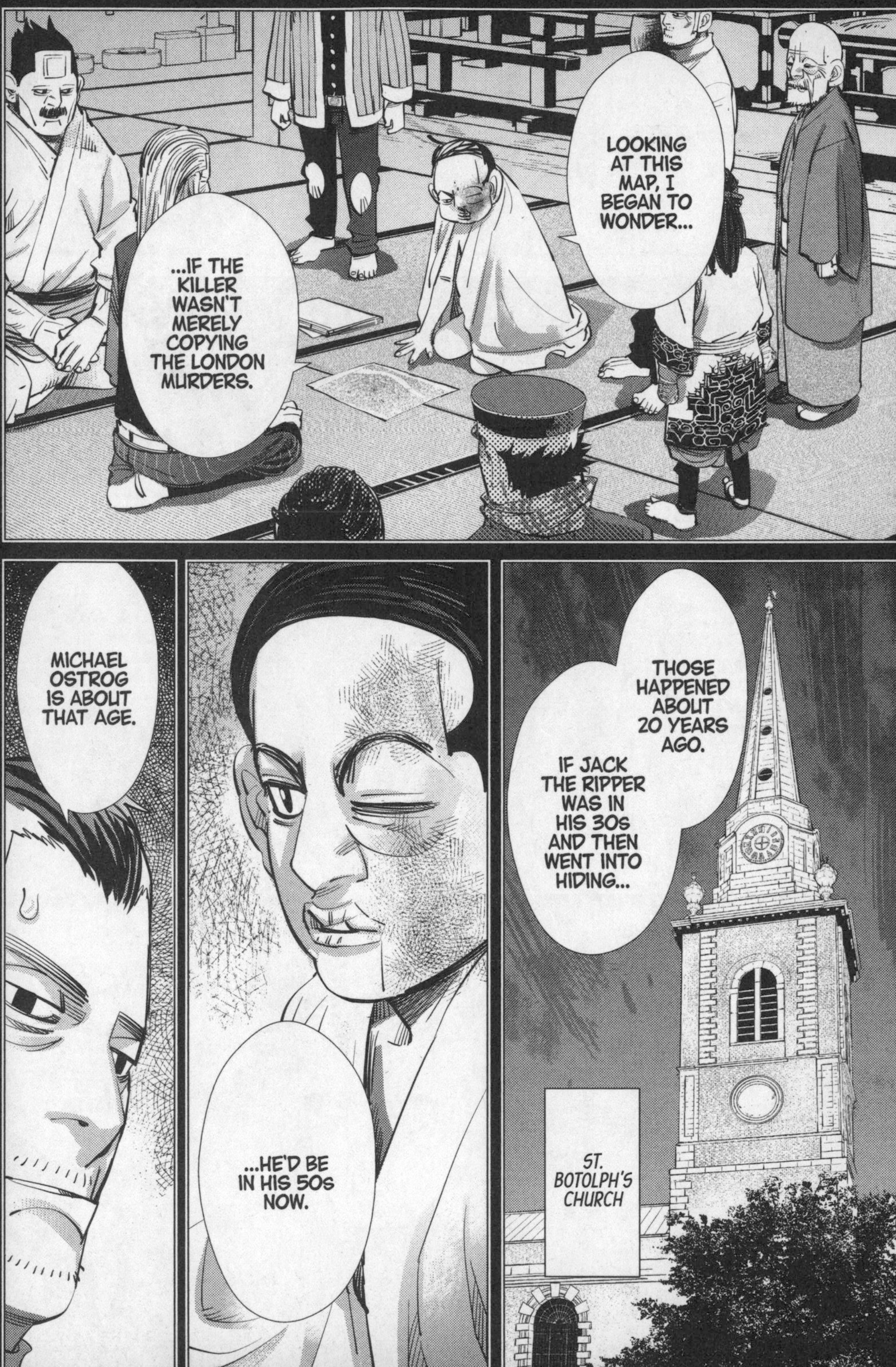
LOOKING AT THIS MAP, I BEGAN TO WONDER...
...IF THE KILLER WASN'T MERELY COPYING THE LONDON MURDERS.
THOSE HAPPENED ABOUT 20 YEARS AGO.
IF JACK THE RIPPER WAS IN HIS 30s AND THEN WENT INTO HIDING...
ST. BOTOLPH'S CHURCH
...HE'D BE IN HIS 50s NOW.
MICHAEL OSTROG IS ABOUT THAT AGE.

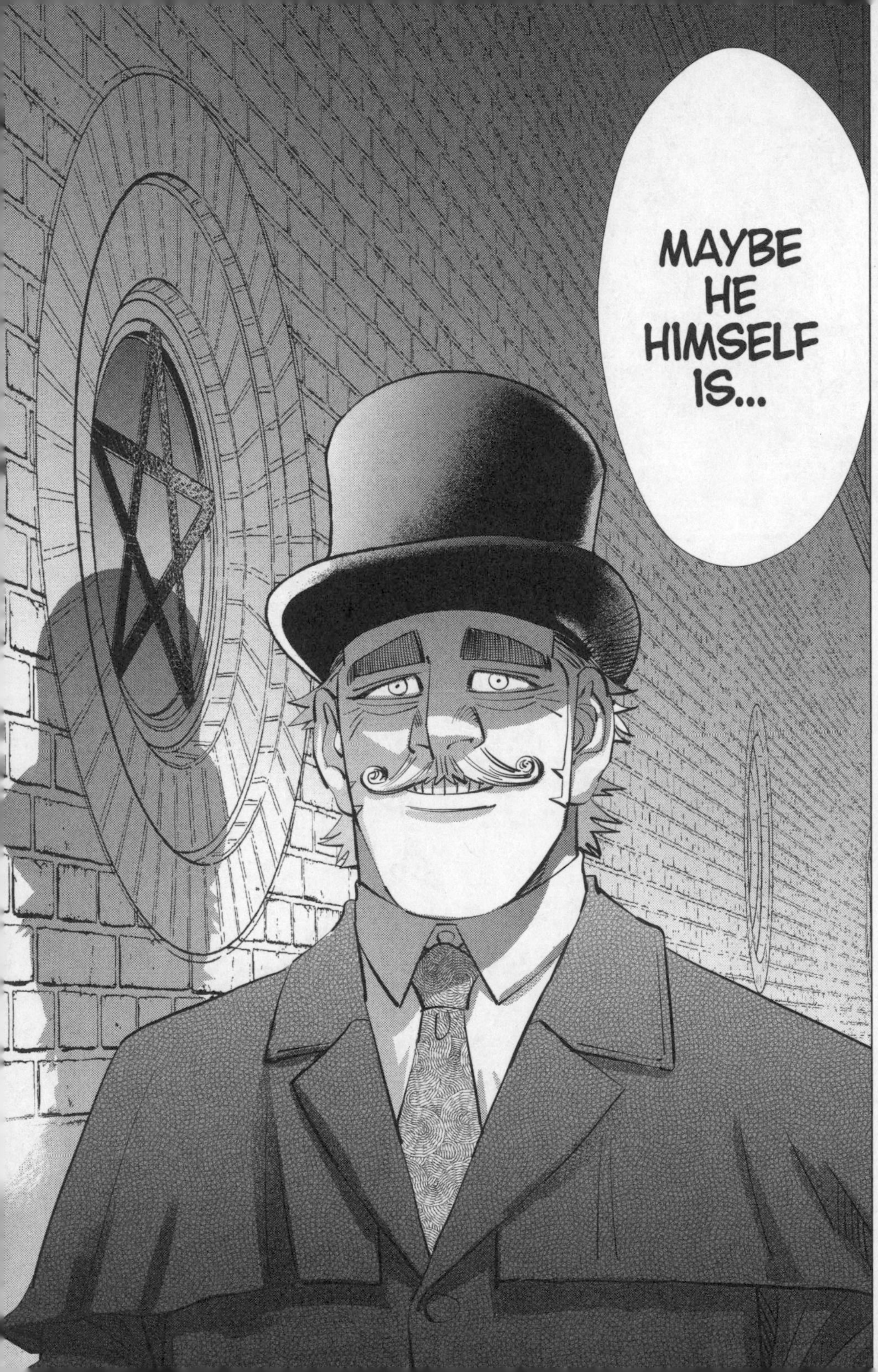
MAYBE HE HIMSELF IS...

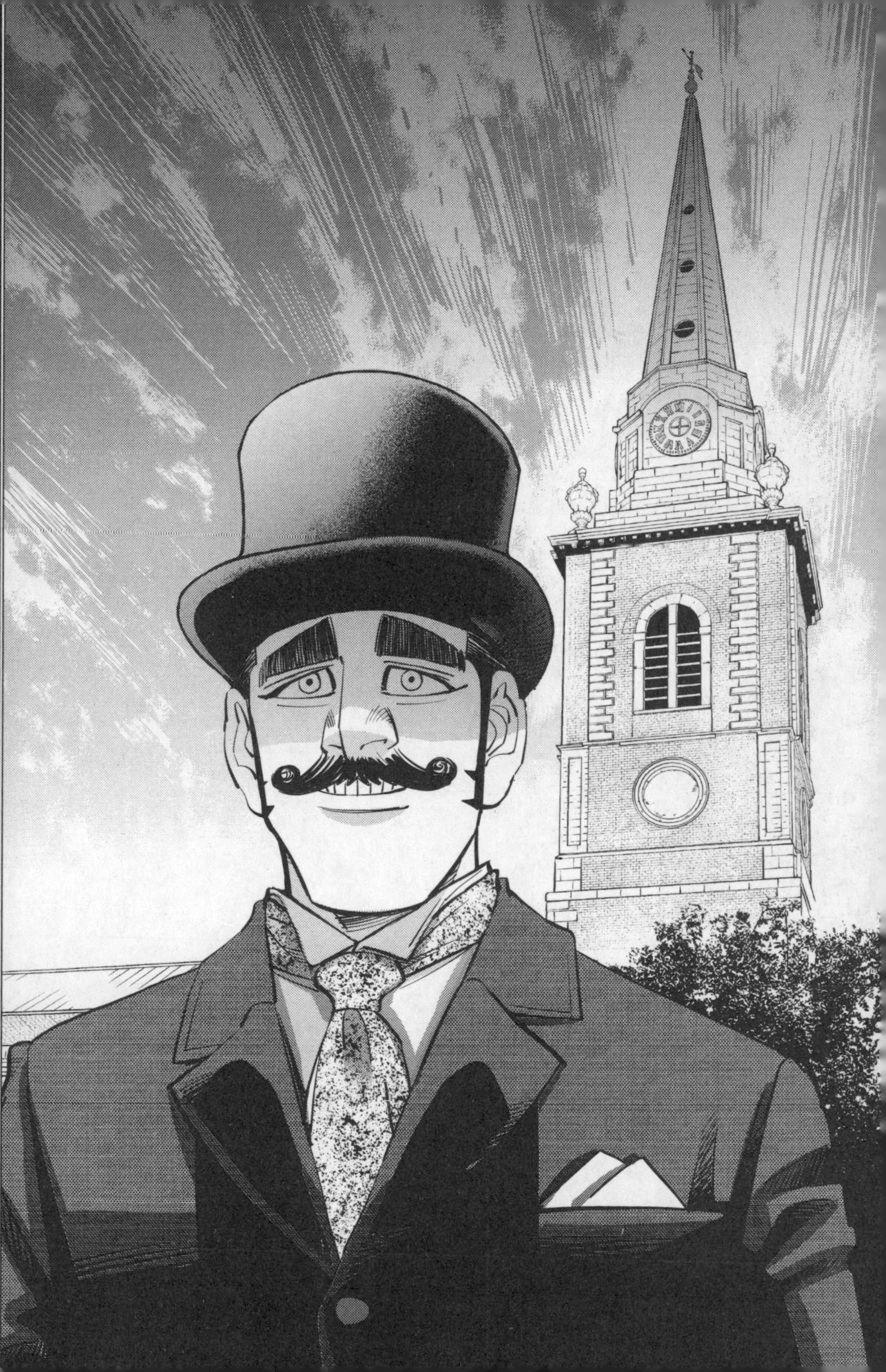

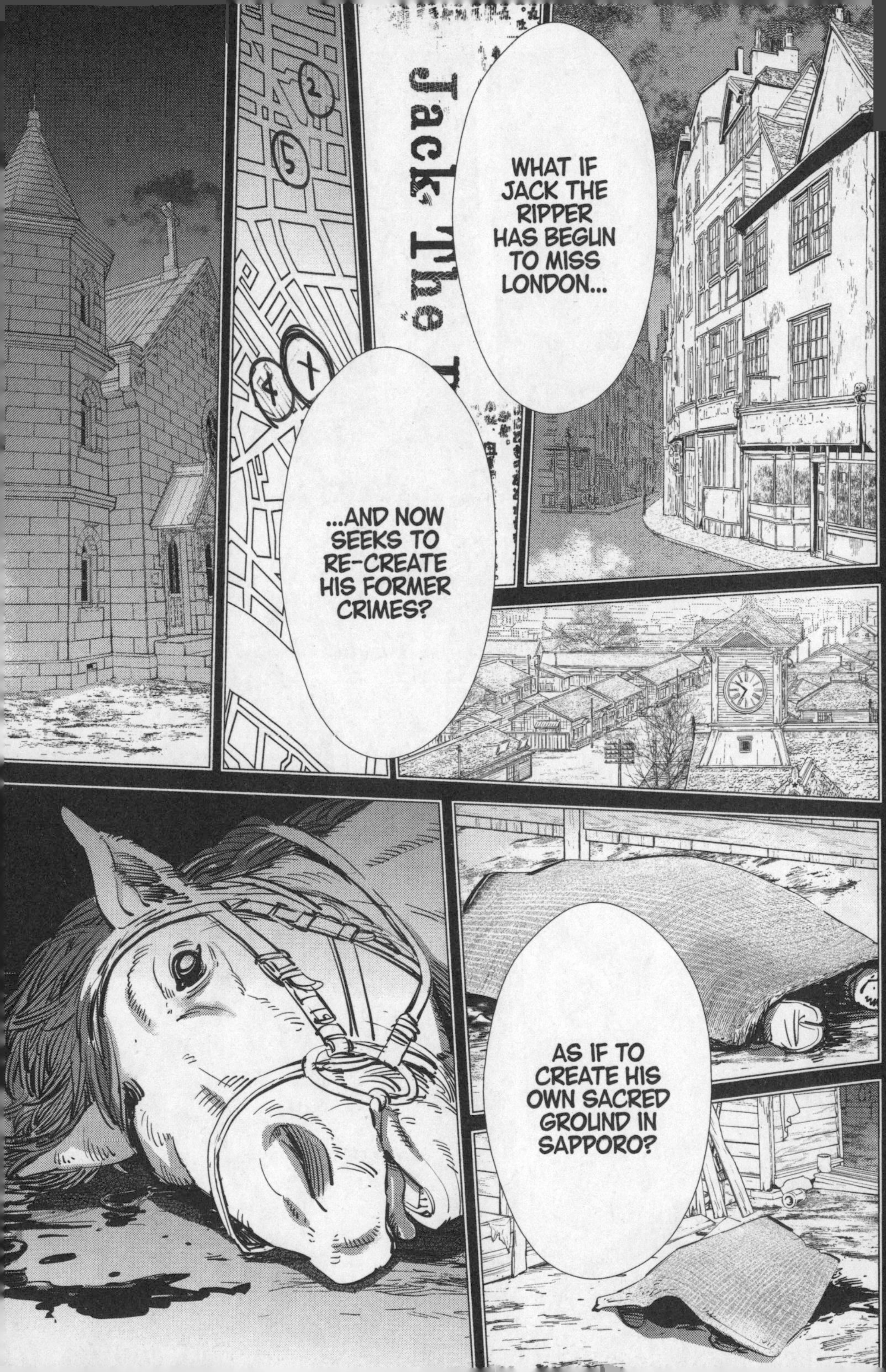
WHAT IF JACK THE RIPPER HAS BEGUN TO MISS LONDON...
Jack The
...AND NOW SEEKS TO RE-CREATE HIS FORMER CRIMES?
AS IF TO CREATE HIS OWN SACRED GROUND IN SAPPORO?

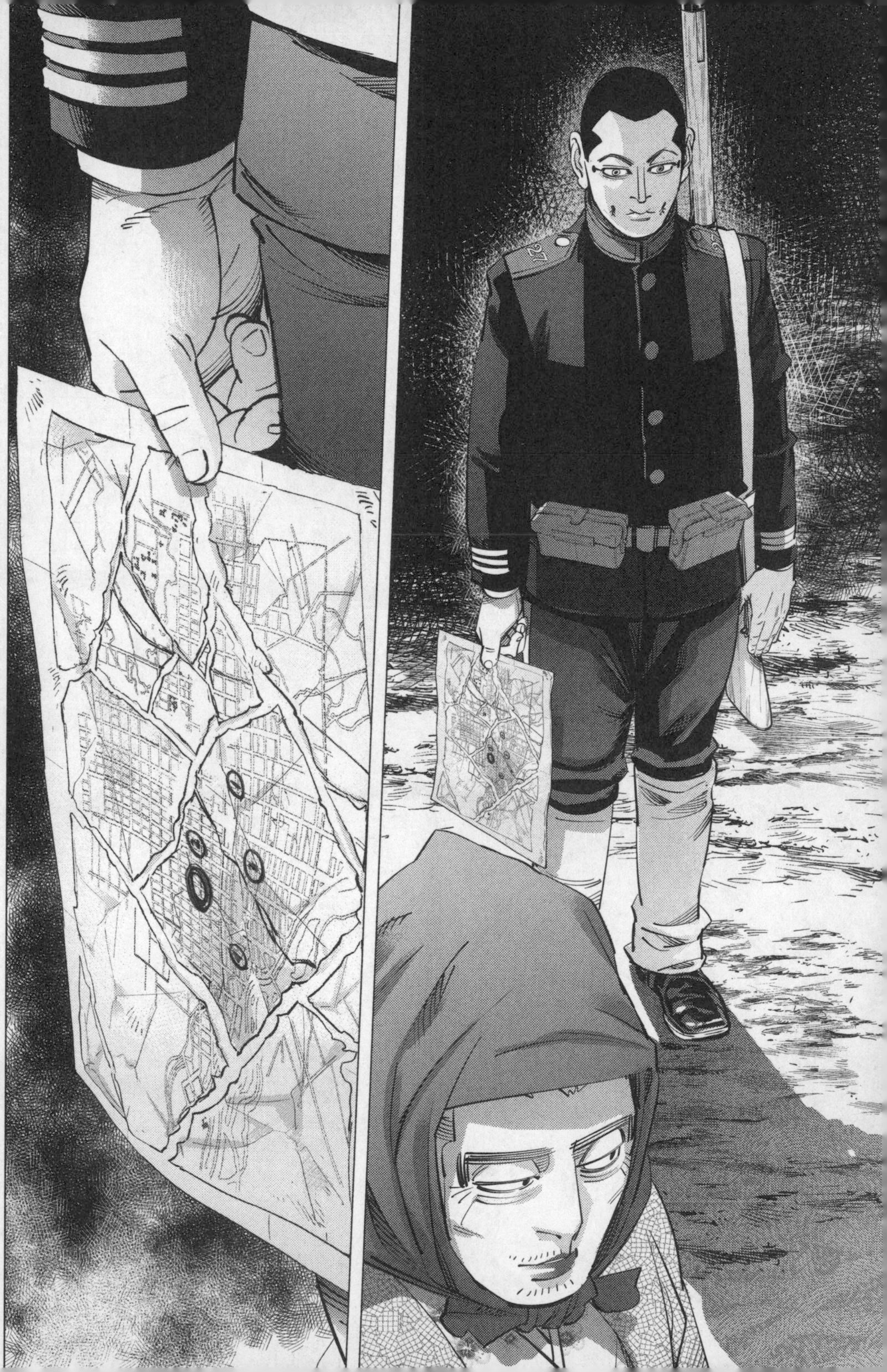

Chapter 250: Skyrocket

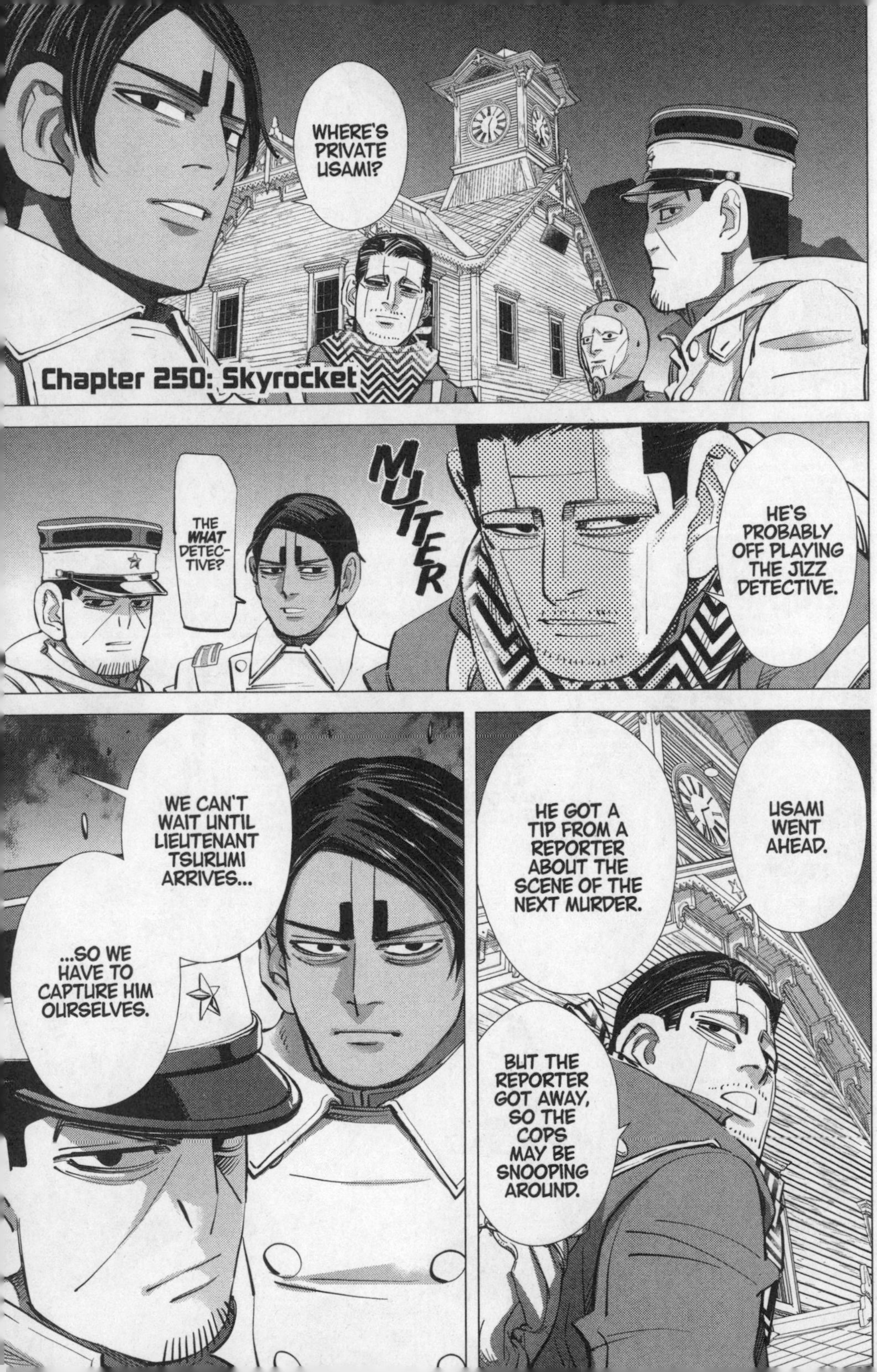
WHERE'S PRIVATE USAMI?
HE'S PROBABLY OFF PLAYING THE JIZZ DETECTIVE.
MUTTER
THE WHAT DETECTIVE?
USAMI WENT AHEAD.
HE GOT A TIP FROM A REPORTER ABOUT THE SCENE OF THE NEXT MURDER.
BUT THE REPORTER GOT AWAY, SO THE COPS MAY BE SNOOPING AROUND.
WE CAN'T WAIT UNTIL LIEUTENANT TSURUMI ARRIVES...
...SO WE HAVE TO CAPTURE HIM OURSELVES.

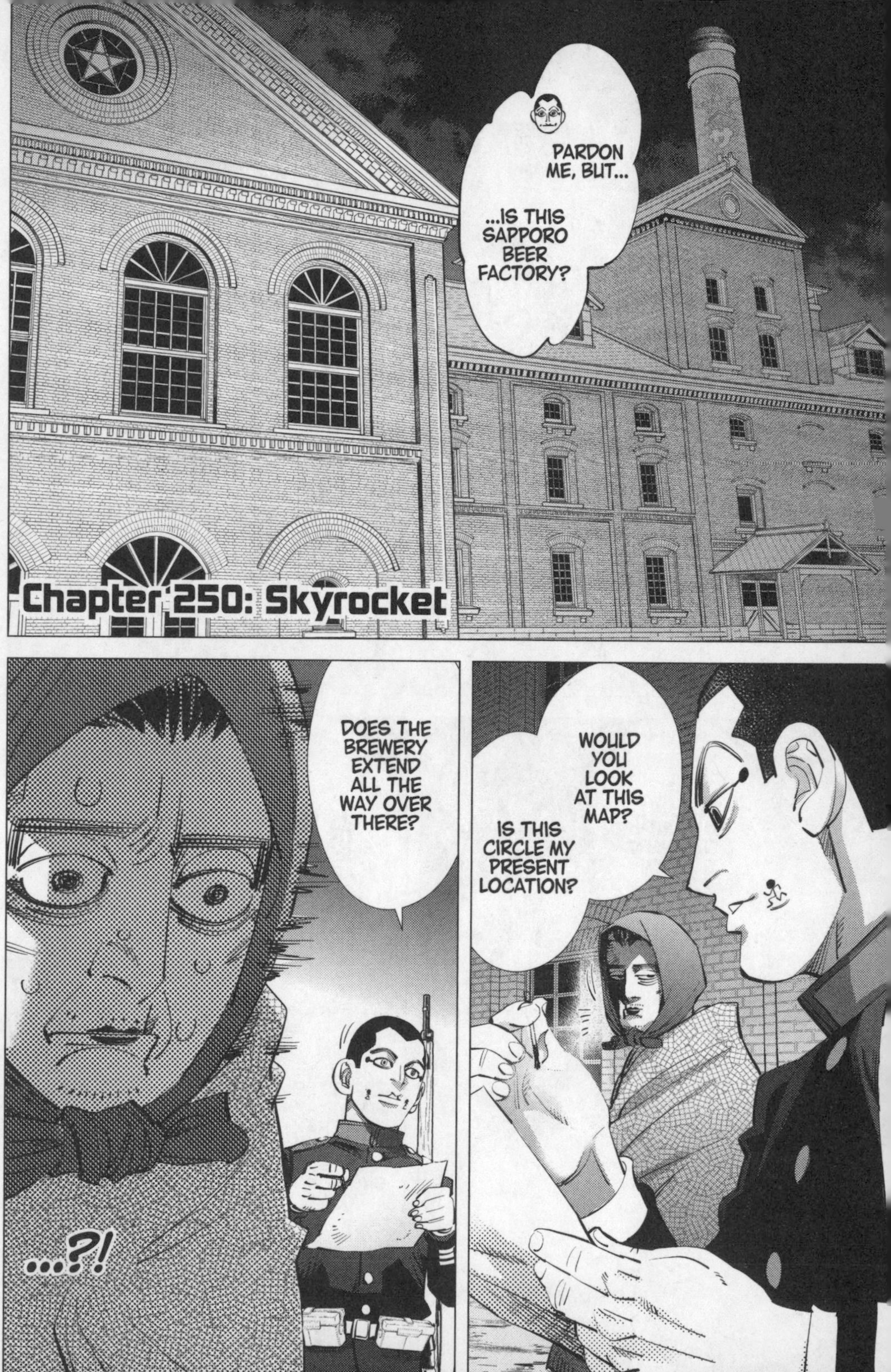
PARDON ME, BUT...
...IS THIS SAPPORO BEER FACTORY?
Chapter 250: Skyrocket
WOULD YOU LOOK AT THIS MAP?
IS THIS CIRCLE MY PRESENT LOCATION?
DOES THE BREWERY EXTEND ALL THE WAY OVER THERE?
...?!

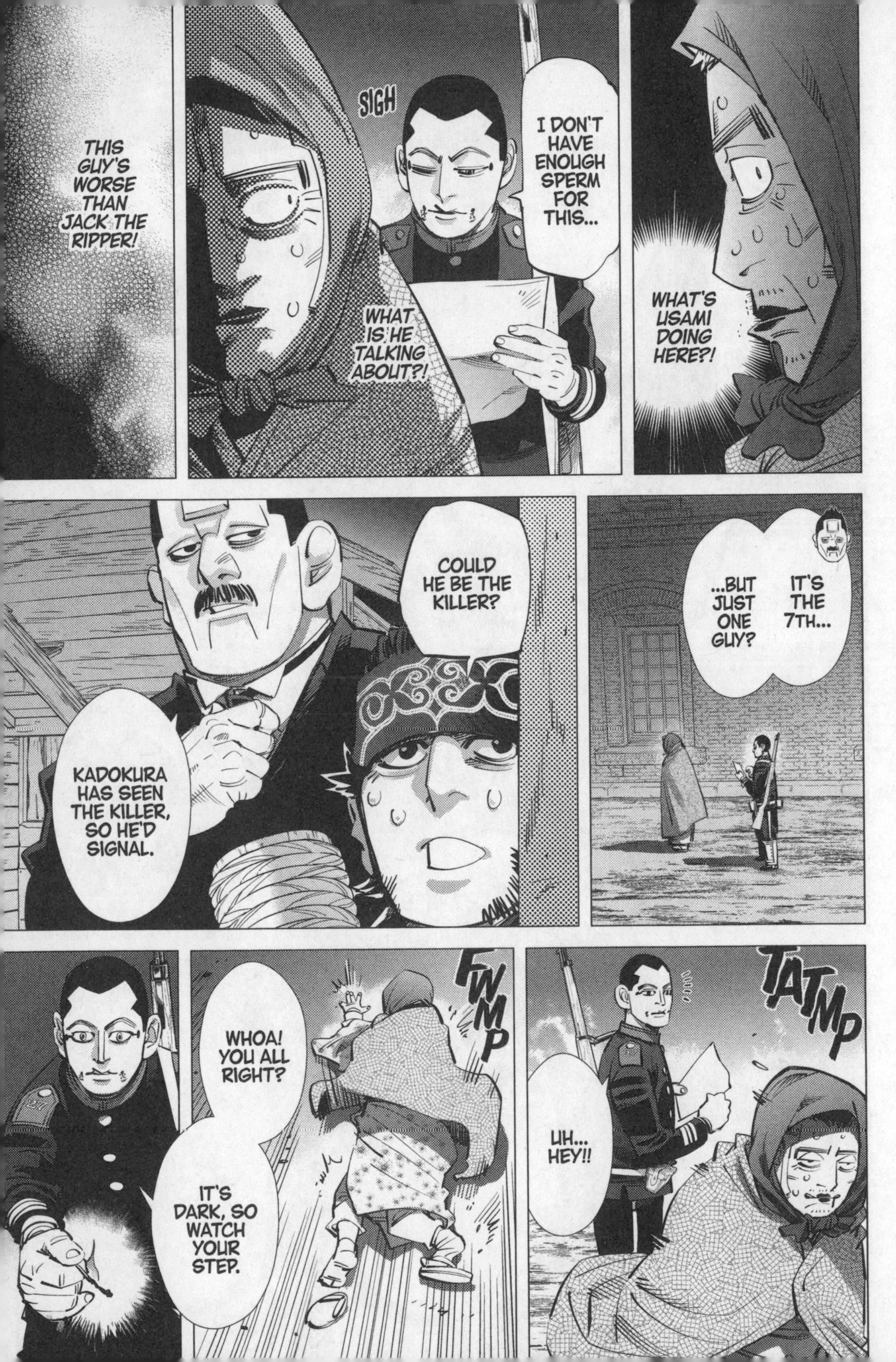
WHAT'S USAMI DOING HERE?!
SIGH
I DON'T HAVE ENOUGH SPERM FOR THIS...
WHAT IS HE TALKING ABOUT?!
THIS GUY'S WORSE THAN JACK THE RIPPER!
IT'S THE 7TH...
...BUT JUST ONE GUY?
COULD HE BE THE KILLER?
KADOKURA HAS SEEN THE KILLER, SO HE'D SIGNAL.
TATMP
UH... HEY!!
FWMP
WHOA! YOU ALL RIGHT?
IT'S DARK, SO WATCH YOUR STEP.

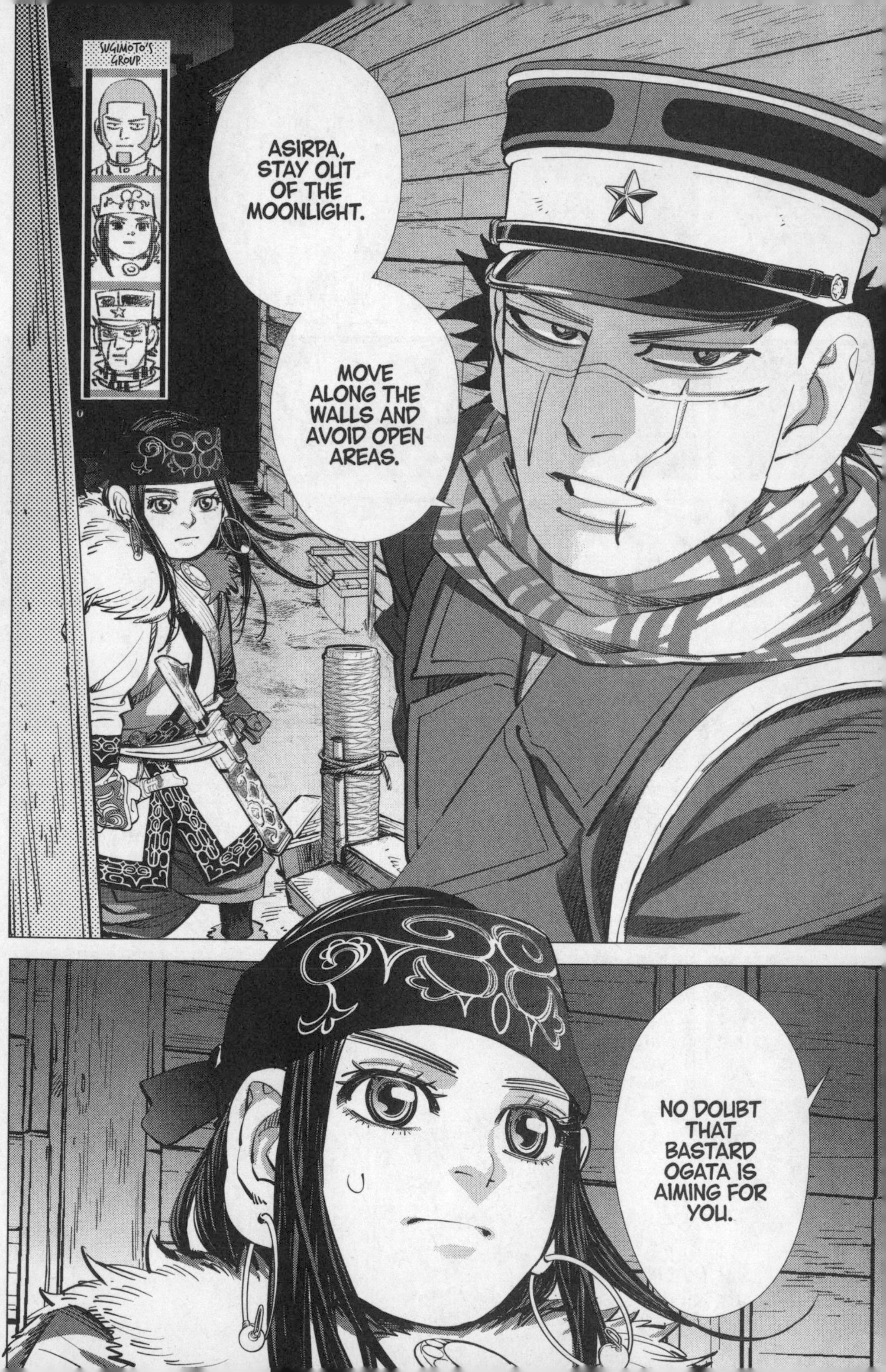
ASIRPA, STAY OUT OF THE MOONLIGHT.
MOVE ALONG THE WALLS AND AVOID OPEN AREAS.
SUGIMOTO'S GROUP
NO DOUBT THAT BASTARD OGATA IS AIMING FOR YOU.

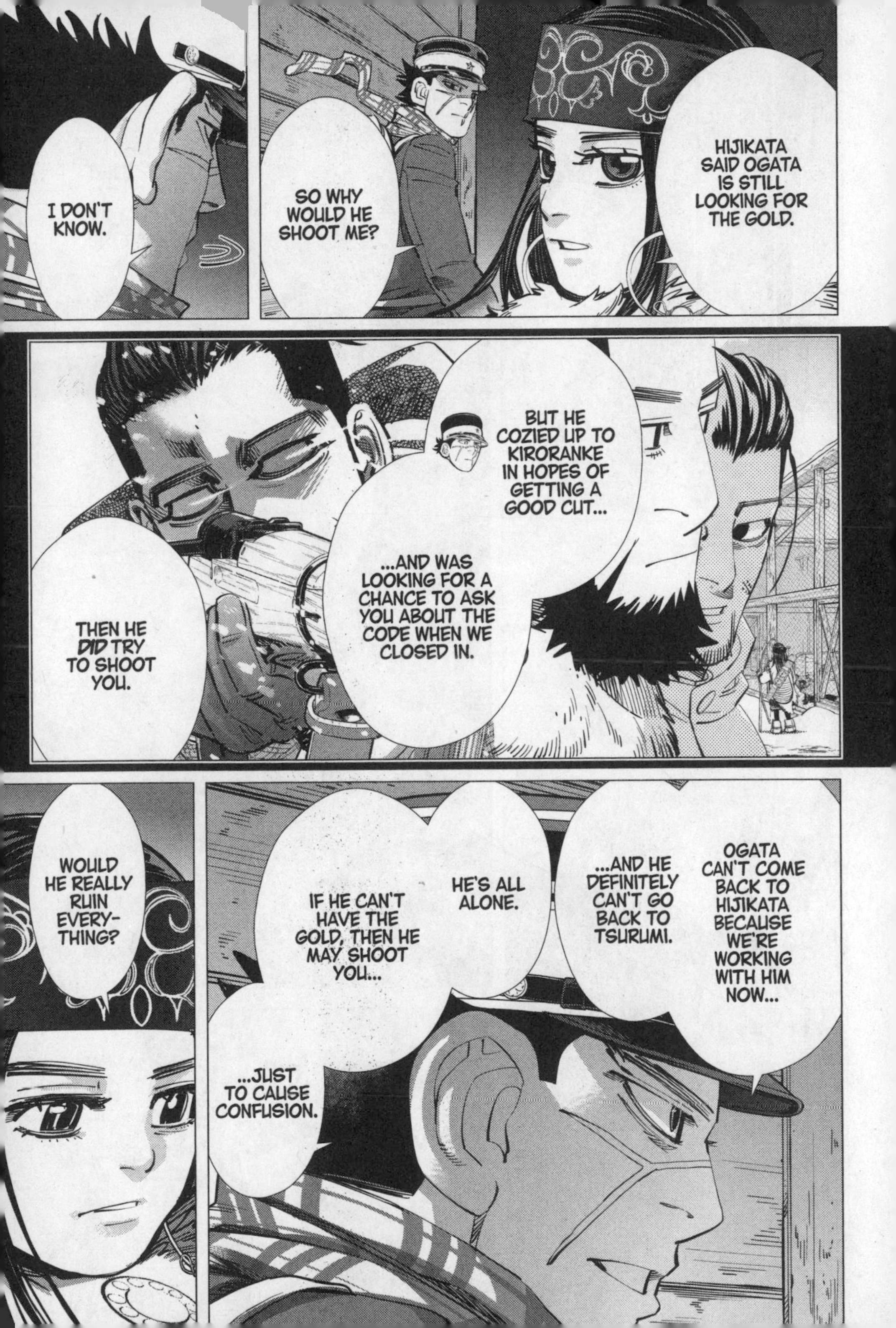
HIJIKATA SAID OGATA IS STILL LOOKING FOR THE GOLD.
SO WHY WOULD HE SHOOT ME?
I DON'T KNOW.
BUT HE COZIED UP TO KIRORANKE IN HOPES OF GETTING A GOOD CUT...
...AND WAS LOOKING FOR A CHANCE TO ASK YOU ABOUT THE CODE WHEN WE CLOSED IN.
THEN HE *DID* TRY TO SHOOT YOU.
OGATA CAN'T COME BACK TO HIJIKATA BECAUSE WE'RE WORKING WITH HIM NOW...
...AND HE DEFINITELY CAN'T GO BACK TO TSURUMI.
HE'S ALL ALONE.
IF HE CAN'T HAVE THE GOLD, THEN HE MAY SHOOT YOU...
...JUST TO CAUSE CONFUSION.
WOULD HE REALLY RUIN EVERY-THING?

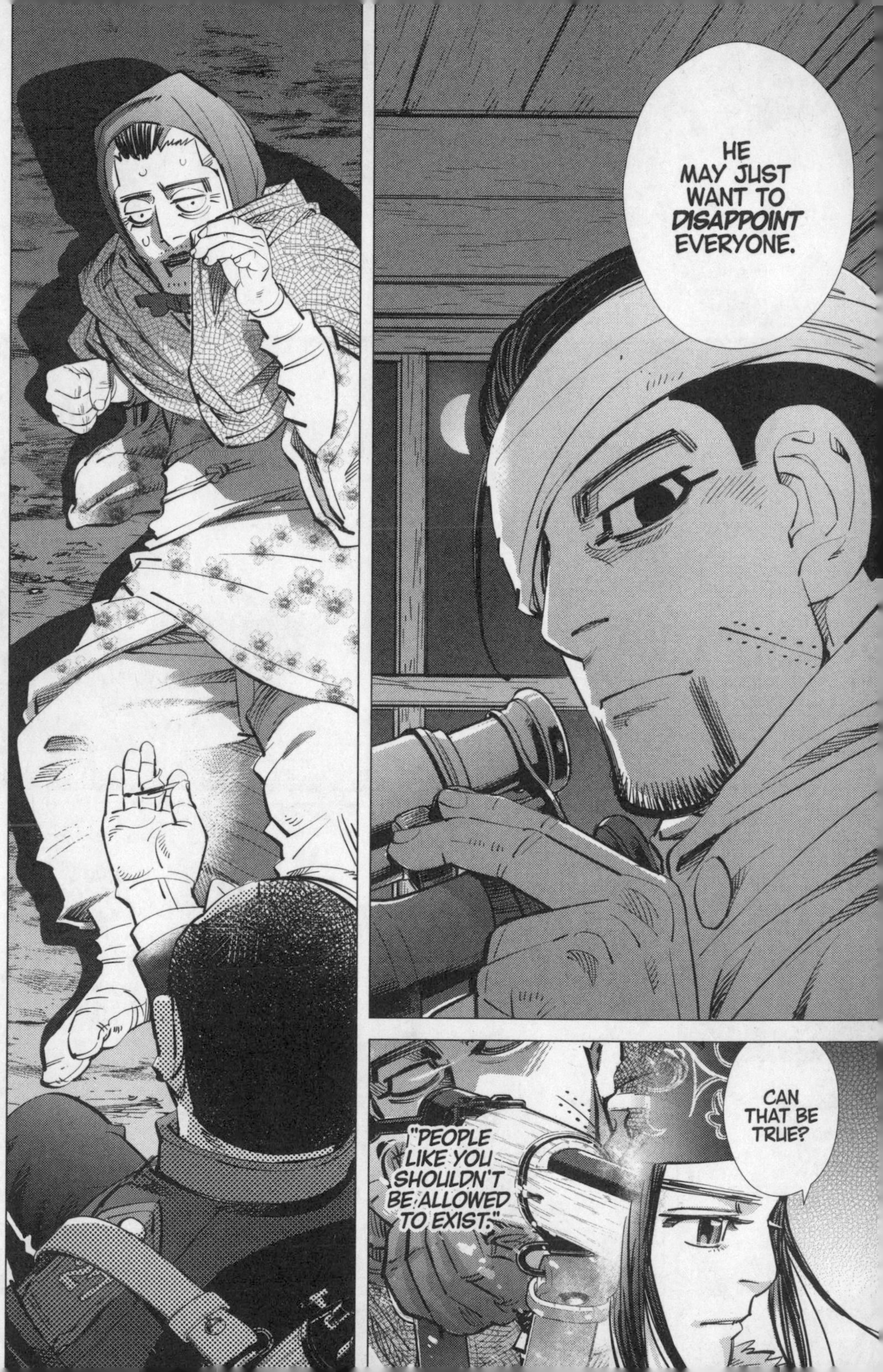
HE MAY JUST WANT TO DISAPPOINT EVERYONE.
CAN THAT BE TRUE?
"PEOPLE LIKE YOU SHOULDN'T BE ALLOWED TO EXIST."

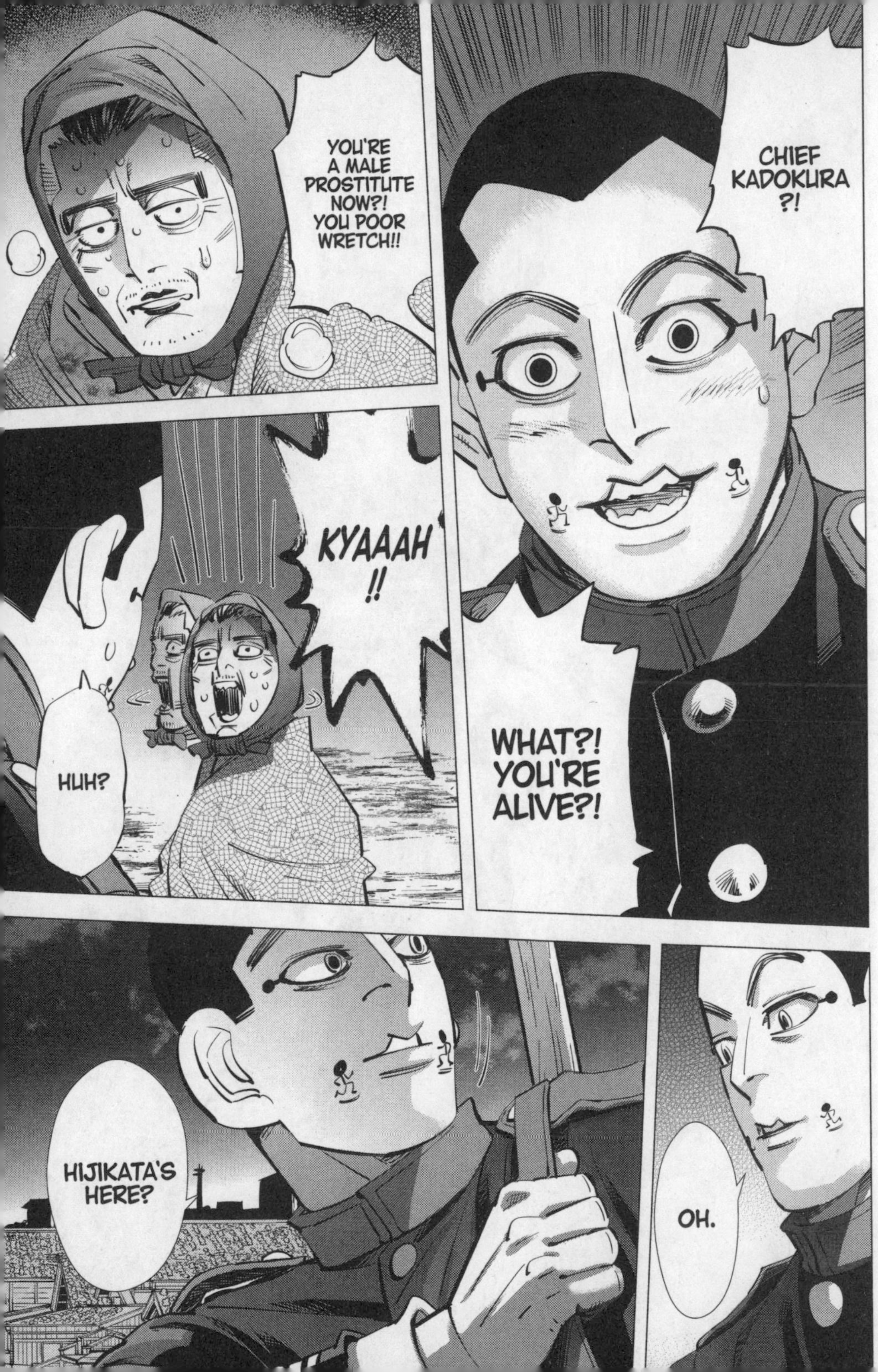
CHIEF KADOKURA?!
WHAT?! YOU'RE ALIVE?!
YOU'RE A MALE PROSTITUTE NOW?! YOU POOR WRETCH!!
KYAAAH!!
HUH?
OH.
HIJIKATA'S HERE?

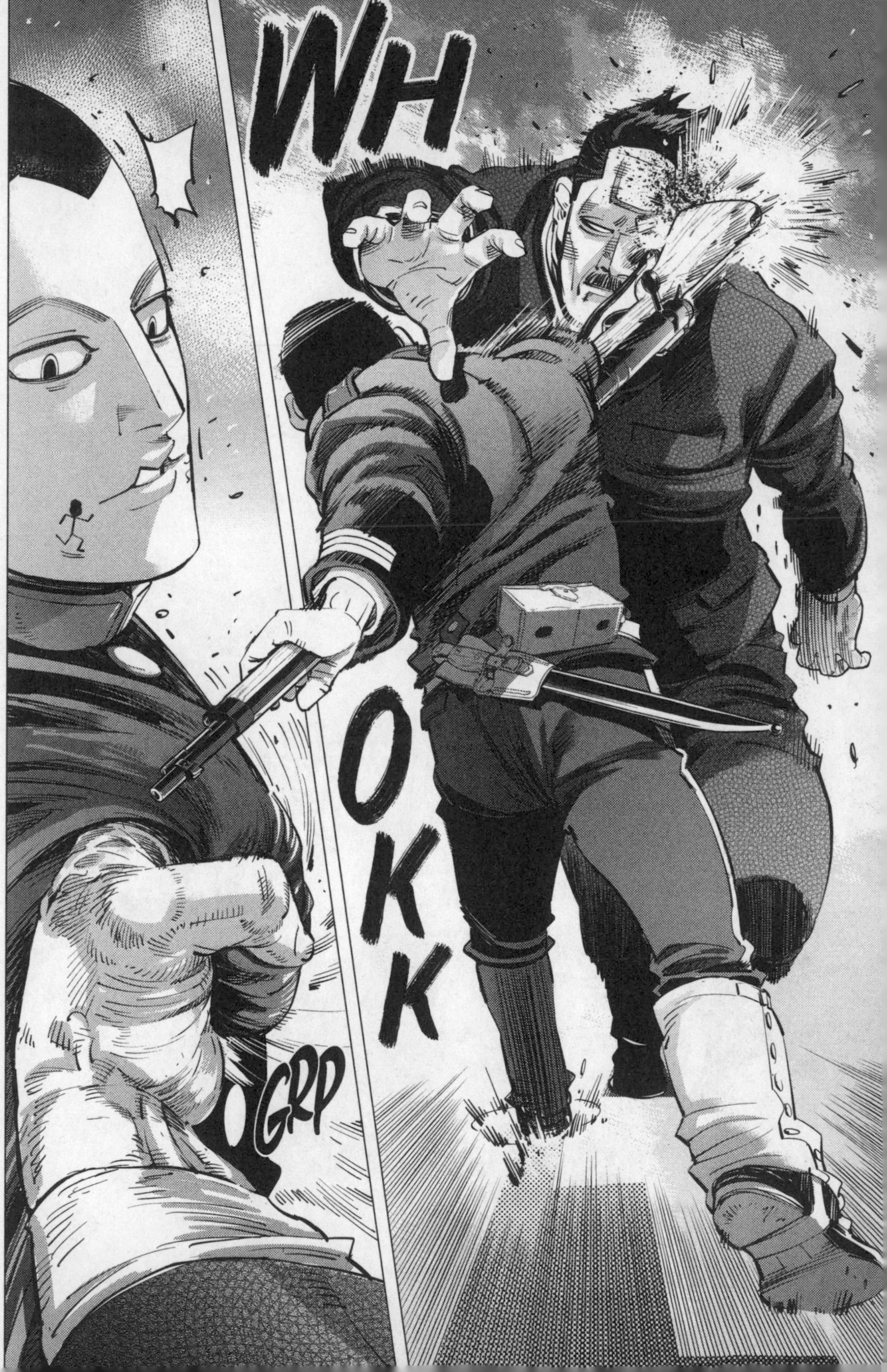
WHOKK
GRP

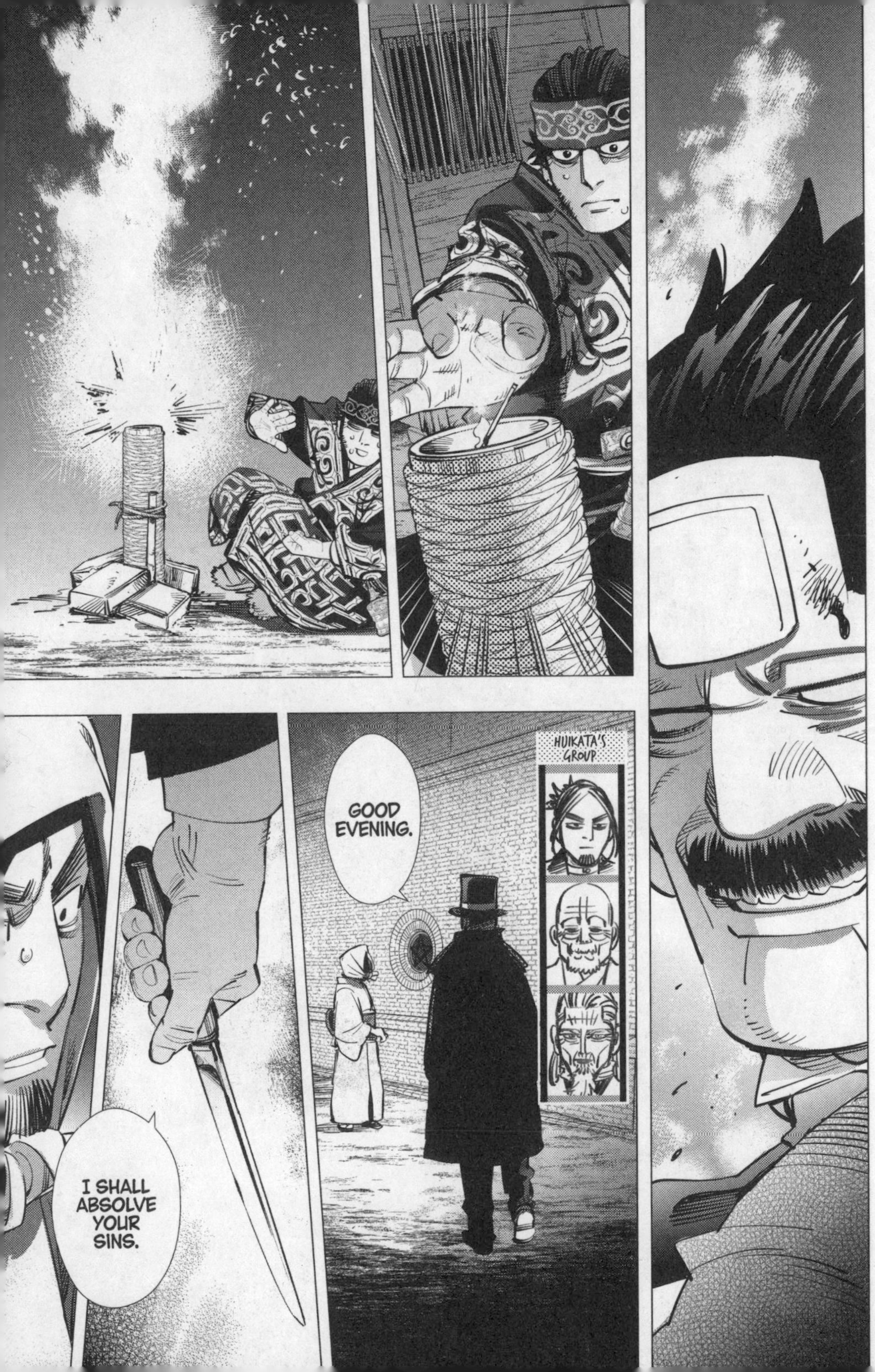
HIJIKATA'S GROUP
GOOD EVENING.
I SHALL ABSOLVE YOUR SINS.

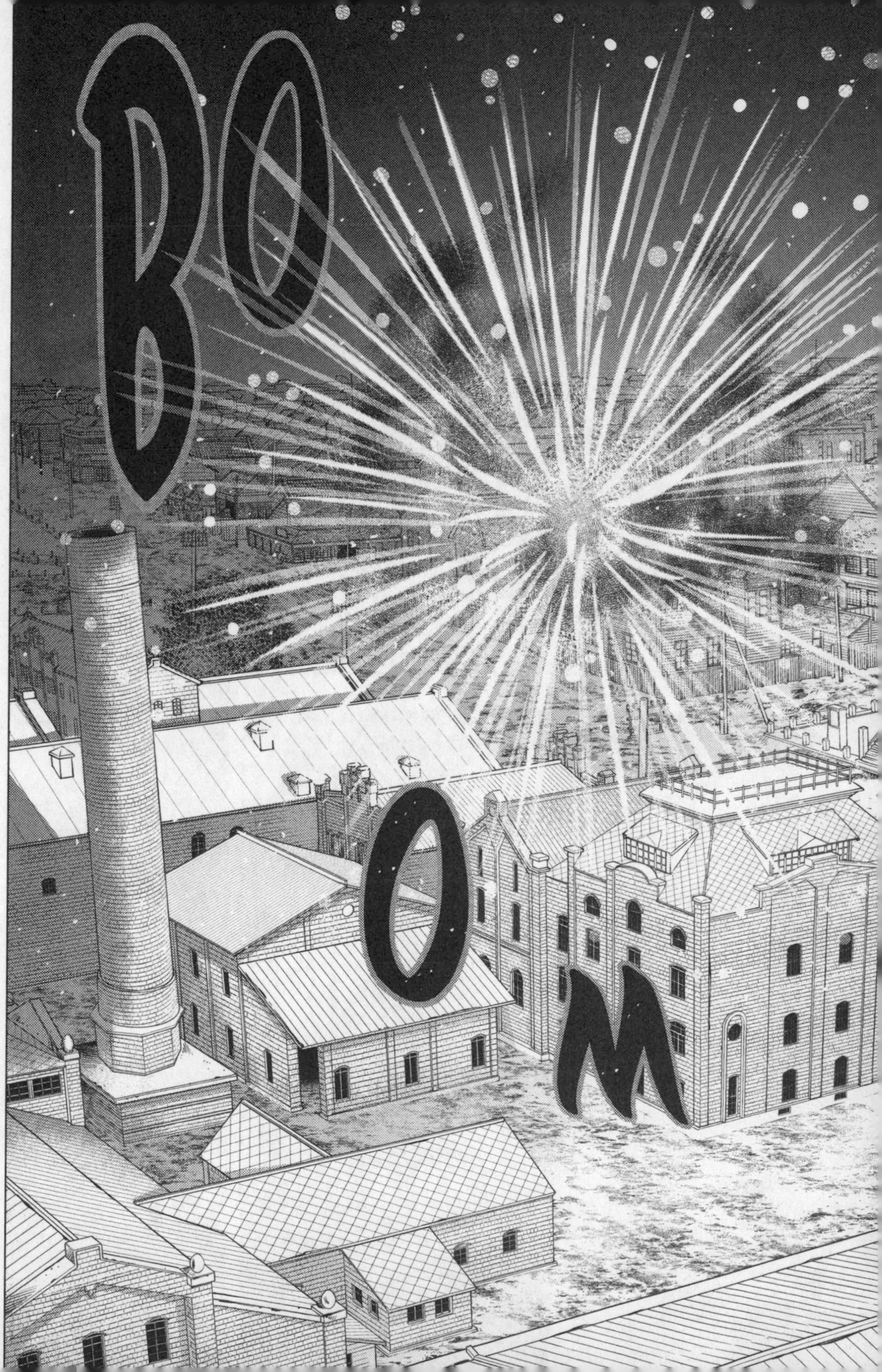
BOOM

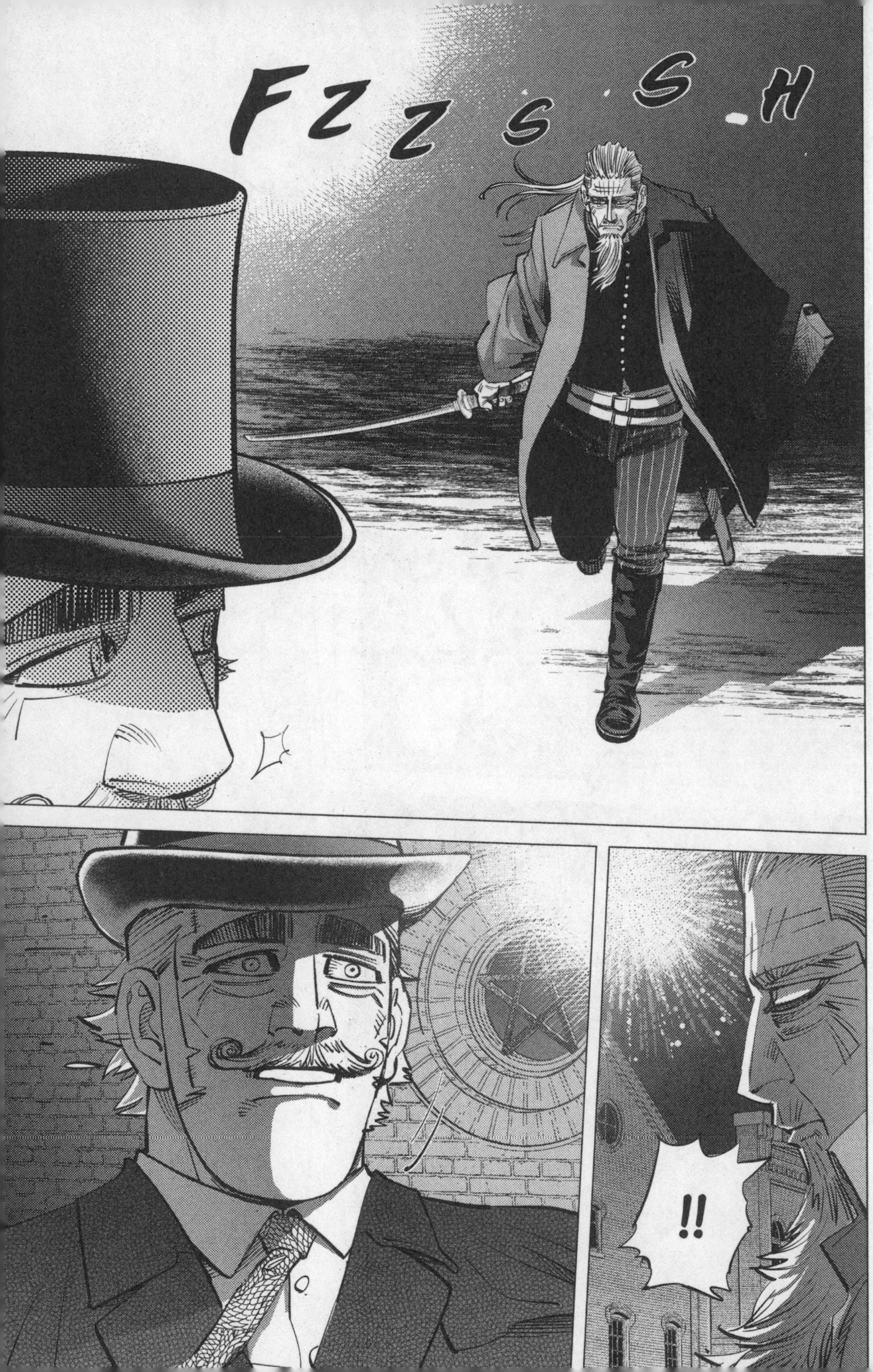
FZZSSSH
!!

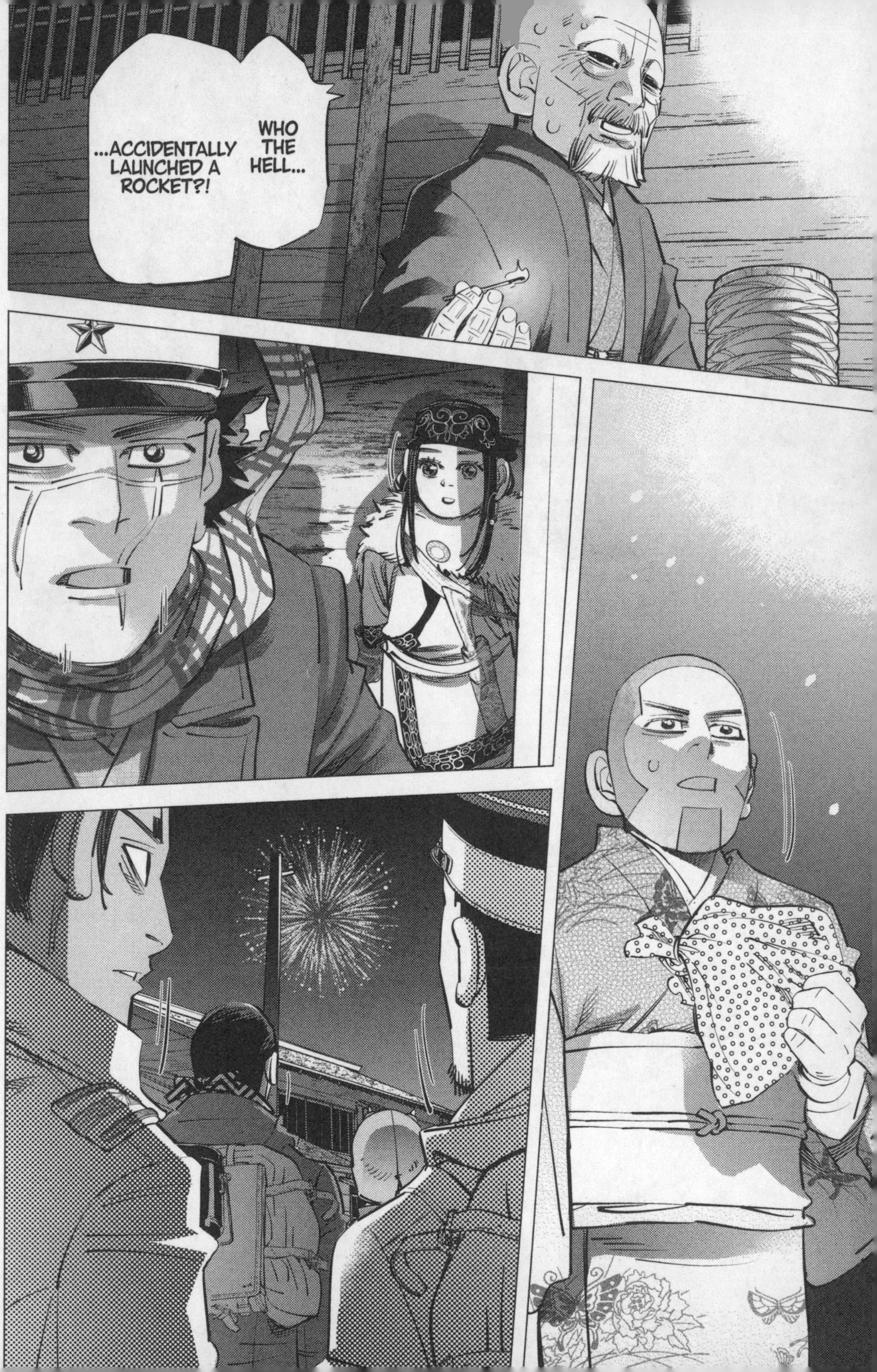
WHO THE HELL...
...ACCIDENTALLY LAUNCHED A ROCKET?!

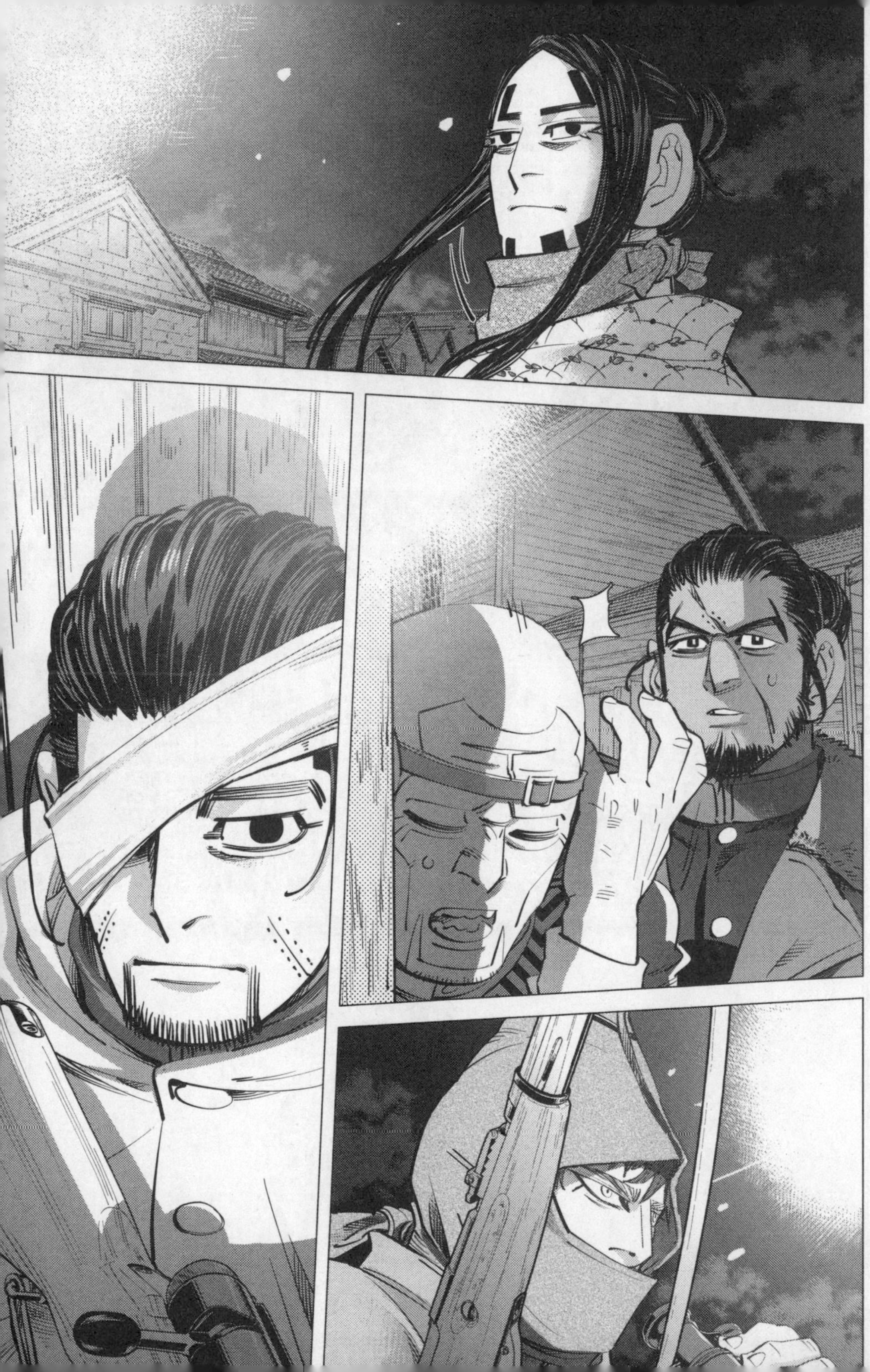

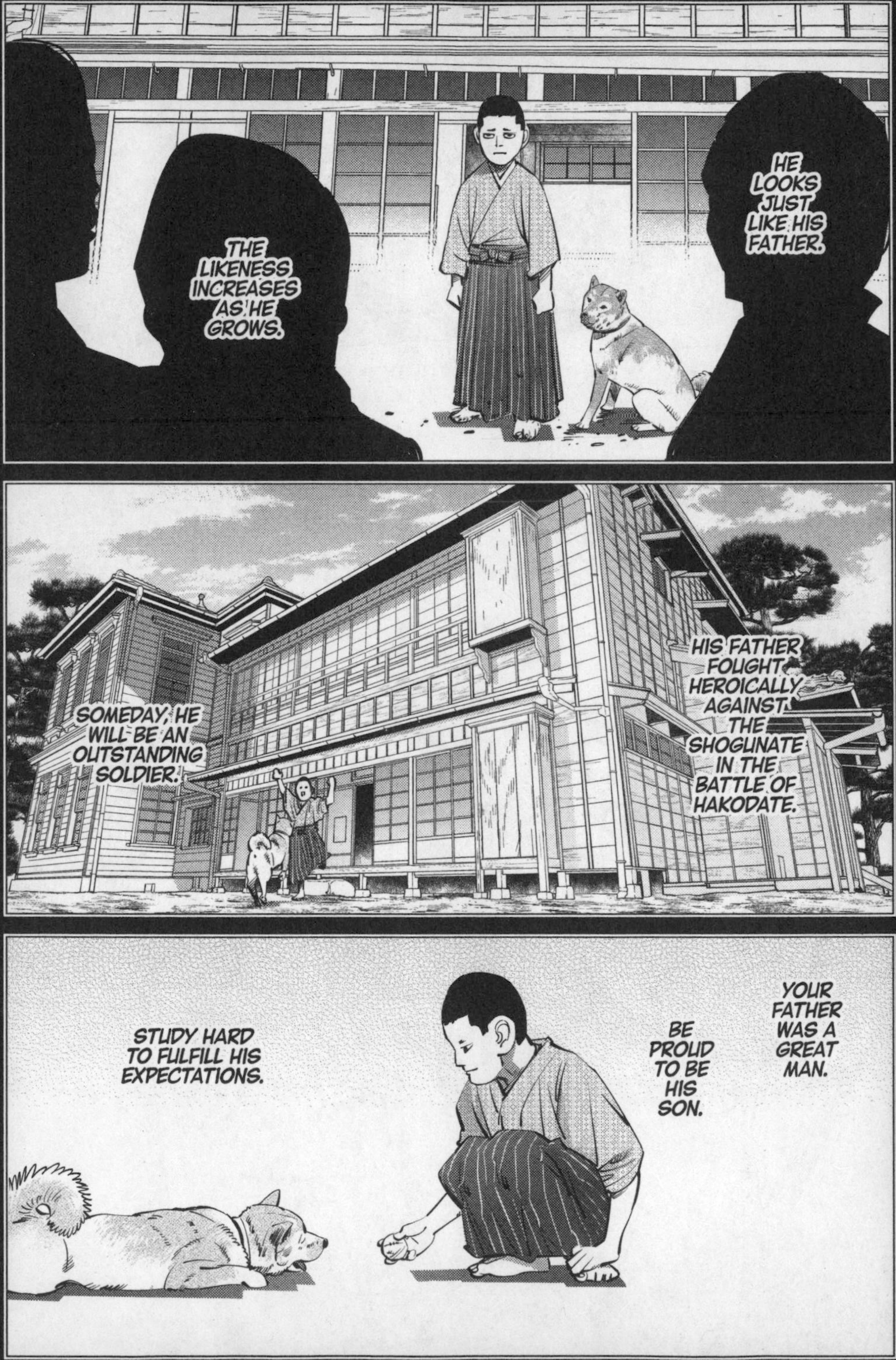
HE LOOKS JUST LIKE HIS FATHER.
THE LIKENESS INCREASES AS HE GROWS.
HIS FATHER FOUGHT HEROICALLY AGAINST THE SHOGUNATE IN THE BATTLE OF HAKODATE.
SOMEDAY, HE WILL BE AN OUTSTANDING SOLDIER.
YOUR FATHER WAS A GREAT MAN.
BE PROUD TO BE HIS SON.
STUDY HARD TO FULFILL HIS EXPECTATIONS.

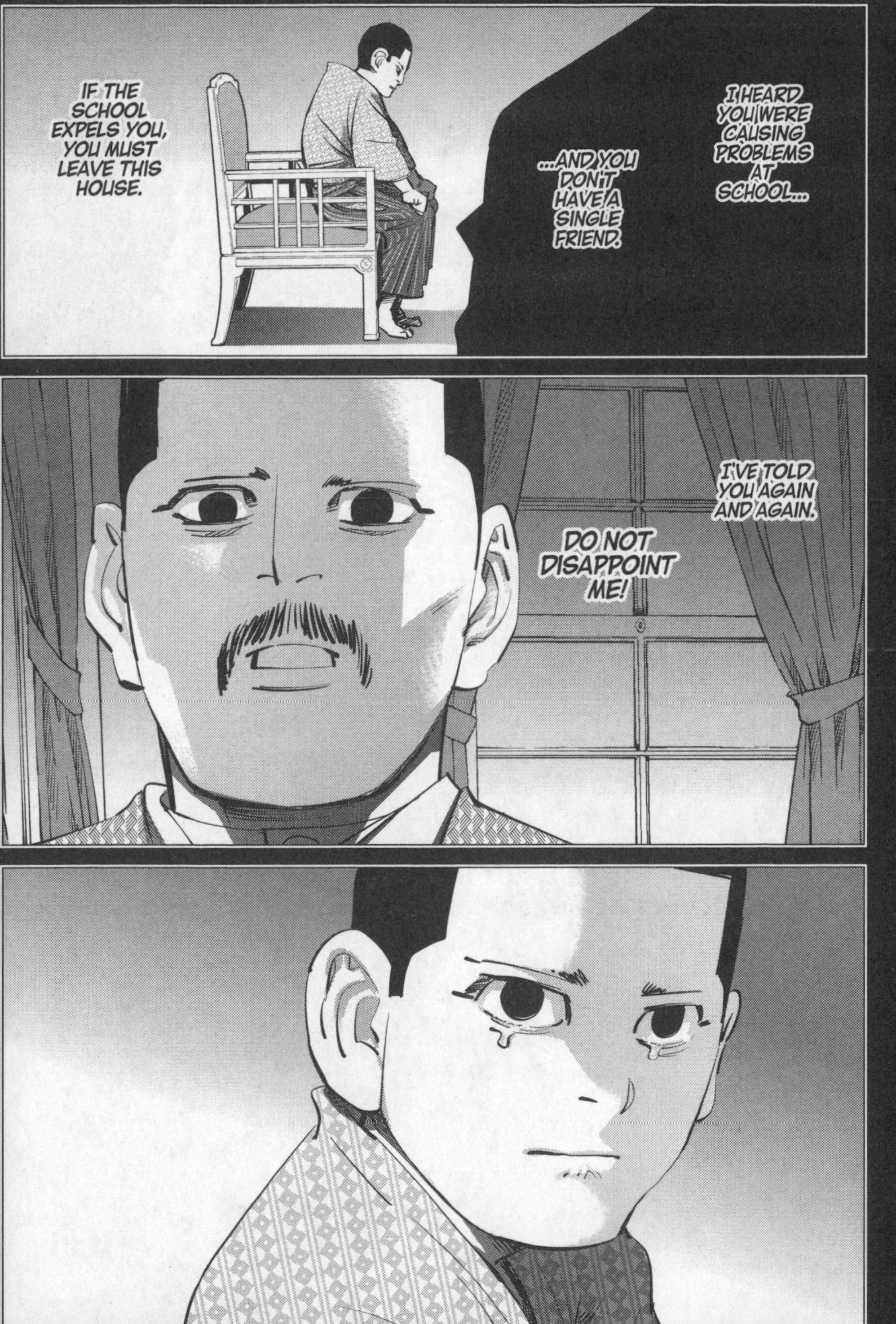
I HEARD YOU WERE CAUSING PROBLEMS AT SCHOOL...
...AND YOU DON'T HAVE A SINGLE FRIEND.
IF THE SCHOOL EXPELS YOU, YOU MUST LEAVE THIS HOUSE.
I'VE TOLD YOU AGAIN AND AGAIN.
DO NOT DISAPPOINT ME!

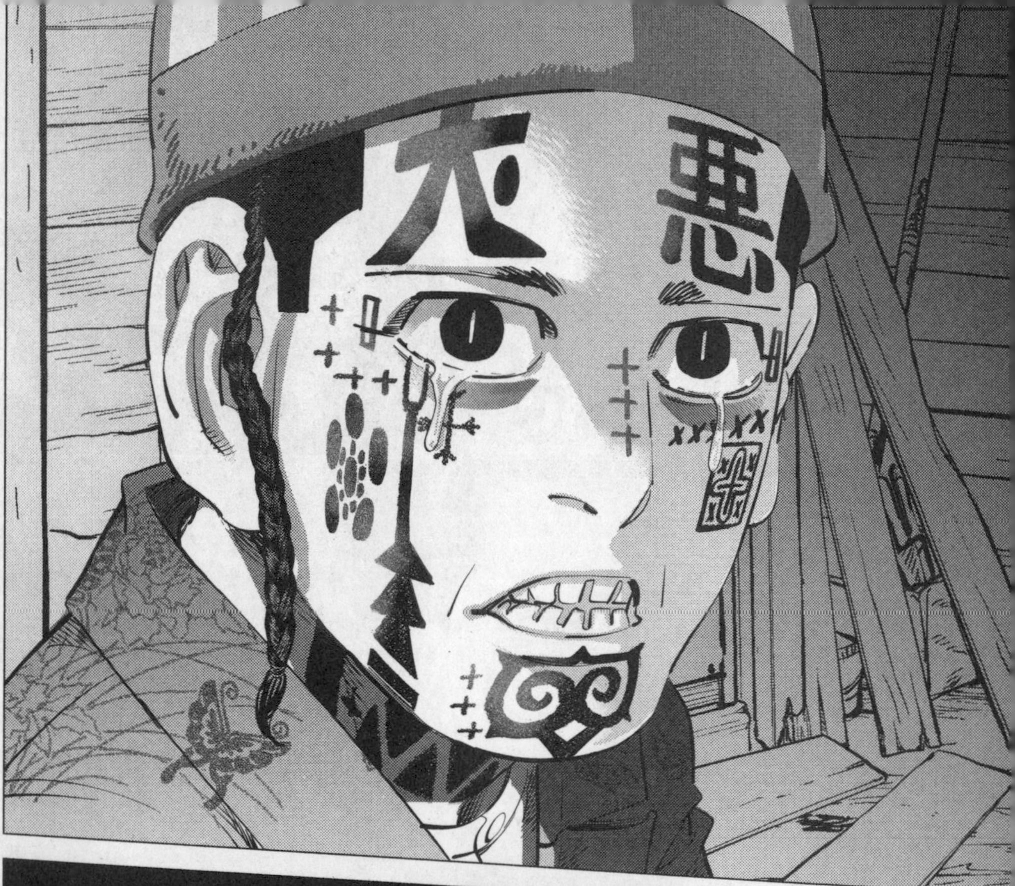

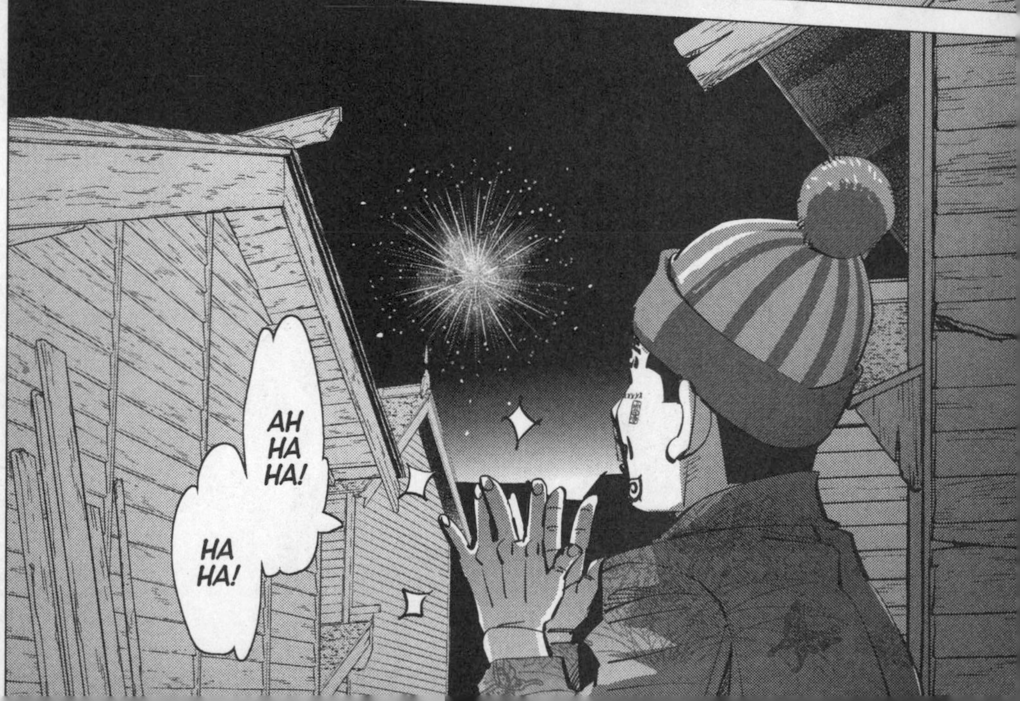
AH HA HA!
HA HA!

BOOM

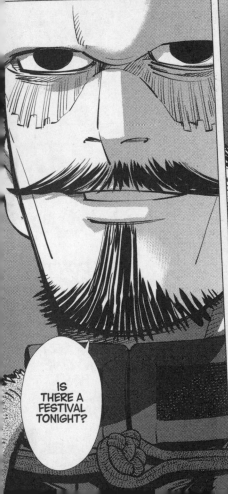

IS THERE A FESTIVAL TONIGHT?

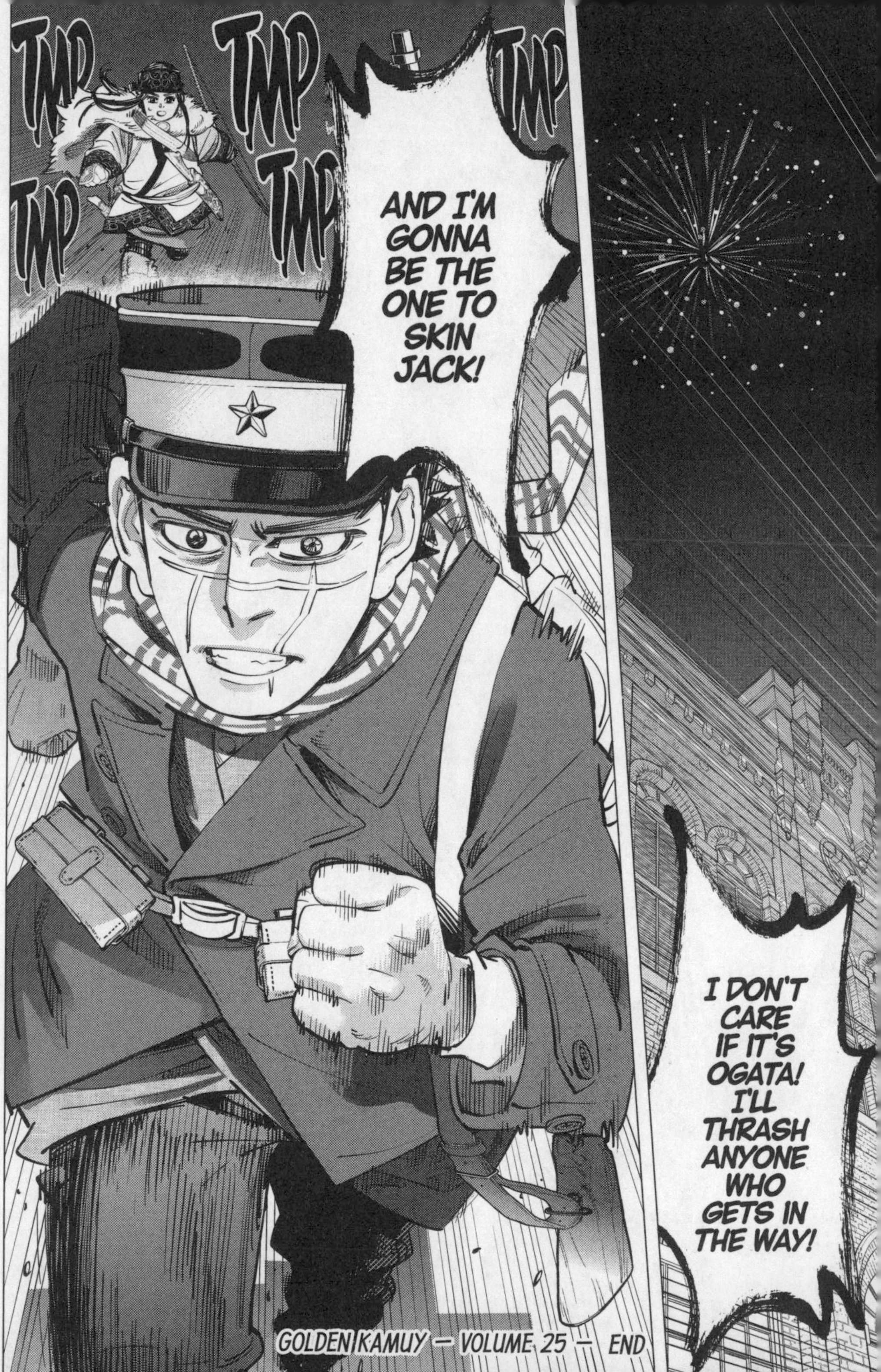
I DON'T CARE IF IT'S OGATA! I'LL THRASH ANYONE WHO GETS IN THE WAY!
TMP
TMP
TMP
TMP
TMP
AND I'M GONNA BE THE ONE TO SKIN JACK!
GOLDEN KAMUY — VOLUME 25 — END

Ainu Language Supervision • Hiroshi Nakagawa •
Russian Language Supervision • Eugenio Uzhinin •
Uilta Language Supervision • Yoshiko Yamada • Satsuma Dialect Supervision •
Shogo Nakamura • Niigata Dialect Supervision • Fumiya Ito

Cooperation from • Hokkaido Ainu Association and the Abashiri Prison Museum • Otaru City General Museum • Waseda University Aizu Museum • Kazunobu Goto, • Botanic Garden and Museum, Hokkaido University • National Museum of Ethnology • Nibutani Ainu Culture Museum • The Ainu Museum • Moon Kabato Museum • Kushiro City Museum • Atsuyo Hisai • Tatsuhiro Tokuda • Shigeharu Terui • All Japan Federation of Karafuto • Tokyo National Museum • Sakhalin Regional Museum • Shiraishi Hidetoshi • Masato Tamura • Historical Village of Hokkaido • Asahikawa City Museum • Hokuchin Museum • Tomakomai City Museum • Museum Meijimura • Sapporo Breweries Ltd.

Photo Credits • Takayuki Monma, Takanori Matsuda, Kozo Ishikawa, Shigekazu Kizu, Minoru Noda

Ainu Culture References

Chiri, Takanaka and Yokoyama, Takao. *Ainugo Eiri Jiten* (Ainu Language Illustrated Dictionary). Tokyo: Kagyusha, 1994

Kayano, Shigeru. *Ainu no Mingu* (Ainu Folkcrafts). Kawagoe: Suzusawa Book Store, 1978

Kayano, Shigeru. *Kayano Shigeru no Ainugo Jiten* (KayanoShigeru's Ainu Language Dictionary). Tokyo: Sanseido, 1996

Musashino Art University – The Research Institute for Culture and Cultural History. *Ainu no Mingu Jissoku Zushu* (Ainu Folkcrafts – Collection of Drawing and Figures). Biratori: Biratori-cho Council for Promoting Ainu Culture, 2014

Satouchi, Ai. *Ainu-shiki ekoroji-seikatsu: Haruzo Ekashi ni manabu shizen no chie* (Ainu Style Ecological Living: Haruzo Ekashi Teaches the Wisdom of Nature). Tokyo: Kabushiki gaisha Shogakukan, 2008

Chiri, Yukie. *Ainu Shin'yoshu* (Chiri Yukie's Ainu Epic Tales). Tokyo: Iwanami Shoten, 1978

Namikawa, Kenji. *Ainu Minzoku no Kiseki* (The Path of the Ainu People). Tokyo: Yamakawa Publishing, 2004

Mook. *Senjuumin Ainu Minzoku* (Bessatsu Taiyo) The Ainu People (Extra Issue Taiyo). Tokyo: Heibonsha, 2004

Kinoshita, Seizo. *Shiraoikotan Kinoshita Seizo Isaku Shashin Shu* (Shiraoikotan: Kinoshita Seizo's Posthumous Photography Collection). Hokkaido Shiraoi-gun Shiraoi-cho: Shiraoi Heritage Conservation Foundation, 1988

The Ainu Museum. *Ainu no Ifuku Bunka* (The Culture of Ainu Clothing). Hokkaido Shiraoi-gun Shiraoi-cho: Shiraoi Ainu Museum, 1991

Keira, Tomoko and Kaji, Sayaka. *Ainu no Shiki* (Ainu's Four Seasons). Tokyo: Akashi Shoten, 1995

Fukuoka, Itoko and Sato, Kazuko. *Ainu Shokubutsushi* (Ainu Botanical Journal). Chiba Urayasu-Shi: Sofukan, 1995

Hayakawa, Noboru. *Ainu no Minzoku* (Ainu Folklore). Iwasaki Bijutsusha, 1983

Sunazawa, Kura. *Ku Sukuppu Orushibe* (The Memories of My Generation). Hokkaido, Sapporo-shi: Miyama Shobo, 1983

Haginaka, Miki et al. *Kikigaki Ainu no Shokuji* (Oral History of Ainu Diet). Tokyo: Rural Culture Association Japan, 1992

Nakagawa, Hiroshi. *New Express Ainu Go*. Tokyo: Hakusuisha, 2013

Nakagawa, Hiroshi. *Ainugo Chitose Hogen Jiten* (The Ainu-Japanese dictionary). Chiba Urayasu-Shi: Sofukan, 1995

Nakagawa, Hiroshi and Nakamoto, Mutsuko. *Kamuy Yukara de Ainu Go wo Manabu* (Learning Ainu with Kamuy Yukar). Tokyo: Hakusuisha, 2007

Nakagawa, Hiroshi. *Katari au Kotoba no Chikara – Kamuy tachi to Ikiru Sekai* (The Power of Spoken Words – Living in a World with Kamuy). Tokyo: Iwanami Shoten, 2010

Sarashina, Genzo and Sarashina, Hikari. *Kotan Seibutsu Ki <1 Juki / Zassou hen>* (Kotan Wildlife Vol. 1 – Trees and Weeds). Hosei University Publishing, 1992/2007

Sarashina, Genzo and Sarashina, Hikari. *Kotan Seibutsu Ki <2 Yacho / Kaijuu / Gyozoku hen>* (Kotan Wildlife Vol. 2 – Birds, Sea Creatures, and Fish). Hosei University Publishing, 1992/2007

Sarashina, Genzo and Sarashina, Hikari. *Kotan Seibutsu Ki <3 Yachou / Mizudori / Konchu hen>* (Kotan Wildlife Vol. 3 – Shorebirds, Seabirds, and Insects). Hosei University Publishing, 1992/2007

Sarashina, Genzo. *Ainu Minwashu* (Collection of Ainu Folktales). Kita Shobou, 1963

Sarashina, Genzo. *Ainu Rekishi to Minzoku* (Ainu History and Folklore). Shakai Shisousha, 1968

Kawakami Yuji. *Sarunkur Ainu Monogatari* (The Tale of Sarunkur Ainu). Kawagoe: Suzusawa Book Store, 2003/2005

Kawakami, Yuji. *Ekashi to Fuchi wo Tazunete* (Visiting Ekashi and Fuchi). Kawagoe: Suzusawa Book Store, 1991

Council for the Conservation of Ainu Culture. *Ainu Minzokushi* (Ainu People Magazine). Dai-ichi Hoki, 1970

Okamura, Kichiemon and Clancy, Judith A. *Ainu no Ishou* (The Clothes of the Ainu People). Kyoto Shoin, 1993

Hokkaido Cultural Property Protection Association. *Ainu Ifuku Chousa Houkokusho <1 Ainu Josei ga Denshou Suru Ibunka>* (The Ainu Clothing Research Report Vol. 1 – Traditional Clothing Passed Down Through Generations of Ainu Women). 1986

Yotsuji, Ichiro. Photos by Mizutani, Morio. *Ainu no Monyo* (Decorative Arts of the Ainu). Kasakura Publishing, 1981

Yoshida, Iwao. *Ainushi Shiryoshu* (Collection of Ainu Historical Documents). Hokkaido Publication Project Center, 1983

Kubodera, Itsuhiko. *Ainu no Mukashibanashi* (Old Stories of the Ainu). Miyaishoten, 1972

Kubodera, Itsuhiko (trans.). *Ainu Minzokushi* (Ainu People Magazine). Dai-ichi Hoki

Inoue, Koichi and Latyshev, Vladislav M. (coed.). *Karafuto Ainu no Mingu* (Karafuto Ainu Folkcraft). Hokkaido Publication Project Center, 2002

Russia ga Mita Ainu Bunka (Ainu Culture as Seen by Russia). The Foundation for Research and Promotion of Ainu Culture, 2013

Russia Minzokugaku Hakubutsukan Ainu Shiryoten—Russia ga Mita Shimaguni no Hitobito (Russia Museum of Ethnology Ainu Materials Exhibition—Island Peoples as Seen by Russia). The Foundation for Research and Promotion of Ainu Culture, 2005

The Foundation for Research and Promotion of Ainu Culture (ed.). *Senjima, Karafuto, Hokkaido—Ainu no Kurashi* (Ainu Life on the Kuril Islands, Karafuto and Hokkaido). The Senri Foundation, 2011

SPb-Ainu Project Group (ed.). *Russia Kagaku Academy Jinruigaku Minzokugaku Hakubutsukan Shozo Ainu Shiryo Mokuroku* (Ainu Collections of Peter the Great Museum of Anthropology and Ethnography Russian Academy of Sciences Catalogue). Sofukan, 1998

Yamamoto, Yuko. *Karafuto Ainu—Jukyo to Mingu* (Residences and Folkcraft of the Karafuto Ainu). Sagami Shobo, 1970

Yamamoto, Yuko (author and ed.). Chiri, Mashiho and Onuki, Emiko co-authors). *Karafuto Shizen Minzoku no Seikatsu* (Lifestyles of Karafuto Natural Peoples). Sagami Shobo, 1979

Chiri, Mashiho. *Chiri Mashiho Chosakushu 3 Seikatsu-shi / Minzokugaku-hen* (Mashiho Chiri Collected Works, Vol. 3: Lifestyles and Ethnology). Heibonsha, 1973

Yamamoto, Yuko. *Hoppo Shizen Minzoku Minwa Shusei* (Northern Natural Peoples Folk Tales Compilation). Sagami Shobo, 1968

Yamamoto, Yuko. *Karafuto Genshi Minzoku no Seikatsu* (Lifestyles of Karafuto Primitive Peoples). ARS, 1943

Nishitsuru, Sadaka. *Karafuto Ainu*. Miyama Shobo, 1974

Kasai, Takechiyo. *Karafuto Ainu no Minzoku* (Folklore of the Karafuto Ainu). Miyama Shobo, 1975

Tanigawa, Kenichi. Kita no Minzokushi-Sakhalin / Chishima no Minzoku (Northern Ethnography—Sakhalin / People of the Kuril Islands). San-Ichi Shobo Publishing Inc., 1997

Takabeya, Fukuhei. *Hoppoken no Ie* (Houses of the Northern Regions). Shokokusha Publishing Co., Ltd., 1943

Abashiri City Northern Folkore Cultural Preservation Society. *Uiruta no Kurashi to Mingu* (Uilta Lifestyles and Folkcraft). 1982

The Foundation for Research and Promotion of Ainu Culture (ed.). *Zaidan Hojin Ainu Bunka Fukko / Kenkyu Suishin Kiko Shuzo Mokuroku 7 (Ishida Shuzo Kyuzo Shashin)* The Foundation for Research and Promotion of Ainu Culture Collection Catalog 7 (Ishida Collection Old Collection Photograph). The Foundation for Research and Promotion of Ainu Culture, 2012

Uilta Society Museum Steering Committee (ed.). *Shiryokan Jakka Duxuni Tenji Sakuhinshu* (Museum Jakka Duxuni Exhibition Works Collection). 2002

Bird, Isabella L. (author), Kobari, Kosai (trans.) *Meiji Shoki no Emishi Tanboki* (Report on Emishi in the Early Meiji Era). Sarorun Shobo, 1977

Munro, N.G. (author), Seligman, B.Z. (ed.), Tetsuro, Komatsu (trans.). *Ainu no Shinko to Sono Gishiki* (Ainu Creed and Cult). Kokushokankokai, 2002

Batchelor, John (author), Tetsuro, Komatsu (trans.). *Ainu no Kurashi to Densho* (Ainu Life and Lore). Hokkaido Publication Project Center, 1999

Shinmyo, Hidehito. *Ainu Fuzokuga no Kenkyu: Kinsei Hokkaido ni Okeru Ainu to Bijutsu* (Study of Ainu Genre Painting: Ainu and Art in Modern Hokkaido). Nakanishi Publishing, 2011

Aoki, Aiko (teller). Nagai, Hiroshi (recorder). Ainu O-san Baa-chan no Upashikuma Densho no Chie no Kiroku (Ainu Midwife Upaskuma: A Record of Traditional Wisdom). Jushinsha, 1998

Segawa, Kiyoko. *Ainu no Konin* (Married Ainu). Miraisha, 1998

Hitchcock, R. (author) Kitakamae, Yasuo (trans.). *Ainujin to Sono Bunka—Meiji Chuki no Ainu no Mura Kara—* (The Ainu People and Their Culture: From the Ainu Villages of the Mid-Meiji Era). Rokko Shuppan, 1990

Landor, A.S. (author). Toda, Sachiko (trans.). *Ezo-chi Isshu Hitori Tabi: Omoide no Ainu Country* (Traveling Alone Around Ezo: Ainu Country as I Remember It). Miraisha, 1985

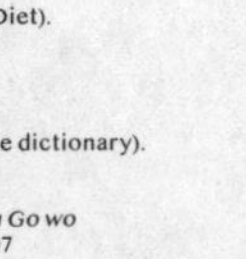
SPECIAL THANKS EDITOR HAKKOU OKUMA

Kanto or wa yaku sak no arankep sinep ka isam.
Nothing comes from heaven without purpose. —Ainu proverb

KAPARAMIPU

COTTON CLOTHING
WITH CUT PATTERNS
AND SEWN WHITE CREPE

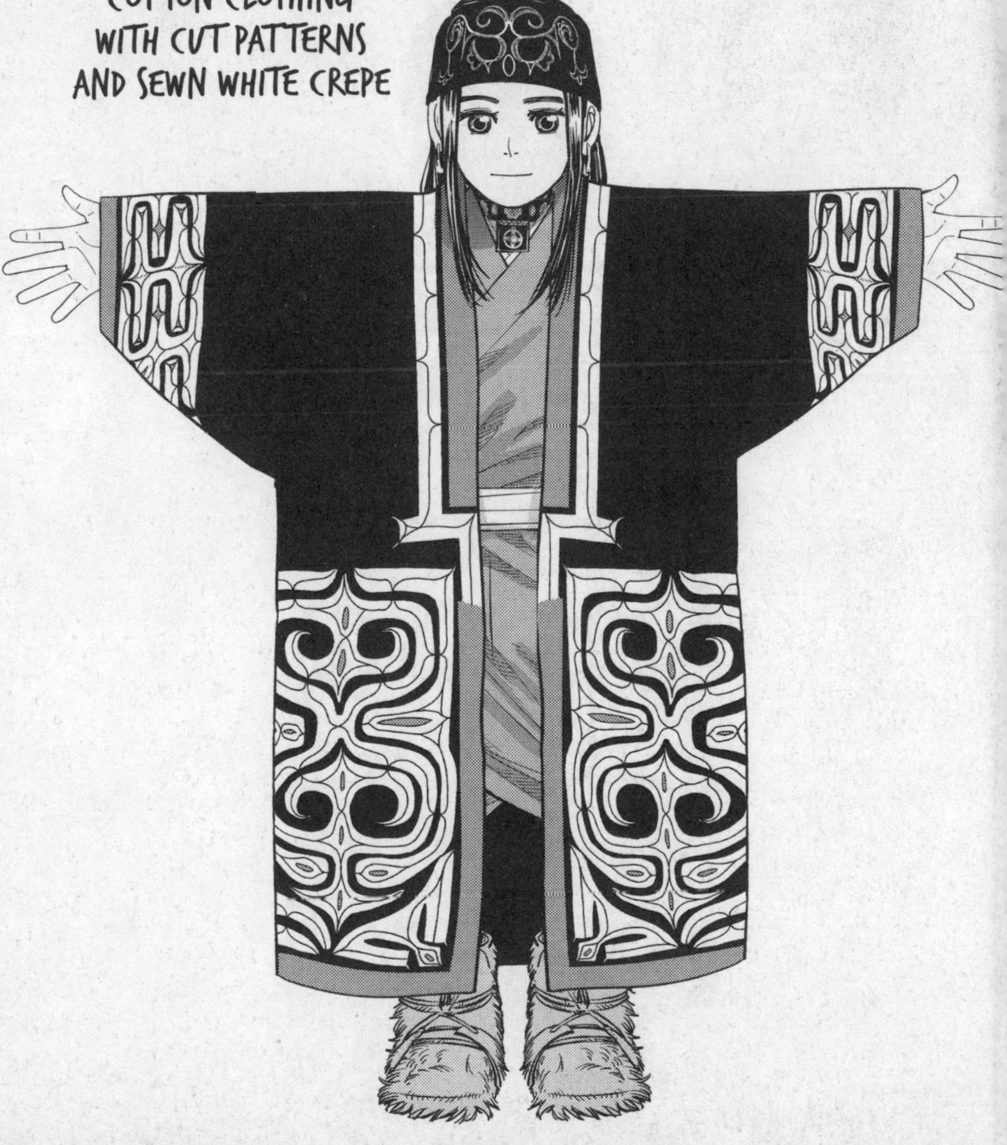

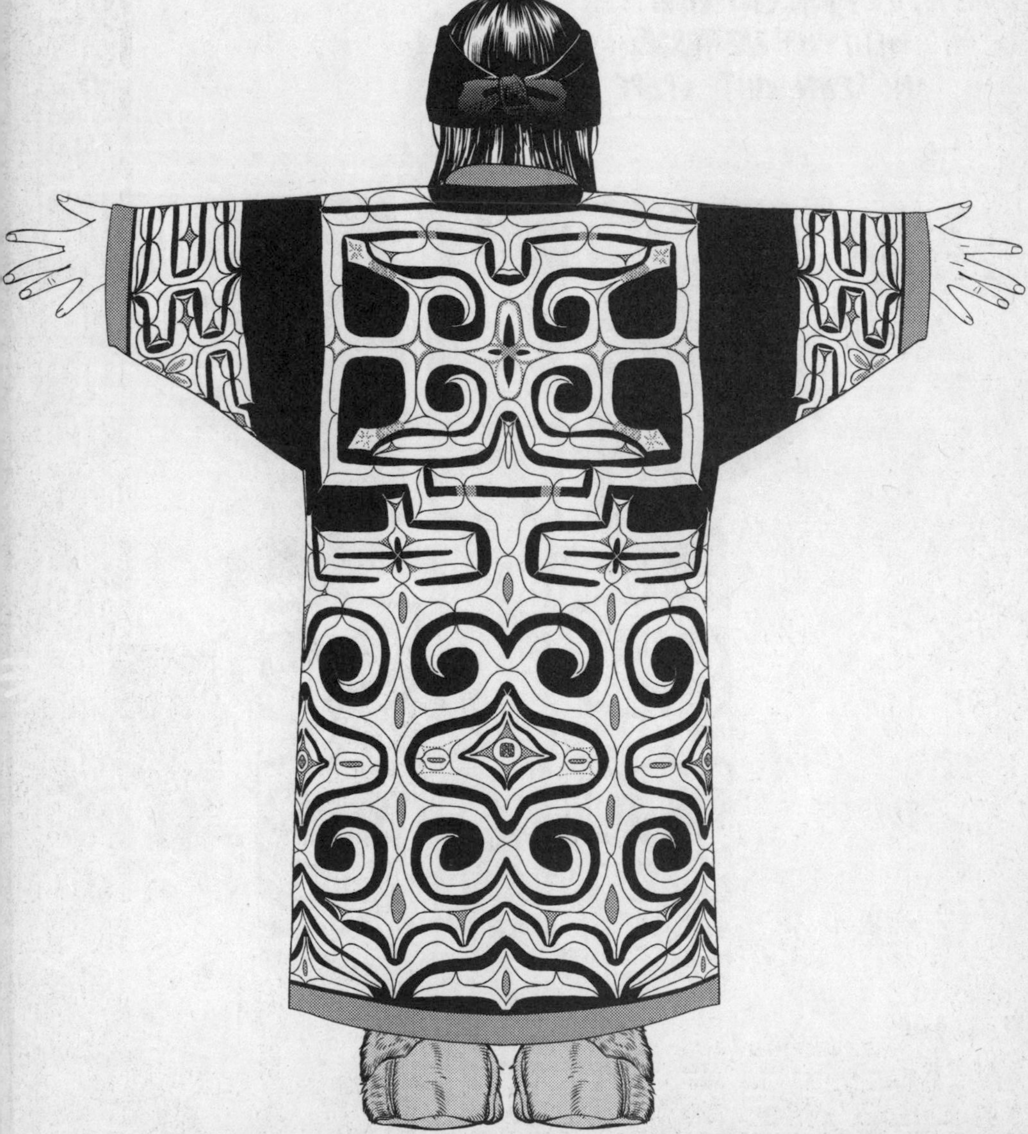

GOLDEN KAMUY

Volume 25
VIZ Signature Edition

Story/Art by **Satoru Noda**

First published in Japan in 2014 by SHUEISHA Inc., Tokyo.
English translation rights arranged by SHUEISHA Inc.

Translation/John Werry
Touch-Up Art & Lettering/Steve Dutro
Design/Shawn Carrico
Editor/Mike Montesa

Printed in Canada

Published by VIZ Media, LLC
P.O. Box 77010
San Francisco, CA 94107

10 9 8 7 6 5 4 3 2 1
First printing, February 2022

VIZ SIGNATURE

VIZ MEDIA
viz.com

ratings.viz.com RATED M MATURE

PARENTAL ADVISORY
GOLDEN KAMUY is rated M for Mature and recommended for mature readers. This volume contains graphic violence, nudity, strong language, and adult themes.